W9-COO-698

THE POSSESSIVE INVESTMENT
IN WHITENESS

GEORGE LIPSITZ

THE POSSESSIVE INVESTMENT IN WHITENESS

HOW WHITE PEOPLE PROFIT
FROM IDENTITY POLITICS

TWENTIETH ANNIVERSARY EDITION

TEMPLE UNIVERSITY PRESS
Philadelphia • *Rome* • *Tokyo*

TEMPLE UNIVERSITY PRESS
Philadelphia, Pennsylvania 19122
www.temple.edu/tempress

Twentieth anniversary edition published 2018. Revised and expanded edition
published 2006.

Cataloging-in-Publication Data is on file with the Library of Congress.
978-1-4399-1638-4 (cloth : alk. paper)
978-1-4399-1639-1 (paper : alk. paper)
978-1-4399-1640-7 (ebook)

♾ The paper used in this publication meets the requirements of the American National
Standard for Information Sciences—Permanence of Paper for Printed Library Materials,
ANSI Z39.48-1992

Printed in the United States of America

9 8 7 6 5 4 3 2 1

Contents

Preface

Bill Moore's Body

I began to suspect that white people did not act as they did because they were white, but for some other reason, and I began to try to locate and understand the reason.

—James Baldwin

This book argues that public policy and private prejudice work together to create a "possessive investment in whiteness" that is responsible for the racialized hierarchies of our society. I use the term *possessive investment* both literally and figuratively. Whiteness has a cash value: it accounts for advantages that come to individuals through profits made from housing secured in discriminatory markets, through the unequal educational opportunities available to children of different races, through insider networks that channel employment opportunities to the relatives and friends of those who have profited most from present and past racial discrimination, and especially through intergenerational transfers of inherited wealth that pass on the spoils of discrimination to succeeding generations. I argue that white Americans are encouraged to invest in whiteness, to remain true to an identity that provides them with resources, power, and opportunity. This whiteness is, of course, a delusion, a scientific and cultural fiction that like all racial identities has no valid foundation in biology or anthropology. Whiteness is, however, a social fact, an identity created and continued with all-too-real consequences for the distribution of wealth, prestige, power, and opportunity.

The term *investment* denotes time spent on a given end, and this book also attempts to explore how social and cultural forces encourage white people to expend time and energy on the creation and re-creation of whiteness. Despite intense and frequent disavowal that whiteness means anything at all to those so designated, research has shown repeatedly that nearly every social choice that white people make about where they live, what schools their children attend, what careers they pursue, and what policies they endorse is shaped by considerations involving race.[1] I use the adjective *posses-sive* to stress the relationship between whiteness and asset accumulation in our society, to connect attitudes to interests, to demonstrate that white supremacy is usually less a matter of direct, referential, and snarling contempt than a system for protecting the privileges of whites by denying communities of color opportunities for asset accumulation and upward mobility. Whiteness is invested in, like property, but it is also a means of accumulating property and keeping it from others. While one can *possess* one's investments, one can also *be possessed* by them. I contend that the artificial construction of whiteness almost always comes to possess white people themselves unless they develop antiracist identities, unless they disinvest and divest themselves of their attachments to white supremacy.

The possessive investment in whiteness is a matter of power, not simply of prejudice. Whiteness is more a condition than a color. It is a structured advantage that is impersonal, institutional, collective, and cumulative. Like all forms of racism, the possessive investment in whiteness exaggerates small differences in appearance to create large differences in condition. It concerns property as well as pigment, assets as well as attitudes. It manifests itself through practices that create differential access to wealth, health, housing, education, jobs, and justice.

I hope it is clear that opposing whiteness is not the same thing as opposing white people. White supremacy is an equal opportunity employer; even non-white people can become active agents of white supremacy as well as passive participants in its hierarchies and rewards. One way of becoming an insider is by participating in the exclusion of other outsiders. An individual might even secure a seat on the Supreme Court on this basis. On the other hand, if not every white supremacist is white, it follows that not all white people have to remain complicit with white supremacy—that there is an element of choice in all of this. White people always have the option of becoming antiracist, although not enough have done so. We do not choose our color, but we do choose our commitments. We do not choose our parents, but we do choose our politics. Yet we do not make these decisions in a vacuum; they occur within a social structure that gives value to whiteness and offers rewards for racism.

I write this book in response to the enduring crisis that confronts us in regard to race. But as with most books, its origins are complex and complicated. Perhaps the best way I can situate my engagement with the possessive investment in whiteness is by relating my connection to a crime that took place more than a half century ago, when I was a teenager. On April 23, 1963, Bill Moore was shot to death at close range alongside a highway in northern Alabama. The thirty-five-year-old father of three children received two .22 caliber slugs in his head and one in his neck.

When Moore was murdered, he was just beginning a one-man civil rights march from Chattanooga, Tennessee, to Jackson, Mississippi. A white man raised in the deep South, Moore had been working as a post office employee in Baltimore. He had been horrified in 1962 by Mississippi governor Ross Barnett's efforts to prevent the desegregation of the University of Mississippi. When a federal court judge had to intervene to order the university to admit a fully qualified twenty-nine-year-old Air Force veteran as its first Black student, Barnett countered with a pledge of total resistance, declaring the state's authority to be superior to that of the federal government. President Kennedy sent National Guard troops to Oxford, Mississippi, to force compliance with the court's order, but a rioting mob of whites resisted with a rampage that left two people dead and almost 400 injured.[2]

Distressed by the violence in Mississippi, Moore asked himself what he could do to help. He had recently moved from Binghamton, New York, to Baltimore for the express purpose of becoming active in the front lines of the civil rights movement. Encouraged by the positive publicity surrounding a march on the Maryland state capital organized by the Baltimore chapter of the Congress of Racial Equality earlier that year, Moore decided that he would stage his own one-man march. Playing on his identity as a postal worker, he decided to "deliver a letter" expressing support for integration to Governor Barnett. In his message, Moore advised the Mississippi governor "not to go down in infamy as one who fought the democracy for all which you have not the power to prevent."[3]

Born in upstate New York, Moore moved with his family to Mississippi as a child. As an adult, he continued to express great affection for the South and its people. He felt particularly embarrassed by Mississippi's image as a bastion of white supremacy. "I dislike the reputation this state has acquired as being the most backward and most bigoted in the land," he asserted in his letter to Barnett. "Those who truly love Mississippi must work to change this image." Before starting his journey, Moore left a letter for President Kennedy at the White House advising the president, "I am not making this walk to demonstrate either Federal rights or state rights, but individual rights. I am doing it to illustrate that peaceful protest is not altogether extinguished down there. I hope that I will not have to eat those words."[4]

Moore rode by bus from Washington, D.C., to Chattanooga, Tennessee, where he began his march on April 21. Pulling a small two-wheeled postal cart containing his belongings, he wore two placards, sandwich-board style, on his chest and back. One read, "Equal Rights for All: Mississippi or Bust"; the other read, "Black and White: Eat at Joe's." On the first days of his trip a white woman smiled at him and another bought him a milkshake. Most of the whites he encountered, however, and at least one of the Blacks, greeted him with jeers and arguments. In Georgia, one group of young white males shouted threats at Moore from a passing car. Another group pelted the postman with rocks and stones. A news broadcaster for Gadsden, Alabama, radio station WGAD later reported that the station had received an anonymous telephone call hours before the shooting reporting Moore's entrance into Etowah County, advising that "there might be a news story of consequence."[5] Moore walked through Gadsden on the afternoon of April 23; a passing motorist discovered his body that night on the pavement of U.S. Highway 11 near Attalia, about ten miles from Gadsden. The sandwich board signs, stained with blood, lay a few feet from his body. Investigators found $51.00 in Moore's pocket and a diary among his possessions. An entry for April 23 noted that he had been confronted by two men who had learned about his walk from television news reports and warned him that he would not finish the march alive. In a final entry he wrote that "a couple of men who had talked to me before, drove up and questioned my religious and political beliefs and one was sure I'd be killed for them."[6]

Even George Wallace, Alabama's notorious segregationist governor, publicly condemned the shooting as "a dastardly act," offering a $1,000 reward for information leading to the arrest and conviction of Moore's assailant.[7] Alabama authorities filed charges almost immediately against the operator of a store and filling station near Fort Payne, Alabama. They accused Floyd L. Simpson, who had been seen speaking with Moore on the day of the murder, with killing William L. Moore "unlawfully and with malice aforethought."[8] An FBI ballistics test on the bullets found in Moore's body and on a .22 caliber rifle belonging to Simpson led to the arrest. The case was referred to a grand jury, and Simpson was released on $5,000 bond. Outside the glare of national publicity, however, the grand jury deliberated slowly. In mid-September, the jury announced its refusal to indict Simpson—or anyone—for Moore's murder. The results of the ballistics tests were not made public. Grand jury foreman Robert Tinsley explained that several witnesses had been called, but he refused to explain why no indictment was issued.[9]

In the meantime, civil rights activists responded immediately to Moore's murder. An integrated group of more than one hundred students in Nashville, Tennessee, marched from the chapel at historically Black Fisk University to the city's Federal Building. They carried signs proclaiming "Moore Died for Love. Let's Live and Act in Love" and "William Moore. Who Will Be Next?"[10] Diane Nash led a delegation of eight Black civil rights workers from Birmingham to Gadsden to take up the letter carrier's march at the spot where he was killed. Not sponsored by any organized civil rights group, the eight participants in the march told reporters that "they hoped to prove that a person preaching love of his fellow man, as Mr. Moore had, could walk safely though Alabama."[11] Members of the group intended to walk all the way to Jackson and were encouraged during the first hour of their march when they received positive comments from white spectators along their route. But Etowah County Sheriff's Office deputies soon arrested all eight marchers, charging them with "peace disturbance."

One week later, civil rights advocates announced another attempt to re-sume Bill Moore's march. Marvin Rich, community relations director for the Congress of Racial Equality, explained from the group's national headquar-ters in New York, "This is to give the people of Alabama and America an-other chance. William Moore traveled through this country to express his hopes for equality and justice and he died. This was a failure for the people of Alabama and the people of America."[12] When the group of six white and six Black demonstrators started their walk from the Greyhound bus station in Chattanooga, bystanders taunted them and threatened them with vio-lence. "Hope you stop a .22," one white man shouted to the group, in refer-ence to the bullets that killed Bill Moore. On the second day of the marchers' journey, a convoy of cars filled with whites chased them across the Alabama–Tennessee border, screaming threats and throwing rocks and bottles. Mem-bers of the mob yelled "Throw them niggers in the river" and "Kill them." Officers of the Alabama Highway Patrol met the march at the state line and arrested the civil rights demonstrators for "breach of peace," manhandling them and attacking them repeatedly with electric-shock cattle prods as they lay on the pavement in nonviolent protest. From their cells in the Kilby State Prison in Montgomery, the arrested demonstrators announced that they would not accept bail. They explained that they intended to remain incarcer-ated as a way of calling attention to the assault on their rights of free speech and free assembly. They remained in jail for nearly a month.[13]

In mid-May, civil rights groups tried once again to deliver Bill Moore's letter to Mississippi's governor. Marchers held a memorial service on the spot where Moore had been killed, but soon Alabama Highway Patrol offi-cers and Etowah County sheriff's deputies arrested and jailed the entire del-egation of five whites and six Blacks for breach of the peace.[14] Later, about thirty African American men, women, and children from a local church joined civil rights workers from around the nation for a memorial service honoring Moore at a roadside park. James Peck, editor of the Congress of Racial Equality's national newsletter, praised Moore as "a genuine idealist—he worked for brotherhood all his life." Reverend E. W. Jarrett of Galilee Baptist Church in Gadsden eulogized Moore as having "died but not in vain." A twenty-six-year-old white participant in the march, a native of Chattanooga then living in New York, explained, "I have come down here to make amends for the way this thing has been going on for the last 200 years. If Christ was on this earth today, I'm sure he would be killed just like Wil-liam Moore."[15]

Bill Moore's murder made many people feel that they had to act, that it was no longer acceptable to be a spectator in the struggle over civil rights. To be sure, many others claimed that Moore had no one to blame but himself, that he had brought about his own death through provocative actions that he should have known would inflame the anger of white supremacists. A *New York Times* editorial on April 26 condemned the murder but at the same time described Moore's march as "a pitifully naive pilgrimage." An investigator for the Alabama State Police reported that he had spoken with Moore thirty minutes before his death and asked the postman to cancel his march or at least remove his signs. "I warned him about the racial situation in Alabama but he wouldn't listen," A. G. McDowell related. "He told me in a very nice way that he wanted to prove something and he couldn't if he turned back."[16] U.S. Attorney General Robert Kennedy withheld the support of the Department of Justice for those attempting to complete Moore's march, arguing that "perhaps their energies might be better used in a different direction than taking a walk."[17]

About six weeks after Moore's murder, Medgar Evers, field secretary for the Mississippi chapter of the National Association for the Advancement of Colored People (NAACP), addressed a mass meeting in Jackson, vowing to carry on the struggle against all forms of segregation in that city. When he returned to his home that night, Evers was killed, shot in the back by a sniper. Although his assassin, Byron de la Beckwith, would successfully avoid a conviction for more than thirty years, the brutal repression required to silence people like Moore, Evers, and their supporters exposed the venomous pathology of white supremacy to people across the nation.[18] In Los Angeles and San Francisco, mass rallies protesting the murders of Moore and Evers attracted more than 20,000 participants.[19] In every region of the country during the summer of 1963, the deaths of Bill Moore and Medgar Evers made people ask themselves what they were prepared to do about the pervasive presence of white supremacy in their society.

I was one of those people. The bullets that killed Bill Moore changed my life. I remember hearing news reports about his disappearance and death on the old gray radio in my bedroom on the second story of my family's home in Paterson, New Jersey. I was fifteen years old. The first broadcasts advised that Moore was missing; the next morning newscasters reported his death. I can still remember the impression that his murder made on me: Moore was a white man murdered by other white men because he opposed white supremacy. I had never encountered a story like that. It made me look into myself and provoked me to think about what I was willing to risk for my own beliefs.

The city that I grew up in was racially diverse, and I had seen enough even at the age of fifteen to realize that good and bad people come in all colors, that both virtue and vice characterize every community. But Bill Moore made me think harder about what it meant for me to be white in a world where the advantages of whiteness were carved out of other people's disadvantages. I knew that those of us dwelling in the almost exclusively white neighborhoods on the east side of Paterson lived in better houses and had more money than our classmates in minority or mixed neighborhoods. I did not know then the way residential segregation and home-loan discrimination skewed life chances along racial lines and inhibited opportunities for asset accumulation among members of aggrieved "minority" groups. Yet I did know that my own neighbors included slumlords who failed to provide decent, sanitary, or even safe living conditions for the tenants they gouged, that profits produced by charging high rates for broken-down tenements in slum neighborhoods in other parts of town paid country club dues and college tuition fees for people in my neighborhood.

The murder of Bill Moore opened up new possibilities and personalized the civil rights struggle for me in dramatic ways. For Bill Moore, disapproving of white supremacy in principle wasn't enough; he felt he needed to put his life on the line trying to end it. Bill Moore fought against white racism because he personally found it intolerable, not just because he imagined it might be intolerable for someone else. Certainly I had been aware of many of the Black martyrs before him in the civil rights movement whose deaths were equally tragic and dramatic. Over the years many writers have justifiably criticized the dynamics whereby white people like Bill Moore martyred in the civil rights movement have received a disproportionate share of attention compared to the overwhelmingly greater number of Black people killed in that struggle. As Rita Schwerner noted when the murder of her husband, Michael, and his fellow civil rights workers James Chaney and Andrew Goodman led to a massive federal investigation and search in Mississippi's rivers and coastal waters for the three victims' missing bodies in 1964, "We all know this search with hundreds of sailors is because Andrew Goodman and my husband are white. If only Chaney was involved, nothing would have been done."[20] Hollywood films, made-for-television movies, and popular books have similarly honored white seminarian James Reeb who was killed in the battles over desegregation in Alabama in 1965, but not Jimmy Lee Jackson, a Black youth murdered in the same struggles. They have chronicled the killing of white civil rights volunteer Viola Liuzzo who was shot to death on the night following the Selma–Montgomery march, but not that of Herbert Lee, a Black farmer and voting rights activist shot and killed by a member of the Mississippi state legislature who was never prosecuted for the killing.[21] History textbooks still routinely credit President Lincoln with freeing the slaves and Presidents Kennedy and Johnson with ending segregation, without mentioning the grassroots pressures from people of color that forced those leaders to take the steps that they did.

Hollywood films about the murders of Medgar Evers (*Ghosts of Mississippi*) and Chaney, Schwerner, and Goodman (*Mississippi Burning*) have rewritten the historical record by placing white FBI agents and white attorneys at the center of a struggle for social justice that actually depended almost entirely upon the determination and persistence of Black people in the face of indifference and even outright hostility among most whites, including those in law enforcement agencies. I hope that my attention to Bill Moore does not contribute to the erasure of Black people from the story of their own struggle for emancipation. I have to admit, however, that the murder of Bill Moore did affect me to an unusual degree, even more than the many reports of the deaths of dozens of Blacks in the civil rights struggle. It is only fair to ask myself if my own conditioning as a white person did not make me somehow value a white life more than a Black life. Yet I also now see how rarely our society produces or even imagines antiracist white people. To be sure, many whites are embarrassed by the benefits they receive from white supremacy, and others are inconvenienced or even threatened by the resentments it creates. Some view white supremacy as economically wasteful and socially destructive, while others may wish they could live in a society without racial distinctions. Yet individuals like Bill Moore are rare. Few white people are willing to risk their lives in the fight against white supremacy, are eager to join a movement with minority leadership, or are cognizant of the fight as something of urgent import for themselves rather than as a favor done for others.

Our history and our fiction contain all too many accounts of whites acting with unctuous paternalism to protect "helpless" people of color but very few stories about white people opposing white supremacy on their own. Members of aggrieved racialized groups appear most often as threatening strangers or servile sidekicks in the stories we tell about our past and present, and only rarely are they depicted as self-active agents operating in their own behalf. The difficulty of imagining an antiracist white subject is part of what made Bill Moore's story so compelling to me years ago and what makes it resonate for me even today. At the moment I learned of Bill Moore's death, I found myself thinking about commitment as well as color. What would it mean to believe in something so powerfully that you would give your life for it? I thought I understood how Moore felt, how tormented he must have been by the terrible injustices in our society and by his own inability to do anything meaningful about them.

Later I would learn about the dangers of individual action, about the ways in which any one person's intentions—no matter how sincere—need to be coordinated with a collective social movement and connected to carefully thought-out strategies and tactics produced by a democratic process that changes individuals and society at the same time. Over the years, I would have the opportunity to come across other examples of principled and effective antiracist action by white individuals, by Bob and Dottie Miller Zellner in the Student Nonviolent Coordinating Committee and the labor movement, by Gail Cincotta in campaigns for community reinvestment, and by Heather Heyer killed for standing up to protest the terrorism of Confederate flag waving neo-Nazis in Charlottesville, Virginia, in 2017.[22]

I discovered eventually that Bill Moore had been advised repeatedly against his one-man march by officers of national civil rights organizations, that he had been a mental patient at the Binghamton State Hospital between 1953 and 1955, and that personal desperation as well as social commitment shaped his decision to march on Mississippi and deliver a letter to the governor.[23] Yet I think it would be a mistake to let Bill Moore's human problems and contradictions overshadow the basic idea that he got absolutely right. Like another man often described as mentally ill—John Brown—Bill Moore found white supremacy an abomination even though he was white. He did not imagine himself innocent of the privileges he had received as a result of being white, nor did guilt drive him to seek the approval of those he might have oppressed. He correctly identified white supremacy as a problem he needed to confront, and he took resolute action toward a solution.

Bill Moore's murder was a terrible crime, but culpability for it does not rest solely with the person who fired the shots that killed him. Bill Moore was murdered because too few people had his kind of courage and commitment, because too many white people kept silent about white supremacy even though they knew it was wrong. Today, I think his example stands as relevant as ever, not because dramatic moments of individual heroism will solve our problems, but because white Americans like myself have not yet come to grips with the structural and cultural forces that racialize rights, opportunities, and life chances in our country. Too many of us continue to imagine that we would have supported the civil rights struggles of years ago, when our actions and opinions today conform more closely to the record of that struggle's opponents. We have so demonized the white racists of 1960s Mississippi that we fail to see the ways in which many of their most heinous practices and policies have triumphed in our own day.

At the time of Bill Moore's murder, Mississippi began to emerge as a public symbol of the sickness at the center of race relations in the United States. In some ways the state deserved that reputation. The rioters in Oxford opposing desegregation of their state's university knew that they could count on overt and covert support from Mississippi's elected officials and leading citizens. Anti-Black vigilantes operated with impunity throughout the state, burning the homes and churches of civil rights leaders, bombing Black-owned businesses, and shooting civil rights workers. A state agency, the Mississippi Sovereignty Commission, gave covert support to white supremacist groups, including those distributing license plate holders emblazoned with slogans like "Federally Occupied Mississippi, Kennedy's Hungary" and "Most Lied About State in The Union." The Sovereignty Commission helped Byron de la Beckwith escape a conviction for the murder of Medgar Evers by helping the defense screen jury members, and its agents conspired with Klansmen to set up the murders of James Chaney, Michael Schwerner, and Andrew Goodman.[24]

In 1964, the challenge by the Mississippi Freedom Democratic Party to the openly white supremacist state delegation to the Democratic National Convention, coupled with the murders of Chaney, Schwerner, and Goodman, attracted national and international attention. Magazine articles and best-selling books attempted to diagnose the conditions that gave rise to the state's racial antagonisms, while popular songs by the Chad Mitchell Trio, Phil Ochs, and Nina Simone criticized Mississippi's practices as outside the pale of civilized society. Nightclub and television audiences viewed Mississippi through the bitter and biting satire of Black comedians Moms Mabley and Dick Gregory, whose topical humor singled out the state's white supremacist culture for special ridicule and critique.[25] Gregory joked that the state was so racist that "a white moderate in Mississippi is a cat who wants to lynch you from a *low* tree."[26]

At the same time, however, a different side of the state of Mississippi became visible through the actions and ideas of the state's African American residents as they mobilized for change along with a small number of white allies. I remember watching the televised testimony of Fannie Lou Hamer before the Credentials Committee at the 1964 Democratic National Convention as she described her attempts to register to vote as well as the harassment and retaliation she suffered for those efforts. As a warning, local authorities once harassed her with a one-month water bill of $9,000, threatening to jail her if she did not pay it.[27] Mrs. Hamer was fired from her job, evicted from her home, and beaten by sheriff's deputies, but she continued to fight for freedom. "Is this America, the land of the free and the home of the brave where we are threatened daily because we want to live as decent human beings?" she asked.[28]

In an election supervised by the Mississippi Freedom Democratic Party (MFDP) and open to all voters regardless of race, Mississippi voters had chosen Hamer and her colleagues to represent their state at the convention. The national Democratic Party, however, seated the all-white segregationist delegation of party regulars, many of whom had already pledged to support Republican nominee Barry Goldwater, who campaigned as an opponent of the 1964 Civil Rights Act. As I learned later, President Johnson sent liberal senator Hubert Humphrey as his representative to a secret meeting at the convention with members of the MFDP in an attempt to persuade them to drop their demands to be seated as official delegates. Hamer had been eager to meet the senator, whom she had admired because of his reputation as a proponent of civil rights, but she was disappointed to find "a little round-eyed man with his eyes full of tears." When warned by the MFDP attorney, Joseph Rauh, that their effort to be seated at the convention would damage Humphrey's chances for nomination as Johnson's running mate, Hamer asked, "Well, Mr. Humphrey, do you mean to tell me that your position is more important to you than four hundred thousand black people's lives?"[29]

Humphrey's inability to answer that question embodied a larger inability among white liberals to distance themselves sufficiently from the possessive investment in whiteness, an inability that plagues them to this day.

At college in St. Louis in 1964, I encountered some Mississippians who had worked with Fannie Lou Hamer and who displayed her kind of courage and commitment. Joyce and Dorie Ladner especially impressed me. They had worked almost alone in Natchez, Mississippi, as civil rights organizers in the early 1960s when nearly everyone else was afraid to challenge white supremacy in that section of the state. I heard the Ladner sisters speak at the campus YMCA at meetings organized by civil rights supporters. The Ladners' knowledge, tactical insights, and commitment left a lasting impression on me. As Charles Payne shows in his excellent study of the civil rights struggle in Mississippi, people like Fannie Lou Hamer and the Ladner sisters emerged from an entire community that made up for a lack of material resources and political power with an abundance of courage and vision. Their example provided hope and inspiration to many people living in circumstances far different from their own.[30]

With the passage of the 1964 and 1965 civil rights laws, Mississippi's brand of white supremacy was revealed as symptomatic of a much broader psychosis. Ending de jure (by law) segregation in the South did little or nothing to end de facto (by fact) segregation in the North. Mississippi, the home of William Faulkner, Chester Himes, and Eudora Welty, of Elvis Presley, Jimmie Rodgers, and Robert Johnson, was not an aberration isolated from the rest of the United States. Although the form differed from state to state and from region to region, the possessive investment in whiteness that poisoned political and private lives in Mississippi was a quintessentially American problem. We discovered that laws guaranteeing the right to eat at a lunch counter did little to correct the elaborate web of discrimination in housing, hiring, and education that left minorities less able to pay for a lunch-counter meal, let alone raise the capital necessary to own a lunch counter. We found that school segregation and unequal education did not end when courts banned "separate but equal" Jim Crow schools, but left intact segregated neighborhoods and school districts. Even the right to vote meant less than we thought when gerrymandering and the high costs of political campaigns left aggrieved minority communities with no one to vote for who would be likely to represent their interests accurately. Those of us who might have been inclined to view white racism as a particularly southern problem at the time of Bill Moore's murder soon saw the wisdom in Malcolm X's observation that as long as you're south of the Canadian border, you're in the South.

This book identifies the ways in which power, property, and the politics of race in our society continue to contain unacknowledged and unacceptable allegiances to white supremacy. I write it, in part, to pay the debts I owe to

Joyce and Dorie Ladner, to Fannie Lou Hamer, and to many other Mississippians. I want to make it clear that Fannie Lou Hamer's appeals did not fall on deaf ears and that Bill Moore's letter can still be delivered after all these years.

Yet I would not be honoring the work of these Mississippians properly if I let it go at that. By the 1990s, I was living and working in California, a state where demagogic political leaders and a frightened electorate repeatedly launched decidedly racist attacks on communities of color. The mendacity and meanness of Governor Pete Wilson, the passage of the anti-immigrant Proposition 187 and the anti–affirmative action Proposition 209, initiatives against bilingual education, and the refusal by legally constituted authorities to enforce laws protecting the civil rights, wages, and working conditions of the people of the state made California in the 1990s the human rights equivalent of Mississippi in the 1960s.

Sixty years ago, Californians could afford to view the events transpiring in Mississippi with pity and contempt. California then was a high-wage and high-employment state where taxpayer support provided quality schools and social service programs geared toward bringing chances for upward mobility to an impressively broad range of its population. The state's political leaders acted with foresight and vision, preparing for the future by speaking honestly and openly with the citizens of their state about the things they needed to do to ensure the common good. Mississippi, on the other hand, used the power of the state to maintain a low-wage, low-employment economy characterized by vivid contrasts between the dire poverty and financial anxiety of most state residents and the monopoly power and luxury lifestyles of a handful of wealthy plutocrats. It trailed most of the other states in educational expenditures per pupil. Its political leaders rarely leveled with citizens, resorting instead to demagogic scapegoating of powerless and nonvoting populations to divide and conquer. As John Dittmer points out in his fine book, *Local People*, one of the intended consequences of racially segmenting the labor force in Mississippi in the 1950s and 1960s was to preserve wealth in a few hands by deterring workers from joining together to seek union representation or legislation regulating the conditions of labor.[31]

By the 1990s, California had caught up with the Mississippi of 1963. State agencies failed to enforce laws regulating wages, hours, and working conditions, much less bans on discrimination in housing, hiring, and education. The growth of unregulated low-wage labor launched a race to the bottom that enabled wealthy consumers to pay less for foodstuffs and food preparation, for construction and maintenance, for child care and domestic cleaning, while the majority of the population confronted the stagnation and even the decline of its real wages. California stood near the bottom in state school spending per pupil—in no small measure because most public school students were not white. We discovered to our sorrow that our elected officials could not lead us, so they lied to us, fomenting hatred against the poor, immigrants, and racial minorities to hide the ways in which their own policies were destroying the economic and social infrastructure of our state. If this book represented an effort to deliver at last the letter that Bill Moore wished to bring to Ross Barnett in 1963, I hoped that it would help send a message to Sacramento as well.

I think I now know why Bill Moore's murder affected me so deeply in 1963. His actions forced my first confrontations with the possessive investment in whiteness—a poisonous system of privilege that pits people against each other and prevents the creation of common ground. Exposing, analyzing, and eradicating this pathology is an obligation that we all share, white people most of all. I hope that this book will be a step in that direction.

In the darkest days of the 1990s, as the governor of California and his political puppets on the board of regents were resorting to the crudest kinds of racist scapegoating to protect the possessive investment in whiteness, a group of young students at the University of California, San Diego, where I was then teaching, created an interethnic antiracist coalition that expressed and enacted a compelling vision of social justice. Their dignity, discipline, and determination to fight every measure designed to increase the "wages of whiteness" provided an inspiring alternative to the unjust and immoral policies advanced by the most powerful and wealthy individuals in their state.[32] They learned the lessons of history well, and their actions pointed the way toward a better and more just future. The members of the No Retreat! coalition inherited the vision and the courage of Fannie Lou Hamer, Bill Moore, and many others. I dedicate this book to them, with deep respect and gratitude.

Introduction to the
Twentieth Anniversary Edition
The Changing Same

*I know what the world has done to my brother, and how narrowly he
has survived it. And I know, which is much worse, and this is the
crime of which I accuse my country and my countrymen, and for
which neither I nor time nor history will ever forgive them, that they
have destroyed and are destroying hundreds of thousands of lives
and do not know it and do not want to know it.*

—JAMES BALDWIN

The publication of this revised twentieth anniversary edition of *The Possessive Investment in Whiteness* provides an opportunity to update, clarify,
and amplify the evidence, ideas, and arguments that appeared in the first
two editions, published in 1998 and 2006. It also offers an opportunity to as-
sess exactly how much has changed over the past two decades and how much
remains the same. The harsh realization that so many of the indecent and
unjust conditions evident twenty years ago remain firmly in place today, and
in fact in most respects have grown worse, should be a source of deep sorrow.
Some readers of the 1998 and 2006 editions contended that the book's evidence about racially disproportionate susceptibility to premature death and
the skewing of opportunities and life chances along racial lines were largely
vestigial remnants of a distant past, merely dying manifestations of historical
slavery and segregation that were fading away and would soon disappear.
They imagined an unbroken upward trajectory of progress over time. Sadly,
however, the racial wealth gap, the racial health gap, and most other measures
of racial stratification and subordination today are even worse than they were
ten or twenty years ago. Time does not heal all wounds. Problems do not solve
themselves. Things will not get better unless we make them better.

Publishers and academic reviewers measure the success of a book by how
many copies are sold, how many times it is cited in research by other scholars, how widely it is assigned in courses, and how frequently its chapters are
reprinted in edited collections. By all of these measures, *The Possessive Investment in Whiteness* has done well. Yet this system of evaluation is a deeply
flawed way of thinking about scholarly research. Books can become popular

simply because they conform to the common sense of their era, because they confirm the ill-conceived ideas or poorly thought out prejudices of readers. Books by scholars ideally should aim to move the conversation along, to challenge dominant assumptions and change prevailing frameworks. Their goal should be to elevate the level of discussion, to complicate how questions are asked and answered, to make people dissatisfied with facile formulations and arguments. The ultimate influence and impact of research rests upon creating a new common sense and forging new frameworks for discussing enduring problems in subtle and sophisticated ways so people can use them to forge solutions.

During the past two decades, *The Possessive Investment in Whiteness* has played a part in shaping a shared social conversation that has changed the frame and shifted the focus of discussions about race. Twenty years ago, scholarly and civic discussions about racism relentlessly portrayed aggrieved racial groups as merely disadvantaged without acknowledging how they are taken advantage of by others. Public policy makers and academic experts at that time generally presumed that the superior life outcomes that whites experienced stemmed from their fortitude, fitness, and family values rather than from the locked-in advantages of the possessive investment in whiteness and its facilitation of opportunity hoarding. Proposed reforms in the past generally presumed that nonwhites had to make themselves better, more fit for freedom, more like whites, not that whites needed to surrender their stranglehold on the unfair gains and unjust rewards they derive from pervasive practices that produce artificial, arbitrary, and irrational discrimination.

Today, it has become commonplace, although hardly universal, to recognize that whiteness is not so much a color as a condition, a structured advantage sustained by past and present forms of exclusion and subordination. It is possible today for people to recognize that racism involves power as well as prejudice, assets as well as attitudes, and the distribution of property and power as well as the particularities of pigment. Twenty years ago, racism was popularly presumed to be the product of individual, aberrant, isolated, and intentional actions by individuals rather than the visible manifestation of processes that are structural, systemic, collective, cumulative, and continuing. The solutions proffered to solve racial problems in the past focused on individual attitudes and behaviors, on improving "race relations" and promoting racial reconciliation. Although better behavior by individuals will always be welcome, it is evident today that it is indecent to settle simply for more cordial and polite relations between the races while grievously unequal and unjust conditions remain in place. True reconciliation cannot take place unless it is preceded by recognition, contrition, atonement, repair, and restitution.

The Possessive Investment in Whiteness has played a role in changing the frame and shifting the focus of civic and scholarly discussions about racism, but it has not done so alone. It has been part of a chorus of many voices, one link in a lengthy chain forged by a wide range of interlocutors. Every antiracist article and book becomes more powerful and more persuasive because of the others and the cumulative impact they exert. The broader conversation profits from our similarities and from our differences, from our agreements and from our disagreements. In shared social conversations about ideas, we do this work together. Everyone contributes and everyone counts. As literary critic Mikhail Bakhtin explains, there is no pure monologue in culture.[1] Everyone enters a dialogue already in progress. Failure to recognize this fact can lead to distorted ways of working. Barbara Tomlinson and I addressed the ramifications of this idea in our 2013 *American Quarterly* article "American Studies as Accompaniment."[2] We noted that the audit culture and prestige hierarchies of academic research can make scholars think they should have the first word or the last word, that they should be the first to discover a new topic or else provide the definitive judgment on the subject so no more research needs to be done. The first and the last word, however, are delusions. Everyone builds on what came before and prepares part of what comes after. The real challenge of research is not to open up or close down debate with the first or last word, but rather to receive gratefully the wisdom of the past (faults and all) and transform its truths so they can be passed on graciously to new generations of critical interlocutors.

The text and footnotes of *The Possessive Investment in Whiteness* reference directly the explicit dialogic partners whose writings shaped it.[3] In retrospect, I can now see how it was also influenced and informed by traces of works by authors not cited.[4] Yet while of the utmost importance to the origins and evolution of this book, scholarly research provided only one part of the dialogue from which it emerged and to which it responded. As Cedric Robinson astutely observed, *The Possessive Investment in Whiteness* is not really a book about whiteness but rather a deployment of tools honed and refined in struggles shaped by radical Black studies and radical Black politics.[5] It came from and sought to contribute to what Martin Luther King, Jr., aptly named "the long and bitter—but beautiful—struggle" for a new and better world.[6]

I started writing what became *The Possessive Investment in Whiteness* in the midst of a series of strategy meetings, public presentations, and classroom lectures designed to respond to attacks on affirmative action in California in the 1990s. The anti-immigrant and anti–affirmative action demagoguery of California governor Pete Wilson played a formative role in the dialogic process that led to the book. The Black Radical Tradition teaches that hegemony can be turned on its head, that poison can be transformed into medicine, that fighting back can maneuver even the most ill-intentioned enemies into becoming unwitting accomplices in our liberation. The mobilizations against Wilson's ballot initiatives Proposition 187 and Proposition 209 that I describe in Chapter 11 provoked me to assemble the evidence, ideas, and arguments that appear on these pages. I described much of what I learned from that struggle first in a presentation at the American Studies Association annual meetings in 1993. That talk became the basis for an article in the *American Quarterly* in 1995, which in turn led to the writing and publication of the first edition of this book in 1998. The ensuing fate of the book has been directly connected to the pulse of the people, to its utility as one of the resources deployed by masses in motion. In conjunction with the creations of many other authors and artists, its framework, terminology, ideas, and evidence have permeated parts of adult education classes for low-wage immigrant women workers, campaigns for educational equity waged by antiracist activists, discussions among church social justice study groups, depositions and friend of the court briefs in fair housing cases, policy briefs by financial equity advocates, lessons and lectures by classroom teachers, and creative works by visual and spoken word artists. Being the author of this book has blessed me with the extraordinary privilege and pleasure of meeting with, speaking with, working with, and learning with—and from—communities in struggle. These acts of accompaniment have taken me to a coalition against lead poisoning meeting at the Prince Hall Mason Lodge in North St. Louis and a fair housing celebration at a country club in the southern suburbs of Chicago, to a son jaorcho fandango in a community center in East Los Angeles and to interviews with fair housing litigants in their living rooms in West Palm Beach, Florida. Everywhere I have been, I have encountered principled people from many different backgrounds working together for social justice, from Ferguson to Flint, from Memphis to Milwaukee, from Boston to Austin.

Much has changed over the past twenty years because of these social movement mobilizations. Billions of dollars of sound investments have been made in racially isolated neighborhoods and communities because of the efforts of the National Community Reinvestment Coalition, the Woodstock Institute, and other social justice organizations dedicated to realizing the promises inscribed in the 1977 Community Reinvestment Act.[7] Fair housing advocates, activists, and attorneys affiliated with the National Fair Housing Alliance have won victories that have opened up a plethora of opportunities for secure, safe, and affordable housing, and have helped people acquire assets that appreciate in value and can be passed down across generations. Creative litigators have used fair housing laws to secure justice for victims of sexual harassment and assault, hate crimes, and environmental racism.[8] Decades of citizen activism at the local level by people of many different races and religions led to the Supreme Court's 2015 ruling in the *Inclusive Communities* case that confirmed the legitimacy and necessity of considering the racially disparate impact of seemingly racial neutral housing policies.[9] Action inside courtrooms has been accompanied by mass mobilizations. Millions of immigrants and their allies poured into the streets in 2006 in a proud display of multiracial, multilingual, and multinational solidarity. This mobilization led to the defeat of legislation pending in Congress at that time that was designed to impose draconian criminal penalties on the quotidian survival strategies of immigrants and their children.[10] Because of #Black-LivesMatter, and #SayHerName protests, police killings of and assaults on unarmed Black people no longer proceed unchallenged but have instead provoked mobilizations by mass movements led by women of color, often by those who identify as queer or trans.[11] Campaigns for educational equity and justice by parents, teachers, and students have foregrounded the idea of education as a public good to be protected rather than simply as a private commodity to be purchased.

Yet for all that has changed, sadly much remains the same. The arguments and analyses written by David Walker in the 1820s, by Anna Julia Cooper in the 1890s and by W.E.B. Du Bois in the 1930s still by and large describe the core features of the racial order we confront and contest today. Words uttered decades ago, including some in this book, could just as easily have been spoken yesterday. David Walker emphasized how the rewards of whiteness corrupt white people. Once group identity makes people accustomed to exploiting the labor of others, he argued, they became blind to the evil acts they perform.[12] These patterns persist today. As New Orleans Ninth Ward spoken word artist, activist, and cultural visionary Sunni Patterson wrote after the devastation her city suffered in 2005, "And we know this place. It's ever-changing yet forever the same: money and power and greed, the game.[13]"

The period preceding this 2018 edition of *The Possessive Investment in Whiteness* was marked by both the organized abandonment and yet punitive confinement of impoverished Black New Orleans residents in the wake of Hurricane Katrina in 2005 and the manipulation of the grand jury process to ensure that no charges were brought against the killer of Michael Brown in Ferguson in 2014. Many of us have come to refer to this as the Katrina-Ferguson Conjuncture, a moment in history that discredits old practices and demands new ones, a time when social movements generate new personalities, new politics, and new polities. Along the way, a racially orchestrated economic crisis produced the greatest loss of assets in history for Black and brown people. Virulent rhetoric, violent acts, and vile policies have targeted immigrants of color, generating mass deportations and detentions. In popular culture and political proclamations, online and in the streets; in private acts of discrimination; and in public policies like "broken windows" policing and the privatization of public education, an unapologetic and unaccountable racism continues to be legislated, learned, and legitimated. Race is still experienced as an identity inscribed on the body that draws negative ascription from members of dominant groups, but it is also instantiated through state and vigilante violence, displacement, dispossession, and disempowerment, systemic processes of criminalization and mass incarceration, and plutocratic policies that revolve around institutionalized privatization and plunder.

We know that these practices and processes are transnational as well as national. They are as deadly in Sao Paolo as they are in San Francisco, as cruel in Manchester as they are in Minneapolis. They mean something different to people suffering from the violence of the U.S. empire outside its borders than they do to those us who live in the metropole. They impact Indigenous people and Muslims with particularly deadly force. Yet these many uneven and different kinds of racism still stem from some common causes. The key categories of economic and social life—no less than the core components of scholarly contemplation and critique—everywhere continue to rest on racist premises, presumptions, and practices that need to be opposed both locally and globally.

We have no choice but to start from where we are, to play the hand we have been dealt by history, to act in the arenas open to us with the modest tools we have at our disposal. In the United States, that means coming to grips with the unresolved and continuing legacies of conquest and colonization, of Indigenous dispossession and immigrant exclusion and exploitation, of sexual racism and of slavery unwilling to die. In the wake of what we have come to name the Katrina-Ferguson Conjuncture, white folks generally still insist on being on top. The old will not die and the new cannot yet be born. When Barack Obama attained the presidency of the United States in 2008, a wide range of civic and scholarly voices predicted that the United States was on the way to becoming a "post-racial" nation. Of course, we knew better. Today, it is clearer than ever that we are not postracial, even if, sadly, we are indeed post-Trayvon Martin, post-Rekia Boyd, post-Eric Garner, post-Sandra Bland, and post-Freddie Gray. The killers of these Black people have never been held accountable for their deeds. The racial and spatial distribution of power, opportunities, and life chances that this violence is enacted to uphold remains firmly in place. Nearly 4 million separate incidents of illegal but unprosecuted housing discrimination take place every year, relegating people of different races to different places, to different neighborhoods, schools, jobs, health conditions, and opportunities for asset accumulation. What the Obama presidency initiated was not a new era of racial liberation but rather a new system of racial subordination, one where the triumphs of a few people of color designated as exceptional serve to rationalize and excuse the exclusion of the masses of racialized people designated as disposable. The direct, referential, and snarling racism of white supremacy's past finds new life through the enactment and celebration of interpersonal hate crimes, ever more lurid and demeaning depictions of nonwhite individuals (including those lauded as exceptional), and the pervasive presence of recreational hate as a perverse but seemingly pleasurable spectacle in political discourse.

At the same time, racially specific denials of dignity, democracy, and opportunity are instituted through structural systematic practices that do not require overt references to race. White supremacy makes its presence felt through hate crimes and hurled insults, but it also works relentlessly and effectively through disproportionate vulnerability to police stops, frisks, arrests, and killings, to mass incarceration and the collateral consequences of a criminal conviction. The possessive investment in whiteness fuels depictions of aggrieved racialized populations as innately risky, as unworthy of protection or support, while subjecting them to housing insecurity, homelessness, foreclosure, and eviction, to labor exploitation and wage theft, and to racialized sexual harassment at work and on the streets. A wide range of policies secure racist effects without announcing racist intent. For example, laws that require would-be voters to have valid current forms of identification with their pictures on them, despite scant evidence of in-person voter fraud, make no overt mention of race. But in a society where racial profiling and poverty combine to make Black people much more likely not to have a driver's license, or more likely to have licenses suspended because they cannot pay fines, the provision functions smoothly and seamlessly as a form of racialized voter suppression.

Yet the Katrina-Ferguson Conjuncture is also an oppositional conjuncture. As has been the case throughout history, new forms of domination produce new forms of resistance. Struggle always emerges from the seeds of a new society that rest inside the shell of the old. The same forces producing seemingly unlimited suffering and sacrifice have also given rise to new politics and new polities. Cedric Robinson reminds us that all systems of social control contain contradictions that can cause their undoing. Even slavery, he notes, "gave the lie to its own conceit: one could not create a perfect system of oppression and exploitation."[14]

The core contradiction of neoliberal society is race. The neoliberal policies, practices, and pedagogies that pervade contemporary society simultaneously require both the deployment and the disavowal of race. Race needs to be deployed as a justification for devaluing the common good. Privatization proceeds primarily by portraying public spaces and public institutions as unclean and unsafe, as the parochial preserve of unworthy people of color. Neoliberalism's core oppositions between public and private, between producer and parasite, proceed through racialized metaphors about lack of responsibility and accountability. Yet race is also deployed as an excuse for the failures of neoliberalism, scapegoating people of color for the absolute inability of the "market" to deliver general prosperity. Concerns with the general welfare are eclipsed by complaints about "those people" receiving welfare. The people who *have* the most severe problems are seen *as* problems through this lens. Yet even while race is relentlessly deployed, it must be disavowed through the erasure of contemporary racism and its relegation to a prior time in history. Racial projects are replete with historical social identities. They reveal the "market" to be a racialized social construct, not an autonomous entity. Racism requires aggrieved groups to expose the illusion of the market, to unmask capitalism as always already racialized. Yet racism also provokes aggrieved groups to draw on archives, create imaginaries, and inhabit identities that are inimical to the interests of market forces, that challenge the hegemony of market time and market space.

In response to the Katrina-Ferguson Conjuncture and its attendant oppressions and abandonments, masses in motion have collectively rejected an unlivable destiny. The cruel treatment of Black New Orleans and the denial of justice for Michael Brown were events designed to humiliate and subordinate. They were public spectacles crafted to demonstrate that Black lives do not matter. Yet for the targets of those messages, these events encapsulated, crystallized, and distilled their experiences with racial subordination over the previous four decades. They exposed the cruelty and mendacity of the people in power. They were seen as injuries that portended an unlivable destiny and as insults that required a collective response. They produced a turning point from which there can be no turning back.

New social movements are emerging in this conjuncture. They are often race based but rarely race bound. They recognize racism as a technology of power, as a justification and excuse for unfair gains and unjust enrichments. They see racism as innately intersectional, as *ever* present, but *never* present in isolation from sexism, homophobia, imperial conquest, and class subordination. These movements acknowledge the long fetch of history, the depressing collective, cumulative, and continuing consequences of slavery unwilling to die, yet they also perceive new possibilities for the present and for the future. They challenge the logics of color blindness and balanced budget conservatism by drawing on the enduring and viable repressed radicalisms of previous eras. They resonate with the call by Charlotta Bass to seek more than "dark faces in high places," with the insistence of Vincent Harding that the goal of the freedom movement had to be more ambitious than merely seeking to desegregate the ranks of the pain inflictors of this world, with the assertion by Martin Luther King, Jr., that "the black revolution is much more than a struggle for the rights of Negroes. It is forcing America to face all its interrelated flaws—racism, poverty, militarism and materialism."[15] Social movements mobilize the insights and energy of people whose backs are not just up against the wall but who have been pushed through the wall. They bring together criminalized youth and adults, houseless survivors of urban development, people who refuse normative sex and gender roles and appearances, targets of police repression, victims of environmental racism, persecuted religious minorities, and immigrants. Their mobilizations challenge the social warrant of neoliberal privatization, personalization, and plunder by promoting plans, policies, and programs speaking to the interests

of those in greatest need, by deepening democratic and deliberative processes through collective decision-making, by developing new leaders and new
understandings of leadership, by finding value in undervalued places and
undervalued people, and by creating new cultures of mutual recognition and
respect.

The pulse of the people in the streets, the music of the masses in motion,
appears in vivid form in a wide range of antiracist mobilizations. It perme-
ates the poetry of the people. Speaking for herself and for millions of others,
Sunni Patterson concludes her poem "We Know This Place" with a clarion
call that resonates with the energy and imagination of our time: "But come,
come children, rally around, and maybe together we can make a sound, that
will shake the trees and rattle the ground, make strong our knees cause we's
freedom bound. Hold On to the Prize. Never Put It Down. Be Firm in the
Stance. No Break, No Bow. Forward dear children, cause freedom is now."[16]
This always changing but forever the same struggle contains both continuity
and rupture, both the depressing weight of stasis and the exhilarating possibility of change. Things will not get better unless we make them better, but
change is in the air.

It can be daunting and depressing to confront the enduring depths and
dimensions of racial oppression, to reckon with the needless suffering that
takes place because of the possessive investment in whiteness. While I can
see some reasons to celebrate the publication of a twentieth-anniversary edition of *The Possessive Investment In Whiteness*, it would have been far prefer-
able from my perspective if the conditions I described twenty years had
become so obsolete that a twentieth-anniversary edition of the book was not
needed. My deepest hope now is that there will not be a need for a thirtieth-
anniversary edition, except perhaps as a historical curiosity delineating how
radically society had changed in the intervening ten years. Whether or not
that happens depends upon all of us, on whether reading this book gives
readers work to do, not just emotions to feel. It is one thing to talk about suffering but quite another to do something about it. It is not enough to craft
eloquent or indignant descriptions of injustice, to wallow in the affects of
alienation and despair, or to savor the peculiar pleasures of cynicism and
resignation, to decry and condemn exploitation but not try to stop it. Racism
is not a text, an ideology, or a secret oath. It is a set of uneven yet fully linked
concrete practices and processes. The racial order gets made and remade
every day. We all have meaningful work to do, and as the lyrics of the venerable gospel song "May the Work I've Done" instruct, in this world, it is the
work you do that speaks for you.

THE POSSESSIVE INVESTMENT
IN WHITENESS

1

The Possessive Investment
in Whiteness

*Blacks are often confronted, in American life, with such devastating
examples of the white descent from dignity; devastating not only
because of the enormity of white pretensions, but because this swift
and graceless descent would seem to indicate that white people have
no principles whatever.*

—JAMES BALDWIN

Shortly after World War II, a French reporter asked expatriate Richard
Wright for his views about the "Negro problem" in America. The author
replied, "There isn't any Negro problem; there is only a white problem."[1]
By inverting the reporter's question, Wright called attention to its hidden
assumptions—that racial polarization comes from the existence of Blacks
rather than from the behavior of whites, that Black people are a "problem"
for whites rather than fellow citizens entitled to justice, and that, unless
otherwise specified, "Americans" means "whites."[2] Wright's formulation also
placed political mobilization by African Americans during the civil rights
era in context, connecting Black disadvantages to white advantages and
finding the roots of Black consciousness in the systemic practices of aversion,
exploitation, denigration, and discrimination practiced by people who think
of themselves as "white."

Whiteness is everywhere in U.S. culture, but it is very hard to see. As
Richard Dyer suggests, "White power secures its dominance by seeming not
to be anything in particular."[3] As the unmarked category against which difference is constructed, whiteness never has to speak its name, never has to
acknowledge its role as an organizing principle in social and cultural relations.[4] To identify, analyze, and oppose the destructive consequences of
whiteness, we need what Walter Benjamin called "presence of mind." Benjamin wrote that people visit fortune-tellers less out of a desire to know the
future than out of a fear of not noticing some important aspect of the present. "Presence of mind," he suggested, "is an abstract of the future, and precise awareness of the present moment more decisive than foreknowledge of

the most distant events."[5] In U.S. society at this time, precise awareness of the present moment requires an understanding of the existence and the destructive consequences of the possessive investment in whiteness that surreptitiously shapes so much of our public and private lives.

Race is a cultural construct, but one with deadly social causes and consequences. Conscious and deliberate actions have institutionalized group identity in the United States, not just through the dissemination of cultural stories but also through the creation of social structures that generate economic advantages for European Americans through the possessive investment in whiteness. Studies of racial culture too far removed from studies of social structure leave us with inadequate explanations for understanding and combating racism.

Desire for land, raw materials, and the profits made possible by slave labor encouraged European settlers in North America to view, first, Native Americans and, later, African Americans as racially inferior people suited "by nature" for the humiliating subordination of involuntary servitude. The long history of the possessive investment in whiteness stems in no small measure from the fact that all subsequent immigrants to North America have come to an already racialized society. As Geonpul scholar Aileen Moreton-Robinson argues, the legal and political institutions of settler colonial societies naturalize the nation as a white possession.[6] Moreover, Indigenous dispossession is not a fixed and finite past event but a continuing and continuously augmented and enhanced set of practices that shape contemporary concepts of law, learning, and land use. From the start, European settlers in North America established structures encouraging a possessive investment in whiteness. The colonial and early national legal systems authorized attacks on Native Americans and encouraged the appropriation of their lands. They protected racialized chattel slavery, limited naturalized citizenship to "white" males, excluded immigrants from Asia as expressly unwelcome (through legislation aimed at China in 1882, India in 1917, Japan in 1924, and the Philippines in 1934), and provided pretexts, rationales, and procedures for restricting the citizenship, exploiting the labor, and seizing the property of Asian Americans, Mexican Americans, Native Americans, and African Americans.[7]

The possessive investment in whiteness is not a simple matter of Black and white; all racialized minority groups have suffered from it, albeit to different degrees and in different ways. The African slave trade began in earnest only after large-scale Native American slavery proved impractical in North America. Efforts to abolish African slavery led initially to the importation of low-wage labor from Asia. Legislation banning immigration from Asia set the stage for the recruitment of low-wage labor from Mexico. All of the new racial hierarchies that emerged in each of these eras revolved around applying racial labels to "nonwhite" groups in order to stigmatize and exploit them while at the same time reserving extra value for whiteness.

Although reproduced in new form in every era, the possessive invest-ment in whiteness has always been influenced by its origins in the racialized history of the United States—by the legacy of slavery and segregation, of "Indian" extermination and immigrant restriction, of conquest and colo-nialism. Although slavery has existed in many countries without any par-ticular racial dimensions to it, the slave system that emerged in North America soon took on distinctly racial forms. Africans enslaved in North America faced a racialized system of power that reserved permanent, he-reditary, chattel slavery for Black people. White settlers institutionalized a possessive investment in whiteness by making Blackness synonymous with slavery and whiteness synonymous with freedom, but also by pitting people of color against one another. Fearful of alliances between Native Americans and African Americans that might challenge the prerogatives of whiteness, white settlers prohibited slaves and free Blacks from traveling in "Indian country." European Americans used diplomacy and force to compel Native Americans to return runaway slaves to their white masters. During the Stono Rebellion of 1739, colonial authorities offered Native Americans a bounty for every rebellious slave they captured or killed. At the same time, British settlers recruited Black slaves to fight against Native Americans with-in colonial militias.[8] In Louisiana in 1729, settler colonialists from France went to war against the Natchez nation in order to seize its land and set up tobacco plantations. Enslaved Africans were compelled to fight on the side of the French along with Choctaws recruited to fight against their Natchez enemies.[9]

The power of whiteness depended not only on white hegemony over sep-arate racialized groups but also on manipulating racial outsiders to fight against one another, to compete for white approval, and to seek the rewards and privileges of whiteness for themselves. Aggrieved communities of color have often sought to curry favor with whites in order to make gains at each other's expense. In the nineteenth century, members of the Cherokee nation began to hold Black slaves, although as Tiya Miles notes, their complicity with the slave system was "not fully transparent, officially sanctioned, or unilateral."[10] Some of the first regular African American units in the U.S. army went to war against Kickapoo and Comanche people in Texas and served as security forces for wagon trains of white settlers on the trails to California. The conquest of the Comanches in the 1870s sparked a mass mi-gration by Spanish-speaking residents of New Mexico into the areas of West Texas formerly occupied by the vanquished Native Americans.[11] Immigrants from Asia sought the rewards of whiteness for themselves by asking the courts to recognize their identity as "white," therefore making them eligible for naturalized citizenship according to the Immigration and Naturalization Act of 1790; Mexican Americans also insisted on being classified as white.[12] In the early twentieth century, Black soldiers already accustomed to fighting

Native Americans in the Southwest participated in the U.S. occupation of the Philippines and the punitive expedition against troops loyal to Pancho Villa in Mexico.[13] Asian American managers cracked down on efforts by Mexican American farmworkers to form unions in the fields, whereas the Pullman Company tried to break the African American Brotherhood of Sleeping Car Porters by importing Filipinx to work as porters. Mexican Americans and Blacks took possession of some of the property confiscated from Japanese Americans during the internment of the 1940s, and Asian Americans, Blacks, and Mexican Americans all secured advantages for themselves by cooperating with the exploitation of Native Americans.

Yet while every racialized minority group has sometimes sought the rewards of whiteness, these groups have also been able to form interethnic antiracist alliances. Native American tribes often harbored runaway slaves and drew upon their expertise in combat against whites. In 1711, an African named Harry helped lead the Tuscaroras against the British.[14] Some runaway slaves took the side of the Natchez in their wars against the French in the eighteenth century. They established maroon settlements where Native Americans and Blacks lived together. Black Seminoles in Florida routinely recruited slaves from Georgia plantations to their side in battles against European Americans.[15] African Americans resisting slavery and white supremacy in the United States during the nineteenth century sometimes looked to Mexico as a refuge (especially after that nation abolished slavery), and in the twentieth century the rise of Japan as a successful nonwhite world power served as one source of inspiration and emulation among African American nationalists. In 1903, Mexican American and Japanese American farmworkers joined forces in Oxnard, California, to wage a successful strike in the beet fields, and subsequently members of the two groups organized an interracial union, the Japanese Mexican Labor Association.[16] Yet whether characterized by conflict or cooperation, all relations among aggrieved racialized minorities stemmed from recognition of the rewards of whiteness and the concomitant penalties imposed upon "nonwhite" populations.

The possessive investment in whiteness today is not simply the residue of conquest and colonialism, of slavery and segregation, of immigrant exclusion and "Indian" extermination. Contemporary whiteness and its rewards have been created and re-created by policies adopted long after the formative stages of Indigenous dispossession, the emancipation of slaves in the 1860s, and even after the outlawing of de jure segregation in the 1960s. There has always been racism in the United States, but it has not always been the same racism. Racism has changed over time, taking on different forms and serving different social purposes in each time period. Antiracist mobilizations during the Civil War and civil rights eras meaningfully curtailed the reach and scope of white supremacy, but in each case reactionary forces engineered a renewal of racism in new forms during succeeding decades.

Contemporary racism has been created anew in many ways over the past half century, most dramatically by the putatively race-neutral, liberal, social democratic reforms of the New Deal era and by the more overtly race-conscious conservative reactions against racial liberalism since the Nixon years. It is a mistake to posit a gradual and inevitable trajectory of evolutionary progress in race relations; on the contrary, our history shows that battles won at one moment can later be lost. Despite hard-fought struggles for change that secured important concessions during the 1960s in the form of civil rights legislation, the racialized nature of social policy in the United States since the Great Depression has actually increased the possessive investment in whiteness among European Americans over the past century.

During the New Deal era of the 1930s and 1940s, both the Wagner Act and the Social Security Act excluded farmworkers and domestics from coverage, effectively denying those disproportionately minority sectors of the workforce protections and benefits routinely afforded whites. The Federal Housing Act of 1934 brought homeownership within reach of millions of citizens by placing the credit of the federal government behind private lending to home buyers, but overtly racist categories in the Federal Housing Agency's (FHA) "confidential" city surveys and appraisers' manuals channeled almost all of the loan money toward whites and away from communities of color.[17] In the post–World War II era, trade unions negotiated contract provisions giving private medical insurance, pensions, and job security largely to the white workers who formed the overwhelming majority of the unionized workforce in mass production industries rather than fighting for full employment, medical care, and old-age pensions for all; at the same time they avoided the fight for an end to discriminatory hiring and promotion practices by employers in those industries.[18] Each of these policies widened the gap between the resources available to whites and those available to aggrieved racial communities.

Federal housing policy offers an important illustration of the broader principles at work in the possessive investment in whiteness. By channeling loans away from older inner-city neighborhoods and toward white home buyers moving into segregated suburbs, the FHA and private lenders after World War II aided and abetted segregation in U.S. residential neighborhoods. FHA appraisers denied federally supported loans to prospective home buyers in the racially mixed Boyle Heights neighborhood of Los Angeles in 1939, for example, because the area struck them as a "'melting pot' area literally honeycombed with diverse and subversive racial elements."[19] Similarly, mostly white St. Louis County secured five times as many FHA mortgages as the more racially mixed city of St. Louis between 1943 and 1960. Home buyers in the county received six times as much loan money and enjoyed per capita mortgage spending 6.3 times greater than those in the city.[20]

The federal government has played a major role in augmenting the possessive investment in whiteness created by systematic racial discrimination in the private sector. For years, the General Services Administration routinely channeled the government's rental and leasing business to real estate agents who engaged in racial discrimination, while federally subsidized urban renewal plans reduced the already limited supply of housing for communities of color through "slum clearance" programs. In concert with FHA support for segregation in the suburbs, federal and state tax monies routinely funded the construction of water supplies and sewage facilities for racially exclusive suburban communities in the 1940s and 1950s. By the 1960s, these areas often incorporated themselves as independent municipalities in order to gain greater access to federal funds allocated for "urban aid."[21]

At the same time that FHA loans and federal highway building projects subsidized the growth of segregated suburbs, urban renewal programs in cities throughout the country devastated minority neighborhoods. Between the 1930s and the 1970s, urban renewal demolished some 1,600 Black neighborhoods in cities north and south. This systematic destruction of individual and collective social and emotional ecosystems exacted an enormous financial and psychic cost on Black communities. Clinical psychiatrist and public health specialist Mindy Thompson Fullilove argues that urban renewal in the mid-twentieth century was of sufficient scale and scope that it produced a profound alienation, a collective traumatic stress reaction that she describes as "root shock."[22] During the 1950s and 1960s, federally assisted urban renewal projects destroyed 20 percent of the central-city housing units occupied by Blacks, as opposed to only 10 percent of those inhabited by whites.[23] More than 60 percent of those displaced by urban renewal were African Americans, Puerto Ricans, Mexican Americans, or members of other minority racial groups. The Federal Housing Administration and the Veterans Administration financed more than $120 billion worth of new housing between 1934 and 1962, but less than 2 percent of this real estate was available to nonwhite families—and most of that small amount was located in segregated areas.[24]

Even in the 1970s, after most major urban renewal programs had been completed, Black central-city residents continued to lose housing units at a rate equal to 80 percent of what had been lost in the 1960s. White displacement during those same years declined to the relatively low levels of the 1950s.[25] In addition, the refusal first to pass, then later to enforce, fair housing laws has enabled real estate brokers, buyers, and sellers to profit from racist collusion against minorities largely without fear of legal retribution. During the decades following World War II, urban renewal helped construct a new "white" identity in the suburbs by helping to destroy ethnically specific European American urban inner-city neighborhoods. Wrecking balls and bulldozers eliminated some of these sites, while others were transformed by an influx of minority residents desperately competing for a declining supply of affordable housing units. As increasing numbers of racial minorities moved into cities, increasing numbers of European American ethnics moved out. Consequently, ethnic differences among whites became a less important dividing line in U.S. culture while race became more important. The suburbs helped turn Euro-Americans into "whites" who could live near each other and intermarry with relatively little difficulty. But this "white" unity rested on residential segregation, on shared access to housing and life chances largely unavailable to communities of color.[26]

During the 1950s and 1960s, local "pro-growth" coalitions led by liberal mayors often justified urban renewal as a program designed to build more housing for poor people. In reality, urban renewal destroyed more housing than it created. Ninety percent of the low-income units removed for urban renewal projects during the entire history of the program was never replaced. Commercial, industrial, and municipal projects occupied more than 80 percent of the land cleared for these projects, with less than 20 percent allocated for replacement housing. In addition, the loss of taxable properties and the tax abatements granted to new enterprises in urban renewal zones often meant serious tax increases for poor, working-class, and middle-class homeowners and renters.[27] Although the percentage of Black suburban dwellers also increased during this period, no significant desegregation of the suburbs took place. Four million whites moved out of central cities between 1960 and 1977, while the number of whites living in suburbs increased by 22 million; during the same years, the inner-city Black population grew by 6 million, but the number of Blacks living in suburbs increased by only 500,000.[28] Cities with large numbers of minority residents found themselves cut off from loans by the FHA. Because of their growing Black and Puerto Rican populations, not a single FHA-sponsored mortgage went to either Camden or Paterson, New Jersey, in 1966.[29]

In 1968, lobbyists for the banking industry helped draft the Housing and Urban Development Act, which allowed private lenders to shift the risks of financing low-income housing to the government, creating a lucrative and thoroughly unregulated market for themselves. One section of the 1968 bill authorized FHA mortgages for inner-city areas that did not meet the usual eligibility criteria. Another section subsidized interest payments by low-income families. If administered wisely, these provisions might have promoted fair housing goals, but FHA administrators deployed them in ways that actually promoted segregation in order to provide banks, brokers, lenders, developers, realtors, and speculators with windfall profits. As a U.S. Commission on Civil Rights investigation later revealed, FHA officials collaborated with blockbusters in financing the flight of low-income whites out of inner-city neighborhoods, and then aided unscrupulous realtors and speculators by arranging purchases of substandard housing by minorities desperate to own their own homes. The resulting sales and mortgage fore-closures brought great profits to lenders (almost all of them white), but their actions led to price fixing and a subsequent inflation of housing costs in the inner city by more than 200 percent between 1968 and 1972. Bankers then foreclosed on the mortgages of thousands of these uninspected and substan-dard homes, ruining many inner-city neighborhoods. In response, the De-partment of Housing and Urban Development essentially redlined inner cities, making them ineligible for future loans, a decision that destroyed the value of inner-city housing for generations to come.[30]

Federally funded highways built to transport suburban commuters to downtown places of employment also destroyed already scarce housing in minority communities, often disrupting neighborhood life as well. Construc-tion of the Harbor Freeway in Los Angeles, the Eastex Freeway in Houston, the I-10 Freeway in New Orleans, and the Mark Twain Freeway in St. Louis displaced thousands of residents and bisected neighborhoods, shopping dis-tricts, and political precincts. The processes of urban renewal and highway construction set in motion a vicious cycle: population loss led to decreased political power, which made minority neighborhoods more vulnerable to fur-ther urban renewal and freeway construction, not to mention more suscep-tible to the placement of prisons, incinerators, toxic waste dumps, and other projects that further depopulated these areas.

The effect of race in government decision-making has significant conse-quences. In Houston, Texas, more than 75 percent of municipal garbage in-cinerators and 100 percent of city-owned garbage dumps sited between the 1920s and the 1970s were located in Black neighborhoods, despite the fact that Blacks made up roughly one quarter of the local population.[31] Today, less than a quarter of Houston is African American—yet both landfills in the city are located in a majority-Black district.[32] A 1992 study by staff writers for the *National Law Journal* examining the Environmental Protection Agency's response to 1,177 toxic waste cases found that polluters of sites near the great-est white populations received penalties 500 percent higher than penalties imposed on polluters in minority areas. Income did not account for these differences; across wealthy and poor communities, the racial disparity held.[33] A 2007 study found that the burden of hazardous waste is still borne un-equally: a national average of 56 percent of residents in neighborhoods with at least one waste site were people of color, compared to only 30 percent of residents in neighborhoods without such sites.[34] The federal Agency for Toxic Substances and Disease Registry's 1988 survey of children suffering from lead poisoning found Black children were two to three times more likely than white children to suffer from excess lead in their bloodstreams.[35] Although blood lead levels declined sharply among children of all races between 1990 and 2012, a 2016 study of Chicago shows a substantial majority of neighborhoods with the highest lead levels continues to be majority Black.[36] Nation-wide, white people are roughly half as likely as people of color to live close to chemical waste facilities—and the facilities in communities of color are al-most twice as likely to be the source of a chemical incident as those in majority-white communities.[37]

Scholarly study reveals that even when adjusted for income and educa-tion, aggrieved racial minorities encounter higher levels of exposure to toxic substances than white people experience.[38] In 2007, the Commission for Ra-cial Justice of the United Church of Christ found race to be the most signifi-cant variable in determining the location of commercial hazardous waste facilities.[39] As of 2014, research shows that African Americans experience nearly twice as much industrial air pollution as do white people, on average, even controlling for socioeconomic resources.[40] In a review of forty-nine studies examining environmental inequities, scholar Evan Ringquist discov-ered that racial disparities outweighed disparities by income.[41] Robert D. Bullard concludes in an article published in 2016 that "race has been found to be an independent factor, not reducible to class" in predicting exposure to a broad range of environmental hazards, including polluted air, contamin-ated fish, lead poisoning, municipal landfills, incinerators, and toxic waste dumps.[42]

Environmental racism makes the possessive investment in whiteness liter-ally a matter of life and death. Nationally, Asian Americans are more than four times as likely to contract tuberculosis as whites. Corporations systematically target Native American reservations when looking for locations for hazardous waste incinerators, solid waste landfills, and nuclear waste storage facilities.[43] As of the mid-1970s, Navajo teenagers developed reproductive organ cancer at seventeen times the national average because of their exposure to radiation from uranium mines.[44] Today, research by the Centers for Disease Control and Prevention (CDC) continues to find elevated levels of uranium in Navajo in-fants.[45] Latinx in East Los Angeles encounter some of the worst smog and the highest concentrations of air toxins in southern California because of prevail-ing wind patterns and the concentration of polluting industries, freeways, and toxic waste dumps.[46] The Chicanx neighborhoods of Barrio Logan, Logan Heights, and National City in San Diego are among the most polluted in the state. Barrio Logan alone contains nearly 128 million pounds of hazardous substances, compared to only 3.2 million in nearby and majority-white La Jolla. Although Barrio Logan covers only 1.2 square miles—less than one tenth of 1 percent of the county's area—it contains 7 percent of the county's air tox-icity "hot spots" and 90 percent of its chromium 6 emissions. In 2010, asthma hospitalization rates for children in National City were 50 percent greater than the average for San Diego County.[47] Black children growing up in the inner city of Washington, D.C., live, on average, twenty-two fewer years than chil-dren raised in the city's white suburbs.[48] According to a 2015 study, if African

Americans had access to the nutrition, health care, and protection against environmental hazards offered routinely to whites, 2.7 million fewer of them would have died between 1970 and 2004.[49]

Minorities are less likely than whites to receive either preventive medical care or costly remedial operations from Medicare. The Kaiser Family Foundation reports that, compared to privately insured white people, privately insured people of color have lower rates of access to and confidence in their ability to pay for medical care.[50] The labor of migrant farmworkers from aggrieved racialized groups plays a vital role in providing adequate nutrition for others, but the farmworkers and their children are disproportionately food insecure.[51] In their important research on health and ethnic diversity, Duane Alwin and Linda Wray argue that health differences among racial and ethnic groups are due to "patterns of institutional racial and ethnic discrimination that produce differential social pathways contributing to different health outcomes."[52]

Just as residential segregation and urban renewal make minority communities disproportionately susceptible to health hazards, their physical and social locations give these communities a different relationship to the criminal justice system. A 2015 study by the Center for Behavioral Health Statistics and Quality revealed that only 14 percent of people who had used drugs in the last year in the United States were Black while 64 percent were white;[53] however, African Americans were ten times more likely to be incarcerated on drug charges than whites.[54] White seniors in high school report 25 percent more drug use than their Black counterparts, and white students visit the emergency room three times more often than Black students do for drug overdoses.[55] Yet while comprising only about 12 percent of the U.S. population, Blacks accounted for 10 percent of drug arrests in 1984 but 38 percent today.[56] In addition, prison terms for African American drug defendants are twenty to fifty times longer than those of white people convicted of comparable crimes. The disparities are not limited to drug offenses. A U.S. Sentencing Commission study found in 2012 that for a wide variety of offenses, sentences for African American men in the federal prison system are 20 percent longer than those given to white men convicted of similar crimes.[57] A study commissioned by the governor of Maryland in 2003 reported that in homicide cases punishable by death, Black people with white victims are two and a half times more likely to receive the death penalty than white people with white victims.[58] A U.S. Sentencing Commission study found in 1992 that half of the federal court districts that handled cases involving crack cocaine prosecuted minority defendants exclusively. The NAACP observes that if Blacks and Latinx benefited from the same incarceration rates as whites, prisons and jails would lose 40 percent of their population.[59]

Racial animus on the part of police officers, prosecutors, and judges accounts for only a small portion of the distinctive experience that racial minorities have with the criminal justice system. Economic devastation makes the drug trade appealing to some people in the inner city, while the dearth of capital in minority neighborhoods curtails opportunities for other kinds of employment. Deindustrialization, unemployment, and lack of intergenerational transfers of wealth undermine parental and adult authority in many neighborhoods. The complex factors that cause people to turn to drugs are no more prevalent in minority communities than elsewhere, but these communities and their inhabitants face more stress while having fewer opportunities to receive private counseling and treatment for their problems.

The structural weaknesses of minority neighborhoods caused by discrimination in housing, education, and hiring also play crucial roles in relations between inner-city residents and the criminal justice system. Cocaine dealing, which initially skyrocketed among white suburban residents, was driven into the inner city by escalating enforcement pressures in wealthy white communities. Ghettos and barrios became distribution centers for the sale of drugs to white suburbanites. Former New York and Houston police commissioner Lee Brown, head of the federal government's antidrug efforts during the early years of the Clinton presidency and later mayor of Houston, noted, "There are those who bring drugs into the country. That's not the black community. Then you have wholesalers, those who distribute them once they get here, and as a rule that's not the black community. Where you find the blacks is in the street dealing."[60] You also find Blacks and other minorities in prison. Police officers in large cities, pressured to show results in the drive against drugs, lack the resources to enforce the law effectively everywhere (in part because of the social costs of deindustrialization and the tax limitation initiatives designed to shrink the size of government). These officers know that it is easier to make arrests and to secure convictions by confronting drug users in areas that have conspicuous street corner sales, that have more people out on the street with no place to go, and that have residents more likely to plead guilty and less likely to secure the services of attorneys who can get the charges against them dropped, reduced, or wiped off the books with subsequent successful counseling and rehabilitation. In addition, politicians supported by the public relations efforts of foundations often portray themselves to suburban voters as opponents of the "dangerous classes" in the inner cities.

Minority disadvantages craft advantages for others. Urban renewal failed to provide new housing for the poor, but it played an important role in transforming the U.S. urban economy from one that relied on factory production to one driven by producer services. Urban renewal projects subsidized the development of downtown office centers on previously residential land, and they frequently created buffer zones of empty blocks dividing poor neighborhoods from new shopping centers and entertainment districts designed for affluent commuters. To help cities compete for corporate investment by making them appealing to high-level executives, federal urban aid favored construction of luxury housing units and cultural centers like symphony halls and art museums over affordable housing for workers. Tax abatements granted to producer services centers further aggravated the fiscal crises that cities faced, leading to tax increases on existing industries, businesses, and residences.

Workers from aggrieved racial minority groups bore the brunt of this transformation. Because the 1964 Civil Rights Act came so late, minority workers who received jobs because of it found themselves more vulnerable to seniority-based layoffs when businesses automated or transferred operations overseas. Although the act initially made real progress in reducing employment discrimination, lessening the gaps between rich and poor and between Black and white workers while helping to bring minority poverty to its lowest level in history in 1973, that year's recession initiated a reversal of minority progress and a reassertion of white privilege.[61] In 1977, the U.S. Commission on Civil Rights reported on the disproportionate impact of layoffs on minority workers. In cases where minority workers made up only 10 to 12 percent of the workforce in their area in 1974, they accounted for 60 to 70 percent of those laid off. The principle of seniority, a trade union triumph designed to protect workers from age discrimination, in this case guaranteed that minority workers would suffer most from technological changes because the legacy of past discrimination by their employers left them with less seniority than white workers.[62]

When housing prices increased dramatically during the 1970s, white homeowners who had been able to take advantage of discriminatory FHA financing policies in the past realized increased equity in their homes while those excluded from the housing market by earlier policies found themselves facing even higher costs of entry into the market in addition to the traditional obstacles presented by the discriminatory practices of sellers, realtors, and lenders. The contrast between European Americans and African Americans is instructive in this regard. Because whites have access to broader housing choices than do Blacks, among other reasons, whites pay 10 percent less than Blacks for similar housing in the same neighborhood. Yet today, the average white person lives in a neighborhood in which property values are 39 and 76 percent higher than values in the neighborhoods inhabited by the average Black and Latino person, respectively.[63]

At the end of the twentieth century, studies showed lenders consistently discriminated against Black applicants, granting them fewer loans than to comparable white applicants.[64] Loan officers were far more likely to overlook flaws in the credit records of white applicants or to arrange creative financing for them than they were with Black applicants.[65] In Houston, for instance, the NCNB Bank of Texas disqualified only 13 percent of middle-income white loan applicants but 36 percent of middle-income Black applicants.[66] By the mid-1990s, however, discrimination in the lending market had shifted to include granting riskier, more expensive loans to people of color than to white people.[67] Although aggrieved racial minorities continue to be denied loans at disproportionate rates—a 2017 Pew Research Center study found that lending institutions deny mortgages to 27.4 percent of Black and 19.2 percent of Latinx applicants but only 10.9 percent of whites—they are now also targeted for subprime mortgages.[68] Such targeting meant that the housing market crash of 2008 disproportionately devastated Black and Latinx families: nationally, 33 percent of Black wealth and nearly 50 percent of Latinx wealth was lost between 2007 and 2011.[69]

When confronted with evidence of systematic racial bias in home lending, defenders of the possessive investment in whiteness argue that the disproportionate share of loan denials to members of minority groups stems not from discrimination but from the low net worth of minority applicants, even those who have high incomes. This might seem a reasonable position, but net worth is almost totally determined by past opportunities for asset accumulation and therefore is the one figure most likely to reflect the history of discrimination. Minorities are told, in essence, "We can't give you a loan today because we've discriminated against members of your race so effectively in the past that you have not been able to accumulate any equity from housing to pass down through the generations." Most white families have acquired their net worth from the appreciation of property that they secured under conditions of special privilege in a discriminatory housing market. In their prize-winning book *Black Wealth/White Wealth*, Melvin Oliver and Thomas Shapiro demonstrate how the history of housing discrimination gives white parents special advantages to borrow funds for their children's college education or to lend money to their children to enter the housing market.[70] In addition, much discrimination in home lending is not based on considerations of net worth; it stems from decisions made by white banking officials based on their stereotypes about minority communities. In 2006, African Americans at high income levels had subprime mortgages at four times the rate of whites at comparable income levels.[71] Even controlling for mortgage risk factors, a National Bureau of Economics Research study noted in 2016 that Black applicants are almost 8 percent more likely to be given a high-cost loan than white applicants.[72]

Yet bankers also profit from the ways in which discrimination creates artificial scarcities in the market. Minorities have to pay more for housing because much of the market is off limits to them. Blockbusters profit from exploiting white fears and provoking whites into panic selling. Minority homeowners denied loans in mainstream banks often turn to predatory lenders who make "low end" loans at enormously high interest rates. If the homeowners fail to pay back these loans, regular banks can acquire the property cheaply and charge someone else exorbitant interest for a loan on the same property.

Federal home loan policies have put the power of the federal government at the service of private discrimination. Urban renewal and highway construction programs have enhanced the possessive investment in whiteness directly through government initiatives. In addition, decisions about where to locate federal jobs have also systematically subsidized whiteness. Federal civilian employment dropped by 41,419 in central cities between 1966 and 1973, but total federal employment in metropolitan areas grew by 26,558.[73] While one might naturally expect the location of government buildings that serve the public to follow population trends, the federal government's policy of locating offices and records centers in suburbs aggravated the flight of jobs to suburban locations less accessible to inner-city residents. Because racial discrimination in the private sector forces minority workers to seek government positions disproportionate to their numbers, these moves exact particular hardships on them. In addition, minorities who follow their jobs to the suburbs must generally allocate more for commuter costs because housing discrimination makes it harder and more expensive for them than for whites to relocate.

The policies of the Reagan and Bush administrations during the 1980s and 1990s greatly exacerbated the racialized aspects of more than fifty years of these social welfare policies. Regressive policies that cut federal aid to education and refused to challenge segregated education, housing, and hiring, as well as the cynical cultivation of an anti-Black consensus through attacks on affirmative action and voting rights legislation, clearly reinforced possessive investments in whiteness. In the U.S. economy, where word of mouth contacts with already employed friends and relatives remain crucial conduits to employment opportunities, attacks on affirmative action guarantee that whites will be rewarded for their historical advantage in the labor market rather than for their individual abilities or efforts.[74]

Attacking the civil rights tradition serves many functions. By mobilizing existing racisms and generating new ones, opponents of racial justice seek to discredit the egalitarian and democratic social movements of the post–World War II era and to connect the attacks by those movements on white wealth hoarding, special privilege, and elite control over education and opportunity to the complaints of despised and allegedly unworthy racial "others." Yet even seemingly race-neutral policies supported by both conservatives and liberals, by both Democrats and Republicans, increased the absolute value of being white. In the 1980s, changes in federal tax laws decreased the value of wage income and increased the value of investment income and inheritance—a move harmful to minorities who suffer from a gap between their total wealth and that of whites even greater than the disparity between their income and white income. The failure to raise the minimum wage between 1981 and 1989 and the decline of more than one third in the value of Aid to Families with Dependent Children (AFDC) payments injured all poor people, but they exacted special on costs on nonwhites, who faced even more constricted markets for employment, housing, and education than poor whites.[75]

Similarly, the "tax reforms" of the 1980s made the effective rate of taxation higher on investment in actual goods and services than on profits from speculative enterprises. This change encouraged the flight of capital from industrial production with its many employment opportunities toward investments that can be turned over quickly to allow the greatest possible tax write-offs. Government policies thus discouraged investments that might produce high-paying jobs and encouraged investors to strip companies of their assets to make rapid short-term profits. These policies hurt almost all workers, but they fell particularly heavily on minority workers, who, because of employment discrimination in the retail and small business sectors, were overrepresented in blue-collar industrial jobs.

Subsidies to the private sector by government agencies also tend to enhance the rewards of past discrimination. Throughout the country, tax increment financing for redevelopment programs offers tax-free and low-interest loans to developers whose projects use public services, often without insisting that these developers pay taxes to local school boards or county governments to support those public services. In St. Louis, tax abatements and tax increment financing for wealthy corporations deprive the city's schools (and their majority African American population) of roughly $12 million a year. Even if these redevelopment projects eventually succeed in increasing municipal revenues through sales and earnings taxes, their proceeds go to funds that pay for the increased services that these developments require (fire and police protection, roads, sewers, electricity, lighting, etc.) rather than to school funds, which are dependent upon property tax revenues.[76] Nationwide, the government granted nearly $245 billion in tax-exempt industrial development bonds in 2015 alone, generating revenue loss that is often made up by ordinary taxpayers.[77] Compared to white Americans, people of color—more likely to be poor or working class—suffer disproportionately from these changes as taxpayers, as workers, and as tenants. A 2016 study by the Citizens for Tax Justice found that the wealthiest 1 percent of people in the United States pay less than nine cents in state and local taxes for every dollar earned, while the poorest 20 percent of residents pay over twelve cents out of every dollar. As groups overrepresented among the poor, minorities have been forced to subsidize the tax breaks given to the wealthy. California's Proposition 13 deprived cities and counties of $10 billion in taxes in the first year of implementation alone while holding the increase in the property tax rate for businesses and some homeowners to about two thirds of its market value, according to a 2016 report from the nonpartisan California Legislative Analyst's Office. The state compensated for the drop in property tax revenue in part through heavily increasing the state sales tax, which disproportionately burdens low-income households. Yet despite this adjustment, total local tax revenue dropped by roughly $150 per person (adjusted for inflation) between 1977 and 2015. Further, the report notes that two thirds of the property tax relief the proposition was intended to provide to homeowners went to people with incomes above $80,000 per year, most of it to those with incomes above $120,000 per year.[78]

Because they are ignorant of even the recent history of the possessive investment in whiteness—generated initially by slavery and segregation, immigrant exclusion and Indigenous dispossession, conquest and colonialism, but augmented more recently by liberal and conservative social policies as well—white Americans produce largely cultural explanations for structural social problems. The increased possessive investment in whiteness generated by disinvestment in U.S. cities, factories, and schools since the 1970s disguises as *racial* problems the general social problems posed by deindustrialization, economic restructuring, and attacks on the welfare state and the social wage. It fuels a discourse that demonizes people of color for being victimized by these changes while hiding the privileges of whiteness. It often attributes the economic advantages enjoyed by whites to their family values, faith, and foresight—rather than to the favoritism they enjoy through their possessive investment in whiteness.

The demonization of Black families in public discourse since the 1970s is particularly instructive in this regard. Reluctance to enforce civil rights laws combined with the racialized consequences of economic restructuring and deindustrialization have injured African American families. During the 1970s, the share of low-income households headed by Blacks increased by one third. Black family income fell from 60 percent of white family income in 1971 to 58 percent in 1980. Even adjusting for unemployment and for African American disadvantages in life-cycle employment (more injuries, more frequently interrupted work histories, confinement to jobs most susceptible to layoffs), the wages of full-time year-round Black workers fell from 77 percent of white workers' income to 73 percent by 1986. In 1986, white workers with high school diplomas earned $3,000 per year more than African Americans with the same education, a surplus that had doubled by 2014.[79] Even when they had the same family structure as white workers, Blacks found themselves more likely to be poor. Yet a wide range of policy makers and pundits has reversed the relationship between cause and effect, identifying the difficulties Black families face as the cause rather than the consequence of their impoverishment.

The deindustrialization and economic restructuring of the 1970s and 1980s imposes continuing racial penalties on wage earners from minority communities, who suffered setbacks while members of other groups accumulated equity-producing assets. Even when some minority groups show improvement, others do not. In 1995, for example, every U.S. ethnic and racial group experienced an increase in income except the 27 million Latinx, who experienced a 5.1 percent drop in income during that year alone.[80]

Forty-six percent of Black workers between the ages of twenty and twenty-four held blue-collar jobs in 1976, but only 20 percent did so by 1984. Earnings by young Black families that had reached 60 percent of white families' income in 1973 fell to 46 percent by 1986. Younger African American families experienced a 50 percent drop in real earnings between 1973 and 1986, with the decline in Black male wages particularly steep.[81] Many popular and scholarly studies have delineated the causes for Black economic decline.[82] Deindustrialization decimated the industrial infrastructure that formerly provided high-wage jobs and chances for upward mobility to Black workers. Attacks on government spending for public housing, health, education, and transportation deprived members of minority groups of needed services and opportunities for jobs in the public sector. A massive retreat at the highest levels of government from the responsibility to enforce antidiscrimination laws has sanctioned pervasive overt and covert racial discrimination by bankers, real estate professionals, and employers. Further, the Great Recession of 2008 had a disproportionately damaging effect on aggrieved racial minorities. Median wealth for Black households dropped almost 50 percent, compared to only 35.8 percent for white households. White unemployment, at the peak of the recession, never rose above the Black prerecession annual unemployment rate, and the Pew Research Center reports the post-recession Black-white income gap has only widened.[83]

Yet public opinion polls of white Americans reflect little recognition of these devastating changes. A study published in 2012 by Harvard Business School professor Michael Norton and Tufts University psychology professor Samuel Sommers reported that a majority of whites actually believe that they face more discrimination for being white than African Americans face for being Black.[84] Sommers and Norton note that whites express these beliefs even though every social indicator in nearly every sphere of life demonstrates that Blacks have drastically less favorable life outcomes than whites. Whites responding to this survey conceded that there has been anti-Black bias sometime in the past, perhaps as late as the 1950s, but they judged that by the year 2000 antiwhite bias began to exceed anti-Black bias by what they estimated was more than one full point on a ten-point scale. The results that Norton and Sommers secured were not an anomaly. Public opinion surveys dating back to the 1960s reveal a consistent pattern of white self-pity and imagined injury. In a poll conducted in 2004, 61 percent of whites claimed that Blacks have the same opportunities for employment and promotion as whites. A 2002 survey found that 81 percent of whites believed that Black children had the same opportunities for a quality education as white children.[85] A 1998 poll revealed that only slightly more than one third of white respondents believed the low socioeconomic status of Blacks could be attributed to discrimination. More than half of the whites surveyed contended that unfavorable life outcomes among Blacks resulted mainly from Blacks' lack of motivation. Almost two thirds predicted confidently that the wealth gap would disappear if Blacks would only "try harder." More than 80 percent of white respondents contended that Black job applicants had exactly the same chances for success as white applicants, and a similar percentage opined that housing discrimination no longer existed in any meaningful form.[86]

A 2012 study led by Harvard researcher Lawrence Bobo revealed that more than 40 percent of U.S. whites viewed Blacks as less hardworking than whites, and over 20 percent viewed them as less intelligent.[87] In 2008, a full 50 percent of white people said that they believed that Blacks suffer from poor housing and employment opportunities because of their own lack of willpower.[88] Roughly 35 percent of whites across the political spectrum contended in 2012 that Blacks tend toward laziness.[89] Even more important, research by Mary Edsall and Thomas Byrne Edsall indicates that many whites structure nearly all of their decisions about housing, education, and politics in response to their aversions to Black people.[90]

The present political culture in this country gives broad sanction for viewing white supremacy and anti-Black racism as forces from the past, as demons finally put to rest by the passage of the 1964 Civil Rights Act and the 1965 Voting Rights Act. Jurists, journalists, and politicians have generally been more vocal in opposing what they call "quotas" and "reverse discrimination"—by which they usually mean race-specific measures designed to remedy existing racial discrimination that inconvenience or offend whites—than in challenging the thousands of well-documented cases every year of routine, systematic, and unyielding discrimination against minorities. It is my contention that the stark contrast between nonwhite experiences and white opinions during the past two decades cannot be attributed solely to individual ignorance or intolerance but stems instead from liberal individualism's inability to describe adequately the collective dimensions of our experience. As long as we define social life as the sum total of conscious and deliberative individual activities, we will be able to discern as racist only *individual* manifestations of personal prejudice and hostility. Systemic, collective, and coordinated group behavior consequently drops out of sight. Collective exercises of power that relentlessly channel rewards, resources, and opportunities from one group to another will not appear "racist" from this perspective because they rarely announce their intention to discriminate against individuals. Yet they nonetheless give racial identities their sinister social meaning by giving people from different races vastly different life chances.

The gap between white perception and minority experience can have explosive consequences. Little more than a year after the 1992 Los Angeles rebellion, a sixteen-year-old high school junior shared her opinions with a reporter from the *Los Angeles Times*: "I don't think white people owe anything to black people," she explained. "We didn't sell them into slavery, it was our ancestors. What they did was wrong, but we've done our best to make up for it." A seventeen-year-old senior echoed those comments, telling the reporter, "I feel we spend more time in my history class talking about what whites owe blacks than just about anything else when the issue of slavery comes up. I often received dirty looks. This seems strange given that I wasn't even alive then. And the few members of my family from that time didn't have the luxury of owning much, let alone slaves. So why, I ask you, am I constantly made to feel guilty?"[91]

More ominously, after pleading guilty to bombing two homes and one car, vandalizing a synagogue, and attempting to start a race war by planning the murder of beating victim Rodney King and the bombing of Los Angeles's First African Methodist Episcopal Church, twenty-year-old Christopher David Fisher explained that "sometimes whites were picked on because of the color of their skin. Maybe we're blamed for slavery."[92] Fisher's actions were certainly extreme, but his justification of them drew knowingly and precisely on a broadly shared narrative about the victimization of "innocent" whites by irrational and ungrateful minorities.

Nearly a quarter century later, another white youth named Fisher also felt picked on. Abigail Fisher wanted to attend the University of Texas at Austin but was not accepted for admission. By the standards used by the university to judge applicants, Fisher would have been able to secure admission if her grades placed her in the top 10 percent of her class. They did not. She could have transferred to the Austin campus after one year at another state university if she earned a grade point average of 3.2 out of a possible 4.0. She chose not to take this option. Instead, she went to court, suing the university on the grounds that she had been rejected from the school because she was white. A white millionaire graduate of the University of Texas financed her lawsuit, which went all the way to the Supreme Court. Even her patron admitted that Fisher did not actually merit admission to the university and that she would not have been accepted even if there had been no affirmative action programs in place. Yet he hoped evidently that her public pouting would help build legal and political momentum for ending affirmative action in college admissions.

In a video that she made to publicize her case, Fisher complained that she had lost her deserved slot in the freshman class to people "with lower grades who weren't in all the activities I was in" and that "the only other difference between us was the color of our skin." Fisher announced that "I was taught from the time I was a little girl that any kind of discrimination was wrong."[93] Yet there was no racial discrimination against Abigail Fisher. Forty-seven students with slightly lower grades and test scores than hers had been offered admission to the freshman class because of documented evidence of special skills and achievements. Five of these were Black or Latinx, but forty-two of them were white. Moreover, 168 Latinx and Black students with grades as good as or even better than Fisher's had also been denied admission to the university in the same year. Most of these students did not have the advantages that Fisher had growing up in suburban Sugar Land, Texas, a city with a median income double the average in the state of Texas, where property values and the percentage of local residents with a bachelor's degree or higher are significantly above the state average, and where only 10 percent of the residents are Latinx and only 7 percent are Black.[94] Since Fisher has informed us that she has been taught since she was a little girl that any kind of discrimination is wrong, perhaps we can look forward to her future work as an opponent of housing discrimination and educational inequality in the state of Texas so that Black and Latinx students like those who outperformed her despite facing greater obstacles will receive due recognition and reward. Yet for that to happen, Fisher's understanding of affirmative action would have to change.

Like many people trained to accept the precepts of the possessive investment in whiteness, Fisher assumes that affirmative action is a special preference that unfairly tilts what would otherwise be a level playing field. Yet affirmative action exists because the playing field is not level, because pervasive and systematic discrimination on the basis of artificial, arbitrary, and irrational factors such as race, gender, sexuality, disability, and religion harm the whole society. Discrimination harms individuals, but it harms all of society as well because it misallocates resources, squanders talents, and undermines fair competition. Affirmative action *exists* because whites ferociously resisted full implementation of civil rights laws and thereby preserved the historical advantages that accrue to them. Affirmative action *persists* because corporations, the military, schools, and government contracting agencies have found that it cancels out some of the effects of racial discrimination and in the process enhances and improves the quality of those institutions.

An illustrative parallel can be drawn with the laws requiring reasonable accommodation for people with disabilities. These laws do not exist because legislators feel sorry for individuals with disabilities but rather because it is both foolish and unproductive to deny someone access to the housing market because apartments don't have curb cuts and ramps, to deny someone employment because the doors of the workplace are too narrow for wheelchairs, or to deny an education to students solely because they are hearing or visually impaired. Businesses should not lose worthy customers, society should not be deprived of the ideas and accomplishments of people with a dis/ability/specialty, and schools should not lose out on capable students because of artificial, arbitrary, and irrational prejudices and obstacles. Racial discrimination is one source of those prejudices and obstacles. Everyone profits when we remove needless impediments to full social membership, when we draw students, employers, and contractors from the broadest possible pool of competitors.

Abigail and Christopher Fisher, like other young whites, often contend that while racist things may have happened in the distant past, it is unfair to hold contemporary whites accountable for them. These young people associate Black grievances solely with slavery, and they express irritation at what they perceive as efforts to make them feel guilty or unduly privileged because of things that they did not do personally. They feel innocent individually and cannot conceive of a collective responsibility for collective wrongs. The claim that one's own family did not own any slaves is intended to end the discussion. It is almost never followed by proposals to find the white families whose ancestors *did* own slaves, to track them down and make them pay reparations. The disavowal of responsibility for slavery never acknowledges how the existence of slavery and the exploitation of Black labor after emancipation created opportunities that penalized *all* Blacks and benefited *all* whites even those who did not own slaves and even those whose families emigrated to the United States after slavery ended. Rather, it seems to hold that because not all white people owned slaves, no white people can be held accountable or inconvenienced by the legacy of slavery. This argument does not address the long histories and contemporary realities of segregation, racialized social policies, urban renewal, or the revived racism of contemporary capitalism. On the contrary, as Christopher Fisher recognized in his remarks, articulation of one's own imagined discomfort with being "picked on" and "blamed" for slavery will be seen as the real injury, one that in his mind gave him good reason to bomb homes, deface synagogues, and plot to kill Black people.

Unfortunately for our society, these young whites accurately reflect the logic of the language of liberal individualism and its ideological predispositions in discussions of race. In their apparent ignorance of the disciplined, systemic, and collective *group* activity that has structured white identities in U.S. history, they reflect the dominant views of their society. In a 1979 law journal article, future Supreme Court justice Antonin Scalia argued that affirmative action "is based upon concepts of racial indebtedness and racial entitlement rather than individual worth and individual need" and is thus "racist."[95] Yet liberal individualism is not completely color-blind on this issue. As Cheryl I. Harris demonstrates, and as we see in Chapter 2, the legacy of liberal individualism has not prevented the Supreme Court from recognizing and protecting the group interests of *whites* in the Bakke, Croson, and Wygant cases, along with many others.[96] In each of these cases, the Court nullified affirmative action programs because they judged efforts to help Blacks as harmful to white expectations of entitlement—expectations based on the possessive investment in whiteness they held as members of a group. In the Bakke case, for instance, where the plaintiff argued that medical school affirmative action programs disadvantaged white applicants like himself, neither Bakke nor the Court contested the legitimacy of medical school admissions standards that reserved five seats in each class for children of wealthy donors to the university or that penalized Bakke for being older than most of the other applicants. The group rights of not-wealthy people or of people older than their classmates did not compel the Court or Bakke to make any claim of harm. But they did challenge and reject a policy designed to offset the effects of past and present discrimination when they could construe the medical school admission policies as detrimental to the interests of whites as a group—and as a consequence they applied the "strict scrutiny" standard to protect whites while denying that protection to people of color. In this case, as in so many others, the language of liberal individualism serves as a cover for coordinated collective group interests.

Group interests are not monolithic, and aggregate figures can obscure serious differences within racial groups. All whites do not benefit from the possessive investment in whiteness in precisely the same ways; the experiences of members of minority groups are not interchangeable. But the possessive investment in whiteness always affects individual and collective life chances and opportunities. Even in cases in which minority groups secure political and economic power through collective mobilization, the terms and conditions of their collectivity and the logic of group solidarity are always influenced and intensified by the absolute value of whiteness in U.S. politics, economics, and culture.[97]

In the 1960s, members of the Black Panther Party used to say that "if you're not part of the solution, you're part of the problem." But those of us who are "white" can only become part of the solution if we recognize the degree to which we are already part of the problem—not because of our race but because of our possessive investment in it. Neither conservative "free market" policies nor liberal social welfare policies can solve the "white problem" in the United States because both reinforce the possessive investment in whiteness. An explicitly antiracist interethnic movement, however—one that acknowledges the existence and power of whiteness—might make some important changes. Antiracist coalitions also have a long history in the United States—in the political activism of John Brown, Sojourner Truth, and the Magon brothers among others, but also in our rich cultural tradition of interethnic antiracism connected to civil rights activism of the kind detailed so brilliantly in rhythm and blues musician Johnny Otis's book, *Upside Your Head! Rhythm and Blues on Central Avenue*. The all too infrequent but nonetheless important efforts by whites to fight racism, not out of sympathy for someone else but out of a sense of self-respect and simple justice, have never completely disappeared; they remain available as models for the present.[98]

Walter Benjamin's praise for "presence of mind" came from his understanding of how difficult it can be to see the present in all of its rich complexity.

But more important, he called for presence of mind as the means for implementing what he named "the only true telepathic miracle"—turning the foreboding future into the fulfilled present.[99] Failure to acknowledge our society's possessive investment in whiteness prevents us from facing the present openly and honestly. It hides from us the devastating costs of disinvestment in America's infrastructure over the past four decades and keeps us from facing our responsibility to reinvest in human resources by channeling resources toward education, health, and housing—and away from subsidies for speculation and luxury. After this long period of disinvestment, the only further disinvestment we need is from the ruinous pathology of whiteness. The possessive investment in whiteness undermines our best instincts and interests. In a society suffering so badly from an absence of mutuality, an absence of responsibility, and an absence of justice, presence of mind might be just what we need.

2

Law and Order

Civil Rights Laws and White Privilege

People who know so little about themselves can face very little in another; and one dare hope for nothing from friends like these.

—JAMES BALDWIN

For more than forty years, the consensus between U.S. liberals and conservatives in favor of the possessive investment in whiteness has been so complete that the issue has not even come under debate. Neither side has been required to make its arguments in explicit racial terms, but both have been able to carry out racialized agendas—the liberals under the name of respecting and promoting market practices, encouraging business investment in cities, and helping the "middle class," the conservatives under the guise of promoting states' rights, protecting private property, and shrinking the welfare state.

Because American society has not acknowledged the ways in which we have created a possessive investment in whiteness, the disadvantages racial minorities face may seem unrelated to the advantages given to whites. The disadvantages of minorities are said to stem from their innate deficiencies rather than from systematic disenfranchisement and discrimination. Especially since the passage of the 1964 and 1965 civil rights acts, the dominant discourse in our society argues that the problems facing communities of color no longer result primarily from discrimination but from the characteristics of those communities themselves, from their purportedly unrestrained sexual behavior and the resulting childbirths out of wedlock, from crime, welfare dependency, and a perverse sense of group identity and group entitlement that stands in the way of individual achievement and advancement.

In this regard, it is vital to look at the actual record of civil rights laws and their enforcement. Contrary to their stated intentions, civil rights laws have actually augmented rather than diminished the possessive investment in whiteness, not because civil rights legislation is by nature unwise or impractical, but because these particular laws have been structured to be ineffective and largely unenforceable. The conservatives are not wrong when they attribute the problems facing aggrieved racial minorities to a crisis of values, rampant violations of law and order, and pernicious group politics; but by attributing these negative characteristics to people of color, they evade the fact that the history of the past seven decades demonstrates that the most fanatical group politics, the most flagrant violations of the law, and the vilest evasions of responsible and moral behavior have been carried out by whites, individually and collectively. Massive white opposition to the implementation (rather than the mere articulation) of antidiscrimination statutes stands as a stunning indictment of the character of European Americans. It shows how the racial problem in the United States remains at heart a white problem. At every stage over the past forty years, whites have responded to civil rights laws with coordinated collective politics characterized by a clear pattern of resistance, refusal, and renegotiation.

Fair Housing

In 1890, San Francisco's Board of Supervisors passed an ordinance mandating the removal of Chinese Americans from neighborhoods close to downtown and ripe for redevelopment. The law ordered Chinese residents to resettle in isolated industrial areas of the city filled with waste dumps and other environmental hazards. Although overturned by the courts eventually, the San Francisco Segregation Ordinance of 1890 prefigured racial zoning laws in many cities that aimed at preventing racial minorities (especially African Americans) from moving into houses on blocks where whites were the majority of the homeowners, while barring whites from moving to houses on blocks where nonwhite people were the majority.[1] All across the nation in the years before World War I, city governments put the force of law behind residential segregation through racial zoning laws. When the Supreme Court declared these ordinances unconstitutional in 1917, some municipalities defied the court outright. Others proceeded as if the court ruling had never happened. West Palm Beach, Florida, adopted a racial zoning ordinance in 1929. Racial zoning in Apopka, Florida, remained on the books until 1968. In Austin, Texas; Atlanta, Georgia; Kansas City, Missouri; and Norfolk, Virginia, city governments used zoning codes as a way to do surreptitiously what the racial zoning ordinances had done openly.[2] Nearly everywhere else, real estate brokers, political leaders, and bankers turned to restrictive covenants and other private deed restrictions to prevent integration and preserve the material rewards of whiteness.

Between 1924 and 1950, realtors throughout the United States subscribed to a national code that bound them to the view that "a realtor should never be instrumental in introducing into a neighborhood a character of property or occupancy, members of any race or nationality, or any individual whose presence will clearly be detrimental to property values in the neighborhood." Local codes were even more explicit in excluding "detrimental" groups from white neighborhoods.[3]

Mob violence and vigilante action accompanied the legal implementation of segregation. As evidenced in the important scholarship of Thomas Sugrue and Arnold Hirsch, northern whites especially succeeded in preserving racially exclusive neighborhoods during the 1940s and 1950s through mob actions that went largely unpunished by law enforcement authorities afraid to challenge crimes enacted on behalf of the possessive investment in whiteness.[4] Most of the time violence was not needed to preserve segregation, however, because restrictive covenants achieved that end through peaceful, although still coercive, means. Restrictive covenants were deed restrictions that pledged to keep houses in white hands in perpetuity. They functioned as the glue that held the white racial cartel together, as collective agreements among white property owners never to sell their homes to people of color (no matter how much money they were offered) and to make sure that the dwellings were sold to whites (no matter how unreliable, unworthy, and unneighborly the purchaser might be). As private agreements written into deed restrictions against the resale of property, restrictive covenants satisfied the courts and effectively constricted the housing market for groups subject to discrimination while providing artificially inflated home equity for whites.

African American community organizations took the lead in opposing restrictive covenants in the courts, attaining partial success in 1948 when the Supreme Court ruled in *Shelley v. Kraemer* that enforcement of these deed restrictions by states violated the Constitution. People denied the opportunity to buy a home (and thus accumulate assets) because of an illegal restrictive covenant, however, had to bear the brunt of challenging it themselves. They had to initiate legal action and bear the complete cost and burden of seeking to have the law enforced.[5] Moreover, even while preventing states from enforcing restrictive covenants, *Shelley v. Kraemer* did not make it illegal for property owners to adhere to them voluntarily, nor did it ban the registration of restrictive covenants with local authorities. For decades after the Supreme Court decision in *Shelley v. Kraemer*, the Federal Housing Administration still persisted in its policy of recommending—and even requiring—restrictive covenants as a condition for receiving government-secured home loans.[6]

White homeowners, realtors, and bankers realized that restrictive covenants could remain in force despite *Shelley v. Kraemer*. In addition, the ruling did nothing to challenge the other major mechanisms for real estate discrimination: redlining (denying loans to areas inhabited by racial minorities), steering (directing minority buyers solely to homes in minority neighborhoods), and block busting (playing on white fears of a change in neighborhood racial balance by promoting panic sales, i.e., getting whites to sell their homes for small amounts and then selling those same homes to minority buyers at extremely high prices).[7]

Despite the *Shelley v. Kraemer* verdict, resistance and refusal to desegregate the private housing market helped preserve the possessive investment in whiteness for white homeowners for the next twenty years. In the life of a nation, twenty years is not long, but in the lives of individuals, twenty years of rights denied can have devastating effects—inhibiting their accumulation of assets, depriving them of the increased equity that comes with homeownership, and devaluating the assets that they might have passed on to their children. Resistance and refusal preserved the possessive investment in whiteness and forced those excluded from its benefits to try to renegotiate the issue of residential segregation through other channels.

In the presidential election of 1960, African American voters in key northern cities provided the crucial margin that elected John F. Kennedy. Afraid to challenge the segregationists in his own party who held key positions in Congress, Kennedy attempted to respond to minority demands for fair housing by issuing presidential executive orders, especially Order 11063 that required government agencies to oppose discrimination in federally supported housing. Once again, white resistance rather than compliance followed. Federal officials quickly realized that the president would not object if they simply did not communicate his order to local housing authorities. The FHA refused to apply Executive Order 11063 even to its own loans, even though that agency ran the largest federally supported housing program.

White resistance to Kennedy's executive order reflected and promoted popular support among whites for racial discrimination. In 1964, California voters overwhelmingly supported a referendum repealing that state's fair-housing law. The state's governor, Edmund G. "Pat" Brown, who supported the open-housing law, later admitted he "was completely out of tune with the white citizens of the state who felt that the right to sell their property to whomever they wanted was a privileged right, a right of ownership, a constitutional right."[8] Widespread acts of resistance and refusal forced a renegotiation of the legal status of open-housing laws, rendering them ineffective even when they were on the books.

The 1964 Civil Rights Act specifically *exempted* federal mortgage insurance programs from antidiscrimination requirements—a stipulation that virtually guaranteed the continuation of discrimination in home lending.[9] When Lyndon Johnson asked Congress to pass a fair-housing bill in 1966, his request produced "some of the most vicious mail LBJ received on any subject," according to White House aide Joseph Califano (and Johnson certainly received more than his share of hate mail on a variety of subjects).[10] Republican minority leader Everett Dirksen attacked the proposed 1966 bill

with particular relish, claiming without supporting evidence that white opposition to fair housing stemmed not from racial prejudice by whites but
from Blacks' bad behavior when they moved into white areas. The House of
Representatives passed a bill that accomplished the opposite of what Johnson
had requested, acknowledging the "right" of individuals to discriminate in
selling their homes and to require their real estate agents to discriminate as
well. Martin Luther King, Jr., and other civil rights leaders argued that the
bill was not worth passing, and only a filibuster by civil rights supporters in
the Senate prevented it from becoming law.[11]

The murder of Dr. King in 1968—and the riots that erupted in its wake—
forced another renegotiation of fair-housing issues. Congress finally passed
a comprehensive fair-housing law, but it was one that actually encouraged
white resistance through provisions that rendered the law virtually unenforceable. Title VIII of the Fair Housing Act authorized the Department of
Housing and Urban Development (HUD) to investigate complaints made
directly to the HUD secretary but forbade that agency from initiating investigations on its own. The act gave the HUD secretary only thirty days to
process complaints and to decide whether action was warranted. Even when
the agency chose to pursue cases, it had no enforcement power. HUD could
only encourage the party guilty of discrimination to accept "conference,
conciliation, and persuasion." In rare instances, HUD could refer cases to
the attorney general for legal action, but Title VIII authorized action by the
Justice Department only when cases "raised an issue of general public importance" or revealed "a pattern or practice" of discrimination. Denial of one
individual's constitutional rights was not considered serious enough for action in this realm. People faced with discrimination in the housing market
were required to file suit within 180 days of the alleged discriminatory act or
within thirty days of the end of mediation. This meant that people suffering
from violations of their rights had to bring action on their own behalf, hire
their own attorneys, pay their own legal fees and court costs, and bear the
burden of proof to establish that "serious" acts of discrimination had indeed
taken place. After all that, even if the plaintiffs won, the act restricted punitive damages in clear-cut cases of discrimination to a maximum of $1,000.[12]

The contours of the 1968 Fair Housing Act make it unique in the annals
of legal discourse. As Patricia Roberts Harris noted when she served as secretary of Housing and Urban Development during the Carter administration, there are very few laws that stipulate that authorities cannot punish
lawbreakers, but only ask if they wish to speak about the matter with their
victims.[13] Yet despite its palpable weaknesses, the 1968 law provoked thousands of complaints about housing discrimination each year. These complaints foundered, however, because of the opportunities for resistance and
refusal built into the act itself. During the 1970s, fewer than 30 percent of the
complaints filed with HUD led to mediation; close to 50 percent of those

remained in noncompliance.[14] By 1986, the antidiscrimination mechanisms established in the 1968 law led to decisions in only about 400 fair-housing cases. Subsequent changes have strengthened aspects of the law's enforcement and punitive mechanisms significantly, although housing discrimination still often goes unpunished. A 2007 report from the U.S. Department of Housing and Urban Development demonstrated that only slightly more than one third of the complaints made to HUD in the preceding year led to conciliation or settlement; only 2 percent of complaints were resolved either through filing of charges or referral to the Department of Justice.[15] Experts estimate more than 3.5 million cases of race-based housing discrimination occur every year without legal action being taken against them.[16]

The process of resistance, refusal, and renegotiation that plagued fair-housing efforts from *Shelley v. Kraemer* through the 1968 Fair Housing Act was not an aberration; it has characterized every judicial, legislative, and executive effort on behalf of open housing for the past fifty years. For example, a group of plaintiffs filed suit in federal court charging racial discrimination by Chicago's public housing authority in the 1960s. A federal judge initially skeptical of their claims eventually found the housing authority guilty in 1969. He ordered the city to construct 700 new units of public housing in white neighborhoods and to locate 75 percent of new public housing outside the inner-city ghetto. The Chicago Housing Authority (CHA) resisted this order initially, but when finally faced with the necessity of compliance, the CHA gutted the judge's ruling by ceasing construction of *all* new public housing in order to evade integration.[17]

Similarly, the St. Louis suburb of Black Jack dissolved its charter, reincorporated under new rules, and changed its zoning laws in 1970 in order to block construction of a low- and middle-income housing development that could possibly open up a few apartments to Blacks in a city that was then 98 percent white. Secretary of Housing and Urban Development George Romney filed a lawsuit against the municipality in federal court as he was required to do by federal law. Attorney General John Mitchell intervened, however, in order to protect Black Jack's resistance to desegregation. He ordered Romney to drop the suit. When the developer then sued the city of Black Jack alleging that the municipality's actions were simply a pretext to evade fair housing laws, city officials countered with the claim that dissolving the charter, reincorporating, and changing the zoning regulations had nothing to do with racial concerns, even though the explosive public debate about those measures focused exclusively on the racial changes that the new housing might produce. The developers won preliminary victories in the courts, but by resisting, refusing and delaying, the city succeeded in making the project eventually so expensive it could not be built.

The executive branch put even more clout behind this kind of resistance when President Nixon announced that he would suspend enforcement of all civil rights laws for a year while his staff studied the situation. Over that year, hundreds of grants were approved by the government without having to comply with federal civil rights laws. Nixon conceded that denying housing to people because of their race was wrong, but he added that he found it equally wrong for cities opposed to federally assisted (and therefore integrated) housing to "have it imposed from Washington by bureaucratic fiat."[18] Nixon's tactic of affirming support for integration in the abstract while acting to undermine the mechanisms that made it possible in practice became the standard response by white politicians to desegregation demands during the civil rights and post–civil rights eras. These politicians soon discovered that their obstructionism made them tremendously popular among white voters.

White resistance expressed as refusal to abide by fair-housing laws continued to guide federal policy in the 1970s and 1980s. A survey conducted by HUD in the 1970s disclosed that Black "testers" sent out to inquire about housing for rent or sale received less information than white testers on housing for sale 15 percent of the time, and less information than white testers about the availability of rental housing 27 percent of the time.[19] As late as 1970, officials of the Federal Home Loan Bank Board redlined postal zip code areas where the Black population was increasing.[20] Training manuals designed for use by private appraisers in 1977 continued to describe desirable neighborhoods as "100 percent Caucasian" along with the phrase "without adverse effects from minorities."[21] Yet federal and state officials remained virtually inactive in the enforcement of fair-housing laws.

Because white resistance and refusal has always led to renegotiation of the terms of open housing, nearly every triumph by fair-housing advocates has turned out to be an empty victory. Opponents of the racially unequal consequences of urban renewal won a long-sought victory in 1970, for example, with the passage of the Uniform Relocation Assistance and Real Property Acquisition Act. This law mandated for the first time that local housing authorities had to replace the low-income units they destroyed (most often occupied by racial minorities). Congress responded by eliminating the urban renewal program altogether, replacing it with community development block grants that emphasized luxury housing for upper- and middle-class homeowners. In St. Louis, the city evicted 500 families (almost all of them African American) from the Pershing-Waterman Redevelopment area, gave $5.8 million in tax abatements to developers, demolished nine buildings at city expense, secured $1.4 million in federal block grant funds, and sold 106 parcels of land to the developers for $122 per parcel. Yet because the Pershing Redevelopment Company was a private enterprise, and because the funding came from block grants rather than urban renewal funds, none of the dislocated families received a single dollar in relocation assistance.[22]

Similarly, Congress passed the Equal Credit Opportunity Act in 1974, which expressly prohibited discrimination in real estate lending, requiring banks to record the racial identities of applicants rejected and accepted for loans. When bankers refused to collect the required data, ten civil rights groups filed suit in 1976. They asked the courts to order the comptroller of the currency, the Federal Deposit Insurance Corporation (FDIC), and the Home Loan Bank Board to obey the 1974 law. These agencies then signed a court order agreeing to collect the required materials, but the comptroller of the currency and the FDIC ceased keeping all records based on race in 1981 when the court order expired. Home Loan Bank Board records revealed that Blacks continued to face rejection rates several times higher than those encountered by white applicants. Having resisted the law initially, the federal agencies complied with the law for a short time when compelled to do so by a court order, then they reverted to absolute refusal as soon as it was feasible for them to do so.

Advocates of fair housing attempted to renegotiate the issue with the passage of the 1975 Home Mortgage Disclosure Act and the 1977 Community Reinvestment Act. These laws required lenders to identify which neighborhoods received their home-improvement and mortgage loans and to demonstrate their willingness to supply capital to worthy borrowers in low-income areas.[23] If enforced fully, these acts might have made a substantial difference, but the Reagan administration rendered them virtually moot by ignoring the law. Reagan's appointee as director of the Justice Department's Civil Rights Division, William Bradford Reynolds, filed only two housing discrimination suits in his first twenty months in office, a distinct drop from the average of thirty-two cases a year filed during the Nixon and Ford presidencies, or even the nineteen per year during the final two years of the Carter administration.[24]

At a time when the number of housing discrimination complaints filed with HUD doubled, the Reagan Justice Department neglected nearly every serious complaint. Instead, it initiated frivolous suits against plans that maintained integrated housing and prevented block busting by regulating the racial balance in housing developments. For example, the administration took action aimed at invalidating deed restrictions in one of the few genuinely integrated areas of Houston, the Houston Oaks subdivision, because the original deeds contained restrictive covenants (which were neither enforced nor honored by the residents). The administration also used the Paperwork Reduction Act as an excuse to stop HUD from gathering data on the racial identities of participants in its housing programs.[25] By refusing to gather data on actual discrimination, the Reagan administration strengthened resistance to fair-housing laws to the point of encouraging outright refusal to obey them.

Precisely because of white resistance to desegregation, the subsidized housing program had the highest percentage of Black recipients of any federal benefits program—38.5 percent in 1979. In 1980, language in an amendment to the Housing and Community Development Act would have allowed local housing authorities to address directly the urgent housing situation of racial minorities by designating housing for those in greatest need, but the Reagan administration came to power shortly afterward. Reagan's appointees made the victory a hollow one by virtually eliminating all federal funding for subsidized housing—from $26.1 billion in 1981 to $2.1 billion in 1985.[26] While cutting allocations for these programs aimed at providing simple subsistence and income maintenance for a primarily Black clientele, the Reagan administration retained the homeowner mortgage deduction, a federal housing policy far more costly to the government, but one that helped a primarily white clientele accumulate assets.

The 1988 Fair Housing Amendments Act, which addressed many important shortcomings in previous fair-housing legislation, came at a time when high housing prices kept many people of color out of the market. In addition, housing in the United States had become so hypersegregated, loan procedures so discriminatory, and enforcement of fair-housing laws so infrequent that federal law acknowledging the rights of all people to secure housing on a fair basis could have little effect on their ability to actually do so. Whites who became homeowners under blatantly discriminatory circumstances condoned and protected by the judicial, legislative, and executive branches of government have also become more formidable competitors for housing, as the value of their homes has increased as a result of appreciation and inflation. Median prices on new homes and on sales of existing homes increased by almost 230 percent between 1970 and 1985, while the consumer price index rose by 177 percent.[27]

The possessive investment in whiteness generated by failure to enforce fair-housing legislation has concrete costs for people of color. Discrimination in subprime lending alone cost Black homeowners between $72 billion and $93 billion in the years from 2000 to 2008.[28] The average Black homeowner is deprived of over $16,000 as a result of the roughly 10 percent higher rate they pay on home mortgages.[29] The costs for those who cannot enter the housing market and who consequently neither build equity nor qualify for the homeowners' tax deduction is, of course, much higher. The appreciated value of owner-occupied homes constitutes the single greatest source of wealth for white Americans. It is the factor most responsible for the disparity between Blacks and whites in respect to wealth—a disparity between the two groups much greater than their differences in income. It is the basis for intergenerational transfers of wealth that enable white parents to give their children financial advantages over the children of other groups. On average, homes owned by whites appreciated $28,000 in value more than homes owned by Black people between 1996 and 2002 alone.[30] Housing plays a crucial role in determining educational opportunities as well, because school funding based on property tax assessments in most localities gives better opportunities to white children than to children from aggrieved racial communities. Opportunities for employment are also affected by housing choices, especially given the location of new places of employment in suburbs and reduced funding for public transportation. In addition, housing affects health conditions, with environmental and health hazards disproportionately located in communities inhabited by people of color.

Whiteness has a value in our society. Its value originates not in the wisdom of white home buyers or the improvements they have made on their property, but from the ways in which patterns of bad faith and nonenforcement of antidiscrimination laws have enabled the beneficiaries of past and present discrimination to protect their gains and pass them on to succeeding generations. These benefits stem directly from the pattern of resistance, refusal, and renegotiation that white individuals and their elected representatives have fashioned in response to antidiscrimination legislation. If these dynamics applied only to housing, they would be damaging enough, but the same process of resistance, refusal, and renegotiation has characterized the history of legislation and court rulings about education and employment as well.

School Desegregation

Unequal opportunities for education play a crucial role in racializing life chances in the United States. Just as the 1948 *Shelley v. Kraemer* decision and the 1968 Fair Housing Act are often credited incorrectly with ending discrimination in housing, the Supreme Court's 1954 ruling in *Brown v. Board of Education* is widely—but wrongly—regarded as the turning point in ending school segregation. Once again, mere articulation of antidiscrimination principles did not lead to their implementation. Like laws against discrimination in housing, official policies designed to end segregated education have been consistently undermined and defeated by white resistance and refusal.

The 1954 *Brown* case culminated sixteen years of school desegregation lawsuits filed by the NAACP and other civil rights and community groups. In that decision, the Court conceded that government bodies had played a crucial role in promoting and preserving racial inequalities by limiting Black students to separate and therefore inherently unequal educations. Yet while ruling against de jure segregation in the abstract, the decision provided no means for dismantling the structures that crafted advantages for white students out of the disadvantages of students of color. The plaintiffs in *Brown* sought more for their children than physical proximity to whites; they pursued desegregation as a means of securing an end to the caste system that stigmatized Blacks as inferior and unworthy and to secure access to the educational resources and opportunities routinely provided to whites. The

Brown decision helped frustrate their aims, however, because it outlawed only one technique of inequality—de jure segregation—without addressing the ways in which discrimination in housing, employment, and access to public services enabled whites to resegregate the schools by placing schools in all white or all Black neighborhoods, by restricting Black student transfers, or by hoarding resources in all white suburban districts. In addition, as Cheryl I. Harris argues, by ordering implementation of its decision "with all deliberate speed," the Supreme Court in *Brown I* and *Brown II* allowed for more deliberation than speed. The Court allowed the white perpetrators of discrimination "to control, manage, postpone, and if necessary, thwart change."[31]

Just as the absence of enforcement mechanisms made violations of fair-housing laws an unusual class of criminal offenses—crimes that carried virtually no penalties—*Brown I* and *Brown II* invented an odd understanding of constitutional rights. In the U.S. constitutional system, rights are generally considered to be "personal and present," meaning that their violation requires immediate redress. But the rights of Black children in *Brown I* and *Brown II* received no such protection. The level of white resistance to desegregation dictated the remedy, an approach that Harris correctly concludes invited "defiance and delay" and, I would add, outright refusal as well.[32] Efforts to desegregate schools provoked massive resistance in the North as well as the South. Yet even with clear evidence of massive refusal on the part of whites to respond to *Brown*, the courts did not accept that the time for "all deliberate speed" had expired and did not begin to evaluate proposed remedies for segregation critically until the 1968 case *Green v. County School Board of New Kent County,* Virginia,[33] Federal courts did not direct school districts to adopt specific remedies like busing until *Swann v. Charlotte-Mecklenberg Board of Education* in 1971, some seventeen years after *Brown I.*

By inviting and allowing decades of delay, the Supreme Court condoned the systematic denial of Black children's constitutional rights, responding instead to the wishes of white parents and their representatives who argued that remediation inconvenienced them and interfered with their expected privileges.[34] Perhaps most important, delay and denial of the rights of Black children encouraged whites to view the inconvenience of busing as worse than the systematic practices of discrimination that provoked it. As in later discussions about affirmative action, characterizing busing as judicial activism and unwarranted federal intervention in community affairs proceeded as if white resistance and refusal had not caused it to be necessary, as if whites were innocent victims of remedies for a disease that did not even exist.

The power of white resistance and refusal to desegregate education was demonstrated most forcefully in the 1973 *San Antonio Independent School District v. Rodriguez* case. In this case, Mexican American students and parents demonstrated that decisions by local school authorities relegated them to inferior schools. The Court did not dispute this assessment of unequal educational opportunity but held that education was not such an important resource that the city and state had to provide Mexican American students with education of high quality. As long as the city and state gave Mexican Americans any education at all, the Court ruled, they were upholding their legal obligations. The San Antonio parents complained that state-drawn district lines and state-mandated reliance on the property tax left them isolated in a district with inadequate resources. The Court, in effect, told them to accept their second-class status, declaring that "any scheme of local taxation—indeed the very existence of identifiable local governmental units—requires the establishment of jurisdictional boundaries that are inevitably arbitrary."[35] The Court's decision not only tolerated these "inevitably arbitrary constructions" in San Antonio but it also endorsed them as the essence of democratic government. The majority opinion in the case held that local entities should determine how local tax monies are spent, celebrating the fact that "each locality is free to tailor local programs to local needs" in a system of pluralism that would enable "experimentation, innovation, and a healthy competition for educational excellence."[36] San Antonio's "experiment" consisted of depriving low-income Mexican American students of an equal education, which met with the approval of the Supreme Court.

The Court established additional precedents purporting to honor local control in the *Milliken v. Bradley* I and II school desegregation cases in Detroit in 1974 and 1977. Lower courts had found that city, county, and state officials designed school district boundaries to provide white students with access to superior schools inside the city and in suburban Detroit. Federal District Court Judge Stephen A. Roth ruled that segregation in Detroit city schools stemmed from deliberate decisions to build new schools in the center of neighborhoods known to be largely white or largely Black, and to permit white students to transfer out of majority Black schools while denying requests by Black students to transfer to majority white schools. Roth noted that the state of Michigan rather than the city of Detroit bore responsibility for these decisions because the Supreme Court of the state repeatedly ruled that education in Michigan "is not a matter of local concern but belongs to the state at large."[37]

Judge Roth found the city, its suburbs, and the state guilty of violating the Fourteenth Amendment rights of Black children. He ordered an interdistrict busing plan that encompassed the city and its suburbs as a remedy. Recognizing that nearly 300,000 children in the three-county area covered by his ruling already rode buses to school, he reasoned that riding the bus for purposes of desegregation should be no more onerous than riding the bus for purposes of segregation. Yet a public outcry against his decision attracted support from political leaders of both major parties and eventually persuaded the Supreme Court to overturn Roth's decision.[38]

The citizens who brought the initial suit to desegregate Detroit's schools included white parents who believed that their children were harmed by state actions that deprived them of an integrated education. Their concerns were dismissed by the Supreme Court, even though they and their Black allies had introduced extensive evidence persuading Judge Roth that private sector actions in real estate and home lending shaped the patterns of school segregation, and that these patterns led residents of Detroit to assume routinely that whites had a right to expect their children's schools to be better funded and better equipped than schools with a majority Black student body. The Supreme Court overruled the Detroit desegregation plan by a 5–4 margin, invoking the sanctity of local control over schools as a guiding principle. "No single tradition in public education is more deeply rooted than local control over the operation of schools," the Court held, noting that "local autonomy has long been thought essential both to the maintenance of community concern and support for public schools and to quality of the educational process."[39]

The "tradition" of local control invoked in the Detroit case was invented for the occasion, saluted only because it offered an excuse for protecting white privilege. As Justice Thurgood Marshall argued in his dissenting opinion, existing school district boundaries covered by the *Milliken* case did not follow neighborhood or even municipal boundaries. The state of Michigan configured school districts so that the Detroit metropolitan area contained eighty-five different administrative units. Some suburbs contained as many as six different school districts. One school district covered five different cities. Seventeen districts extended across two counties, and two districts encompassed three counties. There was no tradition of local autonomy to uphold in Detroit. White privilege rather than local control accounted for the true reason that the Court overturned Judge Roth's ruling.

The majority opinion in *Milliken* contained another blatant fiction about housing segregation. The court record in the case contained evidence of repeated and pervasive violations of state and federal fair housing laws, a pattern of law-breaking responsible for the existence of largely Black cities and largely white suburbs. Yet Justice Potter Stewart's majority opinion ignored this extensive body of evidence, contending with stupefying insouciance that segregation in Detroit and its suburbs stemmed from "unknown or unknowable causes."[40]

In banning interdistrict busing, the *Milliken* decision itself became one more in a long list of fully known and fully knowable causes of segregation. The decision solidified the economic advantages of housing segregation for whites. As Jamin Raskin notes cogently, the decision told whites that it made sense to move to segregated suburbs. It gave "judicial impetus and imprimatur to white flight."[41] *Milliken* rewarded those whites who resisted integration and punished those who supported it. The majority opinion provided rewards for racism and massive subsidies for segregation, granting suburbs that excluded Blacks from residence immunity from school desegregation. It told white parents that the way to secure an optimal education for their children—and in the process deny it to children of color—was to move away from areas where Blacks resided.

White political leadership played an important role in solidifying the resistance to and refusal of school desegregation. Close to 70 percent of northern whites told pollsters that they supported the Johnson administration's efforts to desegregate the South in 1964, but when urban riots, fair-housing campaigns, and efforts to end de facto school segregation reached their localities, a conservative countersubversive mobilization (made manifest in the Goldwater and Wallace campaigns for the presidency and in the efforts by Californians to repeal fair-housing laws) changed public opinion. By 1966, 52 percent of northern whites told pollsters that they felt that the government was pushing integration "too fast."[42] Richard Nixon secured the key support of Strom Thurmond in the 1968 presidential campaign in return for a promise to lessen federal pressure for school desegregation. White southern voters consequently provided him with the crucial vote margin in a closely contested election.[43] Nixon supervised the abandonment of the school desegregation guidelines issued in the 1964 Civil Rights Act, nominated opponents of busing to the Supreme Court, and in his 1972 reelection campaign urged Congress to pass legislation overturning court-ordered busing.[44]

Opposition to school desegregation has enabled whites to preserve de facto advantages they held as a result of an earlier era's overt de jure segregation. As Gary Orfield explains, the superiority of suburban schools is taken for granted as a right attendant to homeownership, while desegregation is viewed as a threat to a system that passes racial advantages from one generation to the next. As he aptly phrases it, "Whites tell pollsters that they believe that blacks are offered equal opportunities, but fiercely resist any efforts to make them send their children to the schools they insist are good enough for blacks." At the same time, "the people who oppose busing minority students to the suburbs also tend to oppose sending suburban dollars to city schools."[45] In a further example of newly apparent ideological inconsistency, whites today profess support for school integration—yet continue to block efforts to desegregate.[46] Wealthy school districts spend money on detectives to investigate whether students of color who claim to live in their districts actually do so.[47] As just one indication of this resistance, the U.S. Government Accountability Office reports that as of 2016 the Department of Justice still has nearly 180 open desegregation cases in federal court.[48]

Efforts to desegregate higher education have also provoked white resistance. In the 1978 *Regents of the University of California v. Bakke* case discussed in the previous chapter, an unsuccessful white applicant to the UC-Davis medical school charged that he had been denied admission to the school because of his race. Bakke claimed that he had compiled a higher undergraduate grade point average (GPA) than the average GPA of minority students admitted through a special admissions program. He did not challenge the legitimacy of the thirty-six white students with GPAs lower than his who also secured acceptance to the UC-Davis medical school the year he applied, nor did he challenge the enrollment of five students admitted because their parents had attended or given money to the school. He did not challenge his exclusion from the other medical schools to which he applied that did not have minority special admissions programs but favored younger applicants over the thirty-six-year-old Bakke. Nor did he mention that he had been the beneficiary of special privileges as an elementary school student in the illegally segregated Dade County, Florida, school district.[49] But Bakke did claim that the sixteen minority special admits to UC-Davis took spots that he deserved, even though the graduation rate for special admission students in the past had ranged from 91 to 95 percent, and at least one of the minority special admits the year Bakke applied had an undergraduate GPA of 3.76, much higher than Bakke's.[50]

In her important and generative article "Whiteness as Property," Cheryl Harris notes that Bakke's case rested on the expectation "that he would never be disfavored when competing with minority candidates, although he might be disfavored with respect to other more privileged whites."[51] While conceding the legality of the UC-Davis minority special admissions program, the Supreme Court nonetheless ordered Bakke's admission to medical school. Justice Powell ruled that while universities could not consider race as a factor in admission procedures merely to correct past injustices, they could consider race as a factor in admissions in order to enhance the educational environment for other (that is, white) students. In this case, the Supreme Court applied to whites the standard of strict scrutiny traditionally used only on behalf of "discrete and insular minorities" likely to suffer "invidious discrimination." In his deciding opinion supporting the state court's level of scrutiny, Justice Lewis Powell did not argue that whites were actually part of a discrete and insular minority likely to suffer invidious discrimination. Instead he opined that white individuals might be so upset by what they viewed as preferential treatment for Chicanx and Blacks that they might *perceive* a denial of equal rights amounting to invidious discrimination.[52] In this case as in many others, guesses about the perceptions and expectations of whites supersede the constitutional rights owed to—and the empirical realities confronting—Blacks and other minorities. It certainly stands in sharp contrast to the 1973 *Rodriguez* decision, which minimized the importance of education as a federally guaranteed right when the case involved Mexican American children. In *Bakke,* white expectations and perceptions of being hindered in their pursuit of the educational opportunities they desired were considered worthy of the highest levels of federal protection.

The value attached to white perceptions by Justice Powell was not an aberration; it is the logical consequence of the success of white resistance and refusal in forcing renegotiation of antidiscrimination law. Its centrality to educational issues is best illustrated by a comparison of the litigation over Bakke with the universally recognized legality of special admissions plans that routinely benefit whites, such as "legacy" admits at elite institutions, including Harvard, Yale, Dartmouth, the University of Pennsylvania, and Stanford. These programs give special preference to children of alumni and children of large donors to the schools. At the University of California and the University of Virginia, alumni children from out of state secure the advantage of being treated as if they were in-state students. As of 2011, Harvard reports accepting 30 percent of applicants whose parents were Harvard alumni, more than four times the rate for nonlegacy applicants.[53] The judicial branch of government that intervened on behalf of Allan Bakke has never found fault with this system, which routinely channels rewards to the children of beneficiaries of past discrimination. A likely member of that group is Jared Kushner, Donald Trump's son-in-law, who as of this writing serves as senior advisor to the president. Kushner secured admission to the freshman class at Harvard at the same time that his real estate developer father pledged to donate $2.5 million dollars to the college. Teachers and administrators at Kushner's high school found Kushner's acceptance to Harvard disappointing because they believed that some of his classmates who deserved admission on merit were turned down. One confided to a reporter, "There is no way anybody in the administrative office of the school thought he would on the merits get into Harvard. His GPA [grade point average] did not warrant it, his SAT scores did not warrant it."[54] As senior advisor to his father-in-law, Kushner may be consulted on one of the key initiatives announced by the Trump administration: having the Department of Justice attack affirmative action programs.

White resistance and refusal in housing and education work to deprive minority children of access to intergenerational transfers of wealth. It denies them access to the skills they will need to better their condition. Inadequate per-pupil funding for heavily Black and Latinx schools means that minority youths frequently encounter effects of underfunding such as larger classes, fewer counselors, more inexperienced teachers, and more poorly equipped laboratories and libraries than their white counterparts.[55] According to a Civil Rights Project study in 2014, over 75 percent of Black students attend schools with a predominately minority enrollment; in the northeastern states over half of Black students and nearly 45 percent of Latinx students attend schools where minority enrollment exceeds 90 percent.[56] Yet, in education as well as in housing, the highest levels of judicial, legislative, and executive power have worked together to preserve white privileges and raise barriers to education and to asset accumulation for members of minority groups. As Cheryl Harris astutely concludes, "When the law recognizes, either implicitly or explicitly, the settled expectations of whites built on the privileges and benefits produced by white supremacy, it acknowledges and reinforces a property interest in whiteness that reproduces black subordination."[57] It also recognizes that white resistance and refusal justifies the renegotiation of opportunities for equality, not just in education, but in housing and hiring.

Fair Hiring

Discrimination in hiring by employers in the private sector produces systematic advantages for white job seekers. Social scientists have found that most job searches in U.S. society rely in part on informal, personal connections to select a candidate,[58] and that using this kind of personal connection increases the number of employment offers extended to job seekers.[59] Personal contacts, further, constitute the best way to find a new position.[60] Moreover, federal labor policies have systematically advantaged whites over minorities, creating and preserving a possessive investment in whiteness with respect to jobs. The Social Security Act of 1935 exempted from coverage the job categories most likely to be filled by African Americans, Asian Americans, and Mexican Americans—farmworkers and domestics—while the National Labor Relations Act put the force of federal law behind racially restrictive union rules and regulations. When the NAACP proposed that the Wagner Act contain a prohibition against racial discrimination by trade unions, the American Federation of Labor announced that it would not support the legislation if it contained such a provision. Thus, organized labor was willing to forgo federally sanctioned collective bargaining to preserve its more important privilege of racial monopolies for white workers. Eventually, the New Deal sided with the unions, granting them federal protection for collective bargaining recognition *and* racial exclusivity.[61]

President Roosevelt's Executive Order 8802 mandated fair hiring in defense industries, but it took concerted direct-action strikes and mass demonstrations by minority workers and their supporters to secure even a modicum of what Roosevelt's executive order promised.[62] When postwar layoffs and discriminatory hiring practices by private employers reversed wartime gains, minority workers initiated twenty years of struggle on a variety of fronts, trying to win access to fair employment opportunities. By 1964, thirty-four states had passed fair-hiring legislation, but these laws had few provisions for enforcement and were largely ineffective. They followed the pattern we have seen earlier of affirming a commitment to nondiscriminatory practices in the abstract while doing nothing to challenge them in practice.[63] Consequently, racially based hiring and racialized segmentation of the labor market remained the norm rather than the exception in the U.S. economy. Employer preferences and trade union discrimination consistently relegated workers from aggrieved racial groups to the worst jobs with the lowest rewards. By the 1950s, Black workers aged twenty-four to forty-four faced unemployment levels three times those confronting their white counterparts. Only half of Black workers labored full time, while nearly 67 percent of white workers had year-round employment. Compared to whites, Black workers endured lower median incomes, a greater likelihood of layoffs, less access to medical and pension plans, and more injuries at work.[64] Because of shorter life spans, lower life earnings, and the regressive nature of Social Security taxes, African American workers paid more into Social Security than they took out, actually subsidizing the Social Security benefits received by more privileged groups. Small wonder then, that at the grassroots level the civil rights struggles so often represented as exclusively concerned with voting rights or desegregating public accommodations often revolved around fair and full employment.

Starting in the early 1960s, Black workers and their allies in Philadelphia, Newark, and New York City staged nonviolent direct-action protests against construction projects financed by taxpayer dollars that hired few, if any, Black workers.[65] In St. Louis, demonstrators led by Percy Green temporarily halted construction on the federally funded Gateway Arch. Green climbed up one leg of the structure and chained himself to it to dramatize his complaints against the project's all-white construction crew.[66] Such demonstrations sought to desegregate the workplace, but in some cities they also had broader social goals. In New York and Philadelphia, community groups linked their demands for construction jobs for minorities to protests against the construction of new schools in all-Black neighborhoods, which they viewed as an effort to ensure segregated and therefore inferior educations for their children.[67]

In Cambridge, Maryland, the militant Cambridge Nonviolent Action Committee conducted a survey of the Black community and disclosed that 42 percent considered unemployment their most pressing problem; 26 percent pinpointed housing, and only 6 percent considered access to public accommodations their top priority.[68] In 1960, a study by the U.S. Commission on Civil Rights condemned "persistent and undeniable" racial discrimination in employment, expressly rebuking the leadership of the trade union movement for its inaction. The massive march on Washington in August 1963, most often remembered as the occasion for Martin Luther King, Jr.'s "I Have a Dream" speech, was officially a march for jobs and justice, with signs prominently displayed calling for stronger fair-employment practices legislation. An investigation by Attorney General Ramsey Clark into the causes of the 1965 Watts riots found employment issues paramount in the minds of community residents.[69]

Confronted with incessant direct-action protests and indirect political pressure, the AFL-CIO reluctantly threw its support behind Title VII of the

1964 Civil Rights Act, a section of the bill ostensibly designed to promote fair hiring. Yet resistance and refusal remained part of the union strategy. According to one highly placed source, the AFL-CIO leadership supported this bill because they believed that a commitment to integration in principle might ward off measures that could bring it about in practice. A leading lobbyist working on behalf of the Civil Rights Act later recalled that the unions "had just been so beaten for their racism that they wanted a bill and then they could blame it on the bill if it wasn't enforced."[70] To that end, they helped write a law that resembled many of the existing ineffective state fair-hiring laws, especially in their assumptions that discriminatory hiring was an individual act and an individual problem rather than a systemic feature of the economy. The law was worded expressly to make clear it did not protect the rights of every job seeker, but was only to be applied in cases of patterns and practices of egregious and large-scale discrimination.

Just as the 1968 Fair Housing Act and the 1954 *Brown* decision established principles about discrimination never designed to be translated into practice, Title VII of the 1964 Civil Rights Act contained provisions that undermined its stated goals. The Equal Employment Opportunity Commission (EEOC) established by the act lacked its own enforcement mechanisms, such as cease-and-desist orders, and could offer only "conciliation" as a remedy to aggrieved individuals.[71] In addition to its weak enforcement provisions, this section of the bill provided explicit special protection for the beneficiaries of past discrimination. As a condition of its support, the AFL-CIO insisted that the bill protect current seniority rights—even those obtained through overtly discriminatory practices. The federation insisted that the mandate for fair hiring applied only to future appointments. Section 703(h) of the bill secured all of these guarantees. In the judgment of Herbert Hill, former national labor director of the NAACP, these provisions offered clear protection to "the racial status quo of seniority systems for at least a generation."[72]

As had been the case in efforts to fight discrimination in housing and education, white resistance prevented fairness in hiring for at least a generation, forcing a renegotiation of the terms, conditions, and procedures of antidiscrimination measures. Even the modest fair-hiring sections of the 1964 Civil Rights Act met with massive resistance by whites—in this case, white employers, white workers, and their political representatives. Some of the St. Louis unions targeted by Percy Green's direct-action protests at the Gateway Arch responded to Title VII by adding a grandfather clause to their apprenticeship regulations, giving extra points on an exam to applicants whose fathers were journeyman construction workers. Construction unions in Philadelphia initiated confidential oral interviews as prerequisites for admission to apprenticeship programs in plumbing, pipefitting, sheet metal work, roofing, and electrical work. All of the Black applicants failed this section of the "exam." Forty percent of the apprentices accepted by the Philadelphia Plumbers Union were the sons of union plumbers. One construction worker in that city bristled when told that Blacks considered these practices discriminatory, explaining, "Some men leave their sons money, some large investments, some business connections and some a profession. I have none of these to bequeath to my sons. I have only one worth-while thing to give: my trade. . . . For this simple father's wish it is said that I discriminate against Negroes. Don't all of us discriminate? Which of us when it comes to choice will not choose a son over all others?"[73] This worker understood very well the value of his whiteness and what it would be worth to his son to pass it across generations. He does not seem concerned by the perpetuation of practices that deny that same intergenerational transfer to Blacks. Like white parents able to leave suburban homes to their children or provide them with legacy admissions to elite colleges, he understood that whiteness is property. Perhaps he also knew that government officials, union leaders, and employers would help him protect that property.

The weaknesses of the EEOC undermined efforts at fair employment. The commission received more than 1,300 complaints about discrimination in its first hundred days of operation. By 1967, it had received more than 8,000 complaints—a total accounting for an average of twenty-three per day. By 1972, little more than half of the 80,000 cases referred to the agency had even been investigated. Frustration with the backlog of complaints at the EEOC forced private individuals to file suits on their own. Between 1965 and 1971, private lawsuits against job discrimination outnumbered actions taken by the Department of Justice by twenty-five to one.[74]

Title VII of the 1964 Civil Rights Act gave the Department of Labor's Bureau of Apprenticeship Training responsibility for ending discrimination in the building trades unions. The bureau failed to take this responsibility seriously. Staffed by individuals with long histories in the trade union movement, it disregarded most of the complaints it received and failed to take any action even when several of its very few investigations revealed clear evidence of discrimination. Three years after the bill became law the agency was still in the process of compiling a list of apprenticeship programs that had been "warned" about discrimination, but even unions notified of violations of the law needed only to issue a statement announcing their intention to comply with the law in the future to get back into the good graces of the government. While the bureau dawdled, unions developed a vast number of tests, oral interviews, and new "education" requirements as a means of continuing to discriminate under the guise of raising standards. In 1968, an exasperated secretary of labor ruled that, in the future, government contractors would not receive any contracts unless they took "affirmative action."[75]

Autoworker Alphonso Lumpkins informed St. Louis Mayor James F. Conway about the weaknesses in fair-hiring law enforcement in a 1980 letter.

Describing his ten-year involvement in a campaign to challenge discrimination in the auto industry, Lumpkins complained, "We have found it very difficult to get local attorneys to stand up to the judges in getting required documents, time to present witnesses, and documents on behalf of our cases."[76] When General Motors (GM) closed its Chevrolet Shell plant, the mostly female and minority workforce learned that they lost all seniority rights and had to seek employment at other GM plants as new workers. Yet when the same company merged its Fisher Body plant with its Chevrolet Truck facility, the workforce at these facilities—89 percent white males at Fisher and 74 percent white males at Chevrolet Truck—kept their seniority rights. That same year, the Equal Employment Opportunity Commission revealed a pattern in St. Louis federal courts that prevented workers like Lumpkins from receiving justice. The EEOC found that federal judges undermined the letter and intent of civil rights laws by denying fees to attorneys for successful plaintiffs in the amounts they would usually receive as reimbursement for their expenses. Thus, the commission's findings confirmed a 1978 brief by the American Civil Liberties Union that charged "an unusual degree of hostility" by federal judges in St. Louis toward people filing civil rights cases. In a successful 1973 suit against discrimination in Iron Workers Local 396 by Black worker Walee Abdul Hameed, one attorney worked 368 hours, and another put in 438, but when they tried to get the losing defendants to pay their usual $60 and $80 per hour fees, Judge James H. Meredith denied their request with no comment. In another case, Judge John H. Nangle gave no award to attorneys for Black firefighters, and in yet another, Judge Kenneth Wangelin awarded an attorney only $300 for a successful suit.[77]

Broader economic changes turned justice delayed into justice denied. When deindustrialization, downsizing, and economic restructuring produced large numbers of layoffs during the 1970s, the seniority rights of white workers insulated them from the worst consequences of these dramatic changes. The provisions in Title VII designed to protect the seniority rights of those workers rewarded them in perpetuity for having benefited from racial discrimination before 1964. As argued in Chapter 1, a study conducted for the U.S. Commission on Civil Rights found that seniority-based layoffs worked particular hardships on Black workers during the 1973–1974 recession. In areas where Blacks made up only 10 to 12 percent of the workforce, they accounted for 60 to 70 percent of the workers laid off.[78] Unprotected by seniority in the present because they had been discriminated against in the past, Blacks paid disproportionate costs for the economic restructuring of the 1970s and 1980s. In addition, because discrimination in hiring did not magically cease with the passage of the 1964 bill, employees who had benefited from discrimination since 1964 also got to retain the seniority rights they had accrued, while others had to struggle against overt and covert discrimination in order to get jobs with lesser seniority. Along with plant closings, layoffs have devastated minority communities. One study found that between 1979 and 1984, 50 percent of Black males in durable goods manufacturing in five Great Lakes cities lost their jobs.[79]

The impact of these seniority-based layoffs might have been less had the laws banning discriminatory practices in hiring been enforced effectively, but here again, white resistance and refusal preserved the possessive investment in whiteness. The Supreme Court has repeatedly thwarted efforts to find fair solutions to the ways in which seniority-based layoffs unfairly and disproportionately affect minority workers. In the 1986 *Wygant v. Jackson Board of Education* case, the Court overturned a voluntary collective bargaining agreement that called for laying off some senior white teachers before junior Black teachers, in order to remedy previous discrimination and to prevent budget crises from causing the district to lose all of its minority teachers. In deciding that this agreement violated the constitutional rights of white workers, Justice Powell posed the decision as a "color-blind" defense of the principle of seniority, arguing that "the rights and expectations surrounding seniority make up what is probably the most valuable capital asset that the worker 'owns,' worth even more than the current equity in his home."[80]

Based on arguments similar to those employed by the Philadelphia construction worker defending nepotism in his union, Powell's comparison to home equity is an appropriate one, but perhaps not for the reasons he intended. Like the equity in homes secured in discriminatory housing markets, white seniority rights secured in discriminatory labor markets routinely receive protection from the courts as if they were constitutional rights. In addition, race rather than seniority stood at the center of this case. Justice Thurgood Marshall observed in his dissent in *Wygant* that all layoffs burden someone, but they are rarely treated as violations of constitutional rights. Marshall noted that the plan the Court rejected did *more* to protect seniority rights than random layoffs would have, but by the Court's reasoning, random layoffs would have been constitutional. Thus, the only kinds of layoffs the majority opinion ruled out were those designed to implement the letter and the spirit of antidiscrimination laws. The violation here was not of seniority but of white expectations that their past advantages would be secured by the courts. As Cheryl Harris explains, "Although the existing state of inequitable distribution is the product of institutionalized white supremacy and economic exploitation, it is seen by whites as part of the natural order of things that cannot legitimately be disturbed."[81]

The Supreme Court carried its protection of white expectations to an extreme degree in the 1989 *City of Richmond v. J. A. Croson* decision. In overturning the Richmond, Virginia, city council's legislation setting aside 30 percent of construction contracts for minority-owned businesses, the

Court ruled that the requirement violated the constitutional rights of white contractors who previously had secured 99.33 percent of city contracting business. In this case, the Court applied to white male business owners the "strict scrutiny" standard originally developed in the 1938 *United States v. Carolene Products Co.* case and later applied to protect "discrete and insular" minorities subject to pervasive discrimination. Justice Sandra Day O'Connor's majority opinion ignored evidence about systematic discrimination in the construction industry, including the fact that between 1973 and 1978 minority businesses received only .67 percent of construction contracts in a city whose population was evenly divided between white and Black. Like Justice Stewart in *Milliken v. Bradley I* and *II*, Justice O'Connor could not fathom why Blacks had not received construction contracts from the City of Richmond prior to the set-aside program. "Blacks may be disproportionately attracted to industries other than construction," she mused, dismissing national statistics on discrimination in the industry because she claimed that they proved nothing about discrimination in the industry in Richmond.[82] Yet while finding no pattern of discrimination against Blacks that might compel remedial action, the majority of the Court did find the claim by a white contractor that he might be relegated to competing for 70 percent of Richmond's construction work instead of 99.33 percent sufficiently serious to warrant strict scrutiny and to overturn the policy of Richmond's democratically elected predominantly Black city council. Unlike the city council of the all-white municipality of Black Jack, Missouri, whose desires to be free of outside "bureaucrats" caused Richard Nixon to suspend enforcement of civil rights laws in 1970, the Richmond city council's actions were overturned as a violation of constitutional rights. The local control that was treated as sacrosanct in the school desegregation cases in San Antonio and Detroit and in housing in Black Jack was nowhere to be found in the court's decision about contracting in Richmond.

This special sensitivity to potential civil rights violations against whites has proven part of a broader pattern. The Supreme Court ruled in *Martin v. Wilks* that white male firefighters in Birmingham who felt they experienced "reverse discrimination" should be allowed to reopen a collective bargaining agreement containing a court-approved affirmative action promotion plan many years after the original case had been settled. Yet in the parallel case in the same year of *Lorance v. ATT Technologies, Inc.*, the Court told female employees that they could not file claims against discriminatory policies in their place of employment because they had waited too long to complain. In fact, the women filed suit as soon as they were aware of the policy's adverse effect on them, but the Court ruled they should have questioned the procedures at the precise moment when they were adopted, even though they could not have possibly known then what results the policies would bring.[83] Thus, the same Supreme Court that granted "suspect-class" status to Birmingham's white male firefighters and Richmond's white contractors denied that status in other cases to women, to minorities, and to persons with below-average incomes.[84]

The Roberts Court: Making It Up as They Go Along

On June 28, 2007, the Supreme Court in the *Parents Involved in Community Schools* case overturned lower court decisions and ignored decades of legal precedent by declaring that modest school desegregation programs in Seattle and Louisville deprived white children and their parents of their Fourteenth Amendment rights to equal protection of the law. In a mendacious and mean-spirited opinion, the Court mobilized the full power of the federal government against local school boards seeking to ensure that rampant housing discrimination in their cities does not deny Black children access to high-quality schools. The Court's ruling clearly contradicted the pledges made by Justice John Roberts and Justice Samuel Alito during their confirmation hearings to uphold precedent and avoid legislating from the bench. The decision mocked the principles of federalism and deference to local authorities celebrated by conservative justices in previous desegregation decisions dating back to *San Antonio v. Rodriguez* in 1973 and *Milliken v. Bradley* in 1974, and articulated as recently as in *Missouri v. Jenkins* in 1995. While claiming to uphold tradition and legal precedent, both the plurality opinion by Justices Roberts, Alito, Scalia, and Thomas and the concurring opinion by Justice Kennedy directly disavowed explicit precedents in previous rulings by the Supreme Court about school desegregation in Charlotte, Cincinnati, Los Angeles, Denver, Fort Wayne, and Pontiac.

The plurality and concurring opinions followed what philosopher Charles Mills calls an "epistemology of ignorance."[85] The Court suffered less from an inability to know than from a firm determination not to know. In order to render this decision, the plurality and Justice Kennedy embraced a series of fictions as if they were facts. The plurality pretended that *Brown v. Board* addressed only the abstract question of whether school boards could recognize race in assigning students to schools. Yet the Warren Court ruled in 1954 that education was a prerequisite for democratic citizenship and that segregated schools deprived Black children of the right to an equal education because segregation composed part of a racial caste system rooted in slavery. Moreover, the court found that the all-Black schools that resulted from segregation suffered from the stigma of inferiority even in the unlikely event that their facilities, curriculum, and teachers were equal to those in white schools. The Roberts Court rewrites this history to find the essence of *Brown* to rest in banning the use of racial identities as a consideration in assigning students to schools. It therefore holds that recognizing the race of a student in order to desegregate schools is the same thing as using race to keep schools segregated.

With this decision the Supreme Court that previously found it improper to intervene when local district officials routinely used patterns of residential segregation to draw attendance lines and to locate new schools in places that guaranteed whites privileged access to better education outlawed actions by local educators trying to respond conscientiously to *Brown's* mandates to end racial isolation and equalize educational opportunity, Closing their eyes to the history of *Brown* and the Thirteenth and Fourteenth Amendments as measures designed to correct the injuries done to Black people by the legacy of slavery, the Court pretended that the relevant constitutional amendments and previous court rulings justify protection of the hereditary privileges that whites derive from past and present racism. As Justice Stevens noted in his concurring dissent from the plurality opinion in *Parents Involved*, it was racial *injustice* rather than racial *recognition* that motivated the plaintiffs in *Brown*. In all the years before the *Brown* decision, no white student ever came to the courts claiming to be stigmatized as inferior for having to attend all-white schools. The white plaintiffs in Seattle and Louisville were not relegated to schools widely known to be inferior. On the contrary, they sought to avoid sending their children to schools that they believed were plenty good enough for Blacks.

Moreover, as Justice Breyer argued in his dissent (joined by Stevens, Ginsburg, and Souter), the Supreme Court has held repeatedly that recognizing race is one of the few ways to desegregate schools successfully, a view clearly articulated in opinions by the Court in *Green v. New Kent County* in 1968 and *Swann v. Mecklenberg* in 1971. Speaking for a unanimous court in the *Swann* case, Chief Justice Warren Burger expressly gave school districts the right to desegregate by using a prescribed ratio of Black and white students. In *Bustop v. Board of Education of the City of Los Angeles* in 1978, Justice Rehnquist declared that local school boards had the right to adopt race-conscious measures to desegregate schools even when no violation of *Brown* had taken place. Yet this entire history was distorted beyond recognition in the *Parents Involved* opinions. Justice Thomas took the revision and distortion of the history of *Brown* to an unprecedented level in *Parents Involved*. He contended that "segregation" only refers to a setup where a school board operates a dual system in which one set of schools is assigned by law to whites and the other to Blacks. Thus, even if every Black student in a district attended all-Black, underfunded, underequipped, and educationally inferior schools, and every white student attended all-white, well-funded, well-equipped, and educationally superior schools, there would be no segregation from Thomas's perspective. Yet it was precisely concerns about residential segregation, racial isolation, and racial inequality in schools that decided previous desegregation cases in Denver, Cincinnati, Boston, and many other cities that never had the kinds of dual systems Thomas claims are a prerequisite for court action.

Despite its flagrant disregard for legal precedent, the Court's decision in *Parents Involved* did continue one tradition of Supreme Court jurisprudence about desegregation: it elevated the convenience and comfort of white people over the constitutional rights of Blacks. Thus, when decisions made by local school boards have benefited whites, the Supreme Court has been an ardent defender of local control. In the school desegregation cases in San Antonio, Detroit, and Kansas City, nonwhite parents and children demonstrated that local school boards deprived minority children of equal educational opportunity. In those instances, Supreme Court decisions went against them because the Court claimed that local control of public education was an overriding public good, a precious principle worthy of constitutional protection. Yet when confronted in the *Parents Involved* cases with local school boards in Louisville and Seattle that acted to help minority children, the Court simply jettisoned the principle of local control. Chief Justice Roberts's opinion went so far as to claim that deference to local school boards "is fundamentally at odds with our equal protection jurisprudence," the opposite of what the Court said in *San Antonio* and *Milliken*.[86]

Protecting whites from the possibility of unfavorable competition with minorities guided the Court in *Parents Involved*. The guardian of kindergarten student Joshua McDonald sued the Louisville school board because the board had rejected McDonald's application to transfer to a school of his choice. In fact, McDonald missed the transfer request deadline because he had moved into the district after the application had to have been submitted. The school board interpreted his application as an attempt to transfer the next year when he would have been in the first grade. They turned him down because the transfer he requested would have had an adverse impact on desegregation in the majority-white school into which he wished to move. When the district realized that McDonald wished to transfer immediately, however, they granted his request. The Louisville school board questioned whether McDonald had suffered an injury in this case worthy of Supreme Court review. He had asked for a transfer and he had received it. The Court ruled, however, that getting into the school McDonald wanted to attend was not sufficient. The Court held that the racial integration system the school board used *might* one day in the future work to McDonald's disadvantage, for example, when he entered middle school or high school. Thus the "injury" in this case that justified the Court's overturning a successful program devised by a local school board was the mere possibility that sometime in the future Joshua McDonald might be disadvantaged in competing for a slot in a majority white school. Yet the routine exclusion of Mexican and Black students from majority white schools in San Antonio and Detroit in the past and in Louisville and Seattle in the present raised no similar question of equal protection for the Court.

The Court's decision in *Parents Involved* offered no opinion on why white students are concentrated on the north side of Seattle or why Louisville was able to integrate successfully only by including the entire metropolitan area in one school district. To the plurality and Justice Kennedy, systematic residential segregation in Seattle and Louisville had no known or knowable causes. Yet the segregated neighborhoods of these cities are actually prima facie evidence of widespread defiance of the 1968 Fair Housing Act. Justice Thomas proved especially creative in evading this fact in his concurring opinion. Deploying the petty malevolence that characterizes many of his writings, Thomas writes that while "presently observed racial imbalance might result from past de jure segregation, racial imbalance can also result from any number of innocent private decisions including voluntary housing choices."[87]

Although the Burger Court recognized in the 1971 *Swann* case that segregated and unequal schools shape housing choices, most subsequent rulings have attempted to deny that link out of hand.[88] While holding the Denver school system responsible for policies that intentionally segregated Black and Latinx students in the 1973 *Keyes* decision, for example, Justice Powell absolved the district of responsibility to remedy "geographical separation of the races" that "resulted from purely natural and neutral non-state causes." In a 1976 decision on segregation in Austin, Texas, Justice Rehnquist likewise asserted (without proof) that "economic pressures and voluntary preferences are the primary determinants of residential patterns." He expanded on that theme in reviewing the Columbus, Ohio, case in 1977, claiming that residential segregation in the region resulted from a "mélange of past happenings prompted by economic considerations, private discrimination, discriminatory school assignments or a desire to reside near people of one's own race or ethnic background."[89] Rehnquist mentions private discrimination and discriminatory school assignments only to dismiss them, to relegate them to less importance than the desire by whites to live in segregated neighborhoods, which apparently in his view is a constitutional right protected by law even though it violates the letter and spirit of the 1968 Fair Housing Act.

In attributing residential segregation to "natural," "neutral," and "voluntary" desires, the Supreme Court has written into law the fictions advanced by guilty defendants in desegregation cases. Attorney James P. Gorton, who represented school districts in suburban St. Louis and Atlanta against desegregation orders, boasted to a reporter that he and his colleagues had established that "people live in specific school districts and urban areas based on job needs, personal preferences, and other factors—not because of race."[90] Yet an enormous body of unchallenged and uncontradicted evidence demonstrates the contrary. Researchers have found consistently that the racial composition of a neighborhood is more important to whites than housing quality, levels of crime, environmental amenities, and location.[91] Even putatively nonracial considerations such as the reputation of local schools often contain perceptions about the racial identities of the student body.[92] Moreover, as Richard Rothstein demonstrates convincingly in his 2017 book *The Color of Law*, residential segregation has been created and maintained consistently by state action, not by "neutral and non-state" decisions.[93]

In the early years of school desegregation cases, judges drew upon this overwhelming evidence to rule that residential segregation stemmed from a combination of private discriminatory acts, including mortgage redlining, real estate steering and blockbusting, and discriminatory public policies such as urban renewal programs that concentrated minorities in overcrowded neighborhoods by offering relocation housing only in those areas. State action structured residential segregation by allocating Section 235 funds only to ghetto and barrio neighborhoods and by making placement decisions about public housing projects, subsidized developments, and schools.[94] As late as 1987, a circuit court established a mutually constitutive relationship between housing and school segregation in Yonkers, New York, fashioning a remedy that required integrated housing as well as integrated schools.[95] In St. Louis, the federal courts ordered the state of Missouri to craft remedies for school segregation that included developing plans for encouraging integrated housing.

The *Parents Involved* decision deployed deeply contradictory logic and language in explaining why school boards in Seattle and Louisville may not use race as a factor in making school assignments. In the Seattle case the plurality opinion notes that the district had never been found guilty of de jure school segregation and therefore could not be subject (even voluntarily) to remedies designed for districts covered directly by *Brown*. Yet the findings in this case by the Ninth Circuit Court reveal that Black parents in Seattle had long charged the school board with locating schools deliberately in neighborhoods where their population would consist of members of only one race, and with allowing white students to transfer freely but making it difficult for Black students to do so. Yet because the school district settled with these parents (to avoid litigation in which it would likely have been found guilty of deliberate de jure discrimination), the Court rules that these charges have not been proven in court and therefore must be treated as if they do not exist. In contrast, in the Louisville case, the Court acknowledged that the district had been found guilty of deliberate de jure discrimination and as a result had implemented desegregation programs including plans like the one under review. Because these programs proved to be successful, however, the district court in 2000 declared Louisville schools to now be unitary and dissolved all desegregation orders. Although Louisville was no longer obligated to desegregate, the district continued to do so because it found integrated schools to be educationally and socially beneficial to the community as a whole. One study found that desegregation played an important role in reducing the Black-white achievement gap in the district. In declaring this to be illegal, however, the Court said not only that Louisville was no longer *obligated* to desegregate but that it was no longer *permitted* to desegregate in this way because the district court ruled in 2000 that the school district had corrected the harm done by its previous policies. Thus, the Seattle school board could not desegregate because it *had not* been found guilty of deliberate segregation, while the Louisville school board could not desegregate because it *had been* found guilty of deliberate segregation and taken remedial action. Desegregation in this view is only a temporary punishment for whites, not a guarantee of constitutional rights for Blacks.

In both Seattle and Louisville, school boards had made concession after concession to white parents over the years. They had constantly refined their desegregation programs to minimize white inconvenience, to limit busing, and to use neighborhood location as an important factor in making school assignments. Rather than rewarding these school boards for their conciliatory efforts, the Supreme Court at each stage condoned, encouraged, and then supported white resistance, refusal, and renegotiation of previously agreed-upon settlements. Consistent with the administrative and judicial policies of the racial state with respect to employment and housing discrimination, the Supreme Court has generally responded to school desegregation suits by exaggerating white injuries and treating antidiscrimination efforts as more egregious civil rights violations than the acts of discrimination by whites that made these efforts necessary in the first place. The injury claimed by the plaintiffs in the Louisville case was that they might be denied admission to the precise educationally advantaged schools of their choosing, a complaint that pales in comparison to the obstacles facing not only Linda Brown in 1954, but Mexican American students in San Antonio in 1973, Black students in Detroit in 1975, and most Black students in Seattle and Louisville today

Justices Roberts, Scalia, Thomas, and Alito had long presented themselves as strict constructionists, as judges who would accept the opinions delivered by previous courts as settled law, who would honor the intentions of Congress by refusing to interfere with statutes on the books, and who would protect local jurisdictions from federal overreach. In this case, however, they practiced the opposite of what they preached. In *Parents Involved* they abandoned fifty years of legal precedent and overturned voluntary local desegregation plans. They characterized *as* discrimination the only practical and plausible means of reducing discrimination.

A similar dynamic guided the Roberts Court in the 2009 *Ricci* case. In that decision, it prevented local officials in New Haven, Connecticut, from enforcing fair employment law. Title VII of the 1964 Civil Rights Act required the city to make sure that tests taken by firefighters seeking promotions contained no built-in biases that impeded the ability of Black and Latinx applicants to pass them. City officials discovered that the test was flawed, that pinning 60 percent of the final grade on the written portion of the test had no legitimate merit rationale and that it served to lower the scores of otherwise qualified applicants. They devised a new exam, one that adhered to what had long been recognized as race-neutral best practices in testing. The lower courts endorsed this move as a matter of equity and fairness, yet the Roberts Court overturned those rulings, commanding the New Haven fire department to accept as valid the results of a test that had been shown to be both defective and racially biased. Their rationale echoed Justice Powell in the Bakke case in claiming that whites who had done well on the original biased tests *might believe* that throwing out the test disadvantaged them for being white. The Roberts Court extended that same special protection to white expectations in the 2013 case of *Shelby v. Holder* when it overturned the clear and express intentions of Congress in passing the Voting Rights Act in 1965 and in amending and renewing it in 1975, 1982, and 2006. The decision ended the pre-clearance requirement imposed on counties and states that had been found guilty of deliberately suppressing minority voters. Writing for the majority, Chief Justice Roberts declared that these government bodies were being retroactively punished for things that happened long ago, that voter suppression was no longer a problem in these jurisdictions. He reached that conclusion despite the fact that the Voting Rights Act has been used to overturn more than 700 clearly discriminatory practices in those very jurisdictions between 1982 and 2006. In the *Parents Involved, Ricci*, and *Shelby* cases, the Roberts Court abandoned its stated commitments to respecting settled law and deferring to the judgment of local authorities and Congress. The justices violated every one of their principles except one, that one being their fidelity to the possessive investment in whiteness.

Resistance, Refusal, Renegotiation, and Racial Progress

Derrick Bell's apt summation of the state of civil rights law in the 1990s is still accurate today: "(1) Because most policies challenged by blacks as discriminatory make no mention of race, blacks can no longer evoke the strict-scrutiny shield in absence of proof of intentional discrimination—at which point, strict scrutiny is hardly needed. (2) Whites challenging racial remedies that usually contain racial classifications are now deemed entitled to strict scrutiny without any distinction between policies of invidious intent and those with remedial purposes. Thus, for equal protection purposes, whites have become the protected 'discrete and insular' minority."[96] White resistance and refusal has led to renegotiation of antidiscrimination law to such a degree that efforts to combat discrimination are now considered discriminatory and efforts to preserve white advantages are treated as civil rights causes.

The problems confronting communities of color in the 2010s are not just the residual consequences of slavery and segregation; they are, as well, the product of liberal and conservative policies that have encouraged resistance, refusal, and renegotiation of antidiscrimination measures. The "disadvantages" facing minority communities have everything to do with having been taken advantage of in the past and present. Without fundamental change, we can only expect the impact of racism on opportunities to increase in the years ahead.

Failure to enforce civil rights laws banning discrimination in housing, education, and hiring, along with efforts to undermine affirmative action and other remedies designed to advance the cause of social justice, render racism structural and institutional rather than purely private and personal. Whites may or may not be openly racist in their personal decisions or private interactions with others, but they nonetheless benefit systematically from the structural impediments to minority access to quality housing, schools, and jobs. Michael Omi makes a useful distinction between *referential* racism (the snarling, sneering, cross-burning displays of antipathy toward minorities) and *inferential* racism (a system of structured inequality that allows white people to remain self-satisfied and smug about their own innocence). Inferential racism allows whites to disown racist statements by popular white politicians and pundits while assuming that the houses they own, the schools they attend, and the jobs they hold have come to them exclusively on the basis of individual merit.

For more than fifty years our nation's public commitments to equal opportunity have been fatally undermined by our practices of resistance, refusal, and renegotiation. Rather than ushering in a golden age when people are judged by the content of their character rather than by the color of their skin, we have augmented and intensified the possessive investment in whiteness. Our policies in the realm of antidiscrimination law conform to the analogy offered more than fifty years ago by Malcolm X. Challenging a reporter who suggested that the passage of civil rights legislation proved that things were improving in the United States, Malcolm X argued that it did not show improvement to stick a knife nine inches into someone, pull it out six inches, and then call that progress. Pulling the knife all the way out would not be progress either. Only healing the wound that the knife had caused would show improvement. "But some people," Malcolm X observed, "don't even want to admit the knife is there."[97]

3

Immigrant Labor and Identity Politics

That victim who is able to articulate the situation of the victim has ceased to be a victim; he, or she, has become a threat.

—JAMES BALDWIN

On election day in 1994, nearly 60 percent of the California electorate voted in favor of Proposition 187, a measure designed to deny medical treatment and education to undocumented workers and their children and to deliver excruciating pain and punishment to the state's most powerless and defenseless residents. The initiative mandated the expulsion from school of close to 500,000 students, required denial of prenatal care to pregnant women, deprived deaf children of sign language instruction, and demanded that doctors refuse to provide their patients with immunization shots and refuse to give them tests and treatment for AIDS, tuberculosis, alcoholism, and all other diseases. Phrased in especially punitive language and fueled by a demagogic and hate-filled public relations campaign blaming "illegal" immigrants from Mexico for the many problems confronting California's economy, the ballot measure created chilling new categories of public obligation and citizenship. It required private citizens to become government informants, ordering doctors, nurses, teachers, social workers, and assorted public employees to report to immigration authorities all persons "suspected" of living in the United States without proper documentation.

In 2010, the state legislature in Arizona enacted S.B. 1070, a law that required police officers to demand proof of citizenship from individuals who might be undocumented. Improperly designating the enforcement of immigration law as a local and state rather than a federal responsibility, this measure mandated racial profiling of the entire Latinx population of the state. It required local law enforcement officials to divert attention away from protecting public safety in order to stage a spectacle affirming the possessive investment in whiteness. That same year, legislators approved H.B. 2281, which attempted to outlaw the teaching of antiracist subject matter to high school students by banning ethnic studies courses in the public schools.

Proclaimed as measures to uphold the law by cracking down on "illegal" immigration, California's Proposition 187 and Arizona's S.B. 1070 and H.B. 2281 were themselves blatantly illegal and unconstitutional measures. Nearly all of their provisions were invalidated by the courts, as opponents of the measures had predicted. Yet bad laws can make for good politics, especially when they pander to the possessive investment in whiteness. The election to the U.S. presidency of Donald Trump in 2016 on a platform that defamed hardworking, low-wage workers from Mexico as criminals and rapists harvested the fruits of the seeds sown by two decades of anti-immigrant hysteria. The long history of hatred directed against immigrants from Mexico, Central and South America, the Caribbean, Asia, the Middle East, and Africa has been a key mechanism for the creation and preservation of white advantage. Hating immigrants makes them easier to exploit. It serves as justification for paying them low wages to do the most onerous work and to neglect their health and housing needs. Focusing attention on the purportedly deficient character of immigrants hides the workings of global capitalism, especially the ways in which the United States is a bounded nation that has become dependent on boundless sources of raw materials, markets, and labor. Immigrants come to the United States from sites that have been totally transformed by U.S. investments and imperial intrusions. Consolidation of agricultural landholdings, military intervention, and the promotion of austerity policies in the global south dispossess and displace millions of people who seek to survive as migrant laborers. Anti-immigrant discourses, laws, and labor policies hide these structures and the ways in which investors and owners in the United States profit from them. They present the United States as the innocent victim of migrant illegality rather than as the beneficiary of migrant desperation.

California Proposition 187: Criminalizing Immigrant Labor

Although surveys showed that many Canadian, Italian, Israeli, and Irish citizens lived and worked in California without proper credentials from the Immigration and Naturalization Service (INS), the popular campaign on behalf of Proposition 187 in 1994 expressly targeted immigrants from Mexico and Central America (and to a lesser extent those from Asia) as the focal point of concern about the alleged "costs" of providing medical care and education to undocumented immigrants. Reinforcing long-standing white supremacist practices of viewing all Latinx and Asians as forever "foreign" while celebrating assimilation as the unique achievement of European immigrants and their descendants, Proposition 187 effectively criminalized

Latinx and Asian American identity, creating a previously unheard of legal category—the "suspected illegal immigrant"—and then subjecting these "suspects" to vigilante surveillance, supervision, and suppression.

Federal jurists delayed the implementation of Proposition 187 as they were required to do by constitutional law. Its provisions improperly granted the power of regulating immigration to the state of California rather than to the federal government. Several of the provisions of the initiative eventually became law, however, through the welfare reform act of 1996 passed by Congress and signed by President Clinton. Although most of its more dramatic and draconian provisions were thrown out by the federal courts, the passage of Proposition 187 marked an important event in the contemporary reinscription of the possessive investment in whiteness. It not only unleashed an inflammatory and hate-filled wave of nativist anti-foreign scapegoating, but it also served as a key component in a campaign to insulate white voters and property owners from the ill effects of neoliberal economic policies. Blaming the state's fiscal woes on immigrants rather than taking responsibility for the ruinous effects of capital flight and a decade and a half of irresponsible tax cuts for the wealthy coupled with disinvestment in education and infrastructure enabled the state's political leaders and wealthy citizens to divert attention away from their own failures. They knew full well that Proposition 187 and the many schemes that surfaced in its wake to deny social services, health care, and education to undocumented and even documented immigrants would have no effect on the numbers of migrants coming to the United States, most of whom migrate to escape even greater austerity in their home countries. They knew that the state would lose more money in federal aid (to education based on school enrollment, for example) than it would save by cutting off benefits to undocumented workers and their families, that denying medical treatment to people in need of care would cause more financial and social damage to the state through unchecked epidemics and untreated diseases than such measures would save in tax revenues.

Moreover, the wealthy white voters who provided the bulwark of leadership in the campaign for Proposition 187 had no intention of giving up the benefits they derived from the unregulated, low-wage work performed for them by immigrant agricultural laborers, short-order cooks, porters, bellhops, janitors, pool cleaners, domestic servants, nannies, gardeners, and construction workers. But these activists knew that creating a climate of terror among racialized immigrants and fostering a lynch-mob atmosphere among whites would constrain minority low-wage workers from organizing unions or demanding state enforcement of existing laws covering minimum wages, safe and humane working conditions, and employer social security contributions. The process of demonizing undocumented workers as "illegal aliens" emanated not from a respect for the law but rather from support for efforts by executives from large corporations, small business owners, and individual homeowners to break the law, to disregard statutes mandating safe working conditions, a living wage, and dignified relations between employers and employees.

Taking advantage of an already vulnerable population, the proponents of Proposition 187 used their ballot initiative as a device to terrorize the low-wage workforce into accepting even worse working conditions and even lower wages. Perhaps more important, they relied on the campaign for Proposition 187 to solidify a countersubversive coalition held together by images that inverted actual power relations—presenting whites, the wealthy, and males as "victims" of the unfair advantages purportedly secured by racial minorities, the poor, and women. Part of a politics of moral panic that characterized the Reagan years and culminated in the capture of Congress by the Republican Party in the 1994 election, this manifestation of privilege masquerading as powerlessness does not really need to convince the electorate at large in order to succeed; its true aim is to build a sense of besieged solidarity within its own group. When the privileged group secures actual victories, as in the case of Proposition 187, doing so simply supplies an added fringe benefit for its adherents—the pleasures of recreational hate.

The proponents of Proposition 187 officially disavowed any racist intent behind their initiative, but their own words and actions indicated otherwise. Linda Hayes, the campaign's media director for southern California, exhibited her group's obsession with race in a letter to the *New York Times* published a few weeks before the election. She explained that illegal immigration stemmed from a secret plan by "Mexicans" to establish Spanish as California's official language, to drive English speakers from the state, and to then hold a plebiscite annexing California to Mexico.[1] Though preposterous as a basis for public policy, Hayes's letter exemplified an important element in the debate over Proposition 187—its role in inviting whites to express openly and in public the racial resentments, prejudices, and paranoid fantasies that they previously entertained largely in private. In the aftermath of the election, a series of ugly incidents illustrated the success of this dimension of the campaign. A fifth-grade teacher ordered her Latinx pupils to write a paper detailing their citizenship status and that of their parents. A counter attendant at a fast-food restaurant refused to serve hamburgers and soft drinks to three English-speaking Mexican American teenagers (all U.S. citizens, it turned out). A restaurant customer entered the establishment's kitchen and demanded proof of citizenship from the cooks. A school security guard told two Latinas, "We don't have to let Mexicans in here anymore." A receptionist at a public health clinic told all Spanish-speaking women that they were no longer eligible for medical treatment. The registrar at a California State University campus submitted a proposal to notify all students with Spanish surnames that they needed to provide proof of citizenship to remain enrolled.[2] At the same time, however, many courageous educators and health care professionals announced their firm intention to defy the new law, to refuse to comply with its provisions requiring them to become informants for the Immigration and Naturalization Service.

Political opportunism accounted for much of the campaign on behalf of Proposition 187. During his first term in office, California governor Pete Wilson saw his approval ratings in public opinion polls drop below 20 percent as the state suffered from a devastating economic recession. Less than 20 percent approval represents a nadir for any incumbent, much less for Pete Wilson, a career politician lavishly subsidized throughout his career by contributions from wealthy attorneys, developers, and bankers in his successful previous races for mayor of San Diego, U.S. senator, and governor.[3] To improve his chances for election, Wilson attempted to deflect anger away from himself and toward some of the most powerless and defenseless people in California. In a state where government allotments to single mothers raising two children already fell $2,645 below the official poverty line, Wilson successfully advocated reducing payments so that these women and their children would be even poorer. He showed himself to be motivated more by spite and contempt than by fiscal restraint when he explained that the new payments should not produce hardships for welfare mothers and their children because the cuts simply meant "one less six pack per week."[4]

Unable to run for reelection on his own record, the only resource Wilson owned to advance his ambitions was his whiteness, which he used ruthlessly and effectively. In his 1994 reelection campaign, he deflected criticism away from his dismal performance as the state's chief executive by scapegoating immigrants for California's problems. His campaign commercials featured a film showing a dozen Mexican nationals running past U.S. border guards as a voice-over narrative seething with racist contempt intoned, "*They* just keep coming." Wilson's speeches and statements in support of his own campaign and on behalf of Proposition 187 made special and nearly obsessive mention of the relatively small number of Mexican immigrant women who give birth to children in California hospitals, taking advantage of stereotypes of Mexicans as sexually unrestrained and acting as if forming families is an illicit activity, as if childbirth is an unnatural and perverse practice of the poor, and as if anyone would be better off if expectant mothers and their children were denied prenatal care and childbirth under safe conditions.

Undocumented workers pay far more in taxes than they receive in services. In addition, they benefit the U.S. economy as productive low-wage laborers, ineligible for direct welfare assistance. They provide surplus profits to employers and help produce lower prices for customers because they are vulnerable to employers who pay them low wages—and in some cases pay them no wages at all—secure in the knowledge that the workers' undocumented status makes it all but impossible for them to file complaints with the legally constituted authorities. To be sure, not all of the federal taxes paid by undocumented workers return to California, and it is true that city, county, and state agencies bear primary responsibility for some of the medical and educational expenses of immigrants. Yet local residents of areas with high immigrant populations also enjoy the overwhelming majority of the economic benefits that come from lower prices for goods and services created by the hard work and legal vulnerability of largely unregulated low-wage immigrant labor.[5]

Particular sectors of the California workforce may well be hurt by the influx of undocumented workers, especially members of other minority groups competing for unskilled low-wage employment. One can see clearly that jobs cleaning and maintaining office buildings, hotels, and restaurants that used to go routinely to African Americans by the 1990s seemed increasingly to be the domain of Central Americans. Employers sometimes favored immigrants over African Americans because those doing the hiring suffered from racist preconceptions about African American workers. Employers also generally preferred to hire workers who did not speak English, who might be unfamiliar with U.S. labor laws, and whose noncitizen status seemingly might make them reluctant to become trade union activists, to file grievances on the job, or to complain to state and federal agencies about violations of labor laws or health and safety regulations. This change was part of a conscious strategy by employers nationwide to create a "union-proof" workforce, a strategy in evidence from the rise of prison labor in the United States to the outsourcing of low-wage data-processing jobs to India, from the entry of Central Americans into jobs as janitors in Los Angeles office buildings to the recruitment of longshore dock workers from the Persian Gulf as replacements for unionized dock workers in Australia, from increases in part-time employment and immigrant labor in the poultry industry in the Midwest and South to the development of computer-generated automation as a means of turning high-paying, high-skill jobs into low-skill, low-wage employment.[6]

After a long educational campaign by civil rights groups, a slight majority of African American voters opposed Proposition 187. The utility of dividing African American from Latinx and/or Asian workers, however, provided an unanticipated fringe benefit for the Republican Party, which put hundreds of thousands of dollars behind the campaign to pass Proposition 187. This turned out to be a rehearsal for the millions they would later spend in 1996 advancing a demagogic ballot proposition against affirmative action. The party directed its efforts mainly at white voters, who comprised an overwhelming majority of the electorate in an off-year election. The strategy aimed at mobilizing anti-immigrant sentiment and using it to slip Pete Wilson past the voters once again despite his poor performance as governor. The Republicans received a major assist from Wilson's opponent, Kathleen

Brown, the state treasurer and Democratic Party nominee for governor. Brown nominally opposed Proposition 187 but failed to challenge its basic premises. Unable and unwilling to oppose the interests of the transnational corporations backing her expensive campaign, the Democratic nominee did not call for improvements in the wages and working conditions of all workers, but instead wound up agreeing with Wilson that undocumented immigrants posed serious problems for California, while demurring only that Proposition 187 was an extreme and ineffective way to address the issue.

The leaders of the Democratic Party, of the trade unions, and of the state's civil rights organizations largely shied away from the fight over Proposition 187. They failed to expose the enormous economic benefits that come to Californians from immigrant workers. They failed to publicize the active role played by big corporations and wealthy individuals in exploiting the labor, resources, and raw materials of the global south in ways that promoted immigration and encouraged the rise of undocumented labor in the United States. They failed to offer proposals to seize the assets of businesses and individuals employing undocumented workers, or to campaign for laws making retailers accountable for selling products secured from illegal sweatshop labor. Offered a choice between the arguments proposed by Pete Wilson—that things are bad and that illegal immigrants were to blame—and the arguments offered by Kathleen Brown—that things are bad but that nothing in particular could be done about them—close to 60 percent of the voters predictably enough chose Wilson's position.

Proposition 187 and the plethora of anti-immigrant measures across the nation that have emerged subsequently draw on a long history of laws designed to ensure the unimpeded importation of low-wage labor in order to drive down wages for all workers while blaming the resulting social and economic catastrophes on the immigrants themselves. In this endeavor, the posture of protecting the property interests of "whiteness" plays an indispensable role. The proponents of Proposition 187 articulated their concerns in unambiguous language when the leader of the campaign to pass the measure described his group as the "posse" and Proposition 187 as "the rope." Key architects of and activists for Proposition 187 received financial backing from the Pioneer Fund, a well-known white supremacist organization dedicated to research in eugenics purporting to prove the biological superiority of the white race and the threat posed to it by interaction with people of color. In television and newspaper advertisements, in public pronouncements and privately circulated propaganda, supporters of Proposition 187 relied on racist and sexist stereotypes, especially the "menace" posed by Mexican women coming to California to have babies at taxpayers' expense. This argument has little basis in fact; the amount of public funds spent on prenatal care and childbirth for undocumented immigrants is both minimal and cost effective. Yet by feminizing and infantilizing the enemy, by connecting the social transgression of nonwhite immigrants coming to California with the fear of unrestrained "Latin" sexuality and procreation, the advocates of Proposition 187 "played the race card," evoking powerful stereotypes that are especially well suited for concealing the real social relations between undocumented immigrants and California's white voters.

Asian American studies scholar Lisa Lowe presented a brilliant and useful analysis of the stereotyping central to the Proposition 187 campaign in an address to the Modern Language Association national meetings in San Diego a little more than a month after the 1994 election. Lowe argued that successful racist stereotypes are not just picturesque untruths but carefully constructed images designed to make lies more attractive than truth.[7] The truth in California in 1994 was that the standard of living enjoyed by the state's middle and upper classes increasingly depended upon the desperation of immigrants, especially low-wage women workers from Mexico, El Salvador, Guatemala, China, the Philippines, and other sites in Latin America and Asia. The labor of these women lowers the price of garments made in primitive sweatshops as well as the price of computer chips vital to the profits of high-tech industries. The low-wage women workers demonized as parasites by Pete Wilson actually do much of the hard work on which middle-class prosperity relies. They clean offices, hotel rooms, and homes. They plant, harvest, prepare, and serve food. They sew clothes they cannot afford to wear. For all their hard and under-rewarded work, they find themselves hated and defamed as lazy dependents living off the largesse of the very people whose lives they make easier and more remunerative. The hypocrisy of Proposition 187's supporters did not need to be well hidden. During the election campaign, reporters discovered that millionaire senatorial candidate and Proposition 187 supporter Michael Huffington had long benefited from the work done for him and his family by an undocumented immigrant housekeeper. Little more than a year after the election, the *Washington Post* reported that Pete Wilson himself employed as his housekeeper an "illegal alien" from Tijuana.[8]

Lowe's analysis uncovers the importance of white identity politics within the immigration issue. The possessive investment in whiteness seeks support for transnational capital by promising to confine its worst effects to communities of color while preserving and extending the benefits of present and past discrimination enjoyed by European Americans. At the same time, it works as a wedge against the welfare state in general, using the denial of benefits to "unworthy" recipients like undocumented (and later even legal) immigrants as the prelude to future campaigns to "privatize" education and health services for everyone, effectively reserving them only for the rich. The portrayal of massive immigration to the United States from Mexico as a consequence of the desire of individual immigrants for welfare benefits completely disregards the neoliberal "reforms" imposed on Mexico by U.S. firms and transnational capitalist institutions that made flight from that country a necessity for many formerly self-sufficient workers and farmers. The U.S. government insisted on free trade and unlimited mobility for U.S. capital; worked to lower wages, cut social spending, and disrupt traditional economies in poor nations; encouraged the growth of low-wage jobs in North America; and then expressed shock and dismay when these decisions all led to increased immigration to the United States.

Arizona HB 2281: Banning Ethnic Studies

The Mexican American Studies Program (MAS) in the Tucson, Arizona, school district achieved an extraordinary record of success using a culturally relevant curriculum and pedagogy that addressed the realities of race and racism in the United States. During the 2010–2011 academic year, 1,300 students took MAS courses in eight different Tucson high schools and middle schools. The classes were voluntary and open to all students. The young people enrolled in them read writings by renowned authors from diverse racial groups and responded to their ideas in discussions, tests, and writing assignments. In a district plagued by a dropout rate of nearly 50 percent among Chicanx students, an astounding 97.5 percent of those enrolled in the MAS classes went on to graduate from high school.[9] MAS students outscored students of all racial and ethnic groups in their schools on standardized tests in reading, math, and writing.[10] A study by education researcher Nolan Cabrera of the University of Arizona found strong empirical evidence that the classes promoted academic achievement, especially among those students who before enrolling in the MAS classes had experienced extremely low levels of academic success.[11]

Despite this clear record of achievement, the legislature in collaboration with the Arizona state superintendent of education declared that the MAS program should be made illegal, alleging that it advocated the overthrow of the U.S. government, promoted resentment toward a race or class of people [which in this context meant whites], was designed primarily for pupils of a particular ethnic group [which here meant Chicanx], and advocated ethnic solidarity instead of the treatment of pupils as individuals. None of these claims were valid. They were a phantasm, a phobic projection of what people possessed by whiteness might imagine ethnic studies courses to be. The courses did not advocate overthrowing the government. They contained critiques of racism, but did not direct resentment against white people. The classes were open to and appreciated by students of all races. They did not eclipse individual identities with group solidarity any more than teaching about the history of westward expansion would promote group solidarity among whites and enmity toward Native Americans. A federal district court judge ruled exactly that in August 2017 in deciding that the ban on ethnic studies enacted by HB2281 stemmed from racial animus rather than concerns about educational quality, that state officials had acted with malicious and expressly race-based motivation in enacting the law, and that its enforcement violated the students' First Amendment rights to freedom of speech and their Fourteenth Amendment rights to equal treatment.[12]

Border Crossers and Double Crossers:
Immigrant Labor and Transnational Capital

The attempt to ban ethnic studies classes in Arizona demonstrates that the focus in political discourse and public policy on *who* is undocumented—low-wage immigrant workers—serves as a smokescreen to hide *what* is undocumented, namely, the actual causes and consequences of contemporary migration. Ethnic studies knowledge projects and political projects can play an important role in making these hidden realities visible. That is why they are targeted for attack. The rhetoric that demonizes low-wage workers for crossing international boundaries elides the existence of the most important border crossers in the Southwest, the U.S. firms that use special tax breaks and the provisions of international trade agreements to set up *maquiladora* plants on the U.S.–Mexico border. Instigated and sustained by tax breaks that offer subsidies to U.S. firms to abandon workers in the United States by fleeing to locations of low-wage labor like Mexico, maquiladora zones provide opportunities for large profits for California businesses and investors. By moving across the border, U.S. firms such as Ford, Chrysler, General Motors, General Electric, and ITT, along with firms owned by investors in other countries, employed over 2 million workers in their Mexican plants in 2014.[13] As of that year, locating these plants in Mexico saved American companies an estimated $30,000 per worker per year.[14] Low wages, low taxes, weak unions, high unemployment, and nonenforcement of environmental protection laws make maquiladora plants a locus of terrible exploitation and disruption in Mexico.[15]

Corporations gain state-subsidized advantages over workers in both the United States and Mexico by crossing the border. For example, in 1992, the Smith-Corona Company closed a typewriter plant in Cortland, New York, dismissing 800 workers from their jobs. The company then relocated its operations to Tijuana, Mexico. Management abuses motivated the Mexican workers to go on strike in October 1994. When the employees announced their work stoppage, the Smith-Corona Company in Mexico "disappeared from the social security records as if it had been shut down," according to Mary Tong of the San Diego Support Committee for Maquiladora Workers. The workers still made the same products at the same plants, but they could not find out the identity of their employer in order to bargain with management. At least sixteen companies "disappeared" in Tijuana in this way in 1994, sometimes simply sneaking out of town, abandoning plants built with subsidies from the Mexican government, and avoiding all payroll and tax obligations including the severance pay required in such situations by Mexican law.[16]

Unconstrained by Mexican environmental laws that are strong but not enforced, companies in one Tijuana industrial park released unlawful and dangerous concentrations of lead, copper, cadmium, chromium, zinc, and arsenic into drainage ditches, polluting sources of drinking water for some 2,000 people living in the *colonia* nestled beneath the industrial park. One study showed that more than 40 percent of the people in this neighborhood suffered from pollution-related illnesses and learning disabilities. Between 1993 and 1995 alone, nine women in this colonia gave birth to anencephalic babies (babies born without brains). Corporate and government officials denied that pollution caused these birth defects, attributing the poor health of mothers and children to deficient amounts of folic acid in the diets of the workers and their families. Yet these workers subsist largely on corn and beans, two foods with high levels of folic acid.[17] Today, flame retardants are found in children's blood at levels four to five times higher in Ciudad Juarez—home to 330 *maquiladoras*—than in that of Mexican children in nonindustrial urban areas.[18] In Tijuana, black carbon air concentrations are twice as high as in nearby San Diego, in part because of Tijuana's 570 *maquiladoras*.[19] Yet one survey of factories that produce electronics found that nearly half had no active environmental policy.[20] Magdalena Cerda, a representative from the Environmental Health Coalition, explained in 2011, "Government oversight [of *maquiladoras*] is poor. There aren't enough inspectors. There is no obligatory inspection scheme, only a voluntary one, and inspections are arranged in advance, with no surprise visits."[21]

The signing of the North American Free Trade Agreement in 1993 compounded already depressed conditions in Mexico's agricultural sector, promoting massive migration to cities like Tijuana. Transnational companies seek out young women workers for their border assembly operations because they believe them to be more obedient and less militant than men or older women. They believe they can work these employees hard for a brief period, and then replace them with other willing recruits fleeing the devastated economic conditions in the agricultural regions of central and southern Mexico. Because Mexican law requires companies to be responsible for the prenatal care and childbirth expenses of women workers, the firms try to force pregnant women to quit their jobs. In one plant owned by a Japanese firm, management put a pregnant worker in a fume-filled soldering room with no ventilation in hopes of making her quit her job. She remained at work because she needed the money. Her baby was born anencephalic.[22]

Maquiladora plants offer great advantages to investors, owners, and their families in the United States, especially California. The plants make products that can be sold for less because of their lower labor costs, while the practice (and even the possibility) of runaway shops constrains the demands of U.S. workers. Economic chaos in Mexico in the wake of peso devaluation and free trade agreements ensured a steady flow of desperate immigrant workers across the border in the 1980s and 1990s. The undocumented status of some of them enabled even greater exploitation, forcing wages and working conditions for all workers even lower.

Immigration, Ideology, and Ethnic Studies

A desire for short-term political advantage propelled Pete Wilson and his allies into politics designed to secure the benefits of past and present discrimination in perpetuity for affluent white voters while at the same time deflecting the anger of downwardly mobile whites against the exploited immigrant workers upon whom the lifestyles of the rich depend. Right-wing attacks on affirmative action and on ethnic studies programs like the Mexican American Studies program in Tucson support this strategy. They aim at suppressing any institutional site capable of generating a critique of racism's role in winning political consent for an emerging economic order that harms the interests of the majority. These attacks, however, also underscore the importance of ethnic studies. When connected to activist efforts to establish cross-border solidarity and to organize low-wage workers into militant collectives, ethnic studies can help shape a popular rejection of politics based on the possessive investment in whiteness.

The Mexican American Studies program in Tucson emerged from the creative minds of caring teachers. It survived and thrived because of its ability to make school a site for critical and contemplative engagement with the harsh realities of racialization and racism. Yet it also owed its origins to the ground plowed by decades of ethnic studies scholarship. Far from the caricatured vision of ethnic studies formulated in the phobic fantasies of the authors and supporters of Arizona's HB2281, ethnic studies research conducted at the college level provided teachers, students, parents, and community members in Tucson and in cities across the nation and around the world with rich resources to analyze, interpret, and contest the possessive investment in whiteness.

Most of the best work in ethnic studies—work often derided as identity politics—in fact addresses the ways in which new social relations have given rise to new coalitions and conflicts that change the meaning of ethnic and racial identity. Rather than seeking to separate society into discrete warring camps, ethnic studies scholars assume that we can be unified eventually only if we examine honestly and critically the things that divide us in the present. They presume that very few social problems can be solved by knowing *less* about them, that racism will not go away by forbidding mention of it. They argue that the same processes that exacerbate old divisions while generating new ones may open the way to unexpected affiliations and alliances based on the pursuit of social justice and on resistance to unjust hierarchies and exploitative practices. The teachers in Tucson organized the MAS classes around the Mayan precept "In Lak'ech" which means I am the other you and you are the other me. The mutual recognition and respect encapsulated in this phrase offers a new pedagogical principle for classroom instruction based on the ideas and practices that have enabled aggrieved communities to survive and thrive for centuries.

Some of the core concepts of ethnic studies research appear vividly in Lisa Lowe's book, *Immigrant Acts*, which explains how the Asian American experience with racialization, economic exploitation, immigrant exclusion, and barriers to citizenship is not the parochial property of Asian Americans alone but rather a legacy important to all Americans. These practices have shaped the meaning of what it means to be a citizen, a low-wage worker, a gendered subject, or an aggrieved racialized "minority." Similarly, in a singularly impressive study, Yen Le Espiritu underscores the importance of normative gender categories in branding all subordinate groups as alternatively "deviant, inferior, or overachieving" while branding each group with a fundamentally distinct race-gender-sex economy.[23] All racialized populations suffer from the possessive investment in whiteness in some ways, but the historical and social circumstances confronting each group differ. Consequently, alliances as well as antagonisms, conflicts as well as coalitions, characterize the complex dynamics of white supremacy within and across group lines.

Lowe identifies hybridity, heterogeneity, and multiplicity as component parts of ethnic identity. In her formulation, people develop ethnic identities through hybridity, a growing together of more than one element—for example, through relations across ethnic lines or through the ways in which one's gender, sexual identification, or class intersects with one's race or ethnicity. Lowe defines ethnic groups as always heterogeneous, as coalitions made up of people with different interests, aims, ages, genders, sexual preferences, religions, languages, and so on. Identities are also multiple in Lowe's formulation; no one lives a life entirely as an ethnic subject. At any given moment, ethnicity might be more important than, say, gender, but under other circumstances gender might become more important. People play different roles under different conditions; their identities emerge though complex interactions with others as well as through constant internal dialogue and negotiation.[24]

The generative insights in Lowe's work emerge in the context of a rich dialogue among scholars in ethnic studies about the dynamism of all social identities, including but not limited to ethnic identities. Juan Flores defines an important component of Puerto Rican identity in New York as "branching out"—"the selective connection to and interaction with the surrounding North American society." Flores notes that the social location of Puerto Rican migrants encourages them to branch out first to Black Americans and to other migrants from Latin America and the Caribbean but later to groups with a similar history of social disadvantage, including Chinese, Arabs, and, "more cautiously," Irish, Italians, and Jews. Consequently, Puerto Rican "assimilation" is not into the dominant culture and does not entail the disappearance of distinct national backgrounds but rather involves a fusion of diverse working-class cultures shaped by marginalization and exclusion to create "a healthy interfertilization of cultures." Jack D. Forbes explores the long history of coalition and conflict that makes Native American and African American identities mutually constitutive as well as mutually exclusive, while Gary Y. Okihiro examines the complex connections and points of convergence between Asian Americans and African Americans. Peter Narvaez's research on the influence of Hispanic music cultures on African American blues musicians reminds us that the proximity of Mexico as a destination for escaped slaves undermined the growth of the slave system in Texas while activists of Mexican origin on both sides of the border provided moral and material assistance to slaves seeking freedom. Kevin Gaines notes that African Americans chafing at the white practice of addressing them by their first names rather than as Mister or Miss or Mrs. subverted the practice by naming their children after anti-imperialist Black heroes from Latin America like Antonio Maceo, a general in the Cuban struggle for independence. James Howard delineates how the Shawnee tribe came to align itself with the antislavery Union forces during the Civil War and how, thirty years later, a band of anti-acculturationist Shawnees emigrated to Mexico in the hope of constructing a pan-Indian nation.[25]

Principled scholars from all backgrounds have carried out important work in ethnic studies, but the situated experiences of scholars from aggrieved minority groups has often proven a source of special insights and analyses. A. Philip Randolph told the 1963 March on Washington that it has often fallen to Blacks to remind other Americans about the importance of giving human rights priority over property rights because their ancestors were transformed by law from human persons into property. In similar fashion, gays and lesbians have often been the most perceptive critics and analysts of heterosexuality as a social force because their situated experiences compel them to recognize, analyze, and understand existing sexual hierarchies and to theorize alternatives to them.[26] It should not be surprising, then, that outstanding research on social identities often emanates from a queer of color critique and from the institutional sites of ethnic studies designed to ask and answer questions that are both particular and universal, that see ethnicity, race, and other social identities both from close up and from far away.

Scholarship in Chicana/o studies has been especially rich in exploring the theoretical and practical causes and consequences of racism. The crises confronting Chicanx communities as a result of the white identity politics put in play by people like Pete Wilson and the complex realities of Chicanx existence have long called into question the simplistic binary oppositions that produce the possessive investment in whiteness. Chicanx communities are connected to the national histories of the United States, Mexico, and Spain, to the immigrant groups from many lands that populate those nations, to indigenous nations and their many social formations, to cultures that include diverse languages, religions, and social practices. Issues of national culture, ethnic identity, and language emerge as parts of complex contradictions in Chicanx history. Consequently, scholars studying Chicanx life and culture need to develop fully theorized definitions of social roles that go beyond the parochial experiences of any one group. The best scholarship in Chicano studies does not simply tack on some new information about Chicanx onto what we already know from the study of other groups, but like all good work in ethnic studies, it uses the situated knowledge and experiences of Chicanx to ask and answer important new questions about the general dynamics of social identities.

Ramon Gutierrez fashioned a compelling narrative about the Spanish and Anglo conquest of Indigenous people in New Mexico between 1600 and 1850 in his book, *When Jesus Came, the Corn Mothers Went Away*. Using Inquisition records and anthropological sources to construct a record of how successive conquests changed the character of both everyday activities and political allegiances, Gutierrez stresses the syncretic and relational nature of ethnic identities, refuting the romantic and essentialist assumptions of previous scholars about Anglos, Indians, and Chicanx. Gutierrez's ability to represent competing and conflicting points of view offers an important alternative to the kind of monologic history that presents only one story told from one point of view. In the process, he demonstrates definitively how ethnic and racial identities always intersect, how they emerge in concert with identities of gender, sexuality, class, religion, and nationality.[27] Gutierrez demonstrates the interconnections between macrosocial structures of power and the experiences of everyday life by showing how all three societies in his study structure inequality through categories of marriage and kinship, but do so in distinctly different ways.

George Sanchez brings a similar dynamism to his history of the Eastside of Los Angeles between 1900 and 1945. In *Becoming Mexican American,* he shows how a specific confluence of residential segregation, class and generational homogeneity, political alliances, and cultural practices coalesced to produce a distinctive Mexican American identity in that city. Like Gutierrez, Sanchez tells a significant story about one community, but in the process he illuminates general principles about the ways in which ethnic and racial identities are constructed dynamically through practical activity. Sanchez shows, for instance, how Mexican migration helped fill the shortage of low-wage labor created by laws mandating the exclusion of immigrants from Asia, how restrictive covenants and racial zoning by whites helped create a Mexican American community with fixed spatial boundaries, and how discrimination against other minority groups occasionally encouraged inter-ethnic alliances based on physical proximity and shared experiences.[28]

One important feature of the scholarship of Gutierrez and Sanchez is their view of ethnicity as relational rather than as atomized and discrete. Group identities form through interaction with other groups. As a result, Spaniards, Mexicans, Pueblo Indians, and Anglos in New Mexico changed each other as well as themselves through complicated experiences of conflict and coopera-tion. Mexican American identity in Los Angeles in Sanchez's account emerged out of complex interactions with Asian Americans, Blacks, and Native Amer-icans to be sure, but also with Molokans, Jews, and Anglo Protestants. Vicki Ruiz argues along similar lines in *Cannery Women, Cannery Lives,* her excel-lent study about Chicana working women in Los Angeles during the 1930s and 1940s. Ruiz's research revealed the ways in which physical proximity in neighborhoods enabled Chicana workers to unite with women of other back-grounds to fight for trade union representation to address their common grievances on the job, including problems they faced specifically as women, such as sexual harassment. Similar research on Chicanx in Texas by David Montejano exposes the importance of Anglo-Mexican relations while Neil Foley's study of the cotton economy in that state demonstrates the mutually constitutive as well as competitive nature of relations among Anglos, Mexi-cans, and Blacks. In a thoughtful and generative study of *testimonios* by nine-teenth-century Californios, Rosaura Sanchez draws upon a stunning repertoire of theories from literary criticism, cultural geography, sociology, and social history to delineate the ways in which the displaced Californio elite both resisted and paradoxically reinforced the racist hierarchies of their Anglo conquerors, establishing themselves as an aggrieved and racialized U.S. ethnic group while simultaneously participating in and endorsing the exclusion and subordination of Native Americans.[29] As a dynamic, fluid, and relational category, ethnic identity emerges as contested within Chicana/o studies scholarship. In *Walls and Mirrors,* a vitally important study of Mexi-can immigration to the United States, David Gutierrez shows how the value of "whiteness" and its concomitant imperatives of racialized exclusion have divided Mexican American communities between those who favor citizen-ship and cultural incorporation in the United States and those oriented more toward maximizing group resources by maintaining solidarity with all people of Mexican origin on both sides of the border. Gutierrez shows how settled descendants of previous immigrants can develop interests and political positions different from those of new immigrants. In an important twist, however, he also identifies the significance of a core contradiction among Anglos who demand low-wage Mexican labor to benefit the U.S. economy while maintaining a racialized view of Mexicans as unwelcome and unfit for cultural or political inclusion.[30] For Gutierrez, the power of the possessive investment in whiteness means that ethnic identity among Chicanx changes its boundaries over time: internal politics and the external opportunity structure help shape Chicanx as assimilationist or separatist, united in defense of immigrants or divided into inclusive and exclusive factions, eager to identify themselves as "white" or determined to ally with other aggrieved communities of color.

This excellent body of historical work helps explain the subtlety and supple nature of Chicanx cultural criticism. Jose Saldivar's innovative *Border Matters* ranges over diverse forms of cultural expression to explore the ways in which the existence of the U.S.–Mexico border shapes Chicanx imagination and expression. In an innovative and persuasive study, Carl Gutierrez-Jones shows how police surveillance, brutality, and incarceration shape the subtexts of a broad range of Chicanx fiction and film representations. Ramón Saldivar explains how oral and written traditions among Chicanx contain a consistent aesthetic sensibility and challenge prevailing power relations by "opting for open over closed forms, for conflict over resolution and synthesis."[31]

One of the main generative achievements of Chicana/o studies scholarship has been to illuminate the ways in which complex cultural meanings become encoded in unlikely sites, unassuming artifacts, and ordinary practices. Rosa Linda Fregoso's *The Bronze Screen,* for example, presents a scintillating study of the ways in which collective memory, popular culture products, religious rituals, and decidedly gendered images and ideas serve as impetus for a feminist politics that revolve around what Chela Sandoval has named "differential consciousness." Similarly, Gloria Anzaldua reads the Virgin of Guadalupe as a complex "religious, political, and cultural image" symbolizing "the mestizo true to his or her Indian values" as well as "rebellion against the rich, upper and middle class; against their subjugation of the poor and the *indio.*" Jose Limon blends cultural critique, ethnography, social history, and folklore in his richly textured and insightful studies of social interactions among Tejanos at barbecues, dance halls, and the myriad other sites where everyday life activities shape and reflect social identities.[32]

Yvonne Yarbro-Bejarano shows how the poisonous legacy of sexism in popular Chicanx narratives, songs, and theatrical traditions works to suppress the experiences and criticisms of women while constituting the community along masculinist lines. Norma Alarcón analyzes the layers of sexism sedimented in the Malintzin legends as well as the problems they pose for Chicana writers and critics. While Chicanx critics have been insightful about the ways in which a shared group identity can hide serious divisions within the group, they have also been brilliant in detailing the ways in which widely divergent interests and practices might emerge from common roots. Steven Loza offers an example of the latter in his pathbreaking and carefully researched examination of the plurality and diversity of Chicanx music from Los Angeles, *Barrio Rhythm*. James Diego Vigil shows how the aesthetics of the *ranflas* (low riders) driven by Chicanx car customizers mimic the methodical, slow, and smooth kinesics manifested in the stylized dress and body language of Chicanx street gangs, while Brenda Bright explores the ways in which low-riding practices in three cities in Texas, New Mexico, and California reveal both unity and division within and across Chicano communities.[33]

These extraordinary works illustrate the importance of ethnic studies scholarship in providing perspective, understanding, and analysis of the problems people face in the present as a result of the cultural transformations transnational capital engenders. Yet, ethnic studies, and especially Chicana/o studies, draws a determinate shape not just from the imperatives of the present but also from the practices of the past. Anxieties about identity that may appear new and daunting to relatively privileged people raised in monolingual environments in metropolitan countries have a long history among aggrieved groups for whom cultural complexity and creative code switching constitute the baseline realities of life. Consequently, some of the most sophisticated vocabularies and grammars of cultural criticism and cultural practice come from groups with comparatively little political and economic power. In the case of Chicano studies, the brilliant innovations of the present draw upon collective resources shaped and honed through the struggles of the past, as exemplified in the enduring relevance of a classic Chicano studies work from the 1950s—Americo Paredes's *With His Pistol in His Hand*.

Paredes's book explores the ballad of Gregorio Cortez, a popular *corrido* from South Texas based (as corridos are) on an actual incident, one that took place in 1901. According to Paredes, the popularity of many versions of the song celebrating the struggles of Gregorio Cortez stemmed from its utility as an allegory about all Tejano people. Relating the story of a peaceful and hardworking man minding his own business who was unjustly attacked and forced to flee in order to avoid being charged for a crime that he did not commit, the ballad's verses systematically unmask the falsity of prevailing Anglo slurs against Mexicans. The incident starts when the Anglo and monolingual sheriff of a Texas county learns that a stolen horse might be in his vicinity. Discovering that Gregorio Cortez recently traded for a mare, the sheriff travels to the Tejano's ranch, accompanied by an Anglo deputy known for his bilingual skills. The deputy does not know Spanish as well as he thinks he does, however. He informs Reynaldo Cortez that the sheriff wishes to speak with Gregorio, and when Reynaldo tells his brother in Spanish "someone wants you" (as in someone wants to speak with you), the deputy translates the words back to the sheriff as "you are a wanted man." Furthermore, when the deputy asks Cortez if he recently traded for a horse, he uses the word equivalent to the generic English term for a horse (*caballo*) rather than the more precise gender-specific Spanish term for a mare (*yegua*). When Cortez replies that he has not traded for a caballo, the deputy tells the sheriff that the rancher is lying. The sheriff pulls out his gun and shoots at but misses Cortez's brother. Cortez returns the fire in self-defense and kills the sheriff.[34] Cortez's skill as a rider enables him to escape the posse assembled by the county and the state to chase him. He becomes a folk hero among Tejanos and even earns the respect of Anglos who recognize that he has been falsely accused of murder for acts committed in self-defense. Cortez is never captured, but in order to save his family and his community from reprisals, he turns himself in to the law, walking in proudly "with his pistol in his hand."

The key elements in the Gregorio Cortez narrative inverted prevailing Anglo stereotypes about Mexicans. In a society in which racist slurs depicting Mexicans as dishonest, stupid, and cowardly served to legitimate Anglo conquest and fraudulent expropriation of land legally held by Tejanos, the ballad of Gregorio Cortez offered an eloquent alternative. Paredes notes that just as white slave owners raped Black women and then portrayed Black males as sex fiends, Anglo Texans stole land from Mexicans and then defamed their victims as people prone to steal. To initiate and legitimate the expropriation of land and labor, they developed stories about Mexicans as unintelligent, lazy, and cowardly. In the ballad of Gregorio Cortez, the charge of thievery turns out to be inaccurate, simply a product of Anglo ignorance and linguistic incompetence. Gregorio Cortez is hardworking, highly skilled, intelligent, and courageous. One particularly important verse inverts one of the most sacred legends of Anglo Texans. For years, admirers of the state law enforcement agency, the Texas Rangers, celebrated the courage of their heroes through a story about a riot in a border town. When local authorities ask the Texas Rangers for help in subduing hundreds and maybe thousands of Mexican insurgents, the state agency sends only one ranger, arguing that there is only one riot. The "humor" of this anecdote relies upon knowledge of a common racist slur that holds the courage of whites to be so great that it takes only one white man to subdue an entire group of Mexicans. In the ballad of Gregorio Cortez, however, these odds are reversed, as just one elusive Mexican frustrates the combined efforts of the Texas Rangers, local sheriffs, and posses. A powerful couplet in the song demonstrates this inversion: "Decia Gregorio Cortez, con su pistola en la mano,/ Ah, cuanto rinche montado para un solo mexicano!" (Then said Gregorio Cortez, with his pistol in his hand,/ Ah, so many mounted Rangers, against one lone Mexican!)[35]

The ballad of Gregorio Cortez and the practices of topical songwriting and singing from which it emerged testify to the presence among Chicanx of what art historian Robert Farris Thompson describes as alternative academies.[36] These sites provide opportunities for personal and collective artistic expression. They offer education in the guise of entertainment, and they serve as conduits for the moral economy that oppressed people need in order to deal with the ideological, political, economic, and police power of their enemies. Paredes's book shows how it fell to one popular song to keep alive historical memory of an incident of injustice, to invert dominant stereotypes, celebrate individual heroism, identify group loyalty as the ultimate moral obligation, and call a community into being through performance.

Of course, changes in historical conditions can also give new meaning to old cultural expressions. The rise of Chicana feminism in the 1970s and 1980s created a consciousness sensitive to the masculinist biases built into the ballad of Gregorio Cortez, what Renato Rosaldo calls its "primordial patriarchy." A song that served emancipatory purposes at one moment may become reactionary in another era, just as a group identity forged in struggle under one set of circumstances may become an obstacle to emancipation at a later moment. Chicana feminists as well as gay and lesbian writers have been particularly active in rereading and reevaluating the traditions of their own communities in order to fuse the traditional antiracism of the Chicano movement with the necessity for projecting what Renato Rosaldo describes as "a heterogeneous, changing heritage into the future."[37]

Yet for all of its grounding in a previous era, Paredes's study of the ballad of Gregorio Cortez remains relevant to understanding, analyzing, and acting upon the oppressive power of enduring racial hierarchies. While adding important and historically specific knowledge to what is already known about Chicanx, *With His Pistol in His Hand* speaks to the experiences of other groups as well. It demonstrates how popular culture and indigenous voices offer evidence about social history, and it challenges us to explore the relationship between all cultural texts and their social and historical contexts. It shows how people act in the arenas that are open to them with the tools they have available. Most important, Paredes's book reminds us that in any moment of danger, people from aggrieved communities can be a source of enormous insight and empowering analysis. Ethnic studies scholarship is no substitute for systematic and coordinated political action, but action without understanding is always doomed to fail. Scholars from aggrieved communities can play a particularly important role in solving pressing problems, not primarily because of who they are but rather because of what they and their communities have been forced to learn from the hands that have been dealt to them by history. Especially when many of the wealthiest and best-educated people in positions of leadership are attempting to escape responsibility for the consequences of their own policies by scapegoating immigrants, non-English speakers, and low-wage workers, ethnic studies scholars have a key role to play in determining what kind of future we will have, or more ominously, whether we will have any future at all.

Unity and Division

We live in an age of painful contradictions. Mass communication and mass migration bring the people of the world closer together in unprecedented ways, uniting diverse populations through common participation in global markets, investments, and mass media. Yet the practices and processes that affect everyone do not affect everyone equally. At the very moment that we find the people of the world becoming more united, we also find that economic inequality, cultural insecurity, and ethnic, religious, and racial rivalries renew old antagonisms and engender new conflicts, leaving us paradoxically more divided than even before.

Ethnic divisions and racial conflicts have a particularly poisonous presence at the present moment. From Bosnia to Belfast, from Rwanda to Russia, from East Timor to Tel Aviv, we see the destructive consequences of ethnic antagonisms everywhere. It is understandable that under these circumstances people might be wary of any kind of "identity politics" in which racial, religious, and ethnic identities become the basis for political solidarity and cultural practice. Writers arguing from a variety of political perspectives have critiqued identity politics as encouraging allegiance to group interests rather than civic responsibility extending across racial and ethnic lines, as an assault on the traditions and values most responsible for human progress, and as a diversion from real social problems, especially economic ones, that they allege have nothing to do with social identities. Alarmist articles in major news magazines bemoan the erosion of a "common" culture in the United States while critics sneer about the emergence of "victim studies" in academia. Minority artists and intellectuals are attacked as guilt-mongering whiners demanding special privileges and seeking to elevate inferior works so as to elevate their own self-esteem. On a broader front, ambitious politicians demagogically dismantle the antidiscrimination mechanisms established as a result of the civil rights movement, mislabeling antiracist remedies as instruments of "reverse racism." All around us, we see evidence of a fundamentally new era for the possessive investment in whiteness, fueled by ferment over identity politics.

Yet once we remember that whiteness is also an identity, one with a long political history, contemporary attacks on "identity" politics come into clear relief as a defense of the traditional privileges and priorities of whiteness in the face of critical and political projects that successfully disclose who actually holds power in this society and what they have done with it. Contrary to claims that they stand for universal interests, the promoters of the politics of whiteness as exemplified by attacks on immigrants and on affirmative action pursue little more than a self-interested strategy for preserving the possessive investment in whiteness, a politics based solely on identity. Conversely, the best ethnic studies scholarship, cultural production, and community organizing aims at opening up an understanding of ethnicity as hybrid, heterogeneous, and multiple—as a political project aimed at creating as Angela Davis advises, identities based on politics, rather than politics based on identities. These projects rely on egalitarian politics and struggles for social justice to counter the identity politics of whiteness that generates identities based on the defense and perpetuation of inequality.[38] Different ethnic groups have different histories and experiences; as long as that is the case, organizing along ethnic lines will always make sense. Yet ethnic groups still must decide which things bring them together and which things divide them, which groups offer them useful alliances and which do not. Mobilizing around a common group identity does not preclude forming strategic and philosophical alliances with other groups.

Under current conditions, defending immigrants requires solidarity among African, Asian, Arab, Latinx, Muslim, and Caribbean communities. Attacks on linguistic diversity create opportunities for coalitions between Latinos and Asians while incidents of racially motivated police brutality bring together immigrants and citizens. Immigration policies about HIV/AIDS led to an unexpected alliance between Haitian and lesbian, gay, bisexual, trans, and queer activists. Efforts to organize trade unions among low-wage workers require coalitions that include African Americans, Latinos, Asian Americans, Native Americans, and European Americans. The Committee against Anti-Asian Violence in New York provided an exemplary model for this kind of organizing when it defended Asian victims of vigilante violence and police brutality but at the same time united with the National Congress for Puerto Rican Rights to stage a Racial Justice Day rally and march, while also publicizing the activities of Project REACH, a multicultural organization established to provide drop-in centers that offer safe havens to gay and lesbian youths, support HIV-positive youth, help women defend themselves against sexual assaults, and train youth leaders.[39] Asian Immigrant Women Advocates (AIWA) in Oakland, California, mobilizes second- and third-generation Asian American women to help empower Asian immigrant women working in the electronics, hotel, and garment industries. AIWA's members come from different national backgrounds, speak different languages, and belong to different classes, yet their shared concern about the lives of low-wage women workers from Asia leads them to political actions that address the class problems women face as workers, the gender problems they confront as women, the legal problems they experience as immigrants, the racial problems they encounter as members of racialized groups, and the language discrimination that they share with Latinx.[40] In the

1990s, organizing efforts among Latinx workers at the New Otani Hotel in Los Angeles drew upon ethnic solidarity in Mexican and Salvadoran communities, but they fueled as well a strategic alliance with Korean veterans of Japanese slave labor camps who had long-standing grievances against the hotel's Japanese owner, the Kajima Corporation, for its role in Japanese imperialism during World War II.[41]

The Bus Riders Union in Los Angeles originated in problems with public transportation in the city that affect all ethnic groups. Yet the group's analysis found that the transportation routes favored by inner-city residents generated funds for the transit system that subsidized the commuter trains used by suburban residents. Arguing that neighborhood race effects accounted for the disproportionate resources made available to commuters from mostly white suburbs, the union brought suit against the transit authority on civil rights grounds. In this case, the 10 to 20 percent of white bus riders in the inner city experienced violations of their civil rights because they relied on services utilized disproportionately by minorities. The Bus Riders Union reached an impressive settlement with the transit authority. Their strategy demonstrated the centrality of race in determining access to public services, yet they mobilized a struggle that was not reduced solely to embodied racial identities but rather one that united members of all races in a common struggle for social justice against the injustices perpetrated by neighborhood race effects.[42]

Action within and across ethnic groups in these struggles is made possible by what the participants know, not simply who they are. Their situated knowledges, historical experiences, and current struggles with power give their ethnic identities their determinant meanings. Like scholars in ethnic studies, their knowledge draws on their experiences. Their strategic insights emanate from the ways in which having less power can make it important to have more knowledge. Political struggle, social analysis, and social theory are mutually constitutive; each is better when linked to the other. As James Baldwin pointed out years ago, "People who cling to their delusions find it difficult, if not impossible, to learn anything worth learning: a people under the necessity of creating themselves must examine everything, and soak up learning the way the roots of a tree soak up water. A people still held in bondage must believe that *Ye shall know the truth, and the truth shall make ye free.*"[43]

4

Whiteness and War

White people were, and are, astounded by the holocaust in Germany.
They did not know that they could act that way. But I very much doubt
whether black people were astounded —at least, in the same way.

—James Baldwin

In her brilliant analysis of the centrality of Indigenous dispossession to the imagination and implementation of the imperial project of the United States, Chickasaw literary scholar Jodi A. Byrd observes that "the United States has used a variety of means 'to make Indian' those peoples and nations who stand in the way of U.S. military and economic desires."[1] Byrd and many other Indigenous scholars demonstrate that dispossession is not a finished past event but an ongoing process that persists in the present. The initial acts of Indigenous dispossession conflated whiteness and warfare in ways that continue to shape contemporary understandings of patriotism and patriarchy.

The U.S. Navy SEALs who tracked and killed Osama Bin Laden in Pakistan in 2011 referred to him as Geronimo, equating the architect of the mass murder at the World Trade Center with the heroic Chiricahua Apache warrior who fought to defend tribal territory from attacks by U.S. and Mexican military forces.[2] The weapons used by U.S troops around the world bear names that register the Indigenous past and present—Black Hawk, Apache Longbow, Lakota and Chinook helicopters, Tomahawk missiles, and Gray Eagle drones. Soldiers who leave military bases overseas are said to be "off the reservation" and in "Indian country."[3] These acts of identifying contemporary military engagements as an extension of the legacy of conquest and colonialism are neither casual nor incidental. They reveal how warfare has been a crucial locus of racial formation and how the possessive investment in whiteness has emerged from, and responded to, a series of racial projects forged in combat.

For example, one of the key figures in the creation of the U.S. Border Patrol in 1924 derived his racial identity and racial frameworks from a history of violence. Born in the early years of the Civil War, Jefferson Davis Milton was named in honor of the president of the slaveholding Confederacy. His father owned slaves and had been governor of the state of Florida. The end of slavery meant the end of the Milton family's life of leisure and luxury. Eager for status and power, Jefferson Davis Milton moved west to work as a law enforcement officer. He participated in the campaigns that captured and incarcerated Geronimo. Early in the twentieth century, he found employment in the U.S. Department of Labor as an officer charged with enforcing the 1882 Chinese Exclusion Act, focused on preventing immigrants from China from entering the United States via Mexico. When the federal government set up the Border Patrol to police the U.S.-Mexico border, mainly to guarantee that sufficient numbers of workers would be available to agribusiness but that as few as possible would be allowed to stay, Milton became a key figure in those efforts and became known as the father of the Border Patrol.[4] The whiteness of Jefferson Davis Milton had its roots in many different instances of racial control in the United States: in Black slavery, dispossession of Indigenous peoples, exclusion of Asians, and strict limitation of Mexican labor.

Similarly, J. Franklin Bell grew up in Kentucky in a family committed to slavery and the secession of the Confederacy. He participated in the 7th Cavalry campaign against the Lakota people in Pine Ridge, South Dakota, and later taught lessons at Fort Apache in Arizona on the tactics of fighting against Indians. Bell organized a regiment to fight against the Filipino nationalist anticolonial forces resisting U.S. control of the Philippines and was promoted to the rank of brigadier general. He served as the U.S. military commander in Manila and then returned home to supervise U.S. troops in Texas in preparation for a possible war with Mexico in the wake of that nation's revolution in 1911.[5] The trajectory that propelled General Bell from wars against Indigenous peoples on the Great Plains to suppression of freedom fighters in the Philippines found colorful expression in the words of President Theodore Roosevelt who described the local Filipino enemies of the United States variously as "Apache," "Comanche," "Malay Bandits," and "Chinese half-breeds."[6]

The life histories of Jefferson Davis Milton and J. Franklin Bell offer a window into the origins of the U.S. military's contemporary invocations of warfare against Indians. They reveal as well the links that connect U.S. wars in Asia to the long history in the United States of Indigenous dispossession, slavery, Asian exclusion, and Mexican suppression. The possessive investment in whiteness is learned and legitimated in many places that at first glance may seem to have little to do with race. One of those places is warfare.

Anti-Asian Violence and U.S. Wars in Asia

In 1982, two unemployed white male autoworkers in Detroit attacked Chinese American draftsman Vincent Chin with a baseball bat. The assailants smashed his skull and beat him to death. Although they later denied any racist intent, one of the autoworkers remarked during the incident, "It's because of you we're out of work"—apparently thinking that Chin was Japanese and therefore responsible for layoffs in the auto industry caused by competition from cars made in Japan. Neither perpetrator ever served a day in prison for the murder.[7] In 1984, a white male high school teacher pushed Ly Yung Cheung, a pregnant nineteen-year-old Chinese American woman, off a New York City subway platform into the path of a moving train that decapitated her. In his successful plea of not guilty by reason of insanity, the teacher claimed that he suffered from "a phobia of Asian people" that led him to murder Cheung.[8] In 1989, a white man wearing combat fatigues fired more than one hundred rounds of ammunition from an AK-47 assault rifle into a crowd of mostly Asian American children at the Cleveland Elementary School in Stockton, California, killing five children and wounding close to thirty others. Four of the children killed were Cambodian refugees—Ram Chun, Sokhim An, Rathanar Or, and Oeun Lim. The fifth was a Vietnamese American, Tran Thanh Thuy. An investigation by state officials found it "highly probable" that the assailant picked that particular school because of his animosity toward "Southeast Asians," whom the gunman described as people who get "benefits" without having to work.[9] In 1992, a group of white males attending a party in Coral Gables, Florida, beat nineteen-year-old Luyen Phan Nguyen to death when he objected to racial slurs directed at him. At least seven of the men ran after Nguyen as he attempted to flee, shouting, "Viet Cong," and hunting him down "like a wounded deer" while bystanders refused to intervene and stop the beating.[10]

Although these incidents sprang from different motivations and circumstances, they share a common core—the identification of Asians in America as foreign enemies, unwelcome and unwanted by white Americans. Hate crimes enact the rage of individual sociopaths, but they also seek justification in patterns of behavior and belief that permeate the rest of society in less extreme form. The logic that legitimated the attacks on Vincent Chin, Ly Yung Cheung, the schoolchildren in Stockton, and Luyen Phan Nguyen stemmed from long-standing patterns and practices in the United States. As Lisa Lowe, Yen Le Espiritu, and Gary Okihiro, among others, have demonstrated repeatedly in their sophisticated research, for more than a century and a half, Asian immigrants have filled the need for cheap labor by U.S. businesses without receiving recognition as vital contributors to the national economy. Diplomats and corporate officers have opened up access to desired markets and raw materials by integrating Asia into the North American economy, yet through law, labor segmentation, and "scientific" racism, Asians in America have been seen as forever foreign and outside the rewards of white identity.[11]

Participation of the United States in wars in Asia over the past seven decades has also contributed significantly to the view of many Americans that Asian Americans and Asians are foreign enemies incapable of being assimilated into the U.S. nation. Military action against Japan in World War II led to the internment of more than 100,000 Japanese Americans in the United States and to the forced sale and seizure of their property. No other group of immigrants and their descendants have been identified with their country of origin in this way, not even German Americans during World War I and World War II. The national groups from countries allied with the United States at different moments in these wars—Chinese, Koreans, Filipinx, Japanese, Vietnamese, and Cambodians—have often found themselves identified as undifferentiated "Asians" in the United States and vilified for the actions of governments and nations that they have actually opposed. Armed conflicts against Asian enemies in the Philippines, Korea, China, Vietnam, Laos, and Cambodia functioned geopolitically to decide control over markets and raw materials in Asia after the demise of direct European imperialism. These wars aimed to contain China and the Soviet Union, and to insure U.S. access to the rim economies of Southeast and Northeast Asia.

During the 1980s, Asians accounted for nearly half of all legal immigrants to the United States. More than a million Southeast Asians entered the country as refugees after the war in Vietnam, and between 1970 and 1990, more than 855,000 Filipinx, 600,000 Koreans, and 575,000 Chinese immigrated to the United States. During the same era, the rise of Japanese businesses as competitors of U.S. firms, the painful legacy of the U.S. war in Vietnam, the stagnation of real wages, and increasing class polarization in the United States combined to engender intense hostility toward Asia and Asian Americans. In the new millennium, the dramatic expansion of China's role on the world economic stage has coincided with a sharp increase in American animosity toward China. As Yen Le Espiritu explains, hostilities toward Asian competitors overseas and Asian American immigrants at home function as components in an interlocking system. "In a time of rising economic powers in Asia, declining economic opportunities in the United States, and growing diversity among America's people," Espiritu observes, "this new Yellow Perilism—the depiction of Asia and Asian Americans as economic and cultural threats to mainstream United States—supplies white Americans with a united identity and provides ideological justification for a U.S. interventionist policy toward Asia, increasing restrictions against Asian (and Latino) immigration, and both the largely invisible institutional racism and the vividly visible physical violence directed against Asians in the United States."[12]

Anti-Asian sentiment in the United States depends upon its necessary correlative—the assumption that true cultural franchise and full citizenship require a white identity. This violence against Asian Americans stems from the kinds of whiteness created within U.S. culture and mobilized in the nation's political, economic, and social life. The "white" identity conditioned to fear the Asian "menace" owes its origins to the history of anti-Indian, anti-Black, and anti-Mexican racism at home as well as to anti-Arab and anti-Latinx racisms shaped by military struggles overseas and by condescending cultural stereotypes at home. White racism is a pathology looking for a place to land, sadism in search of a story.

Reginald Horsman's study of nineteenth-century racism and Manifest Destiny explains how presumptions about racial purity and fears of contamination encouraged white Americans who envisioned themselves as Anglo-Saxons to fabricate proof of the inferiority of other groups. Horsman shows that racialized hierarchies on the home front encouraged imperial expansion abroad, with the rationalizations originally developed to justify conquest of Native Americans eventually applied to Mexicans and Filipinx. Yet the categories created for racist purposes displayed great instability—at one time or another, depending on immediate interests and goals, Native Americans, Blacks, Mexicans, and Asians might be either elevated above the others or labeled the most deficient group of all. Similarly, David Roediger's research shows that the derogatory term "gook" originated among U.S. forces to deride the Nicaraguans fighting with Cesar Augusto Sandino during the U.S. occupation of that nation in the 1920s, long before it was applied as a racial slur against Koreans, Vietnamese, and Iraqis in subsequent conflicts.[13]

Yet whiteness never works in isolation; it functions as part of a broader dynamic grid created through intersections of race, gender, class, and sexuality. The way these identities work in concert gives them their true social meaning. The renewal of patriotic rhetoric and display in the United States during and after the presidency of Ronald Reagan serves as the quintessential example of this intersecting operation. Reagan succeeded in fusing the possessive investment in whiteness with other psychic and material investments—especially in heterosexual masculinity, patriarchy, and patriotism. The intersecting identity he offered gave new meanings to white male patriarchal identities by establishing patriotism as the site where class antagonisms between white men could be reconciled through masculine bonding and through channeling nationalist antagonisms against foreign foes and internal enemies. By encoding the possessive investment in whiteness within national narratives of male heroism and patriarchal protection, Reagan and his allies mobilized a cross-class coalition around the premise that the declines in life chances and opportunities in the United States, the stagnation of real wages, the erosion of basic services, the collapsing infrastructure, and the increasing social disintegration stemmed not from the policies of big corporations and their neoliberal and conservative allies in government but from the harm done to the nation by the civil rights, antiwar, feminist, and gay liberation movements of the 1960s and 1970s. By representing the national crisis as a crisis of the declining value of white male and heterosexual identity, Reagan and his allies and successors built a countersubversive coalition mobilized around protecting the privileges and prerogatives of the possessive investments in whiteness, in masculinity, in patriarchy, and in heterosexuality. Their word provides the cultural and psychological infrastructure for a politics of masculinist militarism that remains dominant in the present.

The murders of Vincent Chin, Ly Yung Cheung, the Southeast Asian schoolchildren in Stockton, and Luyen Phan Nguyen become understandable as more than the private and personal acts of individual criminals when placed in these two contexts: (1) widely shared social beliefs, practices, and images that render Asians as foreign enemies and (2) the decline of life chances and opportunities in the United States viewed as the result of both military defeat in Vietnam and the democratic movements for social change that, among other accomplishments, helped end that war.

The key to the conservative revival that has guided leaders of business and government since the 1970s has been the creation of a countersubversive consensus mobilized around the alleged wounds suffered by straight white men. At the heart of this effort lies an unsolvable contradiction between the leaders' economic goals and the cultural stories they have to tell to win mass support. Those who advocate surrendering national sovereignty and self-determination to transnational corporations rely on cultural stories of wounded national pride, of unfair competition from abroad, of subversion from within by feminists and aggrieved racial minorities, of social disintegration attributed not to systematic disinvestment in the United States but to the behavior of immigrants or welfare recipients. They saturate political culture with stories extolling American national glory that are told by internationalists who seek to export jobs and capital overseas while dismantling the institutions offering opportunity and upward mobility to ordinary citizens in the United States.

The seeming paradox of reconfirmed nationalism during the 1991 Gulf War, the 2003 war in Iraq, and the subsequent and still continuing military actions in Afghanistan, Libya, and other nations during the Obama and Trump administrations, along with the globalization of world politics, economics, and culture that have emerged, represent two sides of the same coin. For more than sixty years, reassertions of nationalism in the United States have taken place in the context of an ever-increasing internationalization of commerce, communication, and culture. Furthermore, some of the most ardent advocates of public patriotism and militant nationalism have been active agents in the internationalization of the economy. Wedded to policies that have weakened the nation's economic and social infrastructures in order to assist multinational corporations with their global ambitions, the nation's political and economic leaders have fashioned cultural narratives of nationalist patriotic excess to obscure and legitimize the drastic changes in national identity engendered by their economic and political decisions. In times of crisis, the illusion that all contradictions and differences would be solved if we would only agree to one kind of culture, one kind of education, one kind of patriotism, one kind of sexuality, and one kind of family often holds widespread appeal.

Exploring the dynamics of nationalistic rhetoric and patriotic display during an era of economic and political internationalization illuminates the role of whiteness as a defining symbolic identity that mobilizes gender and sex in the service of obscuring class polarization. Close study of the patriotic revival of the post–Vietnam era, especially, reveals organic links between discussions of white male identity and the U.S. defeat in the Vietnam War, deindustrialization, changes in gender roles, and the rising emphasis on acquisition, consumption, and display that has characterized the increasingly inegalitarian economy of the postindustrial era. Perhaps most important, analysis of the connections among these events and practices reveals how the whiteness called forth by dominant narratives of "American patriotism" has functioned paradoxically to extend the power of transnational corporations beyond the control of any one nation's politics.

The New Patriotism

In his generative analysis of the 1915 D. W. Griffith film *The Birth of a Nation*, Michael Rogin demonstrates the persuasive power of scenarios depicting "the family in jeopardy" for the construction of nationalist myths. By representing slave emancipation and the radical reforms of the Reconstruction era as threats to the integrity and purity of the white family, Griffith's film forged a renewed narrative of national unity and obligation based on connections between patriotism and patriarchy—between white patriarchal protection of the purity of the white family and the necessity for whites to forget the things that divide them in order to unite against their nonwhite enemies.[14] This trope of patriarchal protection appears prominently in the present in a variety of anti-immigrant discourses and in homophobic and transphobic legislation and executive orders.

The kind of patriotism articulated most often in the United States since the 1970s has successfully updated the formula advanced by Griffith in 1915. It was perhaps best exemplified during ceremonies in 1984 commemorating the fortieth anniversary of the World War II Normandy invasion, when President Ronald Reagan read a letter written to him by the daughter of a veteran who had participated in the 1944 battle. The imagery created by Reagan and his media strategists for this ceremony encapsulated the conflation of whiteness, masculinity, patriarchy, and heterosexuality immanent in the patriotic renewal that revolved around the Reagan presidency. A serious illness had made it impossible for the veteran to attend the anniversary ceremonies himself, but his daughter had promised that she would travel to Normandy in his place and attend the commemoration, visit monuments, and place flowers on the graves of his friends who had been killed in combat. "I'll never forget," she promised him. "Dad, I'll always be proud."

Her father died shortly before the anniversary, but she kept her word and sat in the audience at Omaha Beach as Reagan read her letter to a crowd of veterans and their families. In an image broadcast on network newscasts (and featured repeatedly in an advertisement for the president's reelection campaign that year), tears filled her eyes as the president read her words, his voice quivering with emotion. Media analyst Kathleen Hall Jamieson identifies the imagery encapsulated in that scene as emblematic of the key themes of the Reagan presidency. In one short, sentimental, and cinematic moment, the president depicted military service as a matter of personal pride and private obligation.[15] The drama of a father's military service and a daughter's admiring gratitude reconciled genders and generations (even beyond the grave) through a narrative of patriarchal protection and daughterly obligation. It offered a kind of immortality to the family by connecting it to the ceremonies of the nation-state, and it served the state by locating and legitimating its demands for service and sacrifice within the private realm of family affections. Reagan's rhetoric eclipsed the political purposes ostensibly served by the Normandy invasion—defeating fascism, defending democracy, and furthering freedom of speech, freedom of worship, freedom from fear, and freedom from hunger—in his enthusiasm for a story celebrating personal feelings and family ties.

World War II served as a suitable vehicle for patriotic revival in the post–Vietnam era because of the contrasts between it and the Vietnam War. The United States and its allies secured a clear victory over the Axis powers in the Second World War, the postwar era brought unprecedented prosperity, and the unity forged in the face of wartime emergencies did much to define the nationalism and patriotism of the Cold War era. Yet the deployment of memories about World War II as a "good war" also rested on nostalgia for a preintegration America, when segregation in the military meant that most war heroes were white, when de jure and de facto segregation on the home front channeled the fruits and benefits of victory disproportionately to white citizens.

Reagan's rhetoric had enormous appeal in the eighties. It connected nostalgia for the whiteness of the pre–civil rights era with the affective power of nationalist narratives rooted in private family obligations and the responsibilities of paternal protection. This followed a well-established tradition. From the popularity during the Korean War of Lefty Frizell's song, "Mom and Dad's Waltz," with its improbable rhyme, "I'd do the chores and fight in wars for my momma and papa," to the government distribution of pin-up photos of blonde and snow-white Betty Grable as a symbol of white womanhood and companionate marriage to soldiers during World War II, to Senator Albert Beveridge's description of U.S. annexation of the Philippines in the 1890s as an "opportunity for all the glorious young manhood of the republic—the most virile, ambitious, impatient, militant manhood the world has ever seen," patriotism has often been constructed in the United States as a matter of a gendered and racialized obligation and opportunity.[16]

As Robert Westbrook points out, appeals to private interests as motivations for public obligations in the United States stem from a fundamental contradiction within democratic liberalism as it has emerged in Western capitalist societies. Drawing upon the scholarship of liberal political theorist Michael Walzer, Westbrook explains that liberal states must present themselves as the defenders of private lives, liberty, and happiness. But precisely because they are set up to safeguard the individual, these states have no legitimate way to ask citizens to sacrifice themselves for the government in wartime. Lacking the ability to simply command allegiance as absolutist states do or to naturalize state power in the ways that monarchies do, the liberal capitalist state must cultivate and appropriate private loyalties and attachments in order to mobilize citizens for war.[17]

Westbrook's analysis helps us understand some of the deep-seated emotional appeal of Ronald Reagan's remarks at the Normandy commemoration as well as the political capital they built. Like so much scholarly work of its era, his arguments help us see the connection between the nation and what has come to be called the "imagi-nation."[18] Westbrook captures one aspect of the relationship between citizens and the liberal state quite cogently and convincingly in showing how the state borrows legitimacy and commands obligation by insinuating itself into family and gender roles. But the state also creates those very family and gender roles in a myriad of ways: the state licenses marriages and legislates permissible sexual practices; regulates age, gender, and family identities through rules about labor, commerce, and communication; and allocates welfare benefits, housing subsidies, and tax deductions to favor some forms of family life over others. Just as the state uses gender roles and family obligations to compel behavior that serves its interests, powerful private interests also use the state to create, define, and defend gender roles and family forms consistent with their own goals.

In his speech at Omaha Beach, Ronald Reagan not only used the family to serve a certain definition of the state but he also put the power of the state behind specific definitions of acceptable gender and family roles, with enormous ramifications for the distribution of power, wealth, and life chances among citizens. While clearly colonizing private hopes and fears in the service of the state, Reagan's framing of the Normandy observance also mobilized the affective power of the state to address anxieties in the 1980s about private life, gender roles, jobs, community, and consumption patterns during the president's first term in office.

Reagan's celebration of a daughter's fulfillment of her father's last wish relied on clearly defined gender roles. It situated women as dutiful, grateful, and emotional. By taking her father's place at the ceremony, the letter writer wins the approval of the president, whose tears and quivering voice add a layer of paternal approval for her actions. The ceremony affirmed the continuity of white male heroism, female spectatorship, and national glory as the answer to anxieties about change, death, and decay. In the context of national politics in 1984, the Normandy observance celebrated gender roles and family forms consistent with Reagan's policies as president. It addressed anxieties about combat raised by Reagan's acceleration of the Cold War and the resulting deaths of U.S. service personnel in Lebanon and Grenada. It projected a sense of national purpose and continuity in an age of community disintegration engendered by deindustrialization, economic restructuring, and the evisceration of the welfare state. It offered spectacle without sacrifice, a chance for audiences to recommit themselves to the nation without moving beyond personal emotions and private concerns. By fashioning a public spectacle out of private grief, it combined the excitement of action with the security of spectatorship. In a country increasingly committed to consumption and sensual gratification, it presented the nation-state as a source of spectacle, producing the most elaborate shows of all. As J. A. Hobson noted a century ago, "Jingoism is merely the lust of the spectator."[19] Ronald Reagan's success in establishing himself as both president of the United States and as what some critics have jokingly called "the most popular television character of all time" depended in no small measure upon this ability to project reverent patriotism and confident nationalism.

In 1980, the last year of the Carter presidency, two media events framed the nation's problems in distinctly racialized forms. Extensive media coverage made the Iranian hostage crisis a symbol of the military and diplomatic weaknesses of the United States (perhaps aided by backdoor deals between the Reagan campaign staff and Iranian officials eager to procure the weapons that Reagan eventually did send secretly to that nation). The Iranians released all of their nonwhite captives, a move seemingly aimed at building support in nonwhite communities, but one that guaranteed the national crisis would be viewed as a crisis for whites. In the same year, the victory of the U.S. hockey team over the Soviet Union in the Olympics semi-final round received unprecedented publicity as a Cold War triumph, especially since it came in a sport long dominated by the USSR and Canada in which the U.S. team was a decided underdog. The game was played in the aftermath of the Soviet invasion of Afghanistan. Most important, however, was that unlike many previous victories over Soviet teams by U.S. athletes, the victory in hockey was achieved by a team composed of white men.

Elected to the presidency in the wake of the Iranian hostage crisis and the U.S. hockey team's victory, Reagan cultivated support for his policies and programs by making himself synonymous with beloved national symbols. Making especially skilled use of mass spectacles like the ceremonies marking the Normandy invasion, the opening of the 1984 Olympics, and the centennial of the Statue of Liberty in 1986, the president guided his constituency into a passionate appreciation of displays of national power and pride. Yet for all of Reagan's skills as a performer and politician, he was more the interpreter than the author of the "new patriotism." Revived nationalistic fervor and public displays of patriotic symbols predated and followed his presidency. Popular support for the Gulf War and for the invasion of Panama, the tumultuous parades for soldiers returning home from Operation Desert Storm (and retroactively veterans of Vietnam and Korea), and the outpouring of films, television programs, and popular songs with nationalistic, militaristic, and heroic themes signal a broad base of support for nationalistic public patriotic celebration and display.

During the 1988 presidential election, George H. W. Bush successfully depicted Michael Dukakis as an enemy of the Pledge of Allegiance because the Massachusetts governor supported a court decision exempting Jehovah's Witnesses and other religious objectors from school ceremonies saluting the flag. Dukakis responded, not by delineating the civil libertarian basis for his stance, but by circulating film footage of himself riding in an army tank. In 1992, Bush deflected attention away from his own performance in office with a stream of accusations and insinuations about Bill Clinton's absence from military service during the Vietnam conflict. For his part, Clinton identified himself with the Cold War rhetoric and actions of President Kennedy, and he selected Vietnam veteran Al Gore as his running mate, perhaps to contrast with Bush's vice president, Dan Quayle, whose service in the Indiana National Guard had enabled him to avoid service in Vietnam. At the same time, third-party candidate Ross Perot called attention to his training at the U.S. Naval Academy, to his efforts on behalf of U.S. prisoners of war held in Vietnam, and his selection of a navy officer and former prisoner of war, Admiral James Stockdale, as his running mate.

Yet for all of its apparent intensity and fervor, the "new patriotism" often seemed strangely defensive, embattled, and insecure. Even after the collapse of the Soviet Union and the end of the Cold War, a desperate quality permeated the discourse and display of loyalty to the nation's symbols. Only in the rarest of cases did the new patriotism address aspects of national identity that might truly command the love, loyalty, and lives of citizens, such as the expressive freedoms of speech, press, assembly, and worship guaranteed by the Bill of Rights; the rule of law and its system of checks and balances; and the history of rectifying past injustices as exemplified in the abolitionist and civil rights movements. To the contrary, the covert activities carried on by Oliver North in the Reagan White House; press self-censorship about U.S. military actions in Grenada, Panama, and the Persian Gulf; and popular support for a constitutional amendment to prohibit flag burning all indicate that (to borrow a phrase from singer and activist Michelle Shocked) many Americans are more upset by people like flag burners who would "wrap themselves in the Constitution to trash the flag" than by those like Oliver North who would "wrap themselves in the flag in order to trash the Constitution." Samuel Johnson called patriotism the "last refuge of a scoundrel," but scoundrels evidently had more patience in his day. In the 1980s and 1990s, refuge in patriotism became the first resort of scoundrels of all sorts.

In place of a love for the historical rights and responsibilities of the nation, instead of creating common ground through inclusive and democratic measures, the new patriotism has emphasized public spectacles of power and private celebrations of success. It does not treat war as a regrettable last resort but as an entertaining, frequent, and seemingly casual instrument of policy that offers opportunities to display national purpose and resolve. In several instances, spectacle has seemed to serve as an end in itself, out of all proportion to the events it purported to commemorate. For example, after the thirty-six-hour war in Grenada in 1983, 6,000 elite U.S. troops were awarded 8,700 combat medals for defeating the local police and a Cuban army construction crew. President Reagan announced that "our days of weakness are over. Our military forces are back on their feet and standing tall."[20]

When a group of antiwar Vietnam veterans picketed an appearance by actor Sylvester Stallone in Boston in 1985 because they thought his film *Rambo, First Blood: Part II* simplified issues and exploited the war for profit, a group of teenagers waiting to get Stallone's autograph jeered the veterans and pelted them with stones, screaming that Stallone was the "real veteran."[21] Stallone actually spent the Vietnam War as a security guard at a girl's school in Switzerland, but, like war hawks Pat Buchanan, Newt Gingrich, Dick Cheney, Phil Gramm, Clarence Thomas, and Rush Limbaugh—all of whom conveniently avoided military service in Vietnam themselves—Stallone established credentials as a "patriot" in the 1980s by retroactively embracing the Vietnam War and ridiculing those who had opposed it.

In contrast to previous periods of patriotic enthusiasm like World War II, when Americans justified military action by stressing citizen action in defense of common interests through their participation in armed forces firmly under civilian control, the patriotism of the last twenty-five years of the twentieth century often focused on the actions of small groups of elite warriors. In popular paramilitary magazines like *Soldier of Fortune,* in motion pictures ranging from *Red Dawn* to *Rambo* to *Missing in Action,* and in covert operations directed from the White House by Oliver North and John Poindexter during the Reagan administration, elite warriors defying legal and political constraints to wage their own personal and political battles have presented themselves as the true patriots.[22]

Military spectacles also purport to heal the nation's racial wounds. In Vietnam War era films, precombat racial rivalries disappear when ordeal by fire builds communion among soldiers from different backgrounds. Rambo's character combined German and Native American ancestry in an identity that allowed audiences to root for cowboys and Indians at the same time. Outside of motion pictures, early twenty-first-century life followed art as Republicans and conservative Democrats revered a man they knew little about, General Colin Powell, because his combination of African American identity and military distinction promised a form of cultural unity at no real cost to whites.

Proponents of the new patriotism often cited their efforts as attempts to address the unresolved legacy of the Vietnam War. In their view, antiwar protest during that conflict undermined the welfare of U.S. troops in the field, contributed to the U.S. defeat, and ushered in an era of military and political weakness in the 1970s. Moreover, they claim that Vietnam-era opposition to the war, the military, and the government in general triggered a series of cultural changes with devastating consequences for U.S. society. As William Adams notes, "In the iconography of Reaganism, Vietnam was the protean symbol of all that had gone wrong in American life. Much more than an isolated event or disaster of foreign policy, the war was, and still remains, the great metaphor in the neoconservative lexicon for the 1960s, and thus for the rebellion, disorder, anti-Americanism, and flabbiness that era loosed among us."[23]

Thus, the new patriotism not only sought to address the issues of war and peace, unity and division, loyalty and dissent left over from Vietnam, but it also contained a broader cultural project. While purporting to put Vietnam in the past, it actually tried to go back to that past, to Vietnam particularly, to fight the war all over again, this time not only to win the war but to undo the cultural changes it is thought to have generated. The new patriotism redemonized the Vietnamese enemy, as in the film *The Deer Hunter,* and inverted the power realities of the war by depicting Americans like Rambo as underequipped, feisty guerrilla fighters battling superior numbers and troops with better equipment. Just as former National Endowment for the Humanities director Lynne Cheney called for the replacement of social science textbooks stressing "vacuous concepts" like "the interdependence among people" with textbooks filled with "the magic of myths, fables, and tales of heroes," the rosy new patriotic spectacles of the new patriotism ignored the complex causes and consequences of U.S. involvement in Vietnam to celebrate instead the redeeming virtues of violent acts and heroic stories.[24]

These attempts to put Vietnam in the past began as early as 1976, less than a year after the communist victory in Southeast Asia. President Ford sent an armed force to rescue thirty-eight U.S. merchant sailors aboard the cargo ship *Mayaguez.* The ship and crew had been seized by the Cambodian navy in the confusion of the Khmer Rouge's ascendance to power in that country. Forty-one U.S. Marines died (and forty-nine were wounded) in an effort to free thirty-eight Americans who had already been let go since the Cambodian government had released the *Mayaguez* crew before the U.S. attack began. Yet Senator Barry Goldwater, among many others, hailed the raid as a boost to America's self-image and virility. "It was wonderful," according to the senator. "It shows we've still got balls in this country."[25]

Ronald Reagan boasted that the invasion of Grenada in 1983 and the bombing of Libya in 1985 proved that the United States "was back and standing tall," while George Bush contended that the U.S. invasion of Panama demonstrated the same point. In the mid to late 1980s, many cities including Chicago and New York held massive parades honoring Vietnam veterans—a decade after the conclusion of that war. On the eve of the Gulf War, Bush contrasted the forthcoming campaign with the Vietnam War where, he claimed, U.S. forces fought with "one hand tied behind their backs"; at the war's conclusion he proudly announced that "we've licked the Vietnam syndrome."[26]

When massive public parades welcomed home the veterans of Operation Desert Storm from the Persian Gulf, new patriots lost no opportunity to draw parallels to previous wars. In an opinion piece in the *Los Angeles Times*, a Vietnam-era veteran confessed his jealousy of the Desert Storm vets and their rousing homecoming receptions. Korean War veterans from New York staged a parade on their own behalf two months after the end of the Persian Gulf War, a half century after the hostilities in Korea had ended. They contrasted the immediate gratitude shown to Desert Storm veterans with their own perceived neglect. "My personal feeling was, God, they got it fast," said the executive director of the New York Korean Veterans Memorial Commission, recounting an episode during his group's parade when "some guy came over to me and said is that the memorial for Desert Storm? I said, 'Do me a favor, walk the other way. We've waited 40 years. Desert Storm can wait a couple of months.'"[27]

Yet, no matter how many times they have been declared dead, the memories of Vietnam—and their impact on U.S. society—have not gone away, and that is as it should be. The deaths of more than 50,000 Americans and more than 2 million Vietnamese, Laotians, and Cambodians require our attention, grief, and sorrow. In a guerrilla war with no fixed fronts, savage punishing warfare took the lives of soldiers and civilians alike. U.S. forces detonated more explosives in Southeast Asia during those years than had been exploded by all nations in the entire previous history of aerial warfare. The devastation wrought by bombs, toxic poisons, napalm, fragmentation grenades, and bullets continues in succeeding generations in all of the nations affected by the conflict. Small wonder then that an overwhelming majority of respondents to public opinion polls for decades have continued to affirm that they view U.S. participation in the war to have been not just a tactical error but fundamentally wrong.[28]

The realities of mass destruction and death in Vietnam were not the realities addressed by the new patriotism. They displayed no serious confrontation with the real reasons for the U.S. defeat in Vietnam: the unpopularity and corruption of the South Vietnamese government; the claim on Vietnamese nationalism staked by the communists through their years of resistance against the French, the Japanese, and the United States; the pervasive support for the other side among the Vietnamese people that turned the conflict into an antipersonnel war; and our own government's systematic misrepresentation of the true nature of the conflict to the American people.[29] All the subsequent celebrations of militarism, nationalism, and obedience to the state have not salved the still-open wounds of Vietnam.

Perhaps this is not a failure. Perhaps evocations of Vietnam have been designed less to address that conflict and its legacy than to encourage Americans to view *all* subsequent problems in U.S. society exclusively through the lens of the Vietnam War. This strategy not only precludes learning the lessons of Vietnam, but even more seriously, it prevents coming to grips with quite real current crises—the consequences of deindustrialization and economic restructuring, the demise of whole communities and their institutions, and the social and moral bankruptcy of a market economy that promotes materialism, greed, and selfishness, and that makes every effort to assure the freedom and mobility of capital while relegating human beings to ever more limited life chances and opportunities.

Evocations of powerlessness, humiliation, and social disintegration that the new patriotism ascribes to the Vietnam War perfectly describe what has been happening to U.S. society ever since. They transmit anxieties about social decay through metaphors about threats to the bodies of heterosexual white males, who appear as helpless victims, and present an economic and social crisis as an unnatural disruption of racial and gender expectations. Since 1973, the retreat from racial justice has taken place in the context of deindustrialization, economic restructuring, austerity economics, and the transformation of a market *economy* into a privatized market *society* (in which every personal relation is permeated by commodity relations). Stagnation of real wages, automation-generated unemployment, the evisceration of the welfare state, threats to intergenerational upward mobility, privatization of public resources, and polarization by class, race, and gender have altered the nature of individual and collective life. At the same time, the aggrandizement of property rights over human rights has promoted greed, materialism, and narcissism focused on the pursuit of consumer goods, personal pleasure, and immediate gratification.

These changes have created a society in which people cannot meaningfully take part in making the decisions that affect their lives. Society no longer offers enough jobs at respectable wages. It discourages work while encouraging speculation, gambling, and profiteering. Entertainment spectacles nurture voyeurism, sadism, and sensationalism while stoking envy, avarice, and resentment. Advertising messages invade and exploit—in a word, colonize—the most intimate areas of desire and imagination for profit, while the power of concentrated wealth pits communities against each other in a competition for declining resources and services. As capital becomes more and more mobile—rapidly circling the globe in search of profitable returns on investments—people become less and less mobile, and less and less able to control the ordinary dimensions of their own lives. In such a society, patriotic spectacles serve an important function: the imagined power and majesty of the nation-state seem to compensate for the loss of individual and collective power. As people control their own lives less and less, they look increasingly to images outside themselves for signs of the power and worth they have lost. Patriotism and patriarchy combine to ease anxieties about powerlessness, humiliation, and social disintegration, offering vicarious identification with the power of the state and larger-than-life heroes and authority figures.

Systematic disinvestment in U.S. cities and manufacturing establishments forced millions of people to suffer declines in earning and purchasing power, to lose control over the nature, purpose, and pace of their work, wreaking havoc in their lives as citizens and family members. Plant shutdowns disrupted once-stable communities; truncated intergenerational upward mobility; and made speculation, gambling, and fraud more valuable than work. Investments in plants and equipment by U.S. corporations declined from an average of 4 percent of the gross national product between 1966 and 1970 to 3.1 percent from 1971 to 1975, and 2.9 percent from 1976 to 1980. Unemployment averaged over 7 percent in the United States between 1975 and 1979, a rise from 5.4 percent between 1970 and 1974, and only 3.8 percent from 1965 to 1969. Real median family income, which doubled between 1947 and 1973, fell 6 percent between 1973 and 1980.[30] Despite massive spending on armaments and radical reductions in the tax obligations of corporations and wealthy individuals, capital continued its exodus to more profitable sites of exploitation in other parts of the globe. Thirty-eight million people in the United States lost their jobs in the 1970s as a result of computer-generated automation, plant shutdowns, and cutbacks in municipal and state spending.[31]

At the same time, the emerging postindustrial economy generated sales and service jobs with much lower wages, benefits, and opportunities for advancement than the jobs they replaced. Between 1979 and 1984, more than one fifth of the newly created full-time jobs paid less than $7,000 per year (in 1984 dollars). For the entire decade, the lowest paying industries accounted for nearly 85 percent of new jobs. By 1987, 40 percent of the workforce had no pension plans, and 20 percent had no health insurance. Between 1979 and 1986 the real income of the wealthiest 1 percent of the population increased by 20 percent, while the real income of the poorest 40 percent of the population fell by more than 10 percent. Real discretionary income for the average worker by the early 1980s had fallen 18 percent since 1973. At the same time, housing costs doubled and the costs of basic necessities increased by 100 percent.[32] Changes in tax codes in the 1980s further penalized working people by making them pay more in the form of payroll taxes and user fees, while tax breaks made investment and property income more valuable than wage income.[33]

By presenting national division during the Vietnam War as the root cause of the diminished sense of self and community experienced by many Americans in the last third of the twentieth century, the new patriotism deflected attention and anger away from capital. But it also made a decidedly class-based appeal to resentments rooted in the ways that the working class unfairly shouldered the burdens of the war in Vietnam and unfairly bore the burdens of deindustrialization and economic restructuring afterward. It also made a decidedly race-based appeal by presenting the white U.S. combatant as the only true victim of the conflict, representing antiwar protesters as women or effete men who chose the well-being of Asian "others" over the survival needs of white American men.

The ground war in Vietnam was a working-class war, but not a white war. Out of a potential pool of 27 million people eligible to serve in the military, only 2.5 million went to Vietnam, according to a study by Christian Appy. Eighty percent of those who served came from poor or working-class backgrounds. As one veteran complained, "Where were the sons of all the big shots who supported the war? Not in my platoon. Our guys' people were workers. . . . If the war was so important, why didn't our leaders put everyone's son in there, why only us?"[34] The sons of the important people backing the war, like the sons of most of the important and unimportant people actively opposing it, did not serve in combat because of their class privileges. When protest demonstrations at home and insubordination, desertions, and low morale at the front made it politically dangerous to continue the war, President Nixon and other leaders chose to buy time for a decent interval, allowing them to withdraw gracefully by trying to turn resentment against the war into resentment against antiwar demonstrators. Nixon realized that the public could be persuaded to hate antiwar demonstrators, especially college students, even more than they hated the war. Military leaders picked up on Nixon's cue, telling soldiers that antiwar demonstrators hated them, blamed them for the war, and actively aided and abetted the enemy. Of course, much of the antiwar movement made it easy for their enemies by all too often displaying elitist and anti-working-class attitudes, and by failing to make meaningful alliances with the working-class public, which opposed the war (according to public opinion polls) in even greater numbers than did college students.[35]

The new patriots were certainly correct when they charged that the American people neglected the needs of returning Vietnam veterans, but they revealed more about their own agendas than about neglect of veterans when they focused on the absence of homecoming parades as proof of this maltreatment. The miserable state of Veterans Administration hospitals, the scarcity of education and job-training opportunities for veterans, and corporate/government refusals to acknowledge or address the consequences to veterans of defoliants like Agent Orange all demonstrated far more neglect of Vietnam-era veterans than the absence of parades. Ironically the dishonorable treatment afforded Vietnam veterans came in no small measure as a direct consequence of the conservative attack on the welfare state, which had provided extensive social services for previous generations of veterans. Thus, by directing veteran resentment toward antiwar protesters, conservatives hide from the consequences of their own policies, from what they have done to social welfare programs, to the social wage in the United States, and to the ability of government to respond to the needs of its citizens.

In addition, the new patriots proved themselves extremely selective about which veterans deserved attention. When antiwar veterans attempted to tell their story at the 1971 Winter Soldier hearings, and when they tossed their medals onto the steps outside the halls of Congress to protest the continuation of the war that same year, almost none of the individuals and groups angry about the lack of parades did anything about the veterans' concerns. The dangers faced and overcome in Vietnam by Chicanx, Black, Native American, and Asian American soldiers have not persuaded Anglo-Americans to root out racism from the body politic or recognize the ways in which "American" unity is threatened by the differential distribution of power, wealth, and life chances across racial lines. Most important, by ignoring the ways in which social class determined who went to Vietnam, the new patriots evaded the degree to which the veterans' station in life diminished because they were workers and members of minority groups. Moreover, the erasure of the suffering and deaths inflicted upon the Vietnamese people reflects a sensibility in which only white lives matter.

The mostly working-class veterans of the Vietnam War returned to a country in the throes of deindustrialization. They participated in the wave of wildcat strikes resisting speed-up and automation in U.S. factories during the 1960s and 1970s. They played prominent roles in the United Mine Workers strikes and demonstrations protesting black lung and other industrially caused health hazards. They were visible among the ranks of the unemployed and the homeless. But their status as workers victimized by neoconservative

politics and economics in the 1970s and 1980s was far less useful to the interests of the new patriots than their role as marchers in parades and as
symbols of unrewarded male heroism.

The official story disseminated by new patriots and the news media about
Vietnam veterans obscured the connection between deindustrialization and
the national welfare since the seventies, but many representations of Vietnam
veterans in popular culture have brought it to the surface. Billy Joel's 1982
popular song "Allentown" and Bruce Springsteen's 1984 hit "Born in the
USA" both connected the factory shutdowns of the post-1973 period to the
unresolved anger of Vietnam veterans at broken promises. Joel's "Goodnight
Saigon" became the basis for the climactic moment at his live concert performances; audience members waved lighted matches and cigarette lighters as
they sang the song's anthem-like verse "we said we would all go down together." Similarly, Bobbie Ann Mason's novel *In Country* presents a Kentucky
town filled with fast-food restaurants and advertising images but no meaningful jobs for its disillusioned Vietnam veterans.[36] Unfortunately, even these
progressive representations focus solely on U.S. veterans, obscuring the
people of Southeast Asia and the war's dire consequences for them. They
seem to presume that the psychic damage done to some Americans by the
experience of defeat in Southeast Asia outweighs the nightmare visited on
Vietnam, Cambodia, and Laos by the war itself. Yet, despite their callousness
toward Asian victims of the Vietnam War, these representations call attention to an important unspoken dimension of the war—its class character.

Hollywood films about the Vietnam War have repeatedly drawn on its
class character for dramatic tension and narrative coherence. In contrast to
films about previous wars, where the experience of combat often leveled social distinctions and built powerful alliances among dissimilar soldiers,
Vietnam War films seethe with what one critic called "a steady drone of class
resentment." Perhaps expressions of class resentment only "drone" for those
who feel they are being resented. For working-class audiences in the 1970s
and 1980s, no less than for working-class soldiers in the 1960s and 1970s,
expressions of class anger might be long overdue. In these films, draftees and
enlisted men hate their officers, soldiers hate college students, and corruption almost always percolates down from the top.[37] For example, the Ukrai-
nian American workers portrayed in *The Deer Hunter* fail in their efforts to
protect themselves from life's surprises either in the dying social world of
their hometown in the industrial steel-making city of Clairton, Pennsylvania, or in the equally unpredictable and rapidly disintegrating social world
they enter in combat in Vietnam.[38] The soldiers in *Hamburger Hill* constantly compare themselves to college students who have escaped military service,
while Rambo reserves his greatest rage for the automated technology in his
own supervisor's operations headquarters. Lone-wolf commandos in the
Rambo films, *Missing in Action,* and other action/adventure stories assume

underdog status by reversing reality: this time the Americans fight as guerrillas with primitive weapons against foes with vastly superior arms and technology.[39]

Nearly every Hollywood film about the Vietnam War tells its story from the perspective of white males. Yet the disproportionate numbers of African Americans and Latinx on the front lines in the actual war's combat situations complicate the racial politics of Vietnam War films, preventing a simple binary opposition between whites and Asians. Most often, these films depict initial hostilities between distrustful groups of whites and Blacks, who then bond through the shared experiences of combat. Asian American soldiers are almost absent, Latinx soldiers appear rarely, but combat in Vietnam becomes a site where masculine bonds between Black and white men magically resolve and dissolve racial antagonisms.[40] At the same time, the oppositions that provide dramatic tension in many of these films build upon long-established narrative practices of racialized good and evil—especially the motifs of westward expansion with their hostile and "savage" Native Americans whose purported stealth and ferocity threaten white American troops, and the captivity story that once featured whites captured by Native Americans, reworked for Vietnam War films as a ghostly presence in accounts of U.S. soldiers missing in action or held as prisoners of war by the Vietnamese.

War as the Best Show of All

In spectacles on-screen and off, the new patriotism attempted to channel working-class solidarity into identification with the nation-state and the military. To oppose the government and its policies was portrayed as opposing working-class soldiers in the field. The class solidarity proclaimed in political and entertainment narratives, however, rarely included both genders. If there is a crisis for the working class in the Vietnam as depicted by the new patriotism, it is a distinctly gendered and racialized crisis for working-class white men only. They often become surrogates for all people, as the war is represented as a crisis of masculinity, centered on an alleged erosion of male prestige and power. The exploitation of low-wage women workers in the postwar economy or the burdens imposed on women raising children because of the decline or disappearance of the "family wage" in heavy industry rarely appear in films about the Vietnam War and its aftermath.

In a compelling and quite brilliant analysis, Lynda Boose notes the narcissistic and homoerotic qualities of 1980s and 1990s warrior films. Rather than citizen soldiers, the characters played by Sylvester Stallone and Chuck Norris more closely resembled World Wrestling Federation performers playing out little boys' fantasies of bodily power and domination over other men. *Iron Eagle, Top Gun,* and *An Officer and a Gentleman* all revolve around anxious sons and absent fathers. For Boose, these representations reflect arrested development, "a generation stuck in its own boyhood" attempting to recover the father. She notes that in *The Deer Hunter* there are no fathers, only brothers. In that film and many others like it, the idealized nuclear family dies in Vietnam, providing audiences an opportunity to mourn the loss of patriarchal power and privilege produced not only by defeat in Vietnam but also by deindustrialization at home with its decline in real wages for white male breadwinners and the attendant irreversible entry of women into the wage-earning workforce. But rather than presenting either the war or deindustrialization as political issues, these films and the national political narrative they support present public issues as personal. In Boose's apt summary, "The political is overwhelmed by the personal and adulthood by regressive desire."[41] Regressive desire and a preoccupation with the personal, however, are intensely political phenomena—they nurture the combination of desire and fear necessary to subordination as citizens and consumers. The binary oppositions between males and females reinforced by the Vietnam War narrative of the new patriotism served broader ends in an integrated system of repression and control.

As Boose, Susan Jeffords, Philip Slater, and others have argued, the glorification of the military in our society has served as a key strategy for forces interested in airing anxieties about feminist and gay/lesbian challenges to traditional gender roles.[42] During the 1980s, the core of Ronald Reagan's supporters from the extreme Right viewed patriotism as intimately connected to the restoration of heterosexual male authority. Religious writer Edward Louis Cole complained that in America, "John Wayne has given way to Alan Alda, strength to softness. America once had men," but now it has "pussyfooting pipsqueaks." Similarly, the Reverend Tim LaHaye argued that "it has never been so difficult to be a man," because so many women are working outside the home for pay. In LaHaye's opinion, such women gain "a feeling of independence and self-sufficiency which God did not intend a married woman to have."[43] Yet the solutions offered by the New Christian Right, like the solutions offered by paramilitary culture or consumer society, do not prescribe adult interactions between men and women to determine mutually acceptable gender definitions. Rather, they offer men juvenile fantasies of omnipotence through the unleashing of childish aggression and desire for control over others.

They also encourage the most blatant forms of homophobia, transphobia, and misogyny. By attaching agency and heroism to the identities of heterosexual men and by requiring physical and emotional bonding based on a presumed common identity, the new patriotism seeks to equate social boundaries with natural limits, to present social transgression as biological transgression, and to fuse group loyalty through fear of outsiders. One might think that the desire on the part of previously excluded groups to share the burdens of combat and citizenship would augment rather than diminish one's own service, but the virulent reaction against trans, gay, and lesbian members of the military and against women in combat reveal that primary attachments to identity politics transcend claims about citizenship and patriotic responsibility among large segments of the new patriots. It should come as no surprise that efforts to include women in combat or to acknowledge the obvious presence of gays and lesbians in the military were perceived as threatening by the new patriots rather than as confirming their values. Radio talk-show host Armstrong Williams, a Black neoconservative, summed up much of the Right's anxiety in an October 1996 broadcast, when he explained, "If the feminists and the politically correct people had their way, they would turn our little boys into fairies and queers."[44]

War films and other narratives of military life represent and validate aggressive and regressive male behavior. Psychoanalyst Chaim Shatan observes that basic training can strip recruits of their identities, discouraging their participation in broader communities on or off base. All power is vested in the drill instructors and training leaders. In Shatan's view, "The dissolution of identity is not community, though it can relieve loneliness. Its success is due to the recruit's ability to regress to an earlier stage of development, in which he is again an unseparated appendage of the domain ruled over by the Giant and Giantess, the DIs [drill instructors] of the nursery."[45] Rather than teaching independence and responsibility, the social relations and subjectivities glorified by the new patriotism fuse the narcissism of consumer desire with the nascent authoritarianism of the warfare state.

The glorification of masculine authority and conflation of patriotism with patriarchy in the military might make us think of combat films as exemplars of what our culture often calls an *oedipal journey into adulthood*—a rite of passage through sacrifices that make individuals distinct from others and responsible for their actions. If this were true, the films would help teach discipline, restraint, and responsibility. But the identities encouraged in the military by identification with the group, denials of difference, unquestioning obedience to authorities, and bonding through hatred, anger, and violence conform more closely to what our culture calls *preoedipal traits*—dissolution of the self into a more powerful entity, unleashing normally repressed behaviors and emotions, and fueling hatred for the subjectivities and desires of other people. Rather than teaching responsibility, the new patriotism stages sadomasochistic spectacles that use revenge motifs to justify unleashing the most primitive and unrestrained brutality, imitating the enemies we claim to fear. To manage the anxieties generated by this regression, the new patriots have to affirm all the more intensely their abstract fidelity to leaders, causes, and entities outside themselves.

The dynamics of militaristic spectacles have a self-perpetuating character. Regression to primitive desires generates an anxious longing for identification with powerful patriarchal authority; systematic submission to superior authority gives rise to anxious feelings of loneliness and isolation, which in turn fuels the desire for even more connection to powerful authorities. In *The Origins of Totalitarianism,* Hannah Arendt suggests that people in putatively democratic societies become ready for totalitarianism when loneliness becomes a routine feature of everyday existence. The combined effects of deindustrialization, economic restructuring, and the oppressive materialism of a market society where things have more value than people feed a sense of isolation and loneliness. Privatization prevents people from active engagement in civic society, from participating in processes that might lead to a healthy sense of self. Militarism becomes one of the few spaces in such a society where a shared sense of purpose, connection to others, and unselfish motivation have a legitimate place.

The denial of the political in combat films and fiction no less than in public patriotic rhetoric connected the new patriotism to the narcissism of consumer desire as the unifying national narrative. The ascendancy of greed and materialism in U.S. society during the 1980s was widely acknowledged, but the distinctive form this greed assumed in an age of deindustrialization has attracted less attention and analysis. Changes in investment policies and tax codes during the Reagan years accelerated trends favoring consumption over production, leveraged buyouts over productive investments, short-term profits over long-term investment, and love of gain over collective obligations and responsibilities. People at the highest income levels embraced behaviors previously associated with the poor—seeking short-term sensations and pleasures rather than pursuing disciplined long-range investments, programs, or policies. At the macrosocial level, these policies produced paralyzing levels of public and private debt, squandered the social resources and industrial infrastructure of the nation, and generated long-term costs to individuals and their environments while imposing burdens on future generations. On the microsocial level, they have encouraged the very attitudes displayed most often in adolescent warrior fantasies—regressive desire, narcissistic grandiosity, and anxieties about identity that lead to craving for sensations, distraction, and displays of power.

As president of the United States, no less than in his role as a performer in commercials for General Electric in the 1950s, Ronald Reagan communicated the language of consumer desire with extraordinary skill. He offered more for less, promising that tax cuts would not reduce government revenues because they would stimulate massive economic growth. He claimed that ending government regulation would free the private sector to find market-based solutions to social problems. He told Americans that they could have it all, as in his 1986 State of the Union speech when he announced, "In this land of dreams fulfilled where greater dreams may be imagined, nothing is impossible, no victory is beyond our reach, no glory will ever be too great.

So now, it's up to us, all of us, to prepare America for that day when our work will pale before the greatness of America's champions in the 21st century."[46] When this philosophy led the government to accumulate a larger national debt during Reagan's terms in office than had been incurred by all previous presidents combined, when it produced massive unemployment, homelessness, and health hazards, and when it created the preconditions for massive fraud in the savings and loan industry leading to enormous debts that executives from deregulated industries then passed on to consumers, Reagan continued to insist that his policies were working. In their own way they were, not to solve problems and make the nation stronger, but to transform the political system into a branch of the entertainment industry, into an entity seeking scapegoats for social problems rather than solutions to them.

Of course, the severe economic decline experienced by most people in the United States during the 1980s should not be attributed solely to Reagan; it predated and postdated his terms in office. The stagnation of real wages owed much to long-term imbalances in the U.S. economy between the needs of capital and the needs of the majority of the population. But the political culture that Reagan nurtured in the wake of this devastation perfectly complemented the escape from responsibility promoted by a consumer commodity society fixated on instant gratification. Reagan basked in the glow of the glory he attained by invading Grenada, bombing Libya, and identifying himself with the overwhelming U.S. victory at the 1984 Olympics (gained largely because the Soviet Union and other Warsaw Pact nations did not participate). By timing the Libya bombing for maximum exposure on network prime time, he set the stage for the voyeurism of the Gulf War and the war in Iraq, where news reports often resembled video games or commercials by weapons manufacturers. In return for all of the broken promises and devastated lives of his era, Reagan left the nation with a better-developed taste for spectatorship of the kind described long ago by J. A. Hobson—gloating "over the perils, pains, and slaughter of fellow-men whom he does not know, but whose destruction he desires in a blind and artificially stimulated passion of hatred and revenge."[47]

The new patriotism arose from deeply felt contradictions in U.S. society. It arbitrated anxieties about changes in gender roles, jobs, communities, and collective identity brought on by deindustrialization and economic restructuring. Narratives of national honor took on increased importance as the practices of transnational corporations make the nation state increasingly powerless to advance the interests of its citizens. Private anxieties about isolation, loneliness, and mortality fueled public spectacles of patriotic identification that promise purposeful and unselfish connection to collective and enduring institutions. The new patriotism served vital purposes, providing psychic reparation for the damage done to individuals and groups by the operation of market principles, while at the same time promoting narcissistic desires for pleasure and power that set the stage for ever more majestic public spectacles and demonstrations of military might.

Yet while providing logical responses to the diminution of collective and individual power in an age of deindustrialization, the new patriotism encouraged evasion of collective problems and responsibilities rather than efforts to solve them. It interfered with serious public discussion of the world people had lost and the one being built all around them through deindustrialization and economic restructuring. It promoted male violence and female subordination, built identification with outside authorities at the expense of personal integrity and responsibility, and inflamed desires that can only be quenched by domination over others.

Perhaps most ominously, the new patriotism promoted possessive identification with warfare and violence as solutions to personal and political problems. Although aggression is often portrayed as natural in our culture, the elaborate pomp of patriotic ceremonies and rituals may indicate precisely the opposite—that aggression needs to be endlessly nurtured and constantly cultivated. Contrary to what we see in stories of military glory, it is not easy for humans to kill other humans. One study of the World War II Normandy invasion showed that even among specially trained combat troops, many failed to fire their weapons once the battle started. Nightmares, guilt, and other signs of postcombat stress have plagued veterans of all wars, not just Vietnam. The attention devoted to ceremonial commemoration of past wars may be not so much evidence of how easy it is for people to go to war, but rather how much persuasion, rationalization, and diversion are required to make warfare acceptable.

Unfortunately, elaborate public appeals to honor the memory of slain soldiers only create the preconditions for new generations of corpses. Shatan explains that "ceremonial vengeance" serves to perpetuate rather than resolve the legacy of past wars because it requires repression of the genuine agonies caused by combat. In his eloquent formulation, "unshed tears shed blood," while grief and mourning are transformed into scapegoating and fantasies of revenge. Unresolved grief and guilt foment desires to inflict our wounds on others; reincarnating yesterday's dead as today's warriors "promises collective rebirth to all who have died for the Corps," but at the price of creating more martyrs whose deaths must be avenged in the future.[48]

Ceremonial celebrations of militarism perpetuate dangerous illusions about warfare. They hide the ambiguous outcome of every conflict, the limited utility of force in resolving conflicts of interest and ideology, and the ways in which the resolution of every war contains the seeds of the next one. But even beyond any practical shortcomings of war as a way of resolving conflicts lies its atrocious immorality. Our nation is not the first (and it will not be the last) to believe that participating in the systematic destruction of other humans will not fundamentally compromise our morality and our humanity, but the weight of the historical record is inescapable. Author and Vietnam War veteran Tim O'Brien counsels that moral lessons cannot be learned from warfare. He tells us that a war story "does not instruct, nor encourage virtue, nor suggest models of proper human behavior." O'Brien asks us to cease believing in the morality of war, advising us that any time we feel uplifted or righteous after reading a war story, we have been made the victim of "a very old and terrible lie."[49]

Of course, this is not to say that nothing of value is ever salvaged from war. Certainly many of the people who have seen combat become ferociously antiwar precisely because they have witnessed the waste and destructiveness of warfare firsthand. In addition, as George Mariscal points out in his important book *Aztlan and Vietnam,* for communities of color in the United States, the Vietnam War (like previous conflicts) sharpened contradictions and accelerated demands for racial justice from soldiers who saw themselves asked to fight and possibly die overseas for freedoms that they did not enjoy at home.[50] At the level of soldiers in the field, lessons about mutuality and interdependence often break down prejudice and parochialism. For these individuals and those they influence, warfare holds meanings that counteract the stories of heroism and glory that dominate combat narratives.

On the level of spectacle, however, war can be the best show of all. During World War I, Randolph Bourne argued that war was "the health of the state"—that nothing furthers the totalitarian projects of centralized power as effectively as warfare. During the Gulf War, Todd Gitlin amended Bourne's formulation, claiming that war is also the health of the television networks—and we might add the health of the advertisers, toy makers, film producers, and other merchants of diversion, distraction, and vicarious thrill seeking. Even if only as symbolic compensation, war enables, or at least seems to enable, individuals to negotiate otherwise intolerable contradictions.

The Wages of War

If war remains "the health of the state," it nonetheless does great harm to individuals and groups. Psychoanalyst and cultural critic Joel Kovel reminds us that a false subject needs a false object—people who do not know who they are need demonized enemies in order to define themselves. Hatred of the external enemy does not end when the shooting stops; on the contrary, the spectacles of war and the rituals of ceremonial vengeance promote appetites that need to be sated. It is hardly an accident that with the end of the Cold War, the lobbyists and public relations specialists in right-wing foundations who did so much to promote the new patriotism collaborated with overtly white supremacist organizations like the Pioneer Fund to publicize the most vulgar and discredited forms of white supremacist thought. In Charles Murray and Richard Herrnstein's *The Bell Curve,* but also in Dinesh

D'Souza's *The End of Racism,* and in Samuel P. Huntington's *Clash of Civilizations,* conservatives present people of color at home and abroad as the new enemy to be scapegoated for the lost wages of whiteness. Military veterans of the Vietnam era filled the ranks of anti-immigrant paramilitary and vigilante groups in the late twentieth and early twenty-first centuries in hopes of recapturing the sense of purpose and the security of power they felt decades earlier as young soldiers. The possessive investment in whiteness is thus offered as reparation and consolation for the destructive consequences of economic and political change. Murray, Herrnstein, D'Souza, and Huntington sought to portray the victims of racism as the beneficiaries of unearned privileges given to them because of their race. This move hides the history of the possessive investment in whiteness and inverts the history of racial politics in the United States. Yet while deficient as history and shamefully indecent as intellectual argument, these ideas have formed the core of public relations campaigns that have enjoyed broad success.

In a perceptive analysis of the role of anti-immigrant attitudes in contemporary conservatism, Kitty Calavita observes that "balanced budget conservatism" promises wealth, stability, and security to taxpayers and homeowners but creates an economy characterized by uncertain relations between work and reward, the plunder of public resources for private gain, economic uncertainty, and social disintegration. Moral panics, military mobilizations, and nativist attacks on immigrants provide a useful safety valve for the fear, anger, and frustration fostered by the false promises of the "balanced budget" conservatives. Because of the possessive investment in whiteness and its history, people of color easily become the main targets of this meanness masquerading as morality.[51]

U.S. wars in Asia have pitted U.S. combat troops against soldiers and civilians of nearly every eastern Asian nation. The experiences of warfare in Asia and the propaganda attendant on it have had racist consequences for citizens of those nations as well as for Asian immigrants to the United States. Of course, racism against Asians has a long history in the United States that includes disgraceful acts of mob violence, bigoted legislation denying immigrants from Asia opportunities to become citizens or own property, persistent economic exploitation, and the forced internment of more than 100,000 Japanese Americans, most of them citizens. Yet while not new, anti-Asian racism has taken on an especially vicious character in the context of the U.S. defeat in Vietnam and the rise of Asian economies as competitors with the United States. The hate crimes against Asian Americans enumerated at the beginning of this chapter are only a tiny sample of a much broader pattern of criminal behavior directed against people of Asian origin in the United States.[52] At the same time, the conflation of patriotism with whiteness has also had disastrous consequences for racialized immigrant groups from Mexico, Central and South America, the Caribbean, the Middle East, and the West Indies.

Deliberately inflammatory metaphors by politicians and journalists describing undocumented workers as an invading army prepare the public to see immigrants as the enemy. At the same time, antidrug policies that focus on border interdiction rather than on the suppression of demand and the incentives for supply create actual low-intensity warfare along the border. Government policy and vigilante actions complement one another in bringing the hurts and hatreds of warfare within the nation's borders. In San Diego, a group of young whites active in their high school's Junior Reserve Officers Training program participated in unofficial and unauthorized nighttime excursions on the border during which they fired air rifles at defenseless immigrants. In 1992, a U.S. Border Patrol agent fired rounds from an M-16 rifle into a group of undocumented immigrants traveling on foot near Nogales, Arizona, because he thought they were drug couriers. Although one of the immigrants was wounded by the agent's fire, the incident did not become public until three months later when the same agent shot another unarmed Mexican man who was running away from him, hitting the man in the back two times, using an AR-15 rifle. The agent attempted to cover up his crime by dragging his victim some fifty yards out of sight, leaving him to die, then returning later to bury the body. Another agent encountered him in the act of burial and agreed (reportedly at gunpoint) to keep quiet about the shooting, but fifteen hours later he reported the incident to authorities, who charged the first agent with first-degree murder. At his trial six months later, a jury found the agent not guilty on all charges, accepting defense arguments portraying him as a "law officer on the front line of our nation's war on drugs" whose actions were justified because he was operating in a "war zone."[53]

Immigrants detained for border violations in a private jail contracting with the INS in Elizabeth, New Jersey, succeeded in having the facility closed in 1995 because of inhumane conditions and brutality by guards. Some two dozen of the inmates from that facility then found themselves transferred to the Union County Jail in Elizabeth, where guards punched and kicked them, pushed their heads into toilets, and compelled a line of men to take off their clothes, kneel before the guards, and chant "America is Number One."[54] In May 1996, a group of marines assigned to a secret unit combating drug smuggling along the border shot and killed a teenage U.S. citizen herding goats near his home. A county grand jury recommended that no charges be filed.[55]

Identities are complex, relational, and intersecting. By disguising the social crises of our time as assaults on white male heterosexual power and privilege, the new patriotism has fanned the flames of white supremacy, homophobia, and anti-immigrant hatred. It has encouraged workers to feel their losses as whites, as men, as heterosexuals, but not as workers or community members. It has channeled resentments against foreigners, immigrants, members of aggrieved racial groups, women, gays and lesbians, college students, and intellectuals—but not against transnational capital and the economic austerity and social disintegration it creates and sustains.

The great scholar W.E.B. Du Bois argued long ago that the United States lost its best chance to be an egalitarian and nonracist society in the years after the Civil War because elites successfully manipulated the class resentments of white workers, directing them away from the rich and toward African Americans, Asian Americans, and Mexicans. White workers endured hardships in exchange for the security of knowing that there would always be a group below them, that there was a floor below which they could not fall. Du Bois called this assurance of privilege "the wages of whiteness," what white workers received instead of the higher economic wages they would have earned had they joined with all other workers in an interracial, classwide alliance. Du Bois quotes a populist white Georgia newspaper editor who identified the fatal flaw in going along with the elites' strategy: "Since at least 1865, we have been holding back the Negro to keep him from getting beyond the white man. Our idea has been that the Negro should be kept poor. But by keeping him poor, we have thrown him into competition with ourselves and have kept ourselves poor."[56]

Nearly a century after Du Bois analyzed the wages of whiteness, the egalitarian promise of the social movements of the 1960s has similarly been betrayed by a version of nationalism and identity politics that hides the attack on wages, hours, working conditions, education, transportation, health care, and housing by encouraging a possessive investment in the contemporary version of the wages of whiteness. By investing their identities in these narratives of the nation that depend on the demonization of others, white Americans only serve the interests of the transnational corporations whose policies are directly responsible for the disintegration of the nation's social and economic infrastructure. Accepting the possessive investment in whiteness as consolation and compensation is a bad deal. It guarantees that whiteness is the only thing whites will ever really own.

In the midst of the war in Vietnam, Dr. Martin Luther King, Jr., warned that the war on poverty at home would be lost on the killing fields of Southeast Asia. He spoke out against the war because he believed that the resort to systematic and institutionalized violence that war entailed would desensitize the nation to the suffering of other humans, that it would provoke and perpetuate an unending chain of desire for retribution, retaliation, and vengeance. Dr. King argued that it was indecent for a nation to send young people of different races to fight and die together in the jungles of Southeast Asia and yet claim to be unable to seat them together in the same classrooms in southeast Georgia or house them in the same neighborhoods in places like southeast San Diego.

The politicians and the press roundly condemned Dr. King for his opposition to the Vietnam War. *Time* magazine dismissed him as a demagogue, while the director of the FBI called him the most dangerous man in America. People who had applauded Dr. King for advocating nonviolence in response to white supremacist violence at home denounced him for preaching nonviolence overseas. Yet Dr. King's warnings proved to be right. Divisions at home widened rather than narrowed because of the war. Military violence today continues to plague the people of the world at an ever-escalating rate.

The nation that did not heed Dr. King's appeals in 1967 found itself ill-prepared to pursue peace in the years that followed. The U.S. government trained, financed, and supported violence as a way to repress a revolution in El Salvador and to promote a counterrevolution in Nicaragua. Overt and covert operations by the Reagan administration sold arms to an Iranian government considered an enemy of the United States in order to fund the contras in Nicaragua. CIA operations during that decade funneled $3 billion to Islamic fundamentalists trying to overthrow the Soviet-backed government of Afghanistan. The recipients of that aid became the founders of the organization that attacked the World Trade Center and the Pentagon in 2001.

Each act of war drew justification from the depiction of the enemy as evil incarnate. Anything would be justified, we were told, to stop the Soviets, to overthrow Manuel Noriega in Panama, to end the rule of Saddam Hussein in Iraq, to defeat fanatical Islamic fundamentalists. Yet the Soviets were our allies during World War II because they opposed Hitler. The United States financed and supported Noriega's rise to power because he provided an alternative to pro-Castro forces. The United States armed Saddam Hussein and turned a blind eye to his deployment of chemical weapons against his own people because his forces fought against the Iranian army. The U.S. Central Intelligence Agency (CIA) spent billions to arm Osama Bin Laden and to build the infrastructure that later formed the basis of his terrorist network during the 1980s because Bin Laden and his followers were then fighting against Soviet troops in Afghanistan. Each time, we were told that we have to fight fire with fire, that we need to ally with evil to defeat evil. But in the end, we always wind up with only more oppression, more cruelty, more suffering, more of the very evil our policies purport to prevent.

Little more than a decade after the end of the Gulf War, on September 11, 2001, fundamentalist fascists steeped in their own illusions about the heroic and redemptive nature of violence carried out brutal and deadly attacks on the World Trade Center in New York and the Pentagon in Washington, D.C. When the United States bombed Afghanistan in retaliation for the September 11 attacks, enemy troops ensconced themselves in the very caves that the CIA had helped them build two decades earlier when they were waging war against the Afghan government and its Soviet allies. Just as Dr. King predicted, war did not end violence, it only extended it. Recourse to war as a way of solving problems "once and for all" only fuels the next round of fighting. Military leaders in all countries warn that it is better to be "safe than sorry," but the costs of defining security exclusively in military terms are so enormous that even when actual bloodshed is avoided, no one is safer and everyone is a lot sorrier.

The attacks of September 11, 2001, provoked exuberant displays of nationalism and powerful appeals for unity. One survivor of the attack on the World Trade Center talked with humility and awe of the unity that he witnessed on that day. "There was no gender, no race, no religion. It was everyone helping each other," he explained to a reporter. In a nation deeply divided by economic inequality, by religious differences, by racism, sexism, and homophobia, this utopian vision of unity resonated powerfully.

Yet it soon became clear that the same divisions that perplex the country in peacetime do not go away simply because of war against a foreign enemy. The people from diverse backgrounds who felt so united inside the Twin Towers of the World Trade Center still returned home to a world outside those buildings characterized by economic inequality, residential segregation, racially segmented job markets, racial profiling, differential exposure to environmental hazards, and the persistence of police brutality and private hate crimes. The power of the possessive investment in whiteness quickly convinced some Americans that the terrorist attacks permitted retribution against all Arabs, all Muslims, and all dark-skinned immigrants. The Council on American-Islamic Relations reported 60,000 incidents of harassment within six months of the September 11 attacks. Authorities noted a 300 percent increase in hate crimes nationwide within a year. In Mesa, Arizona, one gun-wielding "patriot" shot at a Lebanese clerk at his job, fired bullets into the home of an Afghan family, and shot to death a Sikh gas station owner. The man accused of the shootings told police "I stand for America all the way."[57] In Dallas, a gunman partially blinded a clerk from Bangladesh, killed an immigrant from India who had been a U.S. citizen for twelve years, and murdered a convenience store clerk from Pakistan. He told each of his victims "God Bless America."[58]

Hate crimes are perpetrated by desperately unhappy and sometimes deranged people. Individuals who do not know who they are need to demonize someone else. A self so uncertain about its own worth needs other people's pain to establish its own identity. Empty, vacuous, and amoral individuals need to perform cruelty to mask their own absence of conviction and purpose. Most Americans do not commit hate crimes, nor do they approve of those who do.

Yet a larger logic provokes and propels hate crimes. It is not accurate to say that the events of September 11 drove people to commit hate crimes; rather, the attacks and the national response to them provided some individuals with justification for what they had wanted to do all along. The sensations, spectacles, and sentiments promoted by politicians and the press in the wake of the attacks exploited a tragic criminal act in order to advance a concept of the nation that would have been unpopular and untenable before September 11. Like the perpetrators of hate crimes, the advocates of this revolutionary change did nothing to honor the victims of September 11 but rather exploited their suffering to advance a calculated, cruel, cynical, and self-serving strategy designed to change the world forever.

When the attacks first occurred, our leaders told us "everything had changed." Then they displayed a giddy enthusiasm for advancing their own longstanding interests in a time of national emergency, proving that very little had actually changed for them. "Terrorism" became the excuse for drilling for oil in the Alaskan wilderness, for eliminating the inheritance tax, for supporting the employers' lockout of dock workers, for checking up on the immigration status of workers on strike against a meatpacking firm in Worthington, Minnesota, and for assaults on the First, Fourth, and Fourteenth Amendments to the Constitution. Two and a half years after the attacks, Secretary of Education Rod Paige claimed that the National Education Association was "a terrorist organization" because it criticized President George W. Bush's failure to fund his own education reforms.[59] At a moment when leaders of the United States could have generated unprecedented unity and shared sense of sacrifice, advancing their own narrow political and economic agenda appealed to them more.

The nation's leaders stoked public fears in order to provoke the kind of unbridled passion that assured them unchecked power. They sought to instigate through fear what they could not inspire by faith. In the name of unity, they demanded unanimity. They wanted a land where everyone danced to their tune. Like the perpetrators of hate crimes, where most people saw a national emergency, they saw an opportunity to advance their own interests.

The war in Iraq became a laboratory to test the profitability of programs that were not yet palatable on the domestic front, notably, privatization of postal services, military supply, prisons, communications, and security. Subcontractors hired by the executive branch received vast sums of money and employed some 10,000 to 20,000 mercenaries, but they remained unaccountable to Congress. The machine-gun toting guards who protected the ruler of Afghanistan and the U.S. chief administrator in Iraq were private security guards, not U.S. military personnel. From protecting missile defense sites to feeding troops to delivering mail to repairing damaged oil rigs, transnational companies secured windfall profits but kept their exact duties, expenditures, and activities secret. They funneled the money they made back into political campaigns to support politicians whose policies offered them even greater opportunities for economic gain.

This privatization is not a by-product of the war against terror; it is one of its main aims. It is no accident that instead of allocating funds to capture actual terrorists, the "war on terror" funded the Defense Advanced Research Projects Agency plan for online traders to win money by speculating on the likelihood of terrorist acts. The privatized nature of the war led to the "Terrorism Information and Prevention System" program, urging completely untrained citizens to police their neighbors by reporting "suspicious activities." Pentagon officials, however, confessed that they had no way to process this information and when people phoned them with "tips," the Defense Department suggested that callers contact the Fox Television Network program "America's Most Wanted."[60] When White House Chief of Staff Andrew Card was asked why the George W. Bush administration began pressing for war in Iraq in September 2002 rather than earlier, he replied that everyone knows that September, not August, is the appropriate time for launching new products.

The lust of the spectator takes center stage in the war on terrorism, eclipsing the responsibilities of the citizen. It has been a war waged without solemnity, without sorrow, without sadness, without civilian soldiers or shared sacrifice. Instead, images of masculinist military heroism and patriarchal power are performed for us as spectacle and sensation, through appeals to both sadism and sentimentality. This is war waged less for territory and position than for photo opportunities, sound bites, and thirty-second campaign commercials. It will not produce winners and losers so much as victims and survivors. Yet its ultimate product is itself: war as a commodity to be consumed and war as a social practice dedicated to the advancement of the commodity system and its increasingly central place in the social world.

Roughly three quarters of a century ago, Walter Benjamin warned that human self-alienation had reached the point where people could now experience their own destruction as an aesthetic pleasure of the first order. The creation of a permanent warfare state, the abrogation of constitutional rights, the funneling of public funds in perpetuity to private firms is enabled by a series of sensations and spectacles designed to "shock and awe" the public into passive roles as spectators.

In a society suffused with hate, hurt, and fear, warfare comes to take on a kind of normative logic. People who have been hurt want to hurt others. People filled with fear wish to make others fearful. But hate, hurt, and fear produce the very evils they purport to prevent. They distract from the arduous but necessary work of citizenship. The fact that others are evil is not enough to make anyone good. Unity and community have to be built from the bottom up, not mandated from the top down. Real security comes from democracy, not from plutocracy; from the activity of citizens not from the passivity of spectators; from righteousness rather than self-righteousness. The work that Dr. King called us to do years ago remains undone today.

5

How Whiteness Works

Inheritance, Wealth, and Health

White Americans have been encouraged to continue dreaming, and black Americans have been alerted to the necessity of waking up.
—JAMES BALDWIN

I n her exemplary study of racial attitudes among white college students, Karyn McKinney documents the tactics that whites often use to deny that privileges accrue to them through the possessive investment in whiteness. She reports that when her students read Peggy McIntosh's highly acclaimed work on the taken-for-granted privileges that white people enjoy daily because of their race, the students zero in only on the micro-level privileges McIntosh identifies. They agree that it would be annoying to be unable to find "flesh colored" bandages that match their skin tones and state they would not like being followed by suspicious security personnel when they enter a department store. Yet they do not address the structural side of McIntosh's examples, evading their privileged access to employment, education, housing, and health care. Instead, they complain that "reverse discrimination" against whites makes their race a liability and that the society in which they live allocates special preferences to people of color.[1]

McKinney's students should not be blamed for their unwillingness to face facts. As James Baldwin noted in another context, the entire history of their nation has conspired to keep the truth from them. Ignorance has its costs, however. By failing to reckon with the rewards that accrue to them as a result of racial privilege, whites prevent themselves from seeing how power actually works in this society, how increasingly undemocratic and unequal their country has become. White workers and professionals eager to police the boundaries of whiteness against challenges from aggrieved communities of color do not see the systematic nature of inequality in their own lives. Whites who feel compelled by self-interest and ideology to defend racial inequality are poorly positioned to understand or critique the class, gender, and regional inequalities that disadvantage them.

As long as they focus on what they perceive to be special preferences given to communities of color, McKinney's students do not see that the wealthiest 1 percent of the U.S. population owns over 40 percent of all the privately held assets in the nation,[2] that the richest 20 percent controls almost 90 percent of the country's wealth, that the 3 million highest earning people in the United States receive roughly the same income as the combined incomes of the 200 million poorest Americans. They do not recognize that the share of the national income garnered by the overwhelming majority of the population—the "bottom" 90 percent—has declined precipitously from two thirds of the national income in 1917 to barely 50 percent in 2013,[3] that working families now perform eleven additional weeks of paid labor annually more than families did forty-five years ago.[4] Since 1979, the wealthiest 1 percent of the U.S. population has seen its income more than double, while the average income of the bottom 99 percent grew by less than 20 percent. Nationally, over 85 percent of income growth between 2009 and 2013, immediately following the Great Recession, went to the highest-income 1 percent of U.S. families.[5] Over 60 percent of the nation's income now goes to the wealthiest fifth of households.[6] The students do not see how preferences are allocated in their society; they do not see how we are actually governed.

Whiteness does its work in the United States as a structured advantage, as a built-in bias that prevents hardworking people from securing just rewards for their labor and ingenuity. It produces unfair gains and unjust rewards for all whites, although not uniformly and equally. As a matter of justice, whites should be interested in abolishing it, in relinquishing the unfair gains and unearned enrichments that flow from it. Yet the possessive investment in whiteness is not an aberration in an otherwise just society. It works in concert with—and flows from—many other forms of inequality and injustice. It is one of the key practices that make unfairness seem necessary, natural, and inevitable. Understanding how whiteness works offers information about more than whiteness. It provides essential information about the nature of inequality in our society, about how privilege is created and sustained but protected from political critique.

Most African Americans know all too well something that McKinney's students do not know—that past and present structural forces shape their lives. Blacks are not likely to number themselves among the 46 million Americans today who can trace the origins of their family wealth to the Homestead Act of 1862 that parceled out land for free to whites but denied it to African Americans.[7] They cannot include themselves among the major beneficiaries of the trillions of dollars of wealth accumulated through the appreciation of housing assets secured by federally insured loans between 1932 and 1962, because 98 percent of FHA loans made during that era went to whites via the openly racist categories utilized in the agency's official manuals for appraisers.[8] Most Blacks know that past discrimination continues to influence contemporary struggles to accumulate assets because wealth is inherited and passed down across generations. In recent years, moreover, changes in the tax code have further skewed opportunities and life chances along racial lines by giving favored treatment to those forms of income most likely to represent the fruits of past and present discrimination like inheritances and capital gains, while lessening the value of income gained through work. The living legacy of past discrimination combines with the impact of contemporary discriminatory practices in mortgage lending, real estate sales, automobile credit financing, and employment to impose artificial impediments against asset accumulation among African Americans.

The persistence of residential segregation, educational inequality, environmental racism, and employment discrimination makes a mockery of the promises of fairness and equality inscribed within civil rights laws. It means that members of aggrieved racial groups experience their racial identities through impediments to the accumulation of assets. People of color confront disproportionate obstacles to acquiring education, marketable skills, and job training. They face unparalleled exposure to health risks. Their racial identities confine them to the segments of the labor market where it is most difficult to bargain over wages and working conditions. They face scrutiny and discipline from law enforcement officials, educators, and cultural brokers intent on restricting their cultural and political expressions. Their unearned disadvantages structure unearned advantages for whites. Yet people of color find themselves portrayed as privileged beneficiaries of special preferences by the very people who profit from their exploitation and oppression.

Young whites like those in McKinney's class can often rely on gifts and bequests from family members for transformative assets that help build wealth, on inheritances that enable them to pay for an education, start a business, or buy a first home. Parents in the median two-parent white family control ten times as much wealth as parents in the median two-parent Black family. In fact, even the median single white parent has more than twice the wealth of the median two-parent Black family.[9] This gap, in part, reflects the fact that almost half of white families receive a bequest on the death of a relative or a large gift from a living family member, compared with only one in ten Black families. Even Blacks who do inherit or receive this kind of gift receive, on average, $30,000 less than whites. Nor is higher education sufficient for overcoming this disparity: half of college-educated whites who inherit money receive more than $55,000, while half of college-educated Blacks who inherit get less than $36,000. The average transfer that white college-educated families receive is $253,353—nearly four times more than the average of $65,755 received by Black college-educated families.[10] In total, among families who do inherit, Black families receive only 10 percent as much wealth as white families do.[11] As successful whites get older, they routinely receive gifts and bequests from relatives, but as successful Blacks age, they have to send money out to elderly relatives who were not able to accumulate the assets that their white counterparts could in the era of overt segregation and discrimination.

Even when Blacks and whites earn the same income, they have very different relationships to wealth. A Black family earning $60,000 per year in income will have less than 30 percent of the wealth owned by white families earning the same amount.[12] The disparity in net financial assets is even greater. Inherited wealth and differential appreciation of property values in Black and white neighborhoods make it impossible for most Blacks to make up through wages the disparities they encounter from the racialized distribution of wealth. A typical Black family earns sixty cents for every dollar earned by a typical white family, but the net worth of the median white family is $144,200—compared to roughly $11,000 for the median Black family. Whites who out-*earn* Blacks by a 5:3 ratio out-*own* Blacks by a 13:1 ratio.[13] The gap is so wide that even middle-class whites have more assets than high-earning Blacks.[14]

It is much easier for middle-income white parents to pass on their class status to their children than it is for parents from aggrieved racial groups. Only 16 percent of white children growing up in the middle-income bracket will fall to the bottom of the income hierarchy, compared to nearly half of middle-income Blacks. It is also easier for low-income whites to move upward than it is for low-income Blacks: nearly 70 percent of whites from the poorest families will move into a higher income quintile, but less than half of Blacks from those families will do the same.[15] The reasons for these disparities stem almost entirely from the ways in which homeownership gives whites in every class more wealth than their Black counterparts with the same incomes, family structures, and work histories. The rate of homeownership among Blacks is more than 40 percent lower than the rate among whites,[16] but even those Blacks who own homes are hindered by the fact that their property appreciates in value less than property owned by whites. Homeownership produces 25 percent less wealth for Blacks than it does for whites.[17] Overall, it is worth $94,426 in net financial assets and $136,173 in net worth to be white.[18] On average, African American homeowners each dole out more than $16,000 in racially inflated interest payments.[19] Residential segregation and discrimination more broadly cost the median Black household nearly $50,000 in lost equity.[20] Because they face an artificially restricted housing market, the current generation of Blacks has lost $82 billion collectively; the next generation is likely to lose $93 billion.[21] Because they face an artificially restricted housing market, Blacks lose significant amounts of money: one study found that reducing Black/white segregation in Chicago by one third would increase Black income by \$3.6 billion in that city alone."[22]

Blacks receive only 2.7 percent of the country's conventional home loans, even though they account for over 13 percent of the population.[23] Even worse, Blacks making over \$150,000 per year in New England are denied home loans more often than whites with an annual income of only \$51,000.[24] Racial discrimination in housing imposes undeserved burdens on minorities while channeling unjust enrichment to whites. While white, young, and upper-income borrowers can secure prime loans at low costs, people of color, the elderly, and low-income households routinely confront higher interest rates and more onerous loan terms from subprime lenders. As white families increasingly turn the appreciated equity in homes they secured in a discriminatory market into diversified stock portfolios, the traditional financial institutions that helped them get into the housing market in the first place abandon mortgage markets to provide them with elite services and opportunities. This relegates people who do not yet own homes to service from subprime and predatory lenders, making their costs of entry into the housing market higher than for those who preceded them. Throughout California, for example, twice as many Latinx and African Americans as whites report that their loans include prepayment penalty provisions designed to strip equity from homeowners and lock borrowers into predatory loans.[25]

The evidence is clear that these inequities are systemwide. A 2001 study found that in Sacramento, the subprime lender New Century Mortgage made ten times as many loans to Black applicants as did the prime lending company that owned New Century Mortgage, U.S. Bank. In Los Angeles, prime lenders including Bank of America, Citibank, U.S. Bank, and Washington Mutual originated fewer refinancing loans in minority neighborhoods than their subprime affiliates—Nations Credit Financial Services, CitiFinancial, New Century Mortgage, and Long Beach Mortgage.[26] These practices culminated in the housing crash of 2006 to 2008, and the structural racism they exemplify resulted in several high-dollar value settlements with the U.S. Department of Justice. In 2012, for instance, Wells Fargo and SunTrust reached separate settlements with the Department of Justice due to stipulations that they had systematically discriminated against qualified African American and Latinx applicants, steering them toward subprime mortgages despite their evident eligibility for better loans.[27] Countrywide settled a similar case in 2015 after targeting over 200,000 Black and Latinx borrowers for subprime mortgages in the four years before the housing market crashed—even when those borrowers were as qualified as white applicants who received prime loans.[28] Overall, over 60 percent of borrowers given subprime mortgages in 2006, just before the crash, should have qualified for conventional loans. Discrimination also pervades the sales and long- and short-term rental markets. A 2012 U.S. Department of Housing and

Urban Development audit conducted in twenty-eight major cities found that real estate sales personnel showed African American home buyers 17.7 percent fewer homes than they showed to white home seekers. The study also found that rental agents discriminated against Black and Latinx applicants, telling them about 11.4 and 12.5 percent fewer available homes, respectively, than comparable whites were informed about.[29] Further, a field experiment examining racial discrimination on Airbnb, a popular website connecting individuals seeking lodging with privately owned rooms or homes, found that individuals with traditionally Black names were rejected by possible hosts 16 percent more often than identical applicants with white-sounding names. This finding suggests that overt discrimination, though somewhat reduced in the traditional rental market through hard-won battles to ensure compliance with civil rights law, may have found a new outlet in the sharing economy.[30]

Unequal access to homeownership and choice rental locations has important health consequences. Access to a limited housing market makes members of aggrieved racial groups more likely than whites to live in communities with toxic hazards and less likely to have access to medical treatment. Whether insured or not, people of color receive fewer preventive medical services than whites. They do not get flu shots, colorectal cancer screening, advice to quit smoking, or elder-specific vaccines such as pneumonia immunization to the degree that they would if they were white.[31] African Americans suffer onerous consequences—like diabetes-related limb amputation—from lack of preventive care and a pattern of delayed medical attention to a much greater degree than is true of members of more privileged groups.[32] The Office of Minority Health in the U.S. Department of Health and Human Services reports that the death rate among Blacks due to diabetes is more than double the rate for whites, that African Americans face a 30 percent greater likelihood of dying from heart disease compared to whites, that whites are 29 percent less likely to die from strokes than are Blacks, and that Black women are twice as likely to die from cervical cancer than are white women.[33] Black men have a lower five-year survival rate than white men do for every type of cancer.[34] Life expectancy overall is three and a half years less for Blacks than life expectancy for whites.[35]

Racial disparities in maternal and infant health are particularly striking. One out of every three African American mothers in 2014 received no prenatal care during the first trimester.[36] Black infants are 50 percent more likely than white babies to be born prematurely, and are two times more likely to die before their first birthday.[37] One third of African American children between the ages of nineteen and thirty-five months were not fully immunized in 2014.[38] In perhaps the most damning single statistic on racial health inequity, Black women's maternal mortality rate in the United States is more than three times higher than white women's.[39]

Moreover, being on the receiving end of racism creates intense and constant stress and increases the risks of depression, anxiety, and anger, a concern in and of itself that also produces or aggravates heart disease. A 2014 study found that people who suffered from racial discrimination were significantly more likely to report psychotic symptoms, even controlling for anxiety and depression levels.[40] Researchers contend that repeated exposure to racial discrimination is associated with higher rates of cardiovascular disease for African American women.[41] A recent meta-analysis of research on perceived racism and health reveals a significant association between discrimination and a broad range of negative mental and physical health outcomes.[42] Childhood blood pressure rates of Black and white girls show no differences, but as adults, Black women's blood pressure increases relative to whites.[43] It drops at night for whites but not for Blacks, a contrast researchers suspect is related to the stress caused by racism.[44] "It's the little things that count," Camara Jones of the Centers for Disease Control and Prevention observes, "like being treated differently by a store clerk. Each event may be insignificant, but the repetition builds up."[45]

Race also affects the quality of medical care. African Americans get sicker and die younger than whites, regardless of social class.[46] Black men in the United States can expect to die 4.4 years earlier than white men, to be more than twice as likely to die of heart disease than white women, and to be over 50 percent more likely to die of strokes than are white men or white women.[47] Increases in income do not necessarily produce increases in health; for darker skinned African American men and women, for instance, blood pressure actually increases at higher levels of income.[48]

Impoverished African American children in cities across the country live in housing with lead-based paint on interior and exterior walls, exposing them to the dangers of developing toxic levels of lead in their bloodstreams.[49] National studies reveal that poor Black children have a far greater chance of contracting lead poisoning than poor white children.[50] Specific cases are even more incriminating. In 2014, emergency managers appointed by the governor and imposed on the majority-Black population of Flint, in flagrant disregard of their democratic rights, changed the municipal water source as part of a privatization scheme. Water drawn from the new source, the Flint River, generated serious complaints about its smell, taste, and color; residents further reported that it caused rashes on contact with skin. For over a year, their concerns were dismissed.[51] By the time state officials took the citizens' complaints seriously, the rates of lead in Flint's children were found to have doubled. The cause was the quality of the river water, which was so corrosive that it was leaching lead from outdated water pipes. In 2017, the Michigan Civil Rights Council released a report concluding that the crisis was caused by systemic racism and its attendant effects on segregation, housing stock, and employment.[52] These problems are hardly limited to Flint, or even to Michigan: new analysis of California Department of Public Health data reveals more than 300 neighborhoods in that state alone whose residents have blood lead rates as high as or higher than those in Flint. A recent *Pediatrics* study estimates that a third of child lead poisoning cases nationwide go undetected.[53] The Centers for Disease Control and Prevention, it is worth noting, have determined that *any* presence of lead in children's blood can cause reduced hearing and speech capabilities, development delay, and brain damage.[54]

The racial health gap is paralleled by the racial wealth gap. At every stage of life and economic level, African Americans face systematic obstacles to asset accumulation, wealth, and health. Inheritance helps whites secure unearned advantages in the form of transformative assets that increase the wealth gap between the races. These workings of whiteness reveal the systemic and structural contours of inequality in the United States. Yet Karyn McKinney's white college students discern no particular advantage to them for being white, and instead present a torrent of complaints about reverse racism and the penalties they imagine they confront for being white. They have been encouraged by the corporate media and the increasingly corporate dominated educational system to ignore the facts and inhabit the fictions of the possessive investment in whiteness, fictions that increasingly revolve around discussions of white fragility, white failure and white fear, as the next chapter delineates.

6

White Fragility, White Failure, White Fear

Whatever white people do not know about Negroes reveals, precisely and inexorably, what they do not know about themselves.

—JAMES BALDWIN

dentifying the existence and power of the possessive investment in whiteness does not presume that all whites are happy, healthy, wealthy, secure, or satisfied. In a society stratified by class, insensitive to the indigent and the ill, and riddled with personal and family dysfunction, many whites are miserable. Yet that is precisely why their whiteness comes to matter to them so much. If people perceive whiteness as the only advantage they have, they will cling to it desperately. No matter how dejected, how discouraged, how aggrieved, or how angry a person may be, whiteness seems to provide a floor below which one cannot fall.

As mentioned in Chapter 4, the classic work *Black Reconstruction in America, 1860–1880,* by W.E.B. Du Bois argues that with the emergence of the Jim Crow system of racial segregation, even the most oppressed and powerless white person secured "wages" of whiteness, psychological wages that guaranteed the illusion of inclusion in a relentlessly and ruthlessly hierarchical exclusionary society.[1] Similarly, Michael Rogin's study of the minstrel show, *Blackface/White Noise*, reveals how lampooning Black identity on the theatrical stage enabled members of despised European immigrant groups to envision and enact an escape from the humiliating subordinations and indignities they suffered from their foreign-looking faces and foreign-sounding names, from the poorly paid labor they performed and from the poorly maintained dwellings in which they lived. Immigrants from Europe embraced anti-Blackness as a way of claiming a measure of the benefits of being white.[2] Yet by directing their anger and ire downward at the communities of color beneath them, whites trapped themselves inside the system that exploited and oppressed them. Du Bois explains that by curtailing the bargaining power of Blacks, whites created competitors who were forced to work for lower wages. Employers could then keep white wages low by threatening to turn to even cheaper Black labor. Thus, the short-term relative advantage that white workers secured from their possessive investment in whiteness created a long-term downward pressure on their wages and working conditions.[3] Black freedom fighter Fannie Lou Hamer phrased it eloquently in the 1960s: "The white man around here don't realize how good it would be to let us up out of the ditch. He can't keep us in the ditch without standing on us, and he can't get out of the ditch without letting us out."[4] As John Bracey demonstrates in his filmed lecture "How Racism Harms White Americans," the United States has a "democratic" system that is not really democratic at all because of white supremacy.[5] The defense of slavery, and later of segregation, became the justification for a plethora of undemocratic practices and structures—from the exclusion of women from the public sphere to the overrepresentation of antidemocratic interests in the electoral college and the U.S. Senate, from the costs in human lives and property of the Civil War to the ways in which discrimination squanders talents, misallocates resources, and inhibits community efficacy and social cohesion.

The possessive investment in whiteness creates a vicious circle. The more fearful, fragile, and headed for failure that whites feel, the more avidly they pursue the idealized fantasy of uninhibited power and agency to which they believe their whiteness entitles them. When this leads to even more failure and frustration, they perceive themselves as grievously victimized and look for scapegoats, these days directing special enmity against the poor, immigrants, Muslims, and people who are lesbian, gay, bisexual, transgender, or queer. In the early twenty-first century, when the organization of the economy, the environment, the educational system, and the political process all increasingly come to serve the interests and aspirations only of the wealthy, more and more whites correctly see themselves as displaced and dispossessed. But in directing their ire against individuals and groups even more aggrieved than they are, they become consumed with hatred for others and unable to diagnose the actual causes of their problems. They come to recognize and understand themselves largely through their enmity. The best thing that could happen to the white poor, the white working class, and the white middle class would be to disinvest in their whiteness and join with other exploited and aggrieved people across racial lines. But without an understanding of how the possessive investment in whiteness serves to sustain a system of racialized capitalism, they do not know that. Instead they become agents of an ever-escalating cycle of moral panics and paroxysms of violence that fuel desires for sadistic power and punishment. In the nineteenth and twentieth centuries, the possessive investment in whiteness often led to lynchings and other forms of mob violence, creating what Du Bois aptly describes as "a sort of permissible Roman holiday for the entertainment of vicious whites."[6] We see those same dynamics at work today in the pervasive violence by law enforcement officers and vigilantes directed against people of color, against religious and sexual minorities, and against immigrants and refugees.

The Charleston Massacre

Early in the evening of June 17, 2015, twenty-one-year-old Dylann Roof walked into the Emanuel African Methodist Episcopal (AME) Church in Charleston, South Carolina. A group of black women and men engaged in Bible study inside the church welcomed the young white visitor to join them in their prayers and discussions. After spending about an hour with the group, Roof abruptly announced "I am here to shoot black people." He pulled out a .45 caliber handgun and eight magazines loaded with hollow point bullets and began firing. When a member of the prayer group tried to persuade Roof to stop the shooting, the killer declared "You rape our women, and you're taking over our country. And you have to go."[7] In a matter of seconds Roof shot and killed six women and three men: DePayne Middleton-Doctor, age forty-nine; Cynthia Hurd, age fifty-four; Susie Jackson, age eighty-seven; Ethel Lance, age seventy; church pastor Clementa Pinckney, age forty-one; Tywanza Sanders, age twenty-six; Daniel Simmons, age seventy-four; Sharonda Singleton, forty-five; and Myra Thompson, age fifty-nine.[8]

When news of the massacre emerged, one of Roof's white friends, twenty-two-year-old Joey Meek, recalled that he had been had been out drinking vodka, smoking marijuana, and snorting cocaine with Roof a few weeks before the shootings. Meek told reporters that Roof complained at that time that "blacks were taking over the world" and that "someone needed to do something about it for the white race."[9] Investigators discovered an online manifesto that Roof had authored and posted alongside an array of anti-Black messages and images that he had gleaned both from white supremacist websites and mainstream political and commercial culture. Roof posted online pictures portraying his allegiance to various symbols of white supremacy and slavery. One picture showed him standing in front of the Confederate history museum in Greenville, South Carolina. In another, he held aloft a Confederate flag. A third depicted Roof sitting on a car with a front license plate that featured several different battle flags of the pro-slavery side in the Civil War.[10] Roof alleged on his website (without supporting evidence) that Blacks have lower IQ scores yet higher testosterone levels than whites. This combination, according to Roof, produces lower impulse control among Blacks, which he contended was "a recipe for violent behavior."[11] Evidently oblivious to his own diminished capacity for impulse control and his own propensity for violent behavior, Roof concluded that the innately violent nature of Blacks meant that whites like himself were obligated to use guns to exterminate them. Roof belittled other whites, especially those who moved to the suburbs, portraying them as cowards running away from the threat posed by Blacks. He counseled that the proper course of action should be for whites to stay in cities, search out Black people, and kill them. In a passage that explained in advance his subsequent attack on the church members in Charleston, Roof explained, "I am not in the position to, alone, go into the ghetto and fight. I chose Charleston because it is [the] most historic city in my state, and at one time had the highest ratio of blacks to Whites in the country."[12] A subsequent investigation by the U.S. Department of Justice found that Roof hoped that his actions would provoke a massive race war waged by whites against Blacks. He selected the church as the site for his crime, according to U.S. Attorney General Loretta Lynch, because Roof believed that the killings at an African American house of worship would "ensure" the highest degree of notoriety and attention.[13]

The Confederate flags that Roof pasted on his car and posted on his website had literal as well as metaphorical meaning for him as emblems of slavery unwilling to die, as they do for all of his fellow white supremacists. The Emanuel AME Church in Charleston that Roof selected as the site for his attempt to provoke a race war was founded by free Blacks in 1818 in a slave state in defiance of the legal and social norms mandated to protect the slave system. As historian Vincent Harding explains, the founding of Emanuel AME constituted an important political act because it "challenged white domination, white control, white definitions of religious life and church polity."[14] The mere existence of the church defied city and state laws that banned Black literacy and mandated that no church could exist unless whites made up a majority of the congregation. City officials routinely arrested members of the Emanuel AME congregation and subjected its leaders to public whippings.[15] Emanuel AME cofounder Denmark Vesey was arrested in 1822 and charged with trying to incite a slave rebellion. Whites condemned Vesey to death at a secret trial. They executed him along with five other "conspirators," and burned the church building to the ground.[16] The members of the Emanuel congregation initially met in secret in response to the burning, but then defiantly rebuilt the church. They had to meet secretly once more, however, when the city again outlawed Black congregations in 1834. One hundred eighty years later when Dylann Roof walked through its doors, this history continued to ennoble and embolden the church's parishioners. Pastor Clementa Pinckney, one of the nine people killed by Roof on June 17, 2015, had previously proclaimed, "What the church is all about is the freedom to be fully what God intends us to be and have equality in the sight of God. And sometimes you got to make noise to do that. Sometimes you may have to die like Denmark Vesey to do that."[17] As it turned out, with that statement, Pinckney both predicted his own death and explained the cause for it and the ultimate meaning of it.

Although Roof's statements and actions were indisputably extreme, the inventory of racist ideas, anxieties, and aspirations that inspired and enabled him to view his unprovoked killing spree as a justified act of self-defense are routinely aired, accepted, and believed in U.S. society. As *New Yorker* editor David Remnick observes, even though Roof was "a loner" and "a solitary fanatic," he nonetheless "derives his hatreds and obsessions from a history of American racism and a still-existing cultural seedbed of white supremacism."[18] Roof's actions were extraordinary and aberrant, but his views about the intellectual inferiority and deviant culture of Black people are ordinary and commonplace. In 1994, the year that Dylann Roof was born, *The Bell Curve* by Charles Murray and Richard Herrnstein was a best-selling book. It was promoted enthusiastically by the American Enterprise Institute, a lavishly funded pro-corporate think tank. *The Bell Curve* claimed that reported racial differences in IQ scores prove that racial differences are fixed and genetic, that intelligence is inherited, and that poverty, criminality, and welfare dependency stem from inherited genes, not social conditions. A decade earlier, Herrnstein had coauthored a book with James Q. Wilson alleging that propensity for crime is an inherited trait.[19] Thus the credentialed social scientists with doctoral degrees from Harvard (Murray and Herrnstein) and the University of Chicago (Wilson) and the high school dropout Dylann Roof share the same intellectually insupportable understanding of race as a series of biologically inherited capabilities. Of course, the action agenda drawn from these premises by the scholars differs from the ones devised by Dylann Roof. None of the scholars would countenance or condone entering a church and killing nine people. The scholars have stated explicitly and clearly, however, that their findings show that differences between the races are innate, and as a result, no money should be spent and no programs should be devised to equalize opportunities, life chances, and conditions. Dylann Roof destroyed the lives of nine people by firing his gun. The arguments made by Charles Murray, Richard Herrnstein, and James Q. Wilson are used to oppose school desegregation, fair housing practices, affirmative action, culturally sensitive curricula and pedagogies, and expenditures on public health. These arguments serve as crucial forms of justification and excuses for practices that destroy millions of lives. The indirect and inferential racism of Murray, Herrnstein, and Wilson is not *less racist* than the direct and referential racism of Dylann Roof. It is simply *more effectively racist*.

In presenting white people as the subordinate and vulnerable group, Roof drew on the readily available frame of "reverse racism." This concept claims that the tables have been turned, that today the only racism that exists is racism against whites. It portrays any perceived diminution of the settled expectations, privileges, and comforts of whites as a grievous racial injury. As explained in Chapter 1, even though Blacks are discriminated against incessantly, leaving them with less wealth, worse jobs, and shorter lives than whites, whites insist that Blacks profit from unearned preferences while whites suffer unjust discrimination. In fact, what they perceive is merely what Luke Charles Harris aptly describes as diminished overrepresentation. Yet while whites discern no meaningful obstacles in the path of Black progress, they do identify black criminality as a clear and evident reality. When Dylann Roof entered the Emanuel AME Church in Charleston on June 17, 2015, he did not really see the actual members of the Bible study group right in front of his eyes. He saw instead the specter of rampant Black criminality. This is an especially off-kilter perception because the only person in the room that Roof knew for sure had a criminal history was himself. In just the few months prior to the shooting, he had been involved in repeated brushes with the law. Roof was arrested in March 2015 on a misdemeanor charge of drug possession. Another time, he was investigated for loitering in a parked car that contained a forearm grip for an AR-15 semiautomatic rifle. In April 2015, Roof was arrested again, this time for trespassing on the grounds of a mall from which he had been banned previously by security guards because he upset store employees by wearing all-black clothing and repeatedly asking them what they felt were unsettling questions.[20]

Dylann Roof was not alone in taking it upon himself to guard the borders of whiteness. He can be considered an exception, but only in the same way that James Jackson can be thought of as an exception. A twenty-eight-year-old white resident of Baltimore, Jackson traveled to New York in March 2017 with the express intention of stalking and killing Black men. On March 20 he found his prey, killing sixty-six-year-old Timothy Caughman, stabbing him repeatedly with a knife in full view of passers-by on a midtown Manhattan street corner. Jackson justified his plot to murder Black men by declaring his anger at them for "mixing with white women." The grand jury that indicted Jackson for murder and a hate crime proclaimed that "Caughman was killed in furtherance of an act of terrorism . . . intended to intimidate and coerce a civilian population, influence the policy of a unit of government by intimidation and coercion, and affect the conduct of a unit of government by murder, assassination and kidnapping."[21]

Dylann Roof and James Jackson are only aberrations in the way that Jeremy Christian is an aberration. While riding the light rail transit system in Portland, Oregon, on May 26, 2017, Christian observed two women board the train, one of them wearing a Muslim hijab. The thirty-five-year-old white supremacist began yelling at them, proclaiming that all Muslims are criminals. He ordered them to "get off the bus, and get out of the country because you don't pay taxes here." When three passengers tried to calm him down, Christian pulled out a knife and stabbed the peacemakers, killing Ricky John Best and Taliesin Myriddin Namkai Meche, and wounding Micah David-Cole Fischer. Reports indicated that Christian's Facebook page championed the idea that only whites should be allowed to live in the Pacific northwest.[22]

Misogyny as well as racism clearly played a key role in the murders committed by Roof, Jackson, and Christian. After charging Black men with "raping our women," Roof murdered six Black women along with three Black men. Jackson took it upon himself to kill Black men because they transgressed the borders he imagined himself ordained to protect when they "mixed" with white women. Christian could not bear the sight of two women whom he believed to be Muslim riding the same public transit car that was available to him. In these cases, possessive investments in whiteness were also investments in white male patriarchal power. The killers in these cases felt entitled, and even obligated, to commit homicides to suppress imagined threats to the narcissistic grandiosity they attached to their race and gender.

Sean Urbanski is also an aberration. On the night of May 20, 2017, the white twenty-two-year-old University of Maryland kinesiology major encountered Richard Collins III at a campus bus stop. Collins was a twenty-three-year-old Black man, a business administration student from nearby Bowie State University who was visiting friends on the Maryland campus. An ROTC student who had been commissioned as a second lieutenant in the Army, Collins was scheduled to receive his undergraduate degree later that week. Urbanski ordered Collins to "step left if you know what's good for you." When Collins refused, Urbanski stabbed him to death. The white killer belonged to a racist Facebook group that called itself "Alt-Reich Nation." Urbanski had posted on it that he liked a message that read "Trump isn't lying that hispanics are taking this land away and that times are bad." Urbanski amended his "like" of the post with the statement "Uh oh here come the Hispanics saying it was their land first." He also "liked" a post that claimed that leftists are murderers who are "freely attacking our race in the media" by promoting Third World immigration, dispensing white guilt propaganda, and "openly promoting us to breed away," again viewing interracial sex by other people as a mortal threat to his own identity. Another post that drew Urbanski's approval spewed hatred against Muslims in the form of a "joke." It claimed "I got arrested for punching this guy at a New Year's party. When you hear an Arab counting down from ten your instincts kick in."[23] Indulging in online recreational hate against Muslims, antiracist whites, and "Hispanics" likely contributed to a state of mind that authorized the killing of a Black man.

Adam W. Purinton is also an aberration. The fifty-two-year-old navy veteran was asked to leave a bar in Olathe, Kansas, on February 22, 2017, because he was harassing two South Asian men. Purinton charged that their appearance proved they were in the country "illegally." He left the tavern, but returned later carrying a pistol which he used to shoot and kill one of the men and wound the other as well as a bystander who tried to intervene.[24] Like Purinton, Wade Michael Page is another aberration, On August 5, 2012, the forty-year-old former army psychological operations specialist barged into a Sikh temple in Milwaukee carrying a Springfield 9mm semiautomatic handgun. He opened fire, killing six worshippers and wounding another three. Page had previously posed for pictures in front of a Nazi flag, supported a white supremacist heavy metal band, and had long talked about his desire to see whites wage a race war against nonwhite enemies.[25]

Roof, Jackson, Christian, Urbanski, Purinton, and Page were likely all disturbed and deranged at the moments when they became violent, but the logic they followed conformed to a well-worn social script authored by respectable people who possess power and prestige. They followed the script laid out for them and reiterated repeatedly in political discourse and popular culture. On the day that Dylann Roof walked into the Emanuel African Methodist Episcopal Church with the intention of killing Black people, the Confederate flag that he displayed proudly on his website also held a place of honor on the flagpole of the South Carolina state house. It was first placed there in 1962 by the governor of the state as a protest against federal court orders enforcing the *Brown v. Board* school desegregation decision. The act of flying that flag was designed to honor and continue a tradition of violence and vituperation in the service of white supremacy that predates the Confederacy itself. In 1856, Preston Brooks, a member of the House of Representatives from South Carolina staged a brutal and nearly fatal attack on Senator Charles Sumner of Massachusetts on the Senate floor, beating him with a cane in retaliation for a speech Sumner had made two days earlier criticizing slave owners. Broken pieces of the cane used in the beating became valued souvenirs for southern legislators who wore them proudly on neck chains to display support for Brooks. The assailant received hundreds of new canes in the mail from supporters, one of which was inscribed "Hit him again."[26] Some 150 years later, in 2009 when Dylann Roof was fourteen years old, South Carolina Representative Joe Wilson interrupted an address to a joint session of Congress by the first African American president of the United States, Barack Obama, by screaming "You lie!" in response to the president's accurate claim that the Affordable Care Act would not cover undocumented immigrants. Wilson received what he described as hundreds of speaking invitations after his outburst, including dozens from fellow members of Congress. A gun-dealing firm in South Carolina offered for sale AR-15 assault rifles with the words "you lie" engraved on them.[27] As of this writing, a statue still stands on the South Carolina state capitol grounds in Columbia honoring the deeds and values of Ben Tillman, a South Carolinian who led an expedition in 1876 that murdered Blacks attempting to exercise their right to vote; Tillman's name also continues to grace the main dining hall at Clemson University, a public state school.[28] If Dylann Roof believed that he would be celebrated for gunning down Black people, the legislature of his state gave him ample reason for that belief.

If Jeremy Christian, Adam Purinton, and Wade Michael Page wanted justification for their beliefs that they had been deputized to engage in anti-immigrant hate crimes, they had only to look to words spoken by prominent politicians. In 2007, the ranking Republican member (and later the chair) of the Homeland Security Committee of the House of Representatives derided the Islamic faith as a facade for terrorism, declaring that there are too many mosques in the United States—institutions he characterized as nothing more than sources of fervent support for radical versions of the religion.[29] A Kansas legislator "joked" at an official hearing in 2011 that illegal immigrants should be shot down like wild pigs. A month earlier, another Kansas legislator concluded that a college student's "olive complexion" proved that she was an illegal immigrant.[30] Little more than a year after Dylann Roof's rampage, a majority of white voters supported and elected as president the candidate who described Mexican immigrants as "criminals" and "rapists," and who insisted that the religion of Islam "hates us."

In his manifesto, Roof explained that the event that "truly awakened me was the Trayvon Martin case." This case might seem to be an odd provocation for Dylann Roof to cite as the impetus that started him on his path to being the white supremacist executioner of Black churchgoers. George Zimmerman was a twenty-eight-year-old neighborhood watch volunteer in Sanford, Florida, who stalked, shot, and killed a Black youth, seventeen-year-old Trayvon Martin, and got away with it. Although the police officers investigating the scene of the crime recommended that charges be filed against Zimmerman, the white police chief simply accepted the killer's claim that the shooting was in self-defense and did not even order an investigation. Local prosecutors failed to charge Zimmerman with any crime until several months of community protests pressured the state of Florida to intervene and appoint a special prosecutor who then overruled local officials and brought charges against him. The son of a wealthy retired army officer and Virginia magistrate, Zimmerman lied to the court about his assets and ordered his wife to hide them in secret accounts in an effort to secure a lower bail bond. His supporters posted messages online describing Trayvon Martin as a thug and the aggressor in the case, even though Martin was unarmed and simply walking back to his father's home carrying a fruit drink and candy he had purchased at a local store.[31] Zimmerman called a police dispatcher to report that he was watching and pursuing the youth whom he continued to stalk even after being advised by the dispatcher not to follow Martin or try to apprehend him. Zimmerman not only pursued Martin, he started a fight with the youth and killed him by shooting him in the heart.

Zimmerman claimed that he followed the youth because there had been recent robberies in the neighborhood committed by Blacks. In his mind, this rendered Martin an object of suspicion, much in the same way that Dylann Roof connected the Bible study group at the Emanuel AME church with rape and violence. Attorney and legal journalist Lisa Bloom examined Zimmerman's claim to be responding to neighborhood break-ins by Blacks in her book *Suspicion Nation*. Bloom found that, at most, in the fourteen months before George Zimmerman killed Trayvon Martin there were eight burglaries and an estimated thirty-six break-ins at the subdivision where Zimmerman lived. Three were committed or attempted by Blacks in an area where Blacks comprised 20 percent of the residents of the neighborhood and 40 percent of the metropolitan area. Thus, as Bloom concludes, Blacks would have been *less* likely to commit burglaries and break-ins than members of other races. Yet over the years, *all* of the forty-six alarmed phone calls made by Zimmerman to the police concerned what he deemed to be suspicious Black people, including one boy estimated to be between seven and nine years old who was walking alone.[32]

Zimmerman had a gun and Martin was unarmed. Zimmerman was ordered by the police dispatcher not to stalk or confront Martin, but he did so anyway. Zimmerman provoked a fight with Martin and shot and killed him. Yet it took sustained community protests and demonstrations to induce prosecutors to even file any charges against Zimmerman. When they reluctantly charged him with second-degree murder, the prosecutors (not the defense) bizarrely denied there was any racial motive in the killing. The prosecutors picked a jury with no Blacks on it, even though African Americans make up 30 percent of the population of the city of Sanford. The prosecution's refusal to allege any racial motivation on Zimmerman's part prevented any intelligible discussion of his motives. The judge instructed the jury to consider only the moment when Zimmerman and Martin struggled, not the racist stalking by Zimmerman that preceded it. As Carol Anderson notes, the judge's instructions succeeding in "transforming a 17 year-old unarmed kid into a big, scary, black guy while the grown man who stalked him through the neighborhood with a loaded gun becomes the victim."[33]

Zimmerman's case for self-defense rested on his story that when he challenged Martin's presence in the subdivision the youth overpowered him and banged his head repeatedly on the concrete sidewalk. Zimmerman alleged that Martin saw Zimmerman's gun and reached for it, and at that point Zimmerman shot the youth to save his own life. Yet Zimmerman's gun was holstered on the back of his belt covered by his T-shirt and jacket. If Zimmerman was truly lying on his back as he claimed, Martin would have had to have Xray eyes to see through Zimmerman's body to discern a gun holstered inside his pants.[34] Moreover, Martin could not have been banging Zimmerman's head on the sidewalk because the incident took place on wet grass, far from any concrete. Police officers found no blood on the sidewalk on the night of the killing. Zimmerman displayed none of the injuries that having his head pounded on the pavement would produce. Zimmerman's attorney even conceded this in his closing argument to the jury.[35]

The prosecution filed the wrong charges, seated a jury favorable to Zimmerman, and neglected to point out the many contradictions in his story.

For example, Zimmerman claimed that when he shot Martin the youth cried out "You got me." The medical evidence, however, shows that the bullet fragments in his lung mean that Martin would have been unable to speak at all. Zimmerman's claim was a physical impossibility.[36] When Zimmerman was acquitted, the prosecutors who failed to convict him gushed that the system had worked, proclaiming that now the facts were out and everyone could decide for themselves what happened between Zimmerman and Martin, a bizarre understanding of the purpose of a trial from the perspective of the prosecution. If the system "worked" in this case, it worked, as it usually does, on behalf of the possessive investment in whiteness. Attorney and television legal commentator Mark Geragos alleged that prosecutors had become so accustomed to portraying young Black men as thugs and predators that they could not imagine any legal strategy to make Trayvon Martin appear sympathetic and render his death as grievable.[37]

Yet Zimmerman, who did not testify during the trial, was perceived with great sympathy inside and outside the courtroom, even though he had a criminal history and Trayvon Martin did not. In 2005, a seemingly inebriated Zimmerman had scuffled with police officers but got charges of "resisting an officer with violence" dropped by agreeing to take alcohol education classes. That same year his former fiancée accused Zimmerman of domestic violence and secured a restraining order against him.[38] A man who worked with him as a security guard at parties reported that Zimmerman was fired from that job because he lost his temper, picked up a woman, and threw her across the room.[39] When depositions were collected in preparation for the trial, Witness No. 9, a cousin of Zimmerman's, accused him of having molested her when they were children. She stated, "I know George. And I know that he does not like Black people. He would start something. He's a very confrontational person. It's in his blood. Let's just say that."[40]

Zimmerman expressed no remorse and took no responsibility for killing Trayvon Martin, describing the shooting as part of "God's Plans," and asserting therefore that to rethink what had happened would be to second guess God and thus be "almost blasphemous."[41] Zimmerman did apportion some blame, however, not to himself, but to Tracy Martin and Sybrina Fulton, the grief-stricken parents of the teenager he killed. "They didn't raise their son right." Zimmerman proclaimed. Accusing Martin of the very acts that he himself had committed, Zimmerman cited as proof of deficient parenting by Martin and Fulton that their son "attacked a complete stranger and attempted to kill him."[42] Zimmerman had no words of reproach for his parents, the ones who raised a son who graduated from high school in 2001 and started an insurance business that failed in its first year; a son who enrolled in Seminole State College but failed classes in algebra and astronomy, received a grade of D in two criminal justice courses, and was placed on academic probation. Ten years after his high school graduation Zimmerman still had not earned enough academic credits to receive even an associate degree.[43] Zimmerman and his wife had $175,000 in assets at the time of his indictment, a sum that they tried to hide from the court through perjured testimony claiming they were indigent.[44] Members of the jury judging him, however, had no difficulty embracing Zimmerman as one of their own, as a heroic defender of white people and white property. In a televised interview, Juror B37 consistently referred to Zimmerman fondly as "George," claiming that there had been many robberies in the neighborhood. She concluded that Zimmerman "wanted to do good. I think he had good in his heart, he just went overboard."[45]

In describing the terror perpetrated against Black people in Sunflower County in Mississippi in the 1960s, Fannie Lou Hamer quipped that every white man who owned a gun and a dog felt free to act as a police officer.[46] The acquittal of George Zimmerman demonstrated that the same principle is still in force today in many places. Before, during, and after the trial, Zimmerman garnered support from people across the United States. Donors contributed more than $200,000 to his defense fund. One entrepreneur sold gun range targets online featuring a facsimile of Martin wearing a hoodie and holding the fruit drink and candy he was carrying when Zimmerman shot him. The seller told CBS news that all of the targets he had for sale were purchased within two days.[47] Todd Kincannon, who served as the executive director of the South Carolina Republican Party for three months, tweeted that had young Trayvon Martin survived into adulthood he would have had to make his living performing fellatio on gay men to get drug money. Later Kincannon tweeted that "Trayvon Martin was a dangerous thug who needed to be put down like a rabid dog."[48] Online newspaper stories about the shooting and subsequent prosecution provoked a torrent of venomous, vicious, and overtly racist responses celebrating the death of Trayvon Martin and encouraging other vigilantes to emulate Zimmerman's behavior.

One person who followed that encouragement was Dylann Roof. Confronted with a case in which the killer of a Black teenager was at first not charged at all, then charged with a lesser crime than the one he committed, and then acquitted completely by a jury with no Black members in a city that is 30 percent Black, Roof saw only white innocence and injury. "I was in disbelief," he wrote. "At this moment I realized that something was very wrong. How could the news be blowing up the Trayvon Martin case while hundreds of these black on White murders got ignored?" The "hundreds of these black on White murders" that Roof referred to came from a list posted on a white supremacist website. In fact, whites are rarely killed by Blacks. A study that examined thirty years of crime statistics found that 86 percent of white murder victims lost their lives at the hands of other whites.[49] Roof did not check to see whether the instances in which whites were murdered by Blacks stemmed from racial motivations as the killing of Trayvon Martin clearly did.

He did not ask whether the killers got the benefit of police chiefs unwilling to investigate or prosecutors unwilling to press charges. He did not investigate how many Blacks who killed whites were acquitted by a jury who feared the innocent victim more than the guilty accused.[50] None of this mattered to Roof. It was a grievous enough injury that people protested in public against the killing of Trayvon Martin, that they believed that his life was worthwhile and his death was worthy of grief, that they insisted that a killer of a Black youth be brought to justice. This was the affront to whiteness that started Roof on his path to massacre black men and women as they sat praying in church.

The Tip of the Iceberg

The seemingly individual, isolated, and aberrant racism displayed by Dylann Roof in the killings at the Emanuel African Methodist Episcopal Church in Charleston is like the tip of an iceberg, the part that is visible because it rises above the surface of the ocean. It is difficult to *not see* the tips of icebergs. Ship captains are well advised to steer clear of them. But even more dangerous than the tip is the part that is harder *to see*, the part of the iceberg that is below the waterline, that although invisible is even more dangerous.[51] The Charleston killings loom large, like the tip of an iceberg, and justifiably so. But below the surface, out of sight—and too often out of mind—the even deadlier pervasive presence of white supremacy continues to poison our shared social life. We should not, and indeed cannot, ignore the overt racist ideas and actions of Dylann Roof. But we leave ourselves in great danger for the future if we attend only to the tip of the iceberg, to overt personal racism, and ignore the submerged but ever so real bottom of the iceberg, the social practices, patterns, processes, and institutions that make up structural racism.

Acts of overt racial violence and the cycle of suffering and slow death that hovers over Black communities are structural as well as individual. As a statement issued by the Rainbow Push Coalition declared, the church shootings in Charleston provoked justified outrage and condemnation, but there has never been concomitant concern over the fact that African Americans are first in infant mortality, first in unemployment, first in incarceration; have the shortest life expectancies; suffer disproportionately from heart disease, liver disease, diabetes and HIV/AIDS; attend segregated schools, live in segregated neighborhoods, and face relentless discrimination in access to bank loans and health care.[52] Since 1950, Blacks have been twice as likely as whites to be unemployed. The highest level of unemployment among whites between 1972 and 2012 was 8.8 percent in 2010. In that same year, the Black unemployment rate was 16.3 percent. During this entire span between 1972 and 2012, the *highest* instance of white unemployment in one year was 2.4 percentage points *lower* than the *average* rate of Black unemployment over the entire forty years.[53]

Gilbert Gee and Chandra Ford proposed the iceberg metaphor as a way of understanding structural racism which they define as the interaction of large systems, forces, ideologies, institutions, and processes that generate and reinforce unequal conditions among different racial groups.[54] The sudden violence perpetrated in the Charleston shootings is as visible and evident as the tip of an iceberg. But there is a less visible slow violence at work in Charleston and elsewhere that is even more deadly because it is structural and systemic.[55] If Dylann Roof had herded 83,000 Black people into a stadium on New Year's Day and gunned them down one by one, everyone would have noticed. But almost no one notices that more than 83,000 Black people are estimated to die prematurely every year because of what the surgeon general of the United States has described as the "pervasive inequalities in America's social, economic and health care systems."[56] At birth, Blacks can expect to live nearly five years fewer than whites. The rate of infant mortality among Blacks is more than twice as high as for whites. Research reveals that even when income and insurance status are corrected for, Blacks have shorter life spans and higher rates than whites of disease, low weight births, infant mortality, and premature adult deaths.[57]

Dylann Roof's counterfactual formulation of Black criminality and white innocence was not merely a personal delusion on his part. It is an equation that has been insistently asserted and widely believed in the instance after instance when innocent and unarmed Black people have been killed by whites. The Charleston shootings produced the deaths of nine people. Yet the Blackness of the victims marked them as vulnerable to premature death long before Dylann Roof entered their house of worship. The notion of using the protection of white interests as a justification for killing Black men and women did not originate with Dylann Roof. It has a long history in U.S. law and social practice and was demonstrated dramatically in the years preceding the Charleston shooting by the criminal justice system's well publicized and disgraceful failures to investigate and fully prosecute police killings of unarmed "suspects" Oscar Grant in Oakland, Eric Garner in New York City, Tamir Rice in Cleveland, Michael Brown in Ferguson, and Freddie Gray in Baltimore. This violence is not directed solely against Black men. Racial violence has never been focused on males alone. Although rarely foregrounded in popular depictions of police brutality, Black women today are beaten, raped, and killed by police officers. In 2015 alone, the year of the Charleston massacre, police officers unjustly killed Alexia Christian, Meagan Hockaday, Mya Hall, Janisha Fonville, and Natasha McKenna. In the previous year, Gabriella Nevarez, Aura Rosser, Michelle Cusseaux, and Tanisha Anderson were killed by law enforcement officers. Chicago police detective Dante Servin shot and killed twenty-two-year-old Rekia Boyd in 2012. In that case, Cook County prosecutors took two years to bring any charges at all, then filed the wrong charge (deliberately under-charging Servin with involuntary manslaughter instead of first-degree murder) in a way that compelled the judge to dismiss the case.[58] In May 2012, the same prosecutor who failed to get George Zimmerman convicted for killing Trayvon Martin won the conviction of Marissa Alexander, a thirty-one-year-old Black woman with no previous record of convictions or even arrests, for aggravated assault with a deadly weapon. Alexander fired a warning shot in self-defense in 2010 because her spouse who had previously abused her was threatening her at the time. The bullet hit a wall and harmed no one, but the jury deliberated for only twelve minutes before finding her guilty, refusing the very self-defense claims that Zimmerman had raised fraudulently but successfully. Alexander was sentenced to twenty years in prison.[59] In 2010, Detroit police officer Joseph Weekly shot and killed seven-year-old Aiyana Stanley-Jones as she slept in her grandmother's home. The officer claimed his gun went off accidentally during a struggle with the girl's grandmother Mertilla Jones. The grandmother said she was reaching out to protect Aiyana. Another officer confirmed Jones's story and testified that there was no struggle. Weekly was cleared of all charges, however, and returned to work.[60] In 2008, a SWAT team in Lima, Ohio, searching for drugs broke into a rented house occupied by Tarika Wilson. Just moments after the officers entered the dwelling they opened fire, killing the unarmed twenty-six-year-old mother of six children and wounding her fourteen-month-old son. One of Wilson's neighbors, Junior Cook, commented, "The cops in Lima, they is racist like no tomorrow. Why else would you shoot a mother with a baby in her arms?"[61]

In 2014, family members called the police to help them tend to thirty-seven-year-old Tanisha Anderson who kept trying to leave the house clad only in her nightgown. Officers dragged her from the home and slammed her face down onto the pavement. During the incident, Anderson cried out for her mother and recited the Lord's Prayer. One officer placed his knee on her back and put his full body weight on her. She stopped breathing and died of cardiopulmonary arrest. The coroner ruled the death a homicide caused by physical restraint in a prone position and agitation that exacerbated her ischemic heart disease and bipolar disorder.[62] Yet the officers involved were not prosecuted for their actions, even though the city paid a settlement of more than $2 million dollars to Anderson's family. In 2015, Sandra Bland was stopped while driving down a street in Waller County, Texas, by a state trooper for allegedly failing to use her turn signal. When she refused to extinguish the cigarette she was smoking, Officer Brian Encina drew his taser and attempted to pull her from the vehicle. In the process he slammed her head against the ground. Three days later she was found dead in her jail cell. County authorities claimed she committed suicide, an allegation that Bland's friends and relatives rejected. Authorities admitted no culpability or responsibility connected to Bland's death, but Officer Encina was later fired and the county agreed to pay a settlement of $1.9 million to Bland's family and to reform jail practices so that the treatment of prisoners could be better monitored.[63]

The deaths of Bland and Anderson occurred within a context of decades of relentless demonization of Black women as deviant, defiant, and dysfunctional. Punitive policies aimed at the poor have long been fueled by phobic fantasies about the alleged misbehavior of nonwhite women. Relentless racially inflected representations of blaming and shaming target the "underclass," immigrants, welfare recipients, the unhoused, inner city youths, single mothers, religious minorities, and people perceived to have non-normative sexual identities.[64] As Dorothy Roberts argues, punishing Black mothers for the poverty of their children provides this system with its central legitimizing trope.[65] These fantasies occlude the intersectional vulnerabilities that Black women face from race and gender discrimination and exploitation. Their economic marginality is coupled with domestic centrality. Low wages keep them from securing shelter, much less accumulating assets. Yet the domestic centrality imposed on them by sexist norms leaves them with the primary responsibility for raising children and the primary blame for not performing miracles in the face of all that deprivation. They are asked to do the most but are given the least resources.[66]

Like Black men, Black women suffer from racist racial profiling, surveillance, and harassment that produce disproportionate numbers of police stops, searches, arrests, charges, convictions, and punishments. In addition, their intersectional identities as women *and* as Blacks make them face gender-specific forms of racialized police mistreatment such as sexual assault, abuse for being pregnant, and additional profiling and abuse if they are lesbian, bisexual, or transgender, or if they have a gender nonconforming appearance or identity. Fully half of the violent acts reported by transgender women in San Francisco in 2000 were committed by police or private security officers. In 2008, law enforcement officers accounted for the third-largest category of perpetrators of violence against lesbian, gay, bisexual, and transgender people.[67] An investigation by reporters affiliated with the Associated Press revealed that more than 500 police officers from forty-one states lost their law enforcement licenses due to sexual assault, but that only a much smaller number faced criminal charges.[68]

Oklahoma City police officer Daniel Holtzclaw viewed his badge and gun as a license to commit multiple sexual assaults against Black women. Holtzclaw routinely and repeatedly molested the Black women he stopped. He ordered women to lift their shirts and open their pants ostensibly to prove they were not carrying drugs.[69] Thirteen women between the ages of seventeen and fifty-seven came forward to testify that between December 2013 and June 2014, Holtzclaw groped them, forced them to have oral sex, and raped them. He warned victims that they would have to perform oral sex on him to avoid going to jail. He asked two of his victims if they had ever performed fellatio before on a white penis.[70] The officer's defense attorney attempted to use the specter of Black criminality to try to discredit the complaints and excuse the officer's actions. Sharing and appealing to the presumption of Black criminality at the core of Dylann Roof's defense of his own crimes, Officer Holtzclaw and his defense attorneys claimed that the words of his accusers could not be trusted because they were poor, had present or prior drug dependency, and had had previous contact with the criminal justice system. Yet that is precisely why Holtzclaw selected them as the victims of his predatory behavior. "He didn't choose C.E.O.s or soccer moms; he chose women he could count on not telling what he was doing," the prosecutor explained in closing arguments, and if they did tell "he counted on the fact that no one would believe them and no one would care."[71] This strategy almost worked, as the jury acquitted him of eighteen counts of assault against five of the women. Most observers agree that the prosecution secured convictions on the remaining counts (half of what he had been charged with) largely because of the testimony of one grandmother who had no criminal record. Had Holtzclaw not picked the "wrong" kind of victim in the jury's eyes, he might have gotten away with all of his assaults.[72] Moreover, the officer's conviction left unresolved the question of how he had been able to perpetrate these deeds for so long. "What about his supervisors?" asked Robert Muhammad of the Nation of Islam; "where are the checks and balances, the audit system that shows accountability for our police and for our tax dollars?"[73]

It is accurate to say that Black men are killed by police officers without due cause in disproportionate numbers. It is accurate to say that deeply ingrained stereotypes about Black men lead police officers to treat them violently. It is not accurate, however, to view police shootings of Black civilians as solely about Black masculinity. Many of the very depictions used to demonize Black men are also deployed against Black women. The fates of men and women who are Black are linked. What happens to one, affects the other. Black women suffer when Black men are killed. Black men suffer when Black women are killed. To focus on racism as mainly an injury to Black manhood is an old and deceptive trick deployed by the oppressors of Black people to divide and conquer and divert attention away from the intersectional qualities of racism and sexism. It protects the privileges of white men by encouraging Black men to make gains at the expense of Black women instead of joining together with them to win advances that benefit all. Focusing only on Black masculinity treats people as isolated and atomized individuals, not recognizing that Black survival, struggle, and success have always depended on mutuality, solidarity, and empowered collaboration. To would-be perpetrators of Black genocide, there are no collateral victims. Every Black body is a threat; every dead one is one step closer to their ultimate goal. Despite unending protestations that racism is provoked by the deficient demeanor, desires, behavior, or beliefs of members of the targeted group, the nature of racial ascription is collective. As sociologist Albert Memmi observes, all members of the group are victimized by it; every single one has already been found "guilty without exception."[74]

Roof's declarations that Black people "must go" because they are "taking over our country" and "raping our women," revealed a poisonous, but not a new or unusual link between racism and sexism. Patriarchy has always been a foundational element in racial terrorism and racial subordination. Roof's fear-laden fantasies about Black men raping white women, about violent Black criminality, about the loss of what he described as "our country" (by which he meant the country of white people, those whose ancestors immigrated to the United States from Europe) are not the personal, private, or parochial perceptions of Dylann Roof as an individual. Things that he thought and said crudely are articulated constantly, if more circumspectly, by politicians, pundits, and public policy experts. Throughout society, everyday decisions about who deserves government protection and who merits government punishment, about which neighborhoods will be filled with amenities and opportunities and which neighborhoods will be plagued with nuisances and hazards, about who gets policed and who the police protect all rest on long-standing practices of demonizing and denigrating nonwhite people. These decisions, grounded in ideologies of a racial threat, position white separation from—and domination over—Blacks and other people of color as rational choices. A familiar set of stories, justifications, and excuses are deployed relentlessly to diminish the dignity and occlude the exploitation of peoples designated as "other." In the case of the Charleston shootings, they provided the killer with justification for snuffing out the lives of nine people simply because they were Black. These are not yesterday's problems. Dylann Roof was born in 1994. He committed his act of racial terrorism as a result of his thorough immersion in ideas and images of our time, more than fifty years after the supposed end of legally mandated white supremacy.

Dylann Roof felt justified in killing African Americans worshipping in a church that their enslaved ancestors established in this country in 1818. He saw them taking over "our" country, not continuing to live in theirs, or perhaps more accurately jointly occupying land stolen from its rightful Indigenous owners. The "country" Roof had in mind is not the constitutional democracy of the United States with its Thirteenth, Fourteenth, and Fifteenth amendments; not the country of Anna Julia Cooper and Martin Luther King, Jr.; not the nation for which soldiers of all races bled and died in wars, but rather a nation of the imagination that is the sole possession of white people. That is why Roof associated himself with other nations that he imagined to be purer and better versions of America. Roof possessed and displayed the flags of settler colonialist Rhodesia and apartheid South Africa as well as the Confederacy. He decorated his website with images of the numerical symbol 1488; this represents Nazism through the number 14, which for white supremacists references the slogan "we must secure the existence of our people and a future for white children," and the number 88, which connotes "Heil Hitler" because H is the eighth letter of the alphabet.[75] Although presenting himself and all other whites as the victims of Black barbarism, it is clear that Roof was driven by aspirations to be barbaric himself, and to get away with it. The whiteness of the United States, like his own personal identity as a white person, may have seemed to Roof to be a fact of nature and an essential part of his imagination of national citizenship and national membership. Yet this whiteness of the nation and of its people are artificial historical constructs brought into existence through intended genocidal wars against the indigenous inhabitants of the nation; the capture, conveyance, and control over enslaved Africans forced to labor for whites; the conquest and appropriation of Mexican lands and the subordination and suppression of the people living on them; and the importation of Asian labor coupled with the absolute prohibition of naturalized citizenship for them. Expressly racist laws like the 1790 Naturalization Act that restricted naturalized citizenship to whites and the laws of many states banning intermarriage between whites and people of color deployed the full powers of the state to produce and protect the privileges and demographic power of whites. Dylann Roof's commonsense perceptions about who should be included and who should be excluded, his presumption that he is both fit and entitled to decide who is fit or unfit for freedom are products of this history. As Ian Haney Lopez demonstrates, the provision of the 1790 Naturalization Act reserving naturalized citizenship to whites, the judicial opinions that interpreted the law as denying naturalization to South Asian and East Asian immigrants, and laws against miscegenation altered the literal complexion of the nation in configuring the physical features of its inhabitants. Dylann Roof and the author and readers of this book might look very different if immigration law had not limited naturalized citizenship to whites and anti-miscegenation laws had not banned interracial marriage. Even after these laws and interpretations were no longer utilized, "the pool of physical features" subsequently present in the nation continued to be reflections of those laws and interpretations.[76] Yet rather than recognizing the continuing costs of the rationales used to justify Indigenous dispossession, slavery, segregation, and immigrant exclusion, white-minded people mired in the equation of the nation with its whiteness and anxious about the white fragility, failure, and fear experienced by Dylann Roof and George Zimmerman have engaged in a cycle of vicious and vile acts of hatred and violence. Although not identical to the possessive investments in anti-Black whiteness manifest in the deeds and words of Dylann Roof and George Zimmerman, anti-immigrant whiteness relies on similar appeals to white innocence, white injury, and white indignation.

Playing the White Card

For more than a decade, Tim Donnelly ran a small business out of the garage of his house in Twin Peaks, California. His firm produced screws for the plastic injection-molding industry. The enterprise had been faltering for years. In 2010, Donnelly was able to report earnings of more than $10,000 from only one customer. He dissolved the business in 2011, leaving $3,000 in unpaid state taxes.[77] Donnelly did not attribute the collapse of his enterprise to the inability of his small business to compete with larger firms for customers and capital. He did not fault his own business plan, management structure, effort, or imagination. Tim Donnelly blamed the government. He alleged that environmental regulations and taxes drove his customers out of the state or out of business. But soon he found a more useful excuse and target. Immigrants, he alleged, were the source of the problems that he faced in his business and the cause of the faltering economy of California.

In 2005, Donnelly placed a rambling manifesto online alleging that the costs of immigration created overcrowded school classrooms and hospital emergency rooms and caused municipal service providers to be on the verge of bankruptcy. He charged that immigration to the United States from Mexico brought with it "rampant illiteracy, drug resistant tuberculosis, drug smugglers, human smugglers, rapists and murderers."[78] In fact, immigrants are significantly healthier than the native-born population, commit far fewer crimes, and serve as an economic boon to consumers who pay lower prices for goods and services because of their low wage labor. The presence of immigrants in communities often recapitalizes areas suffering from disinvestment.[79] The fiscal crisis of public agencies in California and other states stemmed from state tax policies that shifted the costs of government to smaller and smaller local entities, placing them in competition with each other and enabling wealthy districts to hoard resources at the expense of those less well off.[80] Yet even with his business in crisis, Donnelly became so committed to the idea of immigration as the cause of his woes that he decided to neglect that very business and devote his time, imagination, and energy to starting his own chapter of the anti-immigrant Minutemen organization. Donnelly asked supporters to join him at an encampment he set up on the Mexican border, some 180 miles from his home. As the media descended on the site to interview him, Donnelly enjoyed the attention and believed he was skilled in talking to reporters. He phoned his wife and told her enthusiastically, "I don't know how you do this, but I want to talk for a living."[81]

Donnelly's savings were used up by 2010. He decided to run for a position in the state assembly, telling his family, "It was either win the election or go homeless."[82] Without an appeal to the possessive investment in whiteness Donnelly would not have had much to offer as a candidate. He had dropped out of college after a freshman year that included being arrested for stealing a stereo, an incident he characterized as a drunken escapade.[83] His business failure had brought his family to the brink of ruin. He made the decision to cancel his family's health insurance because he believed it was more important to spend what little money they had left on tuition to send the children to a private school.[84] Yet by presenting himself as an opponent of illegal immigration and as a protector of white women against sexually predatory Mexicans, and by predicting that unless immigration from Mexico was stopped, 80 percent of the population of California would be "illegal aliens" within a decade, Donnelly was elected to the assembly from a mostly white, politically conservative district. In the midst of the mortgage foreclosure crisis caused by the predatory and fraudulent conduct of brokers and bankers, he provided his constituency with an explanation for the crisis that protected the historical privileges of white property and power by diverting anger about economic insecurity against Mexican immigrants.

In building his constituency, Donnelly referred repeatedly to his frustration with an incident that took place in 2005. A ten-year-old boy, described in the press as Latino, reportedly made verbal sexual overtures to a white girl in a local school. Donnelly demanded that the boy and his family be deported, even though he had no proof that any of them were undocumented and was evidently not aware that school administrators do not have the legal authority to deport anyone. Donnelly began posting pieces on his website embellishing the story, claiming the boy had molested and threatened eleven girls. He then charged that Muslim extremists were working to convert Mexican immigrants to Islam and unleash them to make war on the United States. Donnelly declared that the slaveholding Confederacy during the Civil War fought heroically on behalf of individual liberty. For good measure, he added that gay people represent the death knell for America.[85]

Donnelly presented himself as a defender of law and order, yet he displayed only a tenuous understanding of the law. He joined an organization committed to ending the practice that anyone born in the United States is automatically a U.S. citizen, even though that right comes directly from judicial interpretations of the Fourteenth Amendment to the Constitution, a document that conservatives generally purport to honor. When one of his friends encountered a group of Mexican men standing in the parking lot of a mini-mart in hopes of picking up day labor jobs, Donnelly complained to the sheriff's department and the Immigration and Customs Enforcement Bureau that these "suspected illegal aliens" should be deported. He vowed to boycott the store when they were not. Yet he treated his own actual law-breaking more casually. In January 2012, Donnelly was caught attempting to board an airplane with a handgun and an ammunition magazine with five additional rounds in his carry-on luggage. The gun was also unregistered in violation of California law. Donnelly explained "he never got around" to registering the weapon, presumably just as he never "got around" to purchasing health insurance for his family or paying his $3,000 tax bill. Moreover, Donnelly protested that he needed to carry the weapon and ammunition onto the airplane, that he had good reason to break the law because purportedly he had been threatened by "illegal aliens."[86]

It is not a disgrace to run a business that fails. It is not a disgrace to be so deeply in debt that one cannot pay taxes. It is not a disgrace to have stolen one stereo in college or to have dropped out after the freshman year. It is not a disgrace to be fined and sentenced to probation for carrying an unregistered firearm onto an airplane. But it is disgraceful conduct to blame one's own personal fragility and failure on other people; to not be responsible or accountable for one's own actions but instead to demonize hard-working, law-abiding immigrants as criminals, terrorists, and sexual predators; to portray oneself as particularly victimized by men standing in a parking lot looking for work, by sick people who come to emergency rooms, and by parents who send their children to a public school. For Tim Donnelly, the possessive investment in whiteness is a get-out-of-accountability-for-free card, a way to secure legitimacy and to excuse and justify personal embarrassments.

Like Dylann Roof and George Zimmerman, Tim Donnelly presents himself as the defender of normative whiteness against nonwhite deviance. He claimed a woman who lived near the border told him that at night she could hear the screams of women being raped by smugglers. Later he changed his account, claiming that he had heard these cries personally, adding they were something he would never forget. He deflected charges that his views reflect racism by pointing to the fact that his wife is a Filipina. Yet he almost immediately gestured again to the 2005 incident involving the ten-year-old school boy, asserting, "I am proud to be a 'racist' if the definition of racist means that you can tolerate being called names in order to protect children from sexual predators."[87]

Yet if Donnelly had a genuine interest in protecting children from sexual predators, he need only have looked no further than the behavior of his Minuteman comrade Chris Simcox. While working as a kindergarten teacher in a private school in the Los Angeles area at the turn of the millennium, Simcox's marriage started to dissolve. His threatening behavior caused his wife to ask the authorities to issue a restraining order against him. On the evening after the September 11, 2001, attacks on the World Trade Center and the Pentagon, Simcox informed his wife by voice mail that he would not speak to their son again until she could recite the preamble to the Constitution. "I am dead serious," he insisted; "that's how much of an American I am." Two days later he left another message on her answering machine vowing that the next time he saw their son he would begin teaching the boy the art of protecting himself with weapons, noting, "I have more than a few weapons."[88]

Simcox later related that the events of 9/11 so disturbed and angered him that he felt he had to get away. He left his family and his job to go camping for forty days in a national park in Arizona. While on that trip he claims to have encountered five groups of "paramilitary drug dealers." He claims he informed the park authorities about this, but when they appeared unconvinced and unconcerned with what he told them, Simcox had an epiphany. He decided to start Civil Homeland Defense, a citizen's group purporting to protect the borders of the United States from this "illegal invasion."[89]

In 2004, Simcox collaborated with Orange County resident and failed accountant Jim Gilchrist to form what they named the Minuteman Project. Gilchrist had been forced to let his license as an accountant expire in 1993 because he declared personal bankruptcy. That declaration enabled him to avoid paying $550,000 he owed to forty-seven creditors. One decade later, however, he presented himself as a fiscal expert, attributing municipal bankruptcies to immigrants, charging that hospitals and school districts were being ruined financially by the demands placed on them for services by the undocumented.[90] When more than 3 million immigrants and their supporters mobilized to protest proposed anti-immigrant legislation in Congress (HR 4437), Gilchrist argued that the appearance of Mexican flags carried by some of the protestors amounted to "the next thing to foreign insurrection." He claimed that if Congress passed immigration laws that regularized the legal status of undocumented workers already in the country, it would cause an insurrection from his side. "I will not promote violence in resolving this," Gilchrist announced, "but I will not stop others who might pursue that."[91]

Both Gilchrist and Simcox were accused of financial mismanagement by other members of the Minutemen. Dissidents complained that Simcox refused to provide an accounting of how the $1.6 million in donations the group collected was spent. Food and resources promised to local chapters did not arrive. Simcox provided no accounting statements about the group's sales of caps, wristbands, bumper stickers, license plate holders, T-shirts, dog tags, and figurines. Simcox contended that he received no salary from the organization but insisted that how he earned his living was "no one's business." He pleaded poverty, complaining that even after selling his life story for a movie "that will soon go into production" he had just enough money to keep himself solvent. He warned that if he did not receive a salary soon from the organization, "it will be necessary for me to leave the organization and return to teaching—or I may need to go get a job at Wal-Mart or Home Depot."[92] In this formulation, teaching or selling and stocking goods in stores are not honorable labors that deserve dignity but rather shameful emblems of fragility and failure. For his part, Gilchrist was fired by the Project's board of directors who took control of the group's website and bank account in 2007. They claimed that as much as $750,000 was missing from the organization.[93]

Simcox went on to found the Minutemen Civil Defense Corps along with J. T. Ready, a man who had been convicted of aggravated assault and criminal mischief as a teenager and was court martialed twice for theft, assault, failure to follow orders, and unauthorized absences while serving in the Marine Corps.[94] In 2012, Ready shot and killed his girlfriend and her daughter, her daughter's partner, and their infant daughter, before committing suicide.[95] Simcox had his own new problems with the law as well. In 2010, a magistrate in superior court in Phoenix issued a protection order barring Simcox from any contact with his wife and children because he had brandished a loaded handgun in front of them for six hours, vowing to kill them and any police personnel who came to their aid. Two former wives had previously accused him of domestic violence.[96]

In 2016, Chris Simcox was convicted of two counts of molesting a five-year-old girl who was a friend of his six-year-old daughter, and of one count of furnishing obscene materials to a minor. He was acquitted of an additional charge of sexual conduct with a minor. During the trial, his three daughters testified against Simcox. One of them was an adult daughter from a previous marriage who testified that when she was young Simcox had molested her on three different occasions. He was sentenced to nineteen and a half years in prison for his crimes, temporarily removing him from his fight against migrant "illegality."[97]

Racism as a Sense of Group Position

Not every anti-immigrant nativist is a swindler, sexual predator, or sociopath, although the fact that some prominent and popular ones have been should be cause for concern. Much more important than the personal character flaws of individuals, however, are the ways in which playing the white card offers opportunities for attention, resources, and power unavailable by other means. It is not that racism is produced by personal dysfunction but rather that dysfunction often gets channeled in racist directions because the reward structures, discourses, and cultural imaginaries of the dominant society encourage people who are fragile, fearful, and flirting with failure to direct their anger and aggression toward racist ends. The possessive investment in whiteness enables a petty criminal like Dylann Roof to imagine himself as a defender of white normativity against Black criminal deviance. Killing Trayvon Martin transforms George Zimmerman from a failed student, a failed husband, and a failed insurance broker into a national hero celebrated in online blogs, provided with large sums of money by supporters, and acquitted by a jury for the killing he committed. The possessive investment in whiteness provides excuses and justifications for the business failures and economic anxieties of Tim Donnelly and Jim Gilchrist, and it motivates their followers to cast votes to elect them to legislative offices. Prominence in the anti-immigrant movement masked, excused, and perhaps exacerbated the criminal impulses and actions of J. T. Ready and Chris Simcox.

Donnelly, Simcox, Gilchrist, and Ready can be depicted as extremists, as exceptions much in the manner that Dylann Roof, George Zimmerman, James Jackson, Jeremy Christian, Sean Urbanski, Adam Purinton, and Wade Michael Page can be portrayed as exceptions. Yet while the claims and conduct of these malefactors are indeed extraordinary, their basic ideas about the possessive investment in whiteness are ordinary and omnipresent, endorsed by economic, political, and academic elites at the highest level. One of the conceits of whiteness (in both senses of the word conceit) has been to attribute violent and vulgar white racism exclusively to the working class or to poorly socialized members of the middle class. Yet Dylann Roof's father is a building contractor who incorporated two businesses and purchased a home in the Florida Keys for more than $400,000 in 2007.[98] His friend Joey Meek reported that both of Roof's parents had houses with swimming pools and that they gave their son everything he wanted.[99] George Zimmerman's father was a career military officer and a retired magistrate judge. Donnelly, Gilchrist, and Simcox were all college graduates, business owners, and political figures with significant support inside the Republican Party. They derived their ideas and attitudes not from harsh experience with poverty and unemployment but from the discourses they encountered continuously at colleges and country clubs, in advertising and entertainment, from bankers and broadcasters, from political pundits and preachers. The memes of Black deviance and dysfunction and of immigrant indolence and dependency did not originate with them but instead came to them as clearly marked cues about proper perspectives and attitudes from credentialed representatives of many of the most significant institutions in U.S. society. As Herbert Blumer established in a path-breaking 1958 article on race relations, racism functions to establish and protect a collective sense of group position among whites. Being part of the dominant group creates an expectation "of being entitled to either exclusive or prior rights in many important areas of life."[100] From Blumer's perspective, when people manifest racist behavior, it is not really the imputed misbehavior and moral deficiency of the subordinate group that motivates them but rather their fear of competition that makes them believe they may lose what they have. These fears are most likely to be activated in times of crisis, especially when a major event compels people who profit from their racial status to think about and respond to the aspirations and actions of subordinate racial groups.[101]

Big events often trigger racist responses. The Savings and Loan Crisis of the 1980s, the 1992 Los Angeles rebellion following the acquittal of the officers who beat Rodney King, the attacks of 9/11, the economic collapse of 2008, and the election of Barack Obama were all major events that placed racial difference at the center of public consciousness. These kinds of big events do not necessarily have to produce paroxysms of racial enmity, Blumer declares. Yet they result in that unhappy outcome when "intellectual and social elites, public figures of prominence, and leaders of powerful organizations" become vocal exponents of the threat to the dominant group allegedly posed by members of the subordinated group.

Elites in U.S. society have behaved in the way that Blumer predicted would lead to racial antagonism. When Dylann Roof conceived of Black churchgoers as murderers and rapists, while George Zimmerman claimed that Trayvon Martin's mother and father had been deficient parents, their formulations resonated with the view of Black life as a tangle of pathology and the Black family's weaknesses as the source of Black poverty articulated in a report by political scientist Daniel Patrick Moynihan initially as a member of the presidential administration teams of Democrat Lyndon Johnson and Republican Richard Nixon, and later as the senator from New York elected on the Democratic Party line.[102] Moynihan received undergraduate and graduate degrees from Tufts University and secured a faculty position at Harvard. It was not the fringe members of the Republican Party like Tim Donnelly, Jim Gilchrist, and Chris Simcox who initially identified immigrants as the cause of white people's problems, but rather Pete Wilson who as governor of California promoted the cruel nativist Proposition 187 as the key to his campaigns for reelection as governor and as a competitor for his party's presidential nomination.[103] Wilson received his undergraduate degree from Yale and his law degree from the University of California, Berkeley. It was not the Minutemen who came up with the idea that the 1964 Civil Rights Act, the 1965 Voting Rights Act, and the Immigration and Nationality Act of 1965 were based on unwarranted feelings of guilt and sympathy toward minorities that threatened to erode the white Anglo-Saxon Protestant essence of national identity. The view of Mexican people and Mexican culture as innately "un-American" threats to the racial and religious homogeneity of the nation flowed from the pen of Samuel P. Huntington in his 2004 book *Who Are We? The Challenges to America's National Identity*.[104] Huntington received his B.A. from Yale, his M.A. from the University of Chicago, and his Ph.D. from Harvard. He taught at Harvard and Columbia and served in the administrations of Democratic presidents Lyndon Johnson and Jimmy Carter. During the past three decades, presidents from both political parties, all of them graduates of elite educational institutions, have relied on these race-bound ideas and arguments by intellectuals. From President Clinton's decisions to implement Operation Gatekeeper, to increase mass incarceration, and to slash the social safety net, to President Bush's racial and religious profiling and abandonment of due process after 9/11, to Barack Obama's timid silence about racial justice but recurrent sermons chastising the behavior of Black families while breaking up families himself through even more deportations than the Bush administration executed, both Republicans and Democrats and liberals and conservatives have pandered to the possessive investment in whiteness.

In 2013, the right-wing Heritage Foundation released a report that purported to document the enormous economic damage done to the U.S. economy by the presence of undocumented immigrants.[105] Ridiculed in *The Economist* as "an abysmally rigged study," the piece was coauthored by Jason Richwine, whose Ph.D. dissertation at Harvard had contended that "Hispanics" innately possess less intelligence than whites. Devastating critiques of Richwine's shoddy scholarship in his dissertation caused the Heritage Foundation to dissociate itself from the subsequent report. Richwine and his supporters complained that he was the victim of political correctness run amok, that he was being "punished" for proclaiming openly what they presumed others already "knew," that people who are Latinx are innately inferior to whites. It did not matter that no other scholar had cited Richwine's dissertation in the four years it had been available or that he was never able to convert any of it into an accepted peer-reviewed publication. His "heroic" individualism was evident to himself and his supporters simply *because* his conclusions were racist.[106] These claims, as W. W. Houston argues, are smoke screens designed to hide "the repugnant prejudice exposed by the shoddiness of his work."[107] That is the way the possessive investment in whiteness does its work.

Not all of the social scientists and humanists working in elite research universities agree with the claims of Moynihan, Huntington, and Richwine. They bemoan the popularity of these frequently disproved and discredited scholarly arguments among police chiefs, politicians, and policy makers, among journalists, judges, and juries. Yet it is no accident that academic inquiry produces such useful legitimating rationales for dominant interests. As historian Craig Wilder demonstrates, most of the elite academic colleges and universities in the United States came into existence originally through the profits made from Indigenous dispossession and slavery. The patrons who established Harvard, Yale, Princeton, Brown, Dartmouth, and other elite academic institutions were settler colonialists, slave owners, and slave traders. The schools they established were set up to serve the interests of the possessive investment in whiteness. "The academy never stood apart from American slavery," Wilder explains; "in fact, it stood beside church and state as the third pillar of a civilization built on bondage."[108] A great deal of good scholarship that serves the needs of social justice is conducted today within these very institutions because of decades of contestation, struggle, and administrative initiatives such as affirmative action. Yet it is the ideas and arguments that are structured in dominance that pervade public policy, both because their authors receive massive subsidies and support from corporate-dominated funders and also because principled investigators willing to interrogate racism's intellectual excuses and justifications have not reckoned fully with the ways in which past complicity with racial regimes of subordination still shapes the questions that are asked and answered and the methods that are validated in academic research.

Whether they are actually white or not, people who are whiteness-minded are trapped by its possessive investments. As individuals they may despise the overt racists in their midst or they may admire them. Regardless of their personal positions, however, they remain cathected to the possessive investment's premises and presumptions. Their commitments are often so deep because they cannot imagine what their identities would be like without the anchor of whiteness to provide the illusion of safety, stability, and security needed to fend off fragility and fear of failure. Cultural theorist Lauren Berlant explains how attachments "to compromised positions of possibility" produce a kind of "cruel optimism." Investing in whiteness means investing in fantasies of fulfilled selfhood that reside outside the self. A false subject needs a false object. People who do not know or like "who they are" crave degraded depictions of "who they are not," depictions that are often simply projections of what they despise or fear most in themselves. They become dependent on what Berlant describes as the continuity of form. Repeated invocations of white vanity and repeated condemnations of the imputed inhumanity of nonwhites provide, in Berlant's words, "something of the subject's continuity of the subject's sense of what it means to keep on living on and to look forward to being in the world."[109]

Popular frustration and elite manipulation connect white fragility, white fear, and white failure to the possessive investment in whiteness. This connection hides from view the interpersonal antagonisms, psychological turmoil, and moral emptiness in white lives. Frenzied attention toward the other inhibits honest and careful reckoning with the self. By promoting enmity against people who are not white, the possessive in whiteness leaves the ills of the self and of society unaddressed, untreated, and uncured. We can never get well if we remain so deeply attached to the things that are making us sick.[110]

7

A Pigment of the Imagination

Even the most thoughtless even the most deluded black person knows
more about his life than the image he is offered as the justification of it.
—JAMES BALDWIN

The preceding chapters of this book have argued that the possessive investment in whiteness makes its presence felt in everyday life through the places where people live, the assets they own, the jobs they hold, the schools they attend, and how they are treated by the police and the courts. The next three chapters explore how these structural injustices are learned and legitimated through cultural constructions that create what Ruben Rumbaut calls a pigment of the imagination. In newspaper stories, television programs, and films, racially specific signs, symbols, images, and ideas encode virtue and vice, refuge and danger, cleanliness and filth. Whiteness relies on never having to speak its name, on never having to own up to the preferences and privileges it entails. Yet whiteness is perpetually defensive and insecure, forever feeling besieged and forever fearful of being betrayed. Protecting yet hiding the workings of whiteness entails a cultural imagination characterized by a seemingly endless chain of evasions, erasures, omissions, occlusions, deflections, and diversions.

Stories of Success

The *New York Times* provided a vivid example of the cultural imagination of whiteness in a feature story about successful young executives in 2003. The article noted a shift in the nature of appointments to boards of directors of large corporations. Previously, these posts went to senior executives who held top positions in their own firms. The new trend identified in this report concerned the elevation of younger executives with little or no previous experience at the highest corporate levels. The prime example given of this trend was the appointment of Nicole Piasecki, an executive at the Boeing airplane manufacturing firm, to the board of directors of the Weyerhaeuser Corporation in the timber and forest products industry. At forty years of age, Piasecki was eighteen years younger than the next youngest person on the board. She was appointed, the article contended, because of her specific skills in marketing and sales. When asked if her appointment to the Weyerhaeuser board surprised her, Piasecki replied, "It was something I was not expecting."[1]

Six days later, the *Times* printed an addendum to the previous story. It noted that the original article did not mention that Piasecki was the great-great-granddaughter of the founder of the Weyerhaeuser Company whose board she had joined. It had also omitted mentioning that her father was the founder of a helicopter manufacturing company that had been sold, before she was born, to the Boeing Company, where she was then vice president for business strategy and marketing. The addendum informed readers that "none of those interviewed for the article, including Ms. Piasecki and Steven R. Rogel, Weyerhaeuser's chief executive, mentioned family connections, nor were they asked about any."[2]

The advantages that Piasecki has secured from her family connections to the corporations she helped direct appeared to be invisible to her, to her supervisors, and to the journalist writing about her. They were not deemed worth mentioning or even inquiring about. Yet they are relevant to her success. As a child, Piasecki accompanied her father to his engineering office and to visit with clients and with military personnel at the Pentagon. "I lived in another world," she once told a reporter; "I was growing up not the way other people grew up."[3] Four of Piasecki's six siblings also work in the aviation industry, and she has expressed hopes that her three children will also enter the industry because "both my husband and I are engineers. I can tell we are shaping them to think engineering."[4] She made no mention of how family connections would give them advantages over other children equally adept at thinking in engineering terms. This is in no way to denigrate or belittle Nicole Piasecki's abilities and achievements. It is to say, however, that the privileges that flow from the possessive investment in whiteness are often invisible to those who possess them, and they rarely find a place in narratives about personal success. Those omissions come into clear relief by contrasting the treatment of Piasecki in the *Times* story with the representations of Luke Charles Harris that appeared in an installment of a television news magazine program.

On January 26, 2007, the ABC television network news feature show *Nightline* focused on childhood poverty in Camden, New Jersey. The program presented poignant vignettes of young people and their parents struggling with hunger, housing insecurity, displacement, and demoralization. The young people did not lack ambition or motivation. They received love and guidance from caring adults. Yet the city where they lived had been devastated by capital flight and deindustrialization, its social cohesion and social networks all but destroyed by concentrated poverty, disinvestment, and racial discrimination.

The script of the broadcast narrated by journalist Diane Sawyer displayed affection and empathy for the struggling, yet appealing, young people it depicted. The program's producers and writers sought to find a glimmer of hope in the midst of the stark realities the show depicted, to explore how a happy ending could be contemplated. They turned to Vassar College political science professor Luke Charles Harris, who had grown up in desperately poor circumstances in Camden. Harris had triumphed in spite of facing obstacles similar to those confronting the children in the program. Because he made it out of the ghetto and attained professional success, the show's message went, the young people in Camden could secure similar results if they followed his example.

Harris's story is certainly dramatic. As he explained to the *Nightline* staff in his pre-interview, his mother was a prostitute addicted to alcohol and drugs who was unable to care for him and his brother. The brothers were taken in and raised by their great-aunt, Mrs. Eva B. Cox, who worked as a domestic in homes around Camden. They lived in a segregated neighborhood and attended a segregated school. A school counselor steered Harris away from the academic track in high school, persuading him that he was not the kind of person who could make it to college and that he would have no use for classes in algebra, chemistry, and physics. Despite the paucity of college prep courses on his high school transcript, Harris was accepted to a state college where he did well. He transferred to St. Joseph's University, then went on to get two law degrees at Yale and a Ph.D. in political science at Princeton.

The production staff of *Nightline* interviewed Harris at length informally and then taped a thirty-minute segment with him. It was clear from their questions that they wanted to use his story to convey the message that anyone could triumph over overwhelming obstacles if one worked hard enough to do so. Harris objected to this premise.[5] In the informal pre-interview he related that his own work habits and character would have meant little if he had not been loved, supported, and helped along the way. He pointed to the care, concern, affection, and guidance he received from Mrs. Cox, a single mother who was not his birth mother. He often described her as his "spiritual shield" against adversity, as the person who taught him propriety, piety, good manners, hard work, selflessness, and modesty. Harris emphasized that he had help outside his family as well. He was able to transfer to St. Joseph and attend Yale and Princeton, he related, only because of the affirmative action programs in place at those institutions. Harris especially objected to the narrative frame positioning him as a "superman" who triumphed on his own, arguing that not only did he have help, but that no one should have to be a superman to succeed. Harris argued that the model *Nightline* was using operated as if everyone is competing in a race where the race track was fairly set up, but some runners are damaged and need extra help. On the contrary, Harris explained, it is not the runners who are damaged and need to be fixed; it is the track that forces them to run in lanes with unfair obstacles—poverty, hunger, second-class schools, slum housing, and race and gender discrimination. Harris has worked as Vassar's affirmative action officer and much of his scholarly research argues that affirmative action corrects the biases that would otherwise dominate school admissions, job hiring, and distribution of contracting opportunities. In his formulation, affirmative action clears the lanes of the race track of the artificial, arbitrary, and irrational impediments placed in them by discrimination.

Nightline's staff used less than five minutes of footage from their conversation with him. They left out his identification of affirmative action programs as the key to his success. They did not include his repeated calls for better funded schools; for unemployment and social support services equal to those in other industrialized nations; nor for investments in jobs, housing, health care, good schools, and infrastructure resources similar to the Marshall Plan programs that rebuilt Europe after the devastation of World War II. The *Nightline* broadcast did include Harris's oblique mention of the help he got from a white man he met while training to run cross country, a man who encouraged him to take college prep courses and to transfer from the state college to St. Joseph's. The program's voiceover narrative translated this one incident into the entire reason for Harris's success, saying "one person, a stranger gave him the gift of support and expectations."[6] Harris already had support from Mrs. Cox and high expectations of his own; what his white running friend gave him was information, and even that would have been useless had it not been for the affirmative action programs that helped him.

Having depicted Harris's success as solely due to one caring white stranger, the *Nightline* narrative went on to propose that all of the problems the program depicted could be solved in that fashion, by caring individuals willing to help the poor, not by challenging the causes of racialized poverty. Harris had stated clearly that children should not have to do superhuman things to have ordinary lives, that they needed good schools with small classes, safe affordable housing, enforcement of civil rights laws, and continuation, and expansion, of affirmative action programs. But this approach would cost money. It would entail addressing the cumulative costs of decades and centuries of racist exclusions and suppression. *Nightline* preferred a cheaper option. Toward the end of the program, the voiceover narrative concluded that the children depicted in the program are all "just one caring adult away from a way out." It presented the children as in need of charity, not justice; in need of attention, not resources.

In different ways, the newspaper story about Nicole Piasecki and the treatment of Luke Charles Harris on *Nightline* reveal how whiteness is learned and legitimated through narratives structured in dominance. The original *Times* story claimed that Piasecki secured a place on the board of directors of Weyerhaeuser because of her "specific skills" as senior executive in marketing and sales, not because her great-great-grandfather founded the company. *Nightline* presented Luke Charles Harris's success as the result of the intervention by a white stranger who gave him support and raised his expectations, even though Harris expressly credited the love and care of Mrs. Cox and the existence of affirmative action programs. Whiteness is presented in these stories as being of no particular help to Piasecki, and of no particular hindrance to Harris. The program portrayed Harris's problems as internal, presenting him as in need of personal inspiration, motivation, and high expectations, all of which he already had in abundance. At the same time, the *New York Times* story portrayed Piasecki's privileges as unrelated to race. It not only omitted the family connections to the founders of the Weyerhaeuser firm that she directs and the Boeing firm that employs her, but also the racialized history of those corporations. Frederick Weyerhaeuser gained control over more timber resources than anyone in the world in the 1890s by gaining access to and control over confiscated Anishinaabeg land. He was among the business executives who profited from the state of Minnesota's seizure of hundreds of thousands of acres of Anishinaaneg land allegedly for delinquent tax payments, from nefarious practices that procured land from people who could not read or write, children attending boarding schools, and soldiers away at war. Along with other lumber industry entrepreneurs, Weyerhaeuser secured funding partially from public sources to build a railroad onto the Leech Lake reservation. When Anishinaabeg resistance threatened to stop that project, the military intervened on Weyerhaeuser's behalf.[7] Today Weyerhaeuser's clearcutting of forests remains a target of Indigenous opposition and activism.[8]

Piasecki's other institutional home is the Boeing Corporation. It too has a history of racialized profiteering. W. E. Boeing, who founded Boeing Aircraft, developed suburbs north of Seattle during the 1930s and 1940s. The property deeds in his developments stipulated that "no property in said addition at any time be sold, conveyed or rented or leased in whole or in part to any person or persons not of the White or Caucasian race."[9] During World War II, Boeing aircraft openly defied President Roosevelt's Executive Order 8802 that stipulated that defense contractors receiving federal funds could not discriminate against Black workers. The company denied Black workers high paying jobs as skilled workers on the assembly line, relegating them instead solely to positions as janitors.[10]

The *Nightline* program contrasted the hardships faced by children in Camden with the amenities and advantages available to young people in nearby Moorestown, a wealthy white suburb, but it offered no explanation for the disparity. It omitted the comments Harris made in his interview that the parents and children in Moorestown did not succeed solely on their own but were "subsidized by a whole range . . . of public policies that gave them the opportunity to fulfill their ambitions, to work and then actually have a pipeline that would . . . make possible their dreams."[11] Moreover, *Nightline* made no mention of how the presence of Blacks and Puerto Ricans in Camden led the Federal Housing Administration in 1966 to refuse to give federal support for even one mortgage in the city.[12] The news magazine had no interest in explaining how the subsidies that flow to wealthy suburban areas through the property tax deduction on federal income tax payments left Camden in 1989 with only $1,140 per student in total federal subsidy while the wealthy city of Princeton garnered $2,399 per student in the same year.[13] The producers and writers who fashioned the *Nightline* story on Camden did not reveal that construction of an interstate highway in Camden obliterated 3,000 low-income housing units between 1963 and 1967, or that an investigative report by the attorney general of the state of New Jersey condemned the route of the highway, finding it "obvious from a glance" that the path chosen aimed to eliminate Black and Puerto Rican neighborhoods while increasing the value of property owned by suburban whites by creating a path toward "facilitating their movement from the suburbs to work and back."[14]

Stories of Failure

Similar patterns of omission and commission permeate another pair of stories spun by reporters about a black and a white protagonist. In the midst of the protests that broke out in response to the killing of Michael Brown by Officer Darren Wilson in Ferguson on August 9, 2014, the *New York Times* published a feature story on the unarmed teenaged Black victim. The *Times* story cautioned that the eighteen-year-old Brown was "no angel," a conclusion the reporter purported to have gleaned from interviews with the deceased's family members and friends. Acknowledging that Brown had "promise" as well as "problems" in his life, the story disclosed that the youth lived in a community that had "rough patches," that he had dabbled in alcohol and drugs, had been in one scuffle with a neighbor, and made up rap lyrics that the *Times* described as "by turn both contemplative and vulgar."[15]

A little more than a year after the *Times* published its story on Michael Brown, a white man named Robert Dear loaded numerous handguns, rifles, and propane canisters into his pickup truck. He drove to the offices of Planned Parenthood in Colorado Springs, Colorado, and fired round after round, killing three people and wounding nine others. In a feature story about the killer, the same *New York Times* that depicted Michael Brown as "no angel," wrote that acquaintances described Dear as "a gentle loner."[16] The very act of shooting nine people and killing three of them would seem to call into question Dear's gentleness on the face of it. The story about him also included accounts of domestic violence, of shooting a neighbor's dog, and of stalking and threatening individuals who displeased him. Yet the headline and story singled out "gentle" as the key adjective for describing the shooter.

The contrast between the description of Michael Brown, an unarmed teenager shot and killed by a police officer, as "no angel," and of Robert Dear, who engaged in terrorist violence and murder at a reproductive services center for women, as "a gentle loner" requires some explanation and interpretation. The reporters and editors who crafted these descriptions may have believed they were simply adding interest to the news by playing against readers' expectations. Finding flaws in the life of a young man thought to be an innocent victim and elements of gentleness in the life of a mass shooter and killer might have been imagined as attempts to discover levels of complex personhood in lives defined by single violent events. Yet the ways in which the racial identities of Brown and Dear were alternately amplified and muted in these stories reveals a more powerful dynamic at work: a cultural imagination that exemplifies the perverse effects of the possessive investment in whiteness.

Near the beginning of the article that depicted Brown as "no angel," the reporter identified the youth as a "black teenager" shot to death by a white police officer. Yet after that point, overt mentions of race disappear from the story and racism is completely absent. The *Times* noted that Ferguson police officials released a video which they alleged showed Brown shoplifting cigars from a local store, but there was no mention that the Ferguson police department was almost all white in a city that was two thirds Black, that the charge of shoplifting was proffered to exculpate the white officer who shot and killed Brown, or that Black youths and adults in Ferguson were constantly stopped, searched, charged, and fined for small offenses like jaywalking as part of a deliberate police strategy to finance municipal expenses with fines imposed on the city's impoverished Black residents. The story did not report the presumptions of Black criminality that haunted the lives of young people like Michael Brown. It recounted, but did not evaluate, for example, an episode when a teacher had accused Brown of stealing an iPod but was forced to drop the complaint when Brown's mother came to school and showed administrators the purchase receipt.

The *Times* story presented as evidence of Brown's unsuitability to be thought of as an angel the fact that "he lived in a community with rough patches," making no mention of how or why residential segregation, racial zoning, mortgage redlining, and other manifestations of the possessive investment in whiteness relegated black youths to residence in criminogenic neighborhoods marked by transience, a dearth of employment opportunities, and aggressive, racially motivated policing. The feature story noted that Brown worked hard to graduate from Normandy High School but did not mention that when he started his schooling in kindergarten in 1996, the school district in which he was enrolled had not been accredited for five years, or that the school funding formula in the state of Missouri enabled white suburban areas to monopolize and hoard educational resources and advantages.[17] The *Times* reported that when he was killed, Brown was looking forward to attending a technical college to take courses in heating and cooling technology. It did not mention that the school he planned to attend was a for-profit vocational school that had come under investigation by the federal Department of Education because of charges of deceptive marketing to poor and minority students, burdening students with unpayable debts and with credentials that meant next to nothing on the job market.[18]

No one had in fact claimed that Brown was an angel, only that the loss of his life was grievable and that his killing was a criminal act. The focus in the *Times* article on the allegedly profane lyrics in Brown's songs diverted attention away from the incontestably profane conditions he endured in Ferguson.[19] By condemning Michael Brown for the neighborhood in which he lived, the *Times* story made it seem as if the eighteen-year-old had the choice to live anywhere in the St. Louis region but unaccountably chose to live in a high-poverty and low-opportunity neighborhood. In finding that Brown was "no angel," the *Times* story gave a free pass to the officer who killed the youth as well as to the police administrators and prosecutors who covered up the crime and prevented its perpetrator from being held accountable. The story offered no opinion on whether these people were angels.

While race was overtly minimized in the *Times* story on Michael Brown, it was excised completely from the account depicting Robert Dear as a "gentle loner."[20] His violent terrorist attack on a women's health center was attributed to his anger at videos distributed by opponents of reproductive rights. These videos had been edited fraudulently to give the appearance that Planned Parenthood performed abortions in order to profit from selling fetal tissue to researchers.[21] The *Times* described the videos as "surreptitious" but neglected to mention that they were fraudulent. The story did not connect Dear's attack on a women's health center to his investments in a misogynist understanding of proper gender roles, even though the article included Dear's history of domestic violence, his record of having been accused of being a peeping tom, and evidence that indicated a fascination with sadistic pornography. The headline for the story identified Dear as someone who "preferred to be left alone," but the account that followed contradicted that repeatedly, especially in regard to matters of race. A neighbor remembered Dear handing him political pamphlets that excoriated President Obama; Dear invited the neighbor to come by Dear's place and "talk about this stuff" in the future.[22] Dear made his living as an art dealer, buying the rights to paintings to make prints of original works to sell. The *Times* reported that the art he bought and sold focused almost exclusively on depictions of the Old South, especially street scenes of Charleston, South Carolina; magnolia blossoms; the campus of the Citadel Military College; and "Old South plantation tableaus."[23] Evidently, being "left alone," for Dear, meant being left alone to agitate against a Black president, circulate images lauding the slaveholding Confederacy, and driving to a women's health center and shooting and killing the people in it. The story noted that Dear killed two civilians as well as a police officer during the shootout, but it did not report that the civilian victims were an Asian American woman (a mother with two children) and a Black man (an Iraq war veteran).

Omitting race from the account of Robert Dear's rampage makes his killing spree the work of a sole individual, unconnected to the prompts and provocations communicated to him constantly by the cultural apparatuses of the possessive investment in whiteness. Including race but not racism in the description of Michael Brown makes him personally culpable for the cumulative effects of police profiling, concentrated poverty, and educational inequality. The dignity of complex personhood is extended to a mass murderer, while culpability for his actions is confined to him alone, safely cordoning off from scrutiny and accountability the racial matrix from which it emerged. In contrast, the stigma of collective guilt attached to the neighborhood in which Michael Brown lived and to the music he made is used to render Michael Brown's death as measurably less regrettable than his supporters claimed.

No one had to tell *Nightline*'s producers and writers or the *New York Times*' reporters and editors to leave whiteness out of the stories about Nicole Piasecki and Robert Dear or to mute the expressly racist obstacles facing Luke Harris and Michael Brown. This pattern of selective omission and commission is part of a shared social language, a cultural imaginary that flows inexorably from the power and pervasive presence of the possessive investment in whiteness. The differences in the descriptions of Nicole Piasecki and Robert Dear, on the one hand, and of Luke Harris and Michael Brown, on the other, reveal the dynamics of what sociologist Albert Memmi calls "the mark of the plural." This concept describes how all members of despised and subordinated groups are held accountable for the actions of every other member of that group. If any one of them is believed to be a criminal, lazy, or dirty, all become tainted. The mark of the plural positions members of aggrieved groups not as individuals, but as symbols of a threatening social aggregate. Members of dominant groups, however, are always treated as individuals. Michael Brown's behavior becomes attached to the alleged tangle of pathology that characterizes the Black family, but Robert Dear, like Dylann Roof, Timothy McVeigh, and other white mass murderers are presumed to be individuals unaffected by being positioned as white throughout their lives.

The Mark of the Plural

The mark of the plural appeared prominently in a message sent by Texas senator John Cornyn in the wake of the street violence that erupted in response to the killing of Freddie Gray by Baltimore police officers in 2015. Gray was a twenty-five-year-old Black man who was arrested and placed in a police wagon with no seatbelt, his hands in handcuffs behind his back. He was subjected to what police officers are said to call a "rough ride" that broke his spine and killed him. Black residents of Baltimore have long complained that police officers punish and terrorize handcuffed suspects before they are even charged with crimes by placing them unsecured by seat belts inside police vans and subjecting them to being tossed around the vehicle and bounced off metal benches and walls during trips that entail fast turns and sudden stops.[24] A Baltimore jury in 2005 awarded $7.4 million to Dondi Johnson, Sr., who had been arrested for public urination and subjected to a rough ride in a police vehicle that left him a quadriplegic.[25] The officers involved in the death of Freddie Gray were only placed on paid administrative leave until daily protest demonstrations demanding justice pressed local officials to indict the officers. Two weeks after the killing, on the day of Gray's funeral, police officers attacked a group of protesting high school students who fought back, touching off an insurrection. Rioters smashed windows and looted stores. Arsonists set more than one hundred vehicles and fifteen buildings on fire. Some $9 million in property was destroyed. It was only after the riots that the local prosecutor brought charges against the police officers involved in Freddie Gray's death. All of the defendants were subsequently acquitted or the charges against them were dropped. According to the criminal justice system, no one was responsible or accountable for the death of Freddie Gray.[26]

Surveying the terrible destruction of the riots, Senator Cornyn used his Twitter account on May 8, 2015, to proclaim, "Liberals, admit it: Baltimore riots are part of a story of absent fathers." Accompanying the tweet was a link to a Bloomberg News story about black children being raised by unmarried parents or in female-headed households.[27] Less than ten days after Cornyn took to Twitter to blame the violence in Baltimore on broken Black families, two biker gangs with white supremacist affiliations engaged in a shootout with each other and with police officers in Waco in Cornyn's home state of Texas. The violence left nine people dead, eighteen wounded, and hundreds charged with criminal offenses. The senator made no comment on the presence or absence of white fathers in the homes of the perpetrators of the Waco violence.

By focusing attention on the absence of black fathers, Senator Cornyn deflected attention away from the presence of the possessive investment in whiteness and its impact on opportunities and life chances in Baltimore. The senator's tweet directing attention toward alleged deficiencies in Black families occluded scrutiny of the actual causes of the insurrection by desperate and angry people refusing an unlivable destiny. Cornyn's analysis of the riot had no place for the Baltimore police department's history of unconstitutional stops, searches, arrests, beatings, and killings of black residents; for the documented record of police officers planting incriminating evidence on suspects; for the legacy of police violence against suspects and the neglect of duty by prosecutors discounting citizen accounts of brutality.[28] The city of Baltimore had to pay millions of dollars in court judgments and settlements to more than one hundred victims of police brutality between 2011 and 2014 alone.[29] An investigation conducted by the Civil Rights Division of the Department of Justice after the Freddie Gray killing found that the Baltimore Police Department routinely used excessive force, retaliated against people engaged in constitutionally protected free expression, and engaged in enforcement strategies designed to produce "severe and unjustified disparities" in the numbers of African Americans stopped, searched, and arrested.[30]

Moreover, Senator Cornyn's focus on the family ignored the history and continuing effects of oppressive residential segregation in Baltimore. Research by scholars including Harold McDougall, Edward Orser, Samuel Kelton Roberts, and Rhonda Williams has thoroughly documented the harm done to Blacks in Baltimore over the years by racial zoning, restrictive covenants, mortgage redlining, urban renewal, block busting, transit racism, and predatory lending. In 2005, a federal judge found the U.S. Department of Housing and Urban Development guilty of creating, promoting, and exacerbating residential racial segregation in Baltimore in violation of the 1968 Fair Housing Act. It was the presence of the possessive investment in whiteness, not the absence of fathers in Black households, that caused the concentrated poverty, environmental pollution, transience, lack of employment and educational opportunities, and police brutality that created the preconditions for the riots.[31] Long before Freddie Gray was killed by police officers, his life had already been deemed disposable. The Sandtown-Winchester neighborhood where Gray lived and where officers arrested him had an unemployment rate of 51.8 percent. A third of the homes in that neighborhood were vacant. Gray suffered from lead poisoning as a child, as do some 8 percent of the children in Sandtown-Winchester. Freddie Gray's neighborhood sends more of its residents to prison than any other neighborhood in the state of Maryland.[32] The average life expectancy of people in Sandtown-Winchester is five years shorter than the Baltimore average and sixteen years shorter than for residents of the primarily white neighborhood in Baltimore that has the longest life expectancy.[33] The rioters were not unruly adolescents in need of fatherly discipline but were exploited, aggrieved, and insurgent men and women using the only means they could see at their disposal to refuse the unlivable destiny to which they had long been relegated.[34]

The focus on the absence of Black fathers from the home stems from the presumption that the Black family is the "tangle of pathology" described in the 1965 Moynihan Report discussed in Chapter 6. For more than a half century, the Moynihan Report has served as the lynchpin of the argument that Black behavior rather than white racism causes Black poverty. Moynihan did not originate this argument; the myth of the lazy, indolent, irresponsible, and hedonistic Black male was forged by white supremacists as soon as slavery ended, and it was deployed as justification and excuse for the mechanisms designed to preserve white rule: Black codes, mass incarceration, prison labor, and Jim Crow segregation.[35] The policies that flowed from this stance had a self-fulfilling quality. Incarceration interrupted work histories and fragmented families. Low wages and unemployment forced workers to leave home in search of wages to send back to their families. In several locales, including Forsythe County in Georgia; Pierce City, Missouri; and Harrison, Arkansas, Black success in farming and business led to pogroms in which whites simply drove Blacks from the area and stole their property.[36] Racist discrimination imposed artificial, arbitrary, and irrational impediments to upward mobility severing the link between work and reward. State and federal welfare programs granted aid to needy whites but systematically denied the same benefits to needy people of color. When political mobilizations compelled governments to at last extend to Blacks the same social welfare assistance routinely given to whites, states adopted policies designed to deny aid to families that included an able-bodied male in the household, even if unemployment levels and local market conditions left these men without income. As a result, Black fathers had to leave the home in order for their families to survive. When they did so, they were condemned for their absence.[37]

Senator Cornyn's tweet about absent fathers ignores the fact that the majority of Black fathers live with their children.[38] It pays no heed to the results of an extensive 2013 study by the Centers for Disease Control and Prevention that found that Black fathers read to their children more frequently than white fathers do, that they talk more frequently with their children about events in the child's day than white fathers do, and that a larger percentage of Black fathers help their children with their homework every day compared to white fathers.[39] Moreover, the assumption that a father in the home is necessary for good parenting is itself a sexist myth. The testimony of Luke Charles Harris that was left out of the 2007 *Nightline* program about Mrs. Eva Cox's guidance and mentoring of him is only one of millions of stories of successful parenting against enormous odds by single Black women.

Senator Cornyn's tweet was right in one respect, however, although not for the reasons he thought. There are nearly 1.5 million Black men "missing" from families. Black fathers are absent because of early deaths and incarceration, because they die prematurely of heart disease, respiratory illnesses, accidents, and homicides. Black fathers are absent because one out of every twelve black men between the ages of twenty-five and fifty-four, some 600,000 in total, are locked up in jails and prisons, mostly for nonviolent offenses. The absence of these men impedes family formation, lowers marriage rates, and leaves many Black women to raise children on their own.[40] Yet if every single one of these absent fathers could return home tomorrow, they and their families would still be confronted with the effects of low wages, unemployment, environmental racism, school segregation, housing discrimination, and racially targeted policing. As sociologist Moon-kie Jung notes, since 1950 the Black unemployment rate has been twice as high as the rate of white joblessness. The *worst* levels of unemployment that whites have experienced are 2.4 percent better than the *average* unemployment levels faced by Blacks.[41]

Avoiding the hard facts about discrimination and subordination in Black communities enables Senator Cornyn to blame the victims, to indict Black people for their inability to overcome virtually insurmountable odds. Just as the *Nightline* investigation of poverty in Camden spun fables about how impoverished Black and Latinx children could become superhuman and just as the report in the *New York Times* chided Michael Brown for failing to be an angel, Cornyn deflects attention away from the unfair gains and unjust rewards of the possessive investment in whiteness by circulating stories about Black dependency and dysfunction. These narratives have had a long history from the earliest days of slave emancipation to the present. They never change and are impervious to evidence. Phobic fantasies about Black criminality and welfare dependence persist, even though crime has consistently decreased and in many locales is at historically low levels, even though direct social welfare payments to poor people have been almost nonexistent since Republicans and Democrats worked together to "end welfare as we know it" in 1996. The fantasies are more important than the facts, however, because they are what keep whiteness working.

Cultural theorists Peter Stallybrass and Allon White argue that expressive culture often focuses obsessively on people at the margins, on difference and deviance, because that enables those at the center to take their privilege and their virtue for granted. The socially peripheral, Stallybrass and White argue, is often symbolically central.[42] The possessive investment in whiteness has rarely entailed simple aversion to or avoidance of Blacks. On the contrary, Blackness pervades the white imagination and the products of its popular culture. Ralph Ellison captured this uncanny present absence and absent presence in his novel *Invisible Man* in which his protagonist works at the Liberty Paint Company, an establishment that specializes in manufacturing what it calls "optic white" paint. The narrator discovers that the secret of the white paint is that it must contain a drop of black paint that no one sees.[43] While Black people are invisible in segregated neighborhoods, schools, and work sites, opinions about Blackness pervade the discourses of whiteness. These ideas, images, and representations may be degrading or demonizing, or pitying and paternalistic. Yet they need to be present for whiteness to exist. As James Baldwin analyzed astutely a half century ago, "a vast amount of energy that goes into what we call the Negro problem is produced by the white man's profound desire not to be judged by those who are not white, not to be seen as he is, and at the same time, a vast amount of the white anguish is rooted in the white man's equally profound need to be seen as he is, to be released from the tyranny of his mirror."[44] Ruminations about the deficiencies of people of color in Camden, Ferguson, and Baltimore preclude asking about the inherited advantages channeled to Nicole Piasecki or about the criminal violence of police officers torturing and killing Black civilians, of white supremacist gang members shooting each other and police officers in Waco, and Robert Dear opening fire at a women's health center in Colorado Springs.

Why Culture Counts

People can be imprisoned effectively by being incarcerated behind stone walls and iron bars. Less obvious, but no less effective, however, are the ways in which people can be confined and constrained even more securely and even more surely by ideas, images, signs, symbols, and stories. When she conducts workshops on structural racism, Black feminist critical race studies scholar Kimberlé Crenshaw often begins with a slide depicting a phoropter, the instrument used by eye care professionals to determine proper prescriptions for eyeglasses. The letters on the eye chart that appeared blurred when seen with no lenses or with the previous prescription become clear when the right lens is selected. The pigment of the imagination created by the mark of the plural in the stories of success and failure in this chapter teach us to look through the wrong lens. They distort reality and impede our ability to deal with it.

8

White Desire

Remembering Robert Johnson

He who has been treated as the devil recognizes the devil when they meet.

—JAMES BALDWIN

I f white racism manifested itself exclusively through hostility and exclusion it would be easier to understand and to combat. Yet the long history of interracial relations has also created a possessive investment in whiteness that entails embracing people of color and their cultures in condescending and controlling ways. The recurrence of racial stereotypes in art and in life, the frequent invocation of people of color as sources of inspiration or forgiveness for whites, and the white fascination with certain notions of "primitive" authenticity among communities of color all testify to the white investment in images that whites themselves have created about people of color. In his excellent study of blackface minstrelsy, Eric Lott identifies both "love and theft" as components of the white racist imagination. These emotions and acts form the central force in the dynamics of white desire manifested in the reception of the blues music of Robert Johnson.

"Every crossroads has a story" proclaimed the large bold lettering in an advertisement promoting the state of Mississippi to tourists on the back cover of the November/December 1996 issue of *Living Blues* magazine. Told in the first person by an aspiring musician who has "tried to pick out those soulful notes on my guitar, but could never duplicate that feeling you get when Howlin' Wolf lets you know he is 300 pounds of joy," the story in the ad concerns going to Mississippi to get in touch with the spirit of Robert Johnson. "Supposedly he went down to a crossroads and sold his soul to the Devil to play like that," the narrator explains. "So I drove down Highway 61 to Highway 49 where most folks say the deal was struck. I didn't want to sell my soul, or anything. I just wanted to kind of pay my respects. I don't know if the Devil got the soul of Robert Johnson that night. But this intersection has still heard its share of music. B. B. King, Muddy Waters, and Charley Patton all had something to say and crossed these roads many times."[1]

It should not be surprising that the state of Mississippi uses the story of Robert Johnson at the crossroads to sell tourism. The story has proven its extraordinary appeal and exceptional commercial value over and over again. A series of successful books, documentary films, and television programs has celebrated "the search for Robert Johnson." The compact disc reissue of Johnson's recordings sold more than 400,000 units within six months of its release and sales exceeded 900,000 units within six years. When a producer and recording engineer working for Sony discovered original masters of Robert Johnson recordings at that company's archives in New York, a reporter for a music industry trade publication compared their find to the discovery of the tomb of King Tut. Rock guitarist Eric Clapton has long validated his own standing as an artist by claiming a psychic and spiritual connection to Johnson as a spiritual ancestor and through his renditions of Johnson's songs, notably "Crossroads."[2] The crossroads metaphor, both with and without reference to Robert Johnson, has served as the focal point for a number of celebrated art exhibits, films, and popular novels.[3]

It might seem paradoxical that large numbers of European Americans who have a powerful possessive investment in the economic rewards of whiteness in the rest of their lives have such a deep affective investment in the art of Robert Johnson, a Black man. The two investments, however, are not mutually exclusive. Indeed, one depends on the other. The very existence of racism adds to the mystery, distance, and inversions of prestige enacted in the reception of blues music by romantics like Eric Clapton and many of his fans. William Faulkner once argued that white Americans needed the Negro selves they encountered through culture because they were the only selves they've ever really known. By relegating African Americans to purportedly primitive, natural, and mystical domains, the consumption of Black culture salves the alienations and identity problems of European Americans.

The commercial value of the crossroads story depends in no small measure on the ways it erases the story's cultural origins and suppresses its original social intentions. Derived originally from diasporic African legends and trickster tales intended to teach the importance of human agency, the crossroads story here functions instead as a register of Western culture's enduring attachment to romanticism, to separating life and art, to elevating individual emotions over collective connections, and to turning social pain into an aesthetic pleasure. The romanticism that guides the circulation and reception of the story of Robert Johnson at the crossroads hides the hard facts of life and labor in the segregated South in Johnson's day. It obscures the ways in which unquestioned assumptions about artistic expression keep people wedded to the very materialist practices that art often ostensibly deplores. This romanticism contributes to the possessive investment in whiteness by maintaining the illusion that individual whites can appropriate aspects of African American experience for their own benefit without having to acknowledge the factors that give African Americans and European Americans widely divergent opportunities and life chances.

In Yoruba and other West African cosmologies, crossroads can be sites of both danger and opportunity. Collision and confusion occur when paths come together, but the crossroads is also a place where decisions need to be made and choices matter. Robert Farris Thompson suggests that Yoruba art functions largely as practical training for life, as an activity that cultivates the ability to recognize significant communications in preparation for making moral choices. Material places and objects can play a central part in this process because artistic activity in the African worldview often aims at capturing the metaphorical power of the natural world to imbue objects with "intuitions of the power to make right things come to pass."[4] The crossroads mediates power across physical and metaphysical worlds, but it also cultivates an appreciation of activity and imagination as tools for transforming concrete circumstances and conditions. The trickster figure at the crossroads—often interpreted in the Western romantic tradition as the devil—is really Eshu-Elegbara (Legba, Elegba, Esu), not an incarnation of evil, but an unpredictable deity with the power to make things happen, a god described by Thompson as "the ultimate master of potentiality."[5]

The story of the crossroads that emerges with such frequency and power in commercial culture, however, proceeds from very different assumptions than these. Walter Hill's 1986 film *Crossroads* featured Ralph Macchio, the star of *The Karate Kid*, playing a white youth who taps into the power of Black blues. The hero tracks down an elderly African American blues musician in a Harlem hospital and helps him return to Mississippi in return for providing the youth with the treasure of "some long lost songs." We learn that the bluesman originally gained his talent by selling his soul to the devil. The climactic moment of the film comes from a guitar duel between Macchio performing the blues and the devil (played by guitar virtuoso Steve Vai) offering heavy metal music in return. In this case, heavy metal represents the contaminated culture of the commercial music industry while the blues appears as a precommercial form with magical powers owing to its purportedly pure and uncontaminated history.[6]

In a similar vein, Walter Mosley's 1995 novel *R L's Dream* recalls Johnson's music nostalgically as an art form that involved its listeners in depths of feeling unknown to today's audiences. Mosley's central character can "play anything on my guitar," but even when the beauty of his playing brings tears to the eyes of his listeners he knows that "the music they was hearin' was just a weak shadow, just like some echo of somethin', that happened a long time ago. They was feelin' somethin', but not what Robert Johnson made us feel in Arcola. They can't get that naked. And they wouldn't want to even if they could, 'cause you know Robert Johnson's blues would rip the skin right off yo' back. Robert Johnson's blues get down to a nerve most people don't even have no more."[7] Once again, the blues here are deployed as an antidote to the shallowness of contemporary commercial culture, as an art form precious because it is unapproachable and unknowable, locked in the past and superior in its emotional depths to anything imaginable.

The blues music that emerges in the film *Crossroads,* in Walter Mosley's *RL's Dream,* and in Eric Clapton's construction of Robert Johnson as a spiritual ancestor has less to do with the blues itself than with the traditions of romanticism in Western culture that date back to the late eighteenth century. Romanticism imagines an art immune to commercial considerations, an art capable of reconciling members of antagonistic social groups, bringing people from very different circumstances together through aesthetic freedom and emotional affinities. As Nancy Rosenblum explains, "The romantic sensibility is marked by a sense of its own boundless potential for creativity and expression, by revulsion at constriction and closure and at the very thought of being authoritatively defined."[8]

Eric Clapton's career and his professed connections to Robert Johnson exemplify this romanticism. Clapton has hardly had an easy life; he was born out of wedlock and raised by his grandparents. He suffered from drug addiction and experienced the death of a child. Yet the romance of Robert Johnson functions in Clapton's personal and professional narratives as an appropriation that hides the differences between the two men and their life circumstances. While both artists faced their share of difficulties in life, on his very best day Robert Johnson still caught more hell than Eric Clapton has ever imagined. The musical forms that Clapton has investigated as a form of personal exploration and discovery came to Johnson as part of a shared social language honed under historically specific circumstances for eminently practical purposes.

Clapton biographer Harry Shapiro identifies "the search for the spirit of Robert Johnson" as a core component in Clapton's career, noting that both artists "have lived 'the rock life' with periods of self-imposed exile, sudden bouts of wanderlust, drinking and gambling."[9] It would no doubt come as a surprise to Johnson to learn that he lived something called "the rock life," but the validation of the blues that comes from connecting it to the success of rock 'n' roll—and the moral qualities that adhere to rock 'n' roll when connected to its blues heritage—testify to both the power of contemporary commercial culture and its painful contradictions. Audiences and critics want to "own" the pleasures and powers of popular music without embracing the commercial and industrial matrices in which they are embedded; they want to imagine that the art that they have discovered through commercial culture is somehow better than commercial culture itself, that their investment in the music grants them an immunity from the embarrassing manipulation, pandering, and trivialization of culture intrinsic to a market society. More than anything, they want to imagine their consumer pleasures and cultural fantasies as a form of freedom.

In another biography of Clapton titled *Crossroads,* Michael Schumacher identifies "wanderlust, drinking, and womanizing" as activities that link Clapton to Johnson. Schumacher offers quotes from Clapton that illustrate the artist's own investment in being linked with Johnson and the authenticity and depth of feeling he associates with his idol. "It was almost like I'd been prepared each step to receive him," Clapton told Schumacher, describing his involvement with Johnson's music as "a religious experience that started out by hearing Chuck Berry, and then at each stage I was going further and further back, and deeper and deeper into the source of the music, until I was ready for Robert Johnson." It is difficult to see in what sense Johnson could be considered "the source" of blues guitar playing or singing in any strictly musical sense. Clapton's comments, however, stem less from an assessment of Johnson as a musician than from the British guitarist's desire for a shared emotional bond with him. "It was almost as if he felt things so acutely he found it almost unbearable," Clapton explained. "It called to me in my confusion, it seemed to echo something that I had always felt."[10]

While claiming a mystical connection with Robert Johnson as an individual, Clapton ignores the economic and social structures that enable him, rather than an African American, to make a fortune playing African American music. Moreover, Clapton's connection to the pain in Robert Johnson's life has not led him to any degree of sympathy for those in similar straits today. At a moment of intense anti-Black, anti-Asian, and anti-Arab sentiment in the United Kingdom during the summer of 1976, Clapton launched a drunken rant against "foreigners" at a concert in racially volatile Birmingham, telling the audience, "I think we should vote for Enoch Powell," then the leading white supremacist member of the British Parliament. Clapton made things worse in succeeding weeks when he attempted to justify his comments on the basis of his resentment of "Arab money-spending and their total lack of respect for other people's property." For those unmoved by his economic argument, Clapton added a dose of masculine patriarchal protection, explaining that "one foreigner had pinched my missus' bum."[11]

Despite Clapton's easy incorporation of anti-foreign racism with his romanticism about an African American artist, the motivations behind romanticism are not necessarily racist. The enduring appeal of romanticism in art and music in Western culture testifies to the alienation and isolation of bourgeois life as well as to the relentless materialism of capitalist societies. The wounds that romanticism attempts to salve are real, but the categories that undergird romantic thinking perpetuate rather than remediate the alienations and injustices that it seeks to address and redress. The life and legend of Robert Johnson can be made to conform perfectly to the contours of romanticism; it is not difficult to see the ends that Johnson's story serves for Eric Clapton and his many fans, as well as for the Mississippi Tourism Commission and for a host of writers, filmmakers, visual artists, musicians, and television producers. Yet incorporating Robert Johnson into a romantic narrative hides both the social circumstances and the cultural strategies that informed his life and art. Understanding these circumstances and strategies can illuminate how the possessive investment in whiteness distorts history for self-interested purposes.

When Robert Johnson started to play music in public, it was not at all evident that he would one day become known as the king of the Delta blues singers. In the ice houses, juke joints, and general stores around Robinsonville, Mississippi, in 1930, most people felt that the nineteen-year-old Johnson could play the harmonica tolerably well and that his singing was acceptable enough, but they judged him to be one of the worst guitar players they had ever heard. Son House remembers that when he and his fellow musicians would put down their instruments during breaks to go outside and take a break in the cool night air, Johnson often picked up one of their guitars and started playing so poorly that the patrons would beg the band members to come back and play just to make him leave the stage. House remembers scolding the teenager, "Don't do that, Robert. You drive the people nuts. You can't play nothing."[12]

Johnson left Robinsonville in 1931 and moved to Hazlehurst—about forty miles south of Jackson. When he returned to Robinsonville two years later, House saw that the young musician now owned his own guitar. "What can you do with that thing?" House teased. "You can't do nothing with it." Johnson smiled and said, "Let me have your seat a minute." When Johnson started to play, House could hardly believe what he was hearing. "He was so good! Our mouths were standing open," House recalled.[13] Years later, blues scholar Mack McCormick interviewed several of Johnson's relatives who claimed that Robert had gone out to a deserted crossroads just before midnight and met a large Black man. The stranger allegedly took the guitar from Johnson's hands, tuned it to his liking, played a piece, and then handed it back. From that point on, the story goes, Robert Johnson played like an expert.[14]

Despite the seemingly universal appeal of this story, anyone who has ever attempted to play music may prefer to think that *practice* had more to do with Robert Johnson's improved skills as a guitar player than any deal with the devil. Yet the crossroads metaphor should not be dismissed as irrelevant or foolish. Robert Johnson's family members and fans interpreted his history through the lens of their own experiences and beliefs as African people in America. They drew upon a large repertoire of folkways originating in Africa to solve the problems they faced as exploited workers, second-class citizens, and members of a despised racial group. The same people who told the story about the crossroads as a mystical site also put mirrors outside their homes to catch the "flash of the spirit." They left the Bible open at night or tacked newspapers onto their walls to secure the protections offered by "spirit writing." They scattered possessions of the dead such as broken glasses, dishes, and cups on burial sites to acknowledge the ruptures between generations but also to honor the memories and observe the rituals that connected them to their ancestors across generations and continents. They looked to African practices for guidance in everyday life activities such as cooking, healing, and farming, but also for explanation and transformation. African practices and beliefs enabled them to render the hegemony of white supremacy in America relative, provisional, and contingent rather than absolute, overwhelming, and unyielding. By remembering and retaining aspects of Africa in their lives, they could turn themselves in their minds from an oppressed national minority into part of the global majority of nonwhite people.

Robert Johnson may not have actually met a man at the crossroads at midnight, but he did infuse a material object—the guitar—with sufficient spiritual power to earn himself escape from the twin pillars of power in the Depression-era South: the plantation and the prison. The guitar enabled him to earn a living on the road, to move from town to town playing the blues for farmworkers and factory hands all across the country. "He didn't care anything about working in the fields," Son House once remarked to a reporter who asked him why Johnson devoted so much time and energy to his music.[15] Robert Johnson's responses to his life choices resembled those of his Mississippi contemporary Charley Patton, who according to Robert Palmer also used the blues to create a life for himself where "he rarely worked for whites except to furnish a night's entertainment, and he was never tied to a menial job or plot of land for very long." Muddy Waters described his own interest in the blues in similar fashion, telling Robert Palmer that he longed to be a preacher, ballplayer, or musician because "I *always* felt like I could beat plowin' mules, choppin' cotton, and drawin' water. I did all that, and I never did like none of it. Sometimes they'd want us to work Saturday, but they'd look for me, and I'd be *gone*, playin' in some little town or some juke joint."[16]

We can well imagine the labor that awaited Robert Johnson in the cotton fields and timber camps of the Mississippi Delta in the 1930s had he not been able to make a living as a musician. He faced humiliation constantly in a society where brutal police officers, lynch mobs, and labor exploitation combined to shape the contours of a Black worker's existence. Robert Johnson may not have met the devil at the crossroads at midnight, but he certainly met the devil every morning at 6 A.M. when he had to say "Good morning, boss." Leaving home for the life of an itinerant musician was not a romantic venture into the lonely life of the artist for him but rather a way out of the suffocating constraints of a racialized class system.

Nothing underscores the desperation of Johnson's life circumstances more than his struggle simply to find a name. The person we have come to call Robert Johnson was rarely known as Robert Johnson during his lifetime. At different moments, people knew him as Robert Dodds, Little Robert Dusty, Robert Spencer, and R. L. Spencer. Almost no one knew him as Robert Johnson until he took that name when he started his career as a musician. His many names reflect the precariousness and uncertainty of the life he led.

Johnson's mother, Julia Major Dodds, lived in Hazlehurst with her husband, Charles Dodds, and their ten children. Charles Dodds provided for his wife and children by laboring on the farm that he owned and by making wicker furniture for sale. In 1909, however, he got into a disagreement with two wealthy white landowners and had to sneak out of town disguised in women's clothing just ahead of a lynch mob eager to punish him for standing up to white people. Dodds escaped to Memphis, where he changed his name to Charles Spencer, just in case vigilantes from Hazlehurst came looking for Robert Dodds. Julia Dodds sent eight of her children one by one to live with their father in Memphis to protect them from retaliation. Local whites eventually got her evicted from her land, ostensibly because of delinquent tax payments but in reality as retribution for Robert Dodds's successful escape. Left with two children, no husband, no land, and no money, Julia Dodds hired out as a farmworker while living in local labor camps. She met Noah Johnson on a cotton plantation, and their son Robert was born on May 8, 1911.[17]

Julia Dodds persisted in her efforts to reunite with her children and their father in Memphis. Yet even though her husband had himself fathered two children with his mistress from Hazlehurst, he never accepted his wife back because of her liaison with Noah Johnson. He did give in to her wishes in one respect, however, when he allowed Robert to live with him and the other children in Memphis for a few years, starting in 1914. Robert returned to the Delta in 1920, however, to live with his mother and her new husband, Willie "Dusty" Willis, in Robinsonville. As Robert Palmer notes, "With three different fathers before he was seven, a series of sudden uprootings and a succession of name changes, Robert had a confused and confusing childhood."[18]

Robert Johnson took the name by which he is known to us today only when he began playing music for a living. Even then, commercial considerations rather than bloodlines or voluntary identification most likely determined his decision. Audiences already knew blues singers Lonnie Johnson and Tommy Johnson, and Robert found that it helped him secure jobs when people confused him with the other Johnsons, so he helped their confusion along by encouraging them to think that he was related to Lonnie or Tommy. He sometimes introduced himself as "one of the Johnson boys" and claimed that the initials R. L. stood for Robert Lonnie.[19] Tommy Johnson had been telling people as early as the 1920s that he secured his talents by making a deal with the devil at a crossroads, and it is possible that Robert Johnson saw the commercial advantage in telling the same story about himself.[20]

Commercial considerations shaped Johnson's persona at every stage of his career. Journalists and some musicians celebrate him as a "pure" Mississippi blues player, but he actually listened extensively to phonograph records by musicians who played very different styles, including Leroy Carr and Lonnie Johnson. Robert Johnson's versions of "Malted Milk" and "Drunken Hearted Man" reveal Lonnie Johnson's influence. "Love in Vain" owes much to Leroy Carr. His version of "Walkin Blues" came from Son House and James McCoy. The influence of Kokomo Arnold and Peetie Wheatstraw is evident in "Sweet Home Chicago" and "Me and the Devil Blues." Robert Palmer contends that Robert Johnson was "perpetually inquisitive about all kinds of music and would probably have perfected an electric, jazz-influenced brand of modern blues had he lived into the 1940s."[21] His artistry was truly exceptional, but he invented no formal or stylistic devices that were not also common to his fellow Delta blues musicians Charley Patton, Son House, and Skip James.[22]

Romantic critics might prefer to imagine blues musicians as folk artists existing outside the culture industry, but in order to survive, much less record, they had to master the codes of commercial culture, even at the local level. The experiences of Honeyboy Edwards are instructive and typical. He remembers how commercial concerns shaped his repertoire because "sometimes the man who owned a country store would give us something like a couple of dollars on Saturday afternoon. We'd sit in the back of the store on some oat sacks or corn sacks and play while they sold groceries and whiskey and beer up front, and the people would come in and listen to us and pitch in. In the afternoon or maybe in the evenin' we'd go to a movie theater and play between the movies."[23] Securing money to "play" music depended on work, on mastering the songs that would attract customers to the country store and the motion picture house.

Romantic myths about the blues contrast sharply with the actual origins of African American music and the system of racialized labor out of which it emerged. In *Black Culture, Black Consciousness,* Lawrence Levine observes that slaves employed music to send messages to other slaves, sometimes about resistance and running away but also to shame their fellow workers into working harder and pulling their weight.[24] Booker T. Washington claimed that slave owners cultivated the singing talents of their chattel because they believed that exceptionally good singers on their plantations could increase productivity.[25] Cosmopolitan contemporary audiences might find Robert Johnson's music refreshingly free of the conventions of commercial culture, but the materials that he used and the spaces open to him for artistic expression never escaped the logic of labor exploitation or the reach of commercial considerations.

Robert Johnson came into this world shortly after a lynch mob drove Charles Dodds out of Hazlehurst, depriving his mother's husband of his land and his livelihood. The blues singer never knew his biological father, Noah Johnson. He fought so bitterly with his stepfather Dusty Willis that eventually he had to run away from home to play his music. Robert Johnson's rootlessness and restlessness were legendary. Fellow blues musician Johnny Shines remembers that "you could wake him up anytime and he was ready to go."[26] Johnson wandered around the United States playing the three-line twelve-bar blues, a hybrid of African and European forms developed in America on the guitar, an instrument that came to the United States from Mexico but had previously migrated from Spain to Mexico and before that from North Africa to Spain. Johnson turned homelessness into an art and consequently is ripe for appropriation by romantics who prize people they imagine to be free of domestic obligations and lose their identities through art, who pursue pleasure and evoke intense emotions, who develop highly individualized and original means of expression, and who live lives that seem to fall outside the bounds of bourgeois society and the constraints of commercial culture.

Yet all the qualities that seem to mark the legendary artist Robert Johnson as a romantic hero do not apply to the historical Robert Johnson. His identity changes had nothing to do with walking away from the security of bourgeois society. His pursuit of pleasure and emotional intensity stemmed directly from his systematic disenfranchisement as a worker, citizen, and racial subject. His art had less to do with his own originality than with his mastery of shared social codes and forms of expression. His life and art were shaped at every stage by economic and commercial considerations. Even his celebrated womanizing takes on another quality when located within Johnson's actual life experiences. At the age of eighteen Johnson met and married sixteen-year-old Virginia Travis and lived with her on the Klein plantation near Robinsonville, sharing a cabin with his half-sister and her husband. Their marriage was not destroyed by Robert's lust or desire to wander but by the tragic death of Virginia and their child during childbirth a year into the marriage. During his sojourn near Hazlehurst in 1931, where he supposedly made his deal with the devil, Johnson married an older woman who worked to support him while the young guitarist took lessons from Alabama-born musician Ike Zinneman (who claimed to have learned music himself during midnight visits to graveyards). Later, Johnson enjoyed an intimate and ongoing relationship with the mother of his fellow blues musician and pupil, Robert Jr. Lockwood.[27] His death at the hands of a man jealous of Johnson's sexual and romantic conquests has long made him a symbol of reckless passion, but his disconnection from stable relationships has to be viewed in the context of the social conditions facing Black people in that era: the high incidence of female mortality during childbirth, inadequate wages, and the pressures that poverty and racism imposed upon family formation and stability in his era.

It is only at the level of reception and critical commentary that Robert Johnson's life conforms to the contours of romanticism. Much of what we encounter in the lore of Robert Johnson comes from how his story can be made to fit another story already in place. As Chris Waterman observes in his important discussion of commercial culture, folk traditions, and critical categories, Charley Patton and Robert Johnson come to represent the quintessential blues players more than someone like Bo Chatmon who was "a light-skinned, somewhat finicky teetotaler who dressed in suits, owned a model-T Ford, and developed professional skills such as carpentry and gramophone repairing." Chatmon is simply too complex a personality and artist to fit the frame through which Johnson is interpreted, but that frame does a disservice to Johnson's identity and history as well. As B. B. King notes about blues critics, "The scholars love to praise the 'pure' blues artists or the ones, like Robert Johnson, who died young and represented tragedy. It angers me how scholars associate the blues strictly with tragedy."[28]

None of this is to deny the astounding artistry of Robert Johnson, nor would it make sense to downplay the importance of the crossroads story when it is properly and carefully understood. But it is to warn against a kind of romanticism that looks so hard for individuality, emotion, and an aesthetic rendering of social pain that it obscures the collective, material, and political dimensions of social life. All art entails understanding the world as it appears to others; identification with others and their experiences is what enables art to exist. As Mikhail Bakhtin observes, culture is always dialogic and the "word" always half belongs to someone else. But if we are going to be honest about the words we share—and the worlds we share—we have to face the harsh facts that divide us as well as the fond hopes that might one day unite us. Romanticism gives us a wishbone, but combating racism requires us to display some backbone.

Visual artist Renee Stout offers an alternative way of receiving the art and life of Robert Johnson. She shows it is possible to learn from others without colonizing their pain for selfish pleasure. Her installation "Dear Robert, I'll Meet You at the Crossroads" engages with Johnson's life and legend playfully. Stout recreates a Depression-era juke joint, displays the furnishings she imagines to have been in Johnson's living room, and presents a "man trap"—a display of a pair of red shoes, see-through fabric, and a bed that Stout hopes will entice Johnson and capture his love. Yet she plays with the romantic legends about the blues singer as well, placing teethlike spikes around the frame of her bed to hold her prey. Stout uses Johnson as a foil for her own strong identity, confiding, "God put me on the planet to challenge a man like that! So, it is like trying to tame that man and by doing this work on him, I am trying to understand all the power he had over women. . . . In a sense I'm relating him to my father, who tried to mold me into a woman who would listen to a man. He used to tell me, all your boyfriends are going to be henpecked, and I said, so what?"[29] Stout challenges Johnson and promises to heal him at the same time, offering a letter from Madame Ching, a fictional healer, with a suggested cure for the ailment described in Johnson's song "Dead Shrimp Blues"—male impotence caused by worry about an unfaithful spouse.

It is fitting and appropriate that Robert Johnson's encounter at the crossroads inspires Renee Stout, an artist whose extensive engagement with African artistic traditions informs all of her creations and infuses them with a strong sense of moral critique, intellectual complexity, and historical connection. Her figures, constructions, and assemblages deploy Kongo cosmograms, *minkisi* bags, fetishes, *minkondi* figures, and ceremonial mirrors in imaginative and innovative ways, mixing traditional African signs and symbols with contemporary North American cultural concerns and forms of expression. Unlike other artists who have turned to Africa for images and inspiration (Picasso, Brancusi, and the early Aaron Douglas), Stout does more than appropriate designs and decoration. She explores the complex totality of art as a social practice in Africa—as religion, medicine, and philosophy as well as ornamentation. Yet Stout does not pretend to be a traditional Kongo artist making fetishes for spiritual and practical purposes. Instead, she appropriately presents herself as someone who adapts African practices to African American realities.[30]

The art of Renee Stout displays both connection with and separation from Africa; it exudes a rooted independence, using African beliefs and practices as a baseline reality for playful and provocative interventions designed to show how place, space, objects, and images interact to mediate relations among people in the modern world. She returns to the past in order to engage the present; she displays representations that might seem exotic and far away at first, only to reveal through them regimes of power, exploitation, and silencing that are very close to home. As Michael D. Harris observes, "When an artist like Renee Stout examines a particular African object and its context, he or she may find meanings and functions that already are familiar because its form, logic, or function are echoed or resembled in African-American cultural expression."[31] In her strategic redeployment of the African past as an enduring part of the African American present, Renee Stout expresses what Paul Gilroy has described as "diasporic intimacy"—the ability of displaced Africans and their descendants to perpetuate African beliefs, values, and ideas in often hostile environments.[32] Diasporic intimacy enabled enslaved Africans in the American South to keep alive memories of the continent they came from through a wide range

of covert and overt practices. They gathered for secret night meetings in re-
mote corners of plantations to chant songs around overturned pots in the
African manner. They danced the "ring shout," moving slowly counterclockwise in circles that contained cosmic moral significance for them. They pep-
pered their speech with African words and made music based on the West
African pentatonic scale rather than on the European diatonic scale.[33] In the
face of the most brutal forms of repression and the most sinister measures of
surveillance, they kept part of Africa alive in America. African retentions
helped them understand their captivity as a crime. It encouraged them to
resist the European American ideology that defamed them as less than
human, that attributed their subordination to their own nature rather than
to the historical actions of their oppressors.

Denied their native languages, forbidden literacy, and prevented by law
from defending themselves from beatings and whippings, American slaves
turned to elements of African culture as a crucible of covert resistance, as a
way of undermining the domination of white supremacy in America. The
retention and reinvention of African forms in America, however, necessi-
tated perpetual struggle. Ex-slave Ben Sullivan identified part of a much
larger process when he told an interviewer from the Works Progress Administration's Federal Writers Project on the American Slave in the 1930s his
memories of an incident during slavery times: "Old man Okra said he wanted a place like he had in Africa, so he built himself a hut, but Master made
him pull it down. He said he didn't want an African hut on his place."[34] After
emancipation, ex-slaves and their descendants continued that struggle. They
built shotgun houses that resembled dwellings in West Africa and protected
their dwellings through a variety of traditional practices from their home
continent—placing mirrors on outside walls, setting ceramic jars on both
sides of front doors, ringing yards with white-washed stones, and decorating
inside walls with dynamic script called "spirit writing."[35] But their links to
Africa were not limited to the physical presence of African objects. As
Charles Joyner argues, even when slaves and free Blacks found themselves
dependent upon European or American tools and artifacts, they put them to
use in distinctly African fashion.[36] Although rarely acknowledged or accepted by the dominant culture, Africanisms in American society have
shaped the mind and spirit of Black Americans, and, in turn, their cultural
expressions have informed the basic vocabulary of most American music,
dance, speech, style, and visual imagery.[37]

The struggle continues today. Many Americans still don't want an African
hut in their country. They understand that the unity forged through the possessive investment in whiteness depends upon the erasure—or at least the eclipse—
of the African, Asian, Latin American, and Native American pasts. Critics of
Afrocentrism and multiculturalism deny, deride, and denigrate claims of enduring African contributions to American culture. Their vehemence makes

Renee Stout's acknowledgment and celebration of the African presence in America that much more important, not just for what she has to say about Africa but for demonstrating that the aspects of our identity tied to ethnic affiliations do not have to produce prejudice and parochialism but can offer us independence rooted in knowledge, enabling us to see things both from close up and from far away.

In *The Disuniting of America: Reflections on a Multicultural Society*, a best-selling book published at the time Renee Stout was exhibiting "Dear Robert, I'll See you at the Crossroads," Pulitzer Prize–winning historian Arthur Schlesinger, Jr., attacked the idea of African influence in America. He decried efforts by educators to explore the connections between African Americans and the culture of the African continent. Denouncing "Afrocentric" education as part of a "cult of ethnicity" designed to "protect, promote, and perpetuate separate ethnic and racial communities," Schlesinger claimed that "it is hard to see what living connection exists between American blacks today and their heterogeneous West African ancestors three centuries ago." He concedes that "from time to time, black leaders, notably Martin Delany in the mid-nineteenth century and Marcus Garvey in the 1920s, excited passing interest in Africa," but Schlesinger nonetheless maintained that "until very recent times, few black Americans have regarded the African connection as a major theme in their lives." Moreover, he charges that "American Afrocentrism" is a recent and "invented" tradition whose advocates operate from chauvinist and even racist motivations based on "the theory that race determines mentality."[38]

It is hard to imagine a historian being any less historical about the role of Africa in America. Schlesinger's argument displays appalling ignorance of the historical record in nearly every respect.[39] Extensive research has consistently confirmed the judgment that Carter G. Woodson offered back in the 1920s, that "what the Negro accomplished in Africa was not lost. His art tended to revive in the slave on the American plantation. It appeared in the tasks, proverbs, and riddles of the plantation Negroes. The tribal chants of the African paved the way for the spirituals, the religious expression of the slave."[40] Following Woodson's analysis, we know that not just the spirituals but the blues as well derived from Africa—from the AAB three-line form of West African poetry; from the antiphony, pitch changes, and "impure" buzz tones of African musical systems; and from the ways the dynamic tensions between European diatonic and African pentatonic scales produce flatted fifths, thirds, and sevenths in blues music.[41]

Although comments from two distinguished and apparently equally uninformed historians appear on the back cover of Schlesinger's book (C. Vann Woodward called the work "brilliant" and John Morton Blum found it "learned, persuasive, and sound"), most knowledgeable reviewers have deemed Schlesinger's argument seriously deficient. Lawrence Levine, an expert on African American culture, singled it out for an especially devastating critique in his presidential address to the Organization of American Historians.[42] But although Schlesinger's book failed as a historical argument, it proved a public relations success, largely because of the support it received from individuals and institutions with a stake in its ideology. *The Disuniting of America* was originally commissioned and published by the Whittle Corporation, a purportedly education-oriented business that started Channel One, a corporation that donated television equipment to schools in return for the exclusive right to program into classrooms light feature stories bracketed by noisy commercials for candy and soda. The Time-Warner conglomerate held a financial interest in Channel One, and that company's *Time* magazine gave extensive publicity to Schlesinger's book, including a cover story in the July 8, 1991, issue that featured an excerpt from it.[43]

When one of the nation's most powerful multimedia conglomerates joins forces with an influential and politically connected educational entrepreneur and a Pulitzer Prize–winning historian to ridicule claims about the influence of Africa in America, the evidence supporting those claims in Renee Stout's work takes on special significance. Even more important than the physical and ethical proof that pervades her art, Stout's self-reflexive disclosures about her own processes of creation reveal the power and depth of organic popular traditions, community art institutions, and private family memories in nurturing and sustaining African imagery, icons, and ideas in America. Moreover, the compelling moral vision that arises from her work bears no resemblance to the parochial prejudice and "racism" that Schlesinger sees at the root of African American interest in Africa. Instead, Stout encourages an open-minded engagement with all cultures.

Her interest in the senses of separation and loss that shape the African diaspora leads Stout to an empathetic identification with the experiences of immigrants to America from Europe, Asia, Central America, and Haiti. Her honest explorations into her own family's history lead her on a quest to reconnect with the African past, but they also enable her to claim Native American and Irish ancestry. "They are all part of my heritage and influence my work," she affirms.[44] The pluralism and panethnic antiracism of Renee Stout's art and worldview are hardly inhibited by her interest in Africa and the Caribbean. On the contrary, her grounding in African forms and philosophies connects her to powerful traditions of social justice and moral critique capable of generating interest, concern, and attachment from many different kinds of people.

Growing up in the working-class East Liberty section of Pittsburgh, Pennsylvania, Stout encountered diverse forms of art and artisanship through that city's established cultural institutions as well as through informal cultural activities in her home and neighborhood. Saturday morning art classes at the Carnegie Museum exposed her to the institution's natural history and art collections. A display of shrunken heads from South America and a Central African *nkisi nkondi* figure made especially strong impressions on Stout, inspiring some of her later work.[45] When she returned to Pittsburgh subsequently to visit with family and friends, she often visited the *nkisi nkondi* in the Carnegie Museum "because I feel like I'm coming back with a little more knowledge each time."[46] She learned about a wide variety of artistic practices and traditions from her everyday life experiences as well. Stout's father worked as a mechanic, and her grandfather labored in a steel mill. They displayed pride in their skills as artisans and offered her important lessons in economy and ingenuity by never throwing anything out and by using all available resources in their work. Her grandfather also played music, providing her with important lessons about intercultural communication when he frequently entertained an interracial crowd of friends and neighbors at his home on summer evenings.[47] These early experiences shaped Stout's disposition toward music as another artistic, religious, and even medical practice—a way of understanding, experiencing, and perhaps even healing the world.

Stout also received artistic instruction and inspiration at home from her mother's brother, whose passion for painting was not diminished by a dearth of resources—he painted on any available spare surface, even the lids of shoe boxes when that was all that he had at his disposal.[48] Just as her classes at the Carnegie Museum started Stout on the road toward representations based on African imagery and icons, her family's ways of working as artisans and artists set the stage for her subsequent success with sculpture and assemblages made up of everyday items and found objects, including an ironing board, sardine cans, slippers, and a mousetrap.[49]

African practices influenced Stout in indirect ways when she was growing up, although she did not recognize or understand their full significance until later in life. She remembers being fascinated by an old house on Renfrew Street in East Liberty because the woman who lived there filled the yard with dolls, stuffed animals, and a scarecrow—all mounted on poles. Only later did she learn of the close correspondence between this African American yard art and traditional West African practices. As art historian Robert Farris Thompson reminds us, yard art provides "an alternative classical tradition" for Black artists, serving as part of "an invisible academy, reminding them who they are and where they come from."[50] Stout returned to Pittsburgh in 1980 to photograph the dressed figures in front of the house on Renfrew Street as part of her ongoing effort to incorporate physical artifacts from her life into her assemblages.[51] Once Stout became conscious of the African presence in her life history, she began to recognize how pervasive it had been. While working on a 1992 installation at Woodlawn Cemetery in New York, Stout learned from her grandmother of a relative who died at a time when the family had no money for a headstone. "My mother took this jar and put things all over it," her grandmother remembered. Like many other African Americans, Stout's family had commemorated their dead in an African way, placing broken objects, household containers, and personal objects on the grave to mark and heal the rupture created by death. Later, during a trip home to Pittsburgh, Stout stopped at a pharmacy that she had visited many times previously in Homewood, a mostly African American neighborhood. She noticed a collection of products designed for natural healing according to African and African American folk practices. "I didn't know that when you go to the back in the corner you have roots and oils, and it was there all along," she recalls. "And I didn't know until I knew what to look for."[52] Once she knew what to look for, African items and icons appeared all around her.

On a visit to California in 1986, Stout noticed newspapers covering the interior walls of a Black woman's home and recognized their connection to African "protective print" and "spirit writing."[53] The Mande people in Africa, among others, placed religious writing inside leather charms. They brought the African Islamic belief in the protective power of the written word with them to America. Throughout the southern United States, Black people often placed newsprint on walls and in shoes, or left the Bible open at night as a continuation of African ways in America.[54] Awareness of these influences on her life has enabled Renee Stout to incorporate African objects and artifacts into her visual images in imaginative and original ways. Protective writing decorates the mixed-media piece "Instructions and Provisions/Wake Me Up on Judgment Day."[55] Her celebrated "Fetish #2" presents a cast of her own body in plaster layered with black paint and decorated with cowrie shells, parts of her deceased grandfather's watch, braided hair extensions, a pelt of monkey hair, medicine bags, dried flowers, a photograph of a baby, and a postal stamp from Africa. In this work, Stout presents herself as a *nkisi* figure decorated with objects of magic and power, including a mirrored back panel to suggest the necessity of "seeing beyond the visible."[56] The mixed-media assemblage "She Kept Her Conjuring Table Very Neat" combines ceremonial candles, roots, bones, beaded slippers, and a photograph of Colonel Frank, a semifictional character who often appears in her work along with his love interest, Dorothy.[57]

In "Ancestral Power Object" Stout presents a standing figure resembling an African nail fetish decorated with pins, jewelry, and her own fingerprints, among other items. Embellished with the names of Haitian and Yoruba deities, mysterious protective writing, the year of her own birth and that of her maternal grandmother, and adorned with a stamp from the Belgian Congo, this mixed-media work expresses Stout's figurative and literal "correspondence" (the postal stamp) with African ideas and arts. Stout mixes dirt and pebbles from West Africa with African American grave dirt as a means of "symbolically putting the whole back together again." She displays an incomplete circle on the front panel of her "Ancestral Power Object" to express "the incomplete destiny and development of the African American people."[58] Here Stout deploys an old metaphor in a new way. The circle has long been a powerful generative concept in African American life and culture, as Sterling Stuckey's singularly important research on the "ring shout" demonstrates. The counterclockwise circle of the ring shout imported from "the Congo" (Angola) became the crucible of moral uplift and political instruction for generations of Black people in slavery and in freedom. While generated in African American communities and serving critical functions for them, the semiotics of the circle articulated values and beliefs important to all people. As Stuckey shows, when Black intellectuals (including W.E.B. Du Bois, Henry Highland Garnet, and Paul Robeson) applied the lessons taught them by the ring shout about solidarity across generations, national borders, and colors, they articulated a humane and egalitarian vision that educated and inspired people from all backgrounds.[59]

In similar fashion, the art of Renee Stout draws powerfully upon African American traditions and her own history. It uses personal and community knowledge to address the problems of a wider world. For example, her penchant for working with ordinary objects has meaning for Stout not simply because they reflect the traditions of her family and her ethnic group but because they offer instruction for dealing with inequality and injustice. "When I look at society," she explains, "I see the emphasis on money and material things. Everyone is bogged down in competition. The reason I use found objects in my art is to say to everyone, 'Use what you have and be positive, whatever it is that you have, try to make something good from it.' My relatives were always able to make any situation elegant or wonderful. They made 'home' a very secure and nourishing place physically and spiritually." Within her own art, the use of found objects offers her a chance to exercise some control over her own environment. "I realized that I was taking objects from a painfully cruel environment and trying to turn them into something positive by creating with them," she says.[60]

Because she knows her own culture and its struggles so well, Stout finds herself especially appreciative of the spiritual, cultural, and political struggles of others. Discussing her use of images from Native American, Mexican, and Haitian folk traditions, she confesses, "I'm attracted to spiritual societies. . . . It [spirituality] seems like a means of survival in a world that you can't always understand." Her work on the African diaspora has honed her sensitivity to the experiences of immigrants to America from other parts of the world. She expresses particular concern about "how some people who have come to this country have had to change their whole way of thinking and identity in order to be accepted, even though they'll never be fully accepted. It is a hard thing to think about. Even though you tried and adapted to the ways of the existing culture, you are never going to be accepted. So, maybe it is not a good idea to throw away your old beliefs and ideas, maybe you should still hold onto them. I want people to think about those [people of other] cultures who come to the United States and have to totally change who they are. It is so unfair."[61]

Contrary to Arthur Schlesinger's assumption that contemporary interest in Africa evidences "the virus of tribalism" and "a cult of ethnicity" mandating ethnic and racial separation, Stout's engagement with African art expresses understanding of the important inflection that the African presence has always given to American society and culture. Rather than leading to racism or ethnic separatism, her art uses the situated knowledge emerging from the African American experience to illuminate broader truths and to imagine ways of branching out so that all people can draw on useful traditions from all cultures, a purpose Stout has articulated:

I can't understand why people are trying to melt everything down, when what actually makes America interesting is the fact that no one originated here except the Native Americans. You have all these wonderful different flavors going into making this one great whole. I don't understand why people are fighting against that. Why is it that people cannot tolerate differences? I think that if people in America could open themselves up to all the different nationalities and customs that we have right here in this country, it would make every individual more worldly without even having to travel. We have so much right here that people are not taking advantage of.[62]

Her comments may be motivated as much by tactical as by philosophical concerns; with reactionary nationalists around the world seeking foundational certainty in mythologies of pure, discrete, and unified cultural origins for their ethnic or national group, Stout argues for creative responses to contradictions, ruptures, and fissures. Her art displays a clear concern for how difficult it will be to appreciate these "wonderful different flavors" when our histories leave us with unequal access to resources, wealth, and life chances—much less to the mechanisms of cultural expression and their distribution.

Renee Stout's engagement with African aesthetics and ideologies continues a long tradition among African American artisans and artists. The Mississippi-born rhythm-and-blues musician Ellas McDaniel touched on these links when he adopted the stage name Bo Diddley, naming himself for the diddley bow, a one-string instrument of African origin.[63] Like Stout, he turned to a retention of African culture and its uses among African Americans to create an identity and an artistic practice capable of changing the ways people experience their lives. Stout's interest in Robert Johnson's music and life complements perfectly her concentration on objects associated with healing, on devices designed to make life better.

Stout draws directly on a broad range of popular African practices surviving in the United States through diverse forms of vernacular artistic expression; but she also builds on a legacy of struggle by important individuals and community institutions that have insisted on a conscious connection between Africa and America. Her work is reminiscent of that of Henry O. Tanner, who began to select African Americans as the subjects of his genre paintings shortly after he appeared before the week-long Congress of Africa symposium at the 1894 Chicago World's Fair.[64] Stout follows in the tradition established by the Hampton Institute when it acquired one of the first collections of African art in North America at the turn of the century, largely through the efforts of that school's alumnus William H. Sheppard, who collected art in the Congo between 1890 and 1910. Throughout the twentieth century, art historians and artists such as James A. Porter, R. O'Hara Lanier, and John Biggers, working at historically Black institutions, have been in the vanguard of knowledge about and respect for the relationship between African and African American art.[65] Similarly, during the Harlem Renaissance, Alain Locke asked his fellow intellectuals to explore and emphasize the African origins of their art.

The American interest in African art is neither recent nor symbolic; it is a product of the ways in which the history of the United States is organically linked to the history of the rest of the world. In the art of Renee Stout, it reaches new levels of complexity, depth, and imagination. Stout offers us an art as complicated and challenging as our history, an art with great affective power that nonetheless brings us face to face with the social relations that both divide and unite us. Whether in Renee Stout's art or in Robert Johnson's music, the African influences in America contain intellectual, aesthetic, and spiritual meanings important to all people. Anyone open to acknowledging and appreciating the African presence can derive great wisdom and enjoyment from her images. Alarmists like Arthur Schlesinger may continue to resist the many things that the African presence in America can teach all of us, but as Ellas McDaniel might say, they don't know diddley.

9

Lean on Me

Beyond Identity Politics

*Once the victim's testimony is delivered, however, there is thereafter,
forever, a witness somewhere: which is an irreducible inconvenience
for the makers and shakers and accomplices of this world. These run
together, in packs, and corroborate each other. They cannot bear the
judgment in the eyes of the people whom they intend to hold in
bondage forever, and who know more about them than their lovers.*

—JAMES BALDWIN

In making the motion picture *Lean on Me* in 1989, director John Avildsen
interrupted his *Karate Kid* series to turn his attention temporarily toward
education. Defying skeptics who charged that he would probably keep
making *Karate Kid* films until someone drove a stake through his heart, the
director of *Rocky* presented a depiction of the adventures of an inner-city
high school principal in a film that offered viewers a cross between *To Sir
with Love* and *The Terminator*. Television and newspaper advertisements for
Lean on Me boasted that the film told the story of a "real life" hero—Joe
Clark, the African American principal of Eastside High School in Paterson,
New Jersey. But Joe Clark is no hero. He exemplifies a new kind of cowardice,
not a new kind of heroism. By celebrating his actions, this film expresses
nothing that is new, just a very old and very destructive form of racism.

I have a personal connection to this film and to the situations it depicts.
I grew up in Paterson and attended Eastside High School, graduating in
1964. Even then, Paterson was a dying industrial city plagued by high rates
of poverty and unemployment. Half my high school class dropped out before
graduation; four of the minority and white working-class students who graduated were killed in the Vietnam War. During the summer after our graduation, frustrated and angry Black youths and adults staged a civil insurrection
in Paterson, setting fire to ghetto buildings and pelting police vehicles with
rocks and bottles. The distinguished poet, critic, and writer Selden Rodman
described Paterson in an article written for the *New York Times* as "an in-
ferno of burnt-out industries, blackened homes, and crippled lives."

Growing up in Paterson during those years offered a young person an education inside and outside of the classroom. In a school whose population was divided among whites, Blacks, and Puerto Ricans, racial tensions permeated every interaction. We knew that no matter what group we belonged to, somebody hated us. People could get jumped, robbed, and maybe even killed simply for being in the wrong place at the wrong time. Yet we also learned to deal with differences, to make friends with people from all backgrounds, to recognize the things we had in common along with the things that divided us.

Ten percent of my class went on to college, mostly those who came from comfortable middle-class homes like my own. We had known all our lives that we would get college educations. Regardless of how hard we worked or whether we worked at all, no matter how well or how poorly we performed as students, our parents' aspirations, intentions, and material support would see to it that we went to college somewhere. At the same time, most of our classmates knew that for them higher education was out of the question, that no matter how hard they worked or how well they performed in school, their futures almost certainly lay in low-wage jobs in Paterson's declining industrial sector. Soon, even those jobs disappeared. My classmates and I went to school in the same building and seemed to receive the same education, but there was a big difference between those whose class and race made it seem natural and necessary to take college prep courses and those channeled into business and vocational tracks facing at best a future of low-paid labor.

During the years that I attended Eastside, my father served as the principal of Central High, a school with an even larger minority population and dropout rate than Eastside's at that time. My father was a gentle and generous man who cared deeply about the students in his school. He could be a strict disciplinarian when he had to be, but he knew that a positive self-image and a sense of social connection could motivate students more effectively and more permanently than punishment. He befriended the students in his school who had behavior problems, learning their names and inquiring about their interests. He helped them with personal and family problems and worked tirelessly to help them secure employment so they could experience the responsibilities, respect, and sense of purpose that a job can bring to a young person. He turned the schools he ran into community centers, involved parents in the educational process, and fashioned after-school and evening programs that spoke to the broader needs of the neighborhood and the city.

My father and my mother had both attended Paterson's public schools in their childhood years. As children of Jewish immigrant parents, they felt that they owed a great debt to the United States for many reasons, but most of all because of the education they received and the ways in which it encouraged, nurtured, and sustained their growth as critical, contemplative, and creative people and citizens. They knew that had their families remained in Europe, they would certainly have been sent to Hitler's concentration camps. That realization left them with a strong sense of social justice and a deep empathy for all oppressed people, not just their fellow Jews. My mother and father became teachers to repay the debt they felt they owed to this country, to give to others the great gifts that they had received. After my father died from a heart attack at the age of forty-nine during my senior year in high school in 1964, my family remained involved in public education in Paterson. My sister and my mother both taught at Eastside at different times during the 1960s and 1970s and established reputations as the kinds of demanding and dedicated instructors that students remember long after their school years have been completed. Over the years, I have learned a great deal from them about what it means to try to offer a quality education in an inner-city school. My father, my mother, my sister, and many of their colleagues and friends have devoted much of their lives to that effort. I know how hard a job they have, how much patience and love it takes to try to neutralize the effects of poverty and racism even temporarily. I know as well that no amount of good intentions, no mastery of teaching techniques, and no degree of effort by individual educators can alter meaningfully the fundamentally unequal distribution of resources and opportunities in this society.

Neither the true history of Paterson's economic decline nor the actual conditions facing its educators appear in *Lean on Me*. Instead, the director of *Rocky* and *The Karate Kid* presents us with another kind of fairy tale, a story about how serious social problems can be solved simply by reciting rules, how challenges to public order by women and members of aggrieved racial minorities can be quelled by male heroes strong enough and determined enough to bully and intimidate their opponents. This glorification of a small-time demagogue and grandstander ignores the structural problems facing cities like Paterson, the realities of unequal funding for schools, and the health and nutrition problems confronting more and more children growing up in poverty.

Joe Clark rose to public prominence during the mid-1980s as part of a coordinated campaign by conservatives to hide the consequences of their own actions in cutting social programs and educational opportunities during the Reagan years. A favorite of right-wing foundations and their educational spokesperson William Bennett, Clark blamed liberals and the civil rights movement for the sorry state of inner-city schools. He offered his own record as an administrator who ruled with an iron hand as a model for improving the schools without spending any more money on education. He called Reverend Jesse Jackson "a constipated maggot" and claimed that young black men were "barbarians who are out of control."[1] Clark became popular among conservatives because he patrolled Eastside High School carrying a baseball bat and a bullhorn, behavior that titillated politicians and public relations flacks with the prospect of enlisting Black mercenaries (whom they had already demonized as brutal) in a campaign of counterinsurgency against unruly inner-city minority youths. Although Clark never developed any substantial following in—or connection to—African American communities, his ability to enact white fantasies made him a favorite among what James Baldwin called "the makers and shakers and accomplices of this world."

Lean on Me opens with a montage that portrays the predominantly Black students and staff of Eastside High School as lazy, licentious, boisterous, and brutal. With stereotypical caricatures that hearken back to nineteenth-century minstrel shows and D. W. Griffith's 1915 white supremacist film, *The Birth of a Nation,* Avildsen raises the specter of out-of-control Black bodies to set the stage for his authoritarian Black hero. *Lean on Me* glamorizes the way Clark resorts to physical intimidation and verbal abuse to make teachers, parents, and students knuckle under to his version of law and order, a version that contains much more order than law. The film attributes the demise of discipline in Eastside High School to the control over school policy won by black female parents and teachers as a result of the civil rights movement of the 1960s. Like *The Birth of a Nation,* it summons up authoritarian patriarchal power as the necessary antidote to a broad range of misbehavior by Blacks, ranging from lascivious attacks on white women to the laziness of public employees, from the uninhibited speech and body movements of Black teenagers to brutal assaults on white authority figures and on "innocent" fellow Blacks. Fusing elements of previous high school "disruption" films with the theme of the lone vigilante, Avildsen's motion picture displays no awareness of the aspirations, experiences, or feelings of students, parents, and teachers, much less any acknowledgment of the actual social conditions they confront.

As principal of Eastside High School, Clark illegally expelled large numbers of students from school on the grounds that he viewed them all as troublemakers. He fueled fights between teacher and parent factions and—most important for his cinematic image—roamed the halls of his school carrying a baseball bat in order to threaten unruly students. These actions won praise from pundits, but they did nothing to solve the educational problems facing the school and its students. Clark failed to lower the dropout rate, to improve academic performance, or to raise scores on standardized tests. Instead, his incessant self-promotion exacted serious costs on the school, which eventually became clear even to his patrons in conservative foundations.

Clark took a "sick leave" from his $65,000 a year principal's job so that he could continue to collect his salary while he toured the country giving lectures to conservative groups at $7,000 per appearance. He was in Los Angeles preparing to appear on the Arsenio Hall television show when a musical act hired for an Eastside High School assembly featured several G-string-clad male dancers. Clark declared himself innocent of any failure to supervise his school, blaming the whole affair on "the essence of some kind of surreptitious act" and in the process offering his students a negative lesson in avoiding responsibility for one's actions.[2] He sought unsuccessfully an appointment to an unexpired term on the board of freeholders in Essex County (about ten miles from Paterson), explaining that he needed experience in an administrative office as preparation to be president of the United States: "I'm not going to be a Jesse Jackson," he declared, referring to questions about the civil rights leader's lack of administrative experience during his 1984 and 1988 campaigns for the presidency. Clark turned his leave of absence into an extended audition for more support from wealthy conservative foundations, avoiding the actual work of running a school so that he could pontificate about education and pursue more lucrative and less taxing employment as a full-time speaker than he was faced with as an educator.

When his year on leave expired, Clark retired from his post. He filed a workman's compensation claim against the board of education, charging that his endocarditis (deterioration of the aortic valve) had been caused by the board's lack of appreciation of his efforts. Clark vowed that the school district "will pay for the damage they inflicted upon my mortal soul."[3] Conservative foundations are not usually supportive of government workers who defy their superiors, expect taxpayers to support them during sick leaves while they rake in thousands of dollars lecturing about their favorite political causes, and then file highly dubious workman's compensation claims. Nevertheless, the foundations continued to embrace Clark because of his utility to their efforts to increase the possessive investment in whiteness.

The Joe Clark portrayed in *Lean on Me* gave white audiences one more chance to blame the victim, one more opportunity to believe that the anguish in African American ghettos stems from the underdeveloped character of the poor rather than from routine and systematic inequalities in resources and opportunities. Since 1973, when President Nixon abandoned public housing and diverted War on Poverty funds into revenue-sharing schemes designed to lower local taxes on real estate, the crises facing the urban poor had escalated. The value of grants given through the Aid to Dependent Children program fell by one third from 1969 to 1985 when inflation is taken into account. The 1981 Deficit Reduction Act took away from the poor one dollar of benefits for every dollar earned. Critics charged that these policies would have disastrous effects on poor families and their children, and consequently on the nation's future. Time has shown these critics to be correct.

At the same time, federal policies fueled a spending spree by and for the rich. Defense boondoggles, insider trading, unregulated speculative schemes, mergers, and profiteering from bad loans wreaked havoc in the U.S. economy. Yet the taxpayer has always been there to pick up the tab, protecting the

failed auto firms, the savings-and-loan swindlers, and the brokers and predatory lenders responsible for the economic collapse of 2008. How does a
country justify itself to itself when it has spent most of its recent history
abandoning its poor children in order to feed the greed of the rich? How do
politicians and public relations flacks who promise to return us to family
values explain their participation in the construction of a casino economy
that brings an apocalypse on the installment plan to inner-city families? The
answer to both questions is to blame the victims, to channel middle-class
fears into a sadistic and vindictive crusade that racializes the poor and then
blames them for their powerlessness.

The economic orthodoxy of our time has not only widened the gap between rich and poor, between whites and communities of color, but it has
also encouraged the growth of a vigilante mentality, as violent and sadistic
as the crimes it purports to oppose. From Bernhard Goetz's shooting of four
youths on a New York subway car to the Philadelphia Police Department's
bombing of MOVE headquarters, from the Los Angeles police roundups of
fourteen-year-olds in the name of stopping gang violence to the killing of
Eric Garner on a Staten Island street corner, the nation has progressively
dispensed with the due process of law when it comes to the racialized poor.
Most often invoked in the name of fighting criminality, this attitude instead
elevates a criminal mentality to the front lines of social policy. It is an attitude rooted in resentment and fear, exploited by law-and-order politicians
and the makers of vigilante films alike.

One problem with this attitude is that it only works as a way to treat
someone else. Joe Clark's belittling and humiliating of his students won audience approval because listeners and viewers believed that such treatment
would be legitimate and might work against the faceless "others" in the ghetto. If they were to think of those students as their own children, they would
never allow anyone to treat them in that fashion. Indeed, the conservative
pundits who fawned over Clark did not line up to send their own children to
Eastside High School. Yet, as we have seen over and over again, once the erosion of civil liberties and the diminution of human dignity gets started, it
does not stop with its original victims. In this context, it is not hard to see
why there is a major motion picture about Joe Clark—an honor denied Sep-
tima Clark, the Reverend Buck Jones, Paul Robeson, Fannie Lou Hamer, Ella
Baker, and other courageous fighters for the African American community.
Hollywood does not believe that white American audiences want to see
Black heroes who love their own communities and struggle to win resources
for them. In Hollywood, there is no room for adult Blacks operating in their
own interests, only for Black sidekicks and underlings, for terrified victims
in need of white protection. The prototypical example was Alan Parker's
Mississippi Burning, which presented the 1964 civil rights struggle in Mississippi as if black people played only the role of passive spectators. From *The*

Birth of a Nation to *Gone with the Wind,* from *Lean on Me* to *Driving Miss Daisy,* Hollywood has always preferred its faithful Black servants. Joe Clark is only the latest in long line of smiling sycophants on- and offscreen, reassuring white America that it will never have to wake up to its racial record and face its responsibilities.

Yet *Lean on Me* adds a new and frightening aspect to this traditional scenario. Clark's purported heroism stems from no positive accomplishment. He does not help his own students nor does he serve as a role model for other educators. His sole function is to fuel the spite, resentment, and rage of the privileged. His mass-mediated image maintains the myth that counterinsurgency will prevail when justice does not, that schools can succeed by becoming prisons—or more precisely that prisons are more important to society than schools. In keeping with the conservative contempt for public education, Clark brings the model of the military and the penitentiary to urban education. It does not matter to his admirers that such behavior cannot develop the intellectual and personal resources necessary for a lifetime of citizenship and work; what does matter is that it imposes a dictatorial and authoritarian model on the poor and presents people who have problems *as* problems.

Joe Clark is not the problem, nor does his perspective bear any relation to a solution. Once he has exhausted his usefulness to those in power he will be shoved aside, like so many before him. What will remain long after Joe Clark has been forgotten, however, are the problems of the inner-city schools and the sadism in search of a story fueled by these kinds of images. Film viewers need to ask how their imaginations are being colonized and for what ends. Perhaps one cannot really blame filmmakers for opportunistically exploiting the racial hatreds and social vindictiveness of the motion picture audience. Hollywood filmmakers are in business to make money, and they have never hidden their willingness to exploit the darkest recesses of the human character to turn a profit for their investors. But at least they could have given this execrable film an appropriate title. In its internal message and social mission, it is not so much *Lean on Me* as *Step on Them.*

None of this is to deny the crippling effects of crime in our society, most of all on the inner city and its inhabitants. Nor is it to assert the irrelevance of discipline, order, self-control, and character for any individual or group. It is only to argue against simplistic and self-serving diagnoses of deep and complex social problems. Locating the origins of white anxieties in the alleged character deficiencies of people from aggrieved racial groups evades an honest engagement with the materialism, selfishness, and predatory competitiveness of *all* social groups in the wake of the changes that neoliberal economics and politics have brought. Nearly every reputable scholarly study shows that unemployment, inferior educational opportunities, and social inequalities are directly linked to increases in crime. People of color have simply been the ones hardest hit by these structural transformations. Declining numbers of blue-collar jobs, capital flight, discrimination by employers in the expanding retail sector of the economy, location of new businesses in suburban locations, residential segregation, and cutbacks in social programs and government employment have all contributed to increased rates of minority unemployment. Unemployment among African American youths quadrupled between 1961 and 1986, while white youth unemployment remained static. Instead of asking why Black criminals exist, it would be more productive to explore, appreciate, and endorse the restorative and resilient practices in Black communities that have provided positive alternatives to lives of crime.

It is understandable that fear of crime makes many people wish to respond with a strong show of force against lawbreakers. But force can create as well as restrain criminality. It can teach people that force is the preferred way to solve problems, especially when it is applied indiscriminately against whole populations. Studies show that exposure to boot-camp correctional facilities structured around humiliating disciplinary routines makes inmates more rather than less aggressive. Force is even more counterproductive when used against law-abiding citizens—the vast majority of people in poor and minority communities. Nine percent of African Americans report that the police have used excessive force against them in the city where they live, and African Americans are nearly three times as likely to die at the hands of police officers than are whites.[4] Highly publicized cases in the 2010s like the police killings of Michael Brown in Ferguson, Missouri, and Philando Castile in Falcon Heights, Minnesota, convince a large proportion of minority observers (and many who are not minorities as well) that a code of silence protects police officers from the consequences of their actions against members of aggrieved communities. Of the nearly 27,000 police brutality cases tracked by the federal Department of Justice in 2002 alone (the most recent year for which the department provides data), only 8 percent led to disciplinary action against an officer.[5] Most important, the most sophisticated social scientific studies show that while neither poverty nor racial discrimination alone *cause* crime, aggressive acts of violence are more likely to emanate from people under conditions of poverty, racial discrimination, and inequality.[6] As Judith and Peter Blau observed years ago, "Aggressive acts of violence seem to result not so much from lack of advantages as from being taken advantage of."[7]

Fighting crime effectively entails addressing its constituent causes, not indulging in the counterproductive escapism, sermonizing, and muscle flexing advanced in films like *Lean on Me.* Yet while we are waiting for the broad structural solutions that we need, we still must address issues of individual morality, personal accountability, and disrespect for law and order. I propose that we start by strictly enforcing the laws that ban discrimination in hous-

ing and hiring, regulate environmental pollution and unsafe working conditions, and guarantee minimum wages, due process, and equal protection of
the law to all citizens. In that vein, I suggest swift and certain punishment
meted out against one individual who flaunted the law brazenly, who deliberately obstructed justice, and who denied citizens the protections guaranteed to them in the Constitution. In his book *The Color Line*, the great
historian John Hope Franklin describes the actions of this individual clearly. Appointed to a post in the Department of Education by the president of
the United States, this person refused to investigate complaints about racial
and gender discrimination, forcing the plaintiffs to ask that he be placed in
contempt of court for his refusal to do what the law required him to do.
When asked at a hearing if he was violating the time frames established for
civil rights enforcement in *Adams v. Bell*, if he was violating them "on all
occasions" and violating them directly on complaints "most of the time" or
at least "half of the time," this bureaucrat answered, "That's right." When
asked if "meanwhile you are violating a court order rather grievously, aren't
you?" he answered yes.

On the strength of this record, this individual was promoted to chair the
Equal Employment Opportunity Commission. In the first year at that job,
the time needed to process complaints went from five months to nine
months. The backlog of unanswered complaints went from 31,000 at the time
of his appointment to 61,686 complaints four years later. This miserable performance earned him an appointment to a federal judgeship, where in one
case, he refused to recuse himself from a dispute that involved the direct financial interests of his personal and professional patron, instead issuing a
ruling that vacated a judgment of $10.4 million against his patron's family-
owned business.[8] Perhaps readers can help me locate this malefactor and
bring him to justice. His name is Clarence Thomas.

Clarence Thomas and Joe Clark prove that not all white supremacists are
white, that white supremacist policies can be pursued by people from all
backgrounds. This should come as no surprise; it is the way power works. No
oppressed group in history has ever been immune to the opportunism of
individuals who desire to distance themselves from the stigma associated
with their oppression. At the same time, while not all white supremacists are
white, all whites do not have to be white supremacists. Just as Joe Clark's
Blackness did not prevent him from acting on behalf of white supremacy, a
white scholar named George Rawick made his life's work exposing and attacking the possessive investment in whiteness. His life story resonates with
the observations offered by the narrator of Chester Himes's 1945 novel, *If He
Hollers Let Him Go*. Reflecting on the range of identities open to white
people, the narrator ponders "how you could take two guys from the same
place" and "one would carry his whiteness like a loaded stick, ready to bop
everybody else in the head with it; and the other guy would just simply be

white as if he didn't have anything to do with it and let it go at that."⁹ Much
of my education about the role whites can play in antiracist activity came
from Rawick, an irascible and exasperating individual with many shortcomings and an assortment of personal problems who got one thing absolutely
right. He was a white man who knew where he stood in respect to racism.
Through his activism and his scholarship, he battled white supremacy, not
simply out of sympathy for others but out of a sense of self-respect. The
truths that appear in his scholarly writings will never make it onto the big
screens of Hollywood, but they have something important to teach us about
the role whites can play in fighting against white supremacy.

Born in Brooklyn in 1929, Rawick went to Erasmus Hall High School,
where one of his acquaintances was Al Davis, who later became famous for
his temper tantrums, paranoia, and indifference to public opinion as the
owner of the Oakland Raiders football team. Many of Rawick's friends observed that he often displayed social skills similar to those of his high school
classmate. He fought with everyone he knew at one time or another, even his
best friends. He could be obstinate, irritating, and rude. He could also be
flexible, considerate, and caring. He once described himself as a descendant
of radical rabbis and gun-running gangsters, and his professional demeanor
displayed evidence of both lineages.

Educated in and out of school by trade-union militants, Rawick attended
Oberlin College in Ohio after graduating from high school in the mid-1940s.
He traveled by train to Ohio, carrying with him radical pamphlets and wearing a zoot suit, fashionable by Brooklyn standards, but an outfit that provoked considerable consternation in Ohio. Rawick went on to do graduate
work at the University of Wisconsin and the University of Chicago, but he
remained committed to political work through his involvement with a variety of left-wing splinter groups. Rawick's doctoral research examined New
Deal programs aimed at youth. He became an expert on oral history at the
same time that the civil rights movement erupted. He realized that his many
years of study and critique of U.S. capitalism had left him completely unpre-
pared for the mass mobilization by African Americans and their allies, and
consequently he felt compelled to explore other kinds of information and
evidence. Moreover, he realized that his formal education had taught him
little about the history of racism.

In 1964, the great scholar and activist C.L.R. James asked Rawick if he
knew of any materials that portrayed slavery in the United States from the
slaves' points of view. Because of his research on the New Deal, Rawick knew
about the Works Progress Administration (WPA) slave narratives—tran-
scriptions of interviews with elderly Blacks conducted during the 1930s,
probing their memories of slavery. His search led Rawick to microfilm records in the Library of Congress, which provided the raw material for a sev-
enteen-volume series that he got Greenwood Press to publish along with an

introductory volume of his own, *From Sundown to Sunup,* which explained the significance of the collection. In the first six chapters of that book, Rawick presents an extraordinary history and interpretation of the self-activity of slaves that created a community in the midst of bondage, demonstrating a dialectical interplay between accommodation and resistance that characterized their existence. The final two chapters lay out an argument about the causes, functions, and contradictions of white racism based on the centrality of slavery to the history of all people in the United States.

Rawick described how "racism took its strongest hold among those people who most thoroughly participated in the new, revolutionary developments of the modern world." He explained how coalitions between white and Black workers foundered, not just because of the material advantages that racial segregation brought to whites, but because racism provided an outlet for all the repressed anguish and frustration that workers felt from the transformation from preindustrial to industrial society. He explained that white workers created a debased image of African Americans that filled real needs for them; Blacks became a locus of both contempt and envy onto which whites projected their own repressed desires for pleasure and unrestrained free expression. Rawick showed how working-class racism never existed alone, how it emerged out of the hardships and self-hatred imposed on white workers by the humiliating subordinations of class.[10]

I first encountered Rawick in the late 1970s when I was finishing my own dissertation at the University of Wisconsin and working under his supervision as a teaching assistant at the University of Missouri–St. Louis. He suffered from a variety of ailments at the time including diabetes, and his health was further damaged by his refusal to take proper medication or to attend to other measures necessary to protect his well-being. He was prone to mood shifts and long periods of depression. I saw him give some of the best and some of the worst lectures I ever heard during those two years. Once he placed the War of 1812 in the wrong century (not an easy mistake to make) and depicted it as a conflict between competing approaches to exterminating Native Americans (not necessarily a bad idea, but a nuance that had escaped many previous investigators). When he completed that lecture he approached me in the back of the hall and asked, "How crazy was that?" I had to admit it seemed pretty crazy.

When Rawick felt healthy, however, he came through with well-crafted, entertaining, carefully researched lectures replete with brilliant insights and observations. I noticed that these occasions often depended upon the make-up of his audience. When his listeners included white working-class students or African Americans of any background he seemed to have a special understanding of their lives and to feel a special compulsion to reach them; in these situations he became a well-organized, scintillating lecturer capable of connecting the most complicated abstractions to vivid and unforgettable illustrative anecdotes. For me, his examples were always the best part of his lectures because they displayed a seemingly limitless understanding of and empathy with the joys and sorrows of working-class life.

George Rawick's lectures and the long conversations that often followed them provided me with an extraordinary education about social identities and social power. They made me aware of the power of conversation and the importance of the specific and the concrete, the legitimacy of personal stories as a way of understanding the world. From them I learned about a vast range of events and ideas, about the contours and contradictions of social movements ranging from the nineteenth-century Knights of Labor to the Missouri sharecroppers' strikes of the late 1930s, from the sectarian Left of the 1940s to the to the countercultures and antiwar mobilizations of the New Left of the 1960s. Rawick told me about demonstrating against the Korean War in 1950 in New York with Bayard Rustin and David Dellinger, about picketing the U.S. embassy during an antiwar demonstration in London in 1967 with Allen Ginsberg and Mick Jagger. It got to the point where I half expected him to come up with a personal memory of everyone he analyzed, including Terence Powderly and Karl Marx. He had an enormous network of friends and associates with whom he kept in constant touch. They comprised a "who's who" of radical politics, so much so that once when he was running out of money, he decided not to pay his phone bill because he reasoned that the FBI would not tolerate losing the opportunity to eavesdrop on his conversations and consequently would prevent the phone company from discontinuing his service. He could never prove it, but his continued access to telephone service seemed to indicate that he was correct.

Rawick understood that social struggle begins with who people really are, not who we would like them to be; that political contestation takes multiple and varied forms, ranging from religious rituals to popular culture; and that struggle on the factory floor has always been connected to and dependent on struggles in other sites—on plantations and Native American reservations, on street corners and country roads, in high-tech laboratories and libraries. Most important, he understood the connections between the possessive investment in whiteness and the contradictions of the social movements of his time.

Growing up in an ethnic, immigrant, working-class neighborhood during the 1930s gave George Rawick firsthand experience with social movements. During that decade the Great Depression overwhelmed the resources of traditional ethnic organizations such as fraternal orders, burial societies, and credit circles that linked ethnic identities to economic interests. The collapse of ethnic institutions came at a time when chain stores and mass marketing created new communities of consumers, when automated production methods broke down skill monopolies among ethnic groups and encouraged the concentration of diverse groups of unskilled and semiskilled workers in common workplaces, and when the emergence of mass organizing drives by the Congress of Industrial Organizations (CIO) drew young workers into what historian Lizabeth Cohen calls "a culture of unity."[11] Simultaneously, the popular front activities of the Communist Party, the cultural programs of the New Deal, and writings by ethnic activists and journalists including Louis Adamic, Langston Hughes, and Jack Conroy emphasized the multi-cultural origins of the United States. The culture of the 1930s glorified the "common man" and changed the reigning image of the immigrant from the unwanted alien banned by the 1924 Immigration Act into the redemptive outsider who had become American by choice and therefore personified the nation's true spirit. Fiorello La Guardia in New York and Anton Cermak in Chicago attained the office of mayor in their cities by pulling together inter-ethnic electoral coalitions that celebrated their diversity. When Cermak's patrician opponent bragged about being part of a family that came over on the Mayflower and implied that his second-generation Czech immigrant op-ponent (nicknamed "Pushcart Tony") was unfit for high office, Cermak re-sponded that his family might not have come over on the Mayflower, but they got here as fast as they could.[12]

The 1930s' "culture of unity" broke down ethnic antagonisms among European Americans and forged a common identity that grew out of mass mobilizations on factory floors and city streets. Participants in the social movements of the 1930s sought and secured real institutional resources to replace the exhausted and inadequate ethnic self-help structures that had let them down when the Depression came. The culture of unity won bargaining recognition for industrial workers in mass-production industries, but it also secured social security pensions and survivors' benefits, federally subsidized home loans, National Labor Relations Board protection for collective bar-gaining, federal responsibility for welfare, and other direct social benefits. These resources from the state made European Americans less dependent upon separate ethnic identities, and they helped create the standard of liv-ing, the suburban neighborhoods, the workplace opportunities, and the edu-cational subsidies that enabled the children and grandchildren of immigrants to become middle class and to blend together into a "white" identity. Earlier in this book I pointed out at great length the disastrous consequences that ensued from the ways in which these gains excluded communities of color and created a possessive investment in whiteness, but the gains themselves, the collective struggle for them, and the institutions and resources they pro-vided help explain how unity might yet be constructed among members of diverse groups.

Although the victories secured by the culture of unity disproportion-ately benefited whites, the coalitions of the 1930s did cut across color lines out of necessity if nothing else. As James Baldwin recalled in 1976, "In a way, we were all niggers in the thirties. I do not know if that really made us more friendly with each other—at bottom, I doubt that, for more would remain of that friendliness today—but it was harder then, and riskier to attempt a separate peace, and benign neglect was not among our possibilities."[13] The perception that a separate peace was dangerous made all the difference in key campaigns in crucial industries for the CIO, as a temporary alliance across racial lines won unprecedented victories. Unfortunately, not all parts of the coalition reaped the fruits of victory to an equal degree.

The CIO needed the cooperation and participation of African American, Mexican American, and Asian American workers to organize mass-production industries, in part because the same discriminatory practices that relegated those groups to dirty unpleasant jobs like foundry work also gave them key roles in production: if the foundry shuts down, the factory cannot run. Historians Robin D. G. Kelley and Vicki Ruiz (among others) present detailed descriptions of the importance of Black workers to the organization of the CIO in Alabama and the centrality of Chicanx to organization in the canning industry on the West Coast.[14]

Yet postwar opportunities available to whites separated their interests from those of communities of color. In his provocative and enlightening book *Blackface/White Noise*, Michael Rogin presents an important anecdote that illuminates this general process. He describes a predominantly Jewish group of war veterans who participated in a cooperative housing development in the Philadelphia suburb of Abington Township. That area had previously been restricted to white Christians by restrictive covenants, but under pressure from the veterans the new development broke the local barriers against Jewish residency. Yet while experiencing ethnic inclusion, these same veterans practiced racial exclusion, appeasing the anxiety of their new Christian neighbors by agreeing not to open their development to Blacks. "We wanted to let Negroes in—they're veterans too," an organizer of the cooperative confessed, "but we've been advised that mortgage investors, unfortunately, will not take Negroes in a mixed project." When some veterans and Jewish activists objected to this bargain, the cooperative's representative stood firm, explaining that "only after every possibility was exhausted did we reluctantly arrive at the conclusion that we must have a 'white' community if we were to have any at all."[15]

Rogin's anecdote encapsulates the process of ethnic inclusion by racial exclusion that transformed the "culture of unity" of the 1930s into the social democratic version of the possessive investment in whiteness during the 1940s, 1950s, and 1960s. Many white immigrants and their descendants developed especially powerful attachments to whiteness because of the ways in which various Americanization programs forced them to assimilate by surrendering all aspects of their own ethnic organization and identification. As Patricia Williams explains, "Sometimes I wonder how many of our present cultural clashes are the left-over traces of the immigrant wars of the last century and the beginning of this one, how much of our reemerging jingoism is the scar that marks the place where Italian kids were mocked for being too dark-skinned, where Jewish kids were taunted for being Jewish, where poor Irish rushed to hang lace curtains at the window as the first act of climbing the ladder up from social scorn, where Chinese kids were tortured for not speaking good English."[16]

Yet shared experiences in social movements of the 1930s and a lingering concern for social justice helped connect some whites to the civil rights movement of the 1950s and 1960s in ways that called whiteness into question. George Rawick was one of those whites. He later told an interviewer that the politics of the Old Left was destroyed by the suddenness of the civil rights movement's successes. "No one anticipated it," he remembered. "I was fundamentally a racist because I had not thought about it and was challenged by it. Somehow I was convinced that the problem was me and I had to resolve the contradiction."[17]

Reasoning that the fact of exploitation was more important than the identity of the victim, Rawick threw himself into antiracist work in the 1950s and 1960s in both his activism and his academic work. Because he had been part of labor and civil rights groups that had black leaders, it was easier for him to envision antiracist coalitions based on what he called the self-activity—the things people do by and for themselves in the face of repressive power—and social analysis of people of color themselves and to reject white paternalistic approaches, which all too often saw racism as simply a symptom of broader social problems rather than an issue in its own right. His experiences with the slave narratives and his careful reading of the writings of W.E.B. Du Bois gave him an advantage over other theorists of whiteness, because he drew upon the sophisticated version of "white studies" developed out of necessity by Blacks.

Rawick wrote *From Sundown to Sunup* to reveal the connections between contemporary self-activity among African Americans and the rivers of resistance that could be traced back to the days of slavery. His book, along with John Blassingame's important *The Slave Community*, not only helped explain the self-activity of the civil rights movement but revealed the importance of work as a crucible for revolt, and it illuminated the important lessons that could be learned by all workers from the forms of resistance undertaken by slaves to resist their subordination. He managed an incredibly difficult task—to write about oppression without obscuring resistance, and to write about resistance while acknowledging the terrible price that people pay for not having power. In his concluding chapters, he analyzed how and why racism functions in working-class life, how it enables individuals to externalize elements of self-hatred and self-loathing into contempt and fear of others.

Rawick thought his work was over when his introduction and the first seventeen volumes of the slave narratives came out, but during a speaking engagement at Tougaloo College outside Jackson, Mississippi, a friend suggested that they look in the Mississippi state archives to see whether they contained any slave narratives not included in the Library of Congress collection. Five volumes emerged from the search in the Mississippi archives, and Rawick launched an inquiry into similar caches in other libraries and archives in Alabama, Missouri, Indiana, and Oklahoma. Rawick immersed himself in the stories told by ordinary people about the ways in which broad structural forces made their presence felt in everyday life. Today libraries all over the world contain dozens of volumes of WPA-collected narratives listed under the title, *The American Slave: A Composite Autobiography.*

Rawick never sought recognition from the main credentialing institutions of our society. No professional honor would ever have pleased him as much as a good conversation with a young worker. A story he often told about himself illustrates the depth of his feeling. Shortly after *From Sundown to Sunup* was published, Rawick boarded a bus in Detroit. To his amazement and delight he noticed a young Black worker carrying a copy of his book. At the next stop, two more passengers got on the bus, each carrying a copy of the book. Figuring that this was a trend, he tried to calculate how many thousands of copies the book was selling in Detroit if every busload of passengers represented three copies. When the next stop produced a fourth passenger, with a fourth copy of the book, he began composing remarks for the mass conference of revolutionary workers that he was sure would follow from the success of the book. It was only when he could no longer contain his curiosity and he asked one man carrying the book that Rawick found out he had stumbled onto a Black history study group carrying that week's assigned reading. Rawick told the story with self-deprecating humor, but I have always found it significant that the possibility of rank-and-file workers picking up his book meant more to George than all the laudatory reviews and extensive academic sales it secured. Indeed, it would have meant more to him than a Pulitzer Prize or a National Book Award.

Rawick also kept himself alert for the hidden possibilities of struggle in even the most conventional arenas. He once lived across the hall from St. Louis Cardinals football players MacArthur Lane and Ernie McMillan. They became symbols for him of the working class, while their boss, Cardinals owner Bill Bidwill, came to represent management. Rawick could describe all the dynamics of the class struggle through the relationship between Bidwill and his players; for him it was another episode in the history of industrial capitalism. When Bidwill turned his factory into a runaway shop and moved the team to Phoenix, following so many other St. Louis industries to the Sun Belt, Rawick was ready with the appropriate critique of management for its squandering of social possibilities. Because of his stories, the whole history of the working class and its connections across racial lines became accessible and tangible to me in new ways; I began to see patterns for the first time.

Of course, Rawick's best gift to all of us has been his writing; not just the slave narratives and *From Sundown to Sunup,* but decades of articles like the important one on self-activity in an early issue of *Radical America* and several written under pseudonyms for obscure leftist journals. They all evidence Rawick's abiding faith in the ingenuity and perseverance of the working class. They express his delight in the symbolic victories with which people keep alive their hopes for a better future. Most of all, they show his capacity to listen to people, to take them seriously, and to fight alongside them rather than commanding or lecturing them into submission. Some people think that such writing is preaching to the already converted, but I think of it more as entertaining the troops, as showing us what we are capable of even under the most dire circumstances, and reminding us how many kindred spirits there have been and continue to be in this world. I know that the things that Rawick has taught me have informed everything I've written about the working class, and I'm sure that Robin D. G. Kelley, David Roediger, Peter Rachleff, Eileen Eagan, Margaret Creel Washington, Stan Weir, Katharine Corbett, Martin Glaberman, and many others would make similar testimonials. Of course, that's just the tip of the iceberg; if every historian who lifted an idea from *Sundown to Sunup* had paid Rawick five cents, he would have had enough money to buy the Cardinal football team and move them back to St. Louis with MacArthur Lane as coach.

Hollywood will always prefer stories about the Joe Clarks of this world to stories about people like Fannie Lou Hamer. The true and useful history that George Rawick discovered in the WPA slave narratives will never eclipse the popular exposure given to the destructive lies told in *The Birth of a Nation, Gone with the Wind,* or *Lean on Me.* Foundations and mainstream media outlets will always try to hide the possessive investment in whiteness, its causes, and its consequences. The makers of *Rocky* and *The Karate Kid* cannot be expected to understand the WPA slave narratives and the lessons they hold about power and struggle for people from all backgrounds. Gil Scott-Heron used to say that the revolution will not be televised, and we should not expect it to appear in the form of high-budget motion pictures from major studios either. Yet revolutionary potential remains among white people willing to resist racism and to struggle openly against it.

After a series of devastating and paralyzing strokes, George Rawick died in 1990. I miss him very much and wish more people knew how important he was. But I would be a poor student if I did not focus on the main lesson that he tried to bring to our attention. Rawick taught us that fighting racism was everyone's business; that the self-activity of oppressed people holds the key to the emancipation of everybody. For all his personal problems he understood that white people have an important role to play in antiracist work. Whites cannot free ourselves without acting against the poisonous pathologies of white supremacy—both referential and inferential. Anyone can make antiracist proclamations, but antiracist practices come only from coordinated collective action. The rewards offered to people from all races to defend the possessive investment in whiteness are enormous, while the dangers of challenging it are all too evident. But in every era, people emerge to fight for something better. Identifying racism and fighting against it may preclude us from joining the ranks of the makers and shakers and accomplices of this world, but at least it will enable us, in the words of Toni Cade Bambara, "to tell the truth and not get trapped."[18] As W.E.B. Du Bois observed many years ago about the possessive investment in whiteness in his own day, "Such discrimination is morally wrong, politically dangerous, industrially wasteful, and socially silly. It is the duty of whites to stop it, and to do so primarily for their own sakes."[19]

10

Finding Families of Resemblance

"Frantic to Join . . . the Japanese Army"

I began to feel a terrified pity for the white children of these white people;
who had been sent, by their parents, to Korea, though their parents did
not know why. Neither did their parents know why these miserable,
incontestably inferior, rice-eating gooks refused to come to heel, and
would not be saved. But I knew why. I came from a long line of miser-
able, incontestably inferior, rice-eating, chicken-stealing, hog-swilling
niggers—who had acquired these skills in their flight from bondage—
who still refused to come to heel, and who would not be saved.

—James Baldwin

Malcolm X used to say that racism is like a Cadillac: they make a new model every year. The racism of 2018 differs from the racism of 1964, and consequently needs to be analyzed, interpreted, addressed, and redressed accordingly. Yet there is continuity as well as rupture in both racism and Cadillacs. A 2018 Cadillac follows a logic of design and a history of prestige that extends back more than one hundred years. The racism of 2018 derives some of its deadly force from the long history behind it. The next four chapters of this book identify and analyze different models and different moments of racism and antiracism. They encompass the ways in which African Americans found families of resemblance linking their fates to Asians and Asian Americans in the 1940s, the emergence of anti-immigrant and anti–affirmative action politics in California in the 1990s, the organized abandonment of black New Orleans in the wake of Hurricane Katrina in 2005, and the aura of mean-spirited mendacity that marks the moment in 2018 when this edition of *The Possessive Investment in Whiteness* appears. Racism is always in all of these moments, but never exactly the same racism. There is a new model every year, but Cadillacs and racism share some continuity over time as well. For all the differences in their appearance in any given moment or model, Cadillacs and racism alike are big, powerful, dangerous, destructive, and wasteful.

All communities of color suffer from the possessive investment in whiteness, but not in the same ways. No magical essence unites aggrieved victims of white supremacy in common endeavors. All too often, racial minorities feel compelled to secure the benefits of whiteness for themselves by gaining advantages at each other's expense.[1] Yet there are also always positive possibilities residing in polylateral relations among aggrieved groups. These can have unpredictable effects. They can enable communities of color to be aware of one another and to forge unexpected alliances instead of antagonisms. African Americans and Asian Americans, for example, have often had hostile relationships with one another as competitors for scarce resources. Yet they have also often been allies, united by similar if not identical experiences as racialized subjects, sometimes because of the racial undertones of U.S. foreign policy. In this chapter, I examine how cultural constrictions of Asian nationalism emerged as unexpected sources of inspiration for African American liberation in the 1940s.

In his celebrated autobiography, Malcolm X explains how he escaped the draft during World War II. At a time when "the only three things in the world that scared me" were "jail, a job, and the Army," the Harlem street hustler devised a plan to fool his foes. Aware that military intelligence agencies stationed "black spies in civilian clothes" in African American neighborhoods to watch for subversive activity, Malcolm (then named Malcolm Little) started "noising around" Harlem bars and street corners ten days before his scheduled preinduction physical exam. He told everyone within earshot that he was "frantic to join . . . the Japanese Army." Just in case the military found these dramatic displays of disloyalty insufficient, Malcolm informed a psychiatrist at his preinduction physical exam that he was eager to enter the military. "I want to get sent down South." he enthused, "Organize them nigger soldiers, you dig? Steal us some guns, and kill crackers!" Not surprisingly, the Selective Service judged Malcolm Little mentally unqualified for military service, sending him home with a 4-F deferment on October 25, 1943.[2]

The distinguished historian John Hope Franklin secured a similar result for himself by very different means and for very different reasons. Swept up in the patriotic fervor that followed the bombing of Pearl Harbor, Franklin was frantic to join . . . the U.S. Navy. He saw an advertisement indicating that the service needed skilled office workers who could type, take shorthand, and run business machines. At that point in his life, Franklin had six years' experience at secretarial work, had won three gold medals in typing, had taken an accounting course in high school, knew shorthand, and in addition, he had earned a Ph.D. in history from Harvard University. The navy recruiter refused Franklin's offer to volunteer because he was lacking one credential—whiteness. They would not use his services because he was Black.

Franklin next directed his efforts toward securing a position with the Department of War, which at the time was assembling a staff of historians. Once again, whiteness mattered. The department's administrators hired several white historians who did not have any advanced degrees, but they never even responded to Franklin's application. When he went for his preinduction physical, a white doctor refused to let Franklin enter his office. He made him wait for his blood test on a bench at the end of a hall near the fire escape until Franklin's protests got him admitted reluctantly to the physician's office.

Years later, Franklin recalled that these experiences changed his attitude toward the war and toward his country. They convinced him that "the United States, however much it was devoted to protecting the freedoms and rights of Europeans, had no respect for me, no interest in my well-being, and not even a desire to utilize my services." Franklin concluded that "the United States did not need me and did not deserve me. Consequently, I spent the remainder of the war years successfully and with malice aforethought outwitting my draft board and the entire Selective Service establishment." Instead of serving in the military, Franklin devoted his time to teaching, scholarship, and activism aimed at undermining the system of white supremacy.[3]

Although they started out with very different intentions, Malcolm X and John Hope Franklin both ended up avoiding military service during World War II. Their actions were hardly typical; the overwhelming majority of African Americans who were eligible for the draft accepted induction and served effectively. Black draft resisters accounted for less than 5 percent of the 12,343 conscientious-objection cases processed by the Justice Department. More than 1 million Black men and women served in the armed forces during the war.[4] Conflicts with the selective service system experienced by Malcolm X and John Hope Franklin, however, bring into sharp relief the potentially explosive racial contradictions facing the United States during the war. Franklin and Malcolm X expressed more than individual ingenuity and personal pique in their resistance to the draft. They articulated and acted upon suspicion about the relationship between World War II and white supremacy that was widely held in their community, suspicion about the shortcomings of democracy in the United States, about the racialized nature of the war, but also eventually about the potential power of nonwhite nations around the globe, and about the viability and desirability of covert and overt resistance to racism.

Although they expressed a decidedly minority view about the draft itself, Malcolm X and John Hope Franklin touched on shared social perceptions that gained majority approval afterward. Malcolm X emerged in the postwar period as a Black nationalist leader who connected antiracist struggles in the United States with anti-imperialist efforts around the globe. During the 1960s, Martin Luther King, Jr., positioned himself as a vigorous opponent of the U.S. war in Vietnam as well as the leader of civil rights and poor people's movements. Large segments of youth in the same period used the research of scholars (including John Hope Franklin) to fashion resistant and oppositional understandings of their obligations to the nation at home and abroad.

The strategic maneuvers by John Hope Franklin and Malcolm X in their struggles with the selective service system highlight the volatile instabilities permeating the seemingly stable narratives of nation and race. Malcolm X initially presented himself quite insincerely as an admirer of America's enemies and as an active agent of subversion simply so he could stay on the streets and pursue his own pleasures as a petty criminal. Yet his eventual imprisonment for crimes committed on those streets led him to a religious conversion and a political awakening that led him to become an actual and sincere opponent of U.S. foreign policy, turning his wartime charade into an important part of his life's work. John Hope Franklin initially approached the government as a superpatriot eager to enlist in the U.S. war effort, but the racism directed at him by the government led him to evade military service and embark on a lifetime of oppositional intellectual work and activism.

By feigning a desire to join the Japanese army and by announcing his interest in shooting southern segregationists, Malcolm X drew upon ideas and practices with deep roots in his own life and in the politics of his community. He played the part of the trickster as embedded in Black folklore, using guile and deception to fool foes and achieve ends covertly. This particular threat to join the Japanese army in particular carried weight at that moment in history because it played on the paranoia of white supremacy. It posed the possibility of a transnational alliance among people of color. In the process, it brought to the surface the inescapably racist realities behind the seemingly color-blind national narrative of the United States and its aims in the war.[5]

Looking for allies outside the United States has been a well-established strategy by members of oppressed social groups. Slaves and free Blacks directed attention to international realities in the antebellum period, savoring the prospect of escape to Indian Territory, Canada, and Mexico, as well as welcoming the assistance offered by European abolitionists. Robin D. G. Kelley's research on Black communists in Alabama in the 1930s indicates that charges of instigation by outside agitators influenced by Russia had little effect on the descendants of slaves who after all had been freed from bondage in part by an invading army from the North.[6] But the Japanese were not just any outsiders to African Americans in the 1940s; they were people of color with their own independent nation, a force capable of challenging Euro-American imperialism on its own terms and possible allies against the oppressive power of white supremacy.

Paul Gilroy and others have written eloquently about a "Black Atlantic"—about the importance of Africa, the Caribbean, and Europe as influences on the Black freedom struggle in the United States. Yet there has been a "Black Pacific" as well. Images of Asia and experiences with Asians and Asian Americans have played an important role in enabling Black people to complicate the simple racial binary that does so much to shape the contours of economic, cultural, and social life in the United States.[7] In addition, it is not just elite intellectuals who have had an international imagination; working people whose labor in a global capitalist economy often brought them into contact with other cultures have often inflected their own organizations and institutions with international imagery and identification.

The African American encounter with Japan has been especially fraught with contradictions. In their zeal to identify with a nonwhite nation whose successes might rebuke Eurocentric claims about white supremacy, Blacks have often overlooked, condoned, and even embraced elements of Japanese fascism and imperialism. In the United States, Japanese agents sometimes succeeded in promoting the crudest kinds of racial essentialism and male chauvinism among Black nationalist groups. Yet as Laura Mulvey observes, "It cannot be easy to move from oppression and its mythologies to resistance in history; a detour through a no-man's land or threshold area of counter-myth and symbolisation is necessary."[8] The African American engagement with Japan provided a detour through a symbolic terrain sufficiently complex to allow an oppressed racial minority in North America to think of itself as part of a global majority of nonwhite peoples. In addition, as Malcolm X's performance at his physical demonstrated, imaginary alliances and identifications with Japan could sometimes create maneuvering room for dealing with immediate and pressing practical problems. African American affinities with Asia have emanated from strategic needs and from the utility of enlisting allies, learning from families of resemblance, and escaping the categories of Black and white as they have developed historically in the United States. These affinities do not evidence innate or essential characteristics attributable to race or skin color; on the contrary, they demonstrate the distinctly social and historical nature of racial formation. Neither rooted in biology nor inherited unproblematically from history, racial identity is a culturally constructed entity always in flux. During World War II, the racialized nature of the Pacific war; the racist ideals of Nazi Germany; the legacy of white supremacy, segregation, colonialism, and conquest in the United States; and antiracist activism at home and abroad all generated contradictions and conflicts that radically refigured race relations in the United States and around the world.

Both global politics and domestic economic imperatives shaped relations between Asian Americans and African Americans from the start. White planters and industrialists in the nineteenth-century United States favored the importation of Asian laborers to simultaneously drive down the wages of poor whites and gain even greater domination over slaves and free Blacks. As immigrants ineligible for naturalized citizenship according to the terms of the 1790 Immigration and Naturalization Act, and as a racialized group relegated largely to low-wage labor, Asian Americans could offer little resistance to employer exploitation and political domination. White workers in California and elsewhere often took the lead in demanding that Asian immigrants be excluded from the U.S. labor market, but many manufacturers and entrepreneurs as well also came to view Asian immigrants as actual or potential competitors and favored exclusion.[9] The U.S. Congress passed the first of several acts excluding Asians from immigrating to the United States in 1882, shortly after the Compromise of 1877 guaranteed the subjugation of southern Blacks, eliminating employers' needs for a group of racialized immigrants to compete with African American laborers. Significantly, one voice raised against the act in congressional debates was that of Senator Blanche K. Bruce of Mississippi, the only African American in the Senate.[10]

Contradictions between domestic racism and the imperial ambitions of the United States appeared as early as 1899, during the Filipino insurrection against occupying U.S. troops in the aftermath of what the United States calls the Spanish-American War. African American soldiers from the Twenty-fourth Infantry Regiment could not help noticing that white Americans used many of the same epithets to describe Filipinx that they used to describe Black soldiers, including "niggers," "black devils," and "gugus." One Black enlisted man in the regiment felt that the rebellion he was sent to suppress emanated from the fact that "the Filipinos resent being treated as inferior," which he believed "set an example to the American Negro" that should be emulated. Similarly, the regiment's sergeant major, John Calloway, informed a Filipinx friend that he was "constantly haunted by the feeling of how wrong morally . . . Americans are in the present affair with you."[11]

Filipinx fighting under the command of Emilio Aguinaldo made appeals to Black troops on the basis of "racial" solidarity, offering posts as commissioned officers in the rebel army to those who switched sides. Most remained loyal to the U.S. cause, but Corporal David Fagen deserted the Twenty-fourth Regiment's I Company on November 17, 1899, to become an officer in the guerrilla army. He married a local woman, served the insurrectionists with distinction, engaged U.S. units effectively, and eluded capture time after time. Fearing that his example might encourage others to follow suit, U.S. officers offered large monetary rewards and expended enormous energy to capture or kill Fagen. On December 5, 1901, U.S. officials announced that a "native" hunter had produced "a slightly decomposed head of a negro" and personal effects that indicated the skull belonged to Fagen. Although this may have been a ruse on Fagen's part to end the search for him, the gradually weakening position of the rebels made further resistance impossible. One way or the other, Fagen disappeared from the combat theater. But his example loomed large in the minds of military and diplomatic officials, especially whenever they contemplated future military activity against non-white populations.[12] Nearly 500 African American soldiers elected to remain in the Philippines at the conclusion of the conflict. Filipinx civilians later told stories to Black U.S. soldiers stationed in their country during World War II about Fagen and about the Black soldiers who refused to participate in crushing the Moro Rebellion of 1914.[13]

Just as some Black soldiers from the Twenty-fourth Infantry Regiment viewed the Philippine Islands independence struggle as a battle with special relevance to their own fight against white supremacy, individuals and groups in Japan took an interest in Marcus Garvey's Universal Negro Improvement Association (UNIA) around the time of World War I. Charles Zampty, a native of Trinidad and a leader of the Garvey movement in Detroit for more than fifty years, learned about the UNIA from Garvey's newspaper, *Negro World*, which he obtained from Japanese sailors in Panama while he worked at the Panama Canal.[14] As early as 1918, Garvey warned that "the next war will be between the Negroes and the whites unless our demands for justice are recognized," adding that, "with Japan to fight with us, we can win such a war."[15]

Other African American intellectuals also looked to Japan for inspiration. Shortly after the war between Russia and Japan, Booker T. Washington pointed to Japanese nationalism as a model for African American development.[16] W.E.B. Du Bois included the "yellow-brown East" in the "darker world" poised to resist "white Europe," in his novel *Dark Princess: A Romance*, in which he fantasized about an alliance linking a South Asian princess, a Japanese nobleman, and an African American intellectual.[17] In his 1935 classic study, *Black Reconstruction in America*, Du Bois counted U.S. support for colonialism and imperialism in Asia, Africa, and Latin America as one of the enduring consequences of the concessions to the South required to suppress African Americans in the years after the Civil War. "Imperialism, the exploitation of colored labor throughout the world, thrives upon the approval of the United States, and the United States gives that approval because of the South," he argued. Warning that war would result from the reactionary stance imposed upon the United States by its commitment to white supremacy, Du Bois reminded his readers, "The South is not interested in freedom for dark India. It has no sympathy with the oppressed of Africa or of Asia."[18]

At times Black grassroots organizations saw resemblances between their status and that of Asian Americans. In San Francisco in the early years of the twentieth century, Black community groups and newspapers opposed efforts to send Japanese American children to segregated schools because they recognized the demeaning nature of segregation from their own experiences. In addition, in their public mobilizations, they pointed repeatedly to the ways in which opposition to immigration from Japan manifested not just a generalized fear of foreigners, but the racist prejudices of white Americans.[19] Malcolm X's Garveyite father and West Indian mother (from Grenada) encouraged him to be internationalist in his thinking; to look to Africa, the Caribbean, and beyond; to render the hegemonic white supremacy of North America relative, contingent, and provisional. This tradition affected Malcolm X directly, but it also shaped the broader contours of relations between

African Americans and people of Asian origin. In 1921, members of Garvey's UNIA and Japanese immigrants in Seattle joined forces to create a colored People's Union open to all people "except the whites or Teutonic races."[20] In New York, a young Vietnamese merchant seaman regularly attended UNIA meetings and became friends with Garvey himself in the early 1920s. Years later he would apply the lessons he learned about nationalism from Garvey when he took on the name Ho Chi Minh and led his country's resistance against Japanese, French, and U.S. control.[21] Forty members of the Garvey movement in Detroit converted to Islam between 1920 and 1923, largely as a result of the efforts of an Ahmadiyah mission from India. Elijah Muhammad, then Elijah Poole, associated with Garveyites in Detroit during the 1930s before founding the Nation of Islam, which Malcolm Little would later join while in prison during the late 1940s. The Nation of Islam went beyond Garvey's pan-Africanism to include (at least symbolically) all "Asiatic" (nonwhite) people.[22]

During the 1930s, a Japanese national using the names Naka Nakane and Satokata Takahishi (sometimes spelled Satokata Takahashi) organized African Americans, Filipinx, West Indians, and East Indians into self-help groups, among them the society for the Development of Our Own, the Ethiopian Intelligence Sons and Daughters of Science, and the Onward Movement of America.[23] Born in Japan in 1875, Nakane married an English woman and migrated to Canada. He presented himself as a major in the Japanese army and a member of a secret fraternal order, the Black Dragon Society. Nakane promised financial aid and military assistance to African Americans in Detroit if they joined in "a war against the white race."[24]

Deported from the United States in 1934, Nakane moved back to Canada and continued to run Development of Our Own indirectly through the work of his second wife, an African American named Pearl Sherrod. When he tried to reenter the United States in 1939, federal officials indicted him for illegal entry and for attempting to bribe an immigration officer. The FBI charged in 1939 that Nakane had been an influential presence within the Nation of Islam (NOI), that he spoke as a guest at NOI temples in Chicago and Detroit, and that his thinking played a major role in shaping Elijah Muhammad's attitudes toward the Japanese government. As proof, the FBI offered a copy of a speech that the bureau claimed had been saved by an agent since 1933, in which Muhammad predicted that "the Japanese will slaughter the white man."[25]

The Pacific Movement of the Eastern World (PMEW), founded in Chicago and St. Louis in 1932, advocated the unification of nonwhite people under the leadership of the empire of Japan. Led by Ashima Takis (whose pseudonyms included Policarpio Manansala, Mimo de Guzman, and Itake Koo), the group expressed its ideology of racial unity in the colors of its banners—black, yellow, and brown.[26] The PMEW implied that it had the backing of the Japanese government in offering free transportation, land, houses, farm animals, and crop seed to the first 3 million American Blacks willing to repatriate to Africa.[27] Although Marcus Garvey expressly warned his followers against the PMEW, Takis frequently represented himself as an ally and even an agent of the Garvey movement, and his group enjoyed considerable allegiance among Garveyites in the Midwest, especially in Gary, Indiana, and East St. Louis, Illinois.[28] Madame M.L.T. De Mena of the UNIA defied Garvey's prohibitions and arranged speaking engagements for Takis and his Chinese associate Moy Liang before Black nationalist audiences.[29] "The Japanese are colored people, like you," Takis told African American audiences, adding pointedly that "the white governments do not give the negro any consideration." In 1940, Takis told one African American group that war would soon break out between the United States and Japan, and that they would receive rifles from Japan to help them mount an insurrection in the Midwest while Japanese troops attacked the West Coast.[30] In the 1930s, the leader of the Peace Movement of Ethiopia, Mittie Maud Lena Gordon, had asked newly elected president Franklin Roosevelt to help finance Black repatriation to Africa. After the Japanese attack on Pearl Harbor, Gordon described December 7, 1941, as the day "one billion Black people struck for freedom."[31]

Thus, Malcolm X's presentation of himself in 1943 as pro-Japanese and anti–white supremacist picked up on elements of his personal history as well as on significant currents of thought and action among Black nationalists. He also exploited well-founded fears among government officials. Some recognized that the pathology of white supremacy posed special problems for the nation as it sought to fashion national unity in a war against German and Japanese fascism. White racism in the United States undermined arguments behind U.S. participation in the war and made it harder to distinguish the Allies from the Axis. Racial segregation in industry and in the army kept qualified fighters and factory workers from positions where they were sorely needed, while the racialized nature of the war in Asia threatened to open up old wounds on the home front. Most important, asking African American, Asian American, Mexican American, and Native American soldiers to fight for freedoms overseas that they did not themselves enjoy at home presented powerful political, ideological, and logistical problems. But some government officials worried more about conspiratorial collaboration between African Americans and agents of the Japanese government.

As far back as the 1920s, the Department of Justice and agents from military intelligence had expressed fears of a Japanese-Black alliance. One report alleged: "The Japanese Associations subscribe to radical negro literature. In California a negro organization, formed in September, 1920, issued resolutions declaring that negros would not, in case of the exclusion of Japanese, take their place; a prominent negro was liberally paid to spread propaganda for the Japanese; and various negro religious and social bodies were approached in many ways." The report continued: "It is the determined purpose of Japan to amalgamate the entire colored races of the world against the Nordic or white race, with Japan at the head of the coalition, for the purpose of wrestling away the supremacy of the white race and placing such supremacy in the colored peoples under the dominion of Japan."[32]

Similar fears haunted policy makers during World War II. Secretary of War Henry L. Stimson attributed Black demands for equality during the conflict to agitation by Japanese agents and communists. Stimson recognized no legitimate grievances among African Americans but instead interpreted their demands for jobs in industry and positions in combat as evidence of Japanese-initiated efforts to interfere with mobilization for national defense. In the same vein, the Department of State warned against Japanese infiltration of Black protest groups, like A. Philip Randolph's March on Washington Movement, as part of an effort "to direct the Negro Minority in a subversive effort against the United States."[33]

Southern journalist and self-proclaimed racial moderate Virginius Dabney feared African American identification with the Japanese war effort because, "like the natives of Malaya and Burma, the American Negroes are sometimes imbued with the notion that a victory for the yellow race over the white race might also be a victory for them."[34] These predictions could become self-fulfilling prophesies; by showing how frightened they were by the prospect of alliances between African Americans and people of color elsewhere in the world, anxious whites called attention to a potential resource for Black freedom struggles that eventually came to full flower in the 1960s in the form of opposition to the Vietnam War by the Student Nonviolent Coordinating Committee and the Southern Christian Leadership Conference and expressions of solidarity with anti-imperialist struggles in Asia, Africa, the Middle East, and Latin America by more radical groups.

Extensive surveillance and infiltration of Japanese American and African American organizations by intelligence agents conclusively found little reason to fear any significant systematic disloyalty or subversion. Yet once the war started, government officials moved swiftly and decisively against Black nationalist draft resisters and organizations suspected of sympathy with Japanese war aims. F. H. Hammurabi, leader of World Wide Friends of Africa (also known as the House of Knowledge), was indicted in 1942 for delivering speeches praising Japan and for showing his audiences films of the Japanese attack on Pearl Harbor.[35]

Federal agents placed Ashima Takis under surveillance because of the PMEW's efforts to persuade Black nationalists in New York to ready "the dark-skinned races for armed uprisings should Japanese forces invade United States soil."[36] He received a three-year prison sentence for having cashed a fraudulent money order some years earlier, and then served as a star witness

in a federal prosecution of St. Louis area members of the PMEW. His followers reported that Takis spoke German, French, and Spanish; that his English
was perfect in private conversation but heavily accented in public speeches;
and that he enjoyed success as a faith healer in Black neighborhoods.[37] Robert
A. Hill describes Takis as a Japanese who masqueraded as a Filipinx under
the pseudonym Policarpio Manansala, while Ernest V. Allen represents him
as a Filipinx who called himself Mimo de Guzman and Policarpio Manansala but masqueraded as a Japanese national under the pseudonym Ashima
Takis.

Prosecutors brought charges of sedition and inciting draft resistance
against leaders of the Peace Movement of Ethiopia and against the Nation of
Islam. Federal agents arrested Elijah Muhammad in May 1942, and a federal judge sentenced him to a five-year prison term at the Federal Correctional Institution in Milan, Michigan. FBI agents raided the Chicago Temple
of the NOI in September 1942, tearing "the place apart trying to find weapons hidden there since they believed we were connected with the Japanese,"
one suspect later recalled. The agents found no weapons or documents linking the group to the Japanese government, but those arrested all served three
years in prison for draft evasion.[38]

Although Malcolm X later joined the Nation of Islam, where he fashioned an impassioned and precise critique of the connections linking U.S.
imperialism overseas and anti-Black racism at home, there is no reason to
doubt his report in his autobiography that in 1943 his conscious motivations
entailed little more than a desire to avoid "jail, a job, and the Army."[39] But he
could not have failed to notice that the war against Japan gave him leverage
that he would not have had otherwise. In that respect, his vision corresponded to that of millions of other African Americans. Immediately after
the Japanese attack on Pearl Harbor, Robert L. Vann, editor and publisher of
one of the nation's most important Black newspapers, the *Pittsburgh Courier*,
called on the president and Congress "to declare war on Japan and against
racial prejudice in our country." This campaign for "double victory" had actually started before the war, when A. Philip Randolph used the threat of a
mass march on Washington in June 1941 to extract from President Roosevelt
Executive Order 8802, which mandated fair hiring in defense industries.
James Boggs, a Black activist in Detroit working in the auto industry, recalled that "Negroes did not give credit for this order to Roosevelt and the
American government. Far from it. Recognizing that America and its allies
had their backs to the wall in their struggle with Hitler and Tojo, Negroes
said that Hitler and Tojo, by creating the war which made the Americans
give them jobs in the industry, had done more for them in four years than
Uncle Sam had done in 300 years."[40]

Yet, even in the midst of a war against a common enemy, white Americans held onto their historic hatreds and prejudices. At the Packard main

factory in Detroit, white war workers protesting desegregation of the assembly line announced that they would rather lose the war than have to "work beside a nigger on the assembly line." John L. De Witt of the Fourth Army Western Defense Command in San Francisco complained to the army's chief of classification when the badly needed reinforcements that he had requested turned out to be African American soldiers. "You're filling too many colored troops up on the West Coast," De Witt warned. "There will be a great deal of public reaction out here due to the Jap situation. They feel they've got enough black skinned people around them as it is, Filipinos and Japanese. . . . I'd rather have a white regiment."[41]

Black workers had to wage unrelenting struggles to secure and keep high-paying posts in defense industries on the home front, while African American military personnel served under white officers in a segregated military. The high command did its best to keep Black troops out of combat for as long as they could so that those soldiers could not claim the fruits of victory over fascism.[42] On the other hand, in order to promote enthusiasm for the war among African Americans, the military also publicized the heroism of individual Black combatants like Dorie Miller, a steward on the battleship *West Virginia,* which was among the vessels attacked at Pearl Harbor on December 7, 1941. According to the navy, Miller was stationed on the bridge near the ship's commanding officer when the enemy attacked. He reportedly dragged the ship's wounded captain from an exposed spot on the bridge and then manned a machine gun, shooting down two enemy planes, despite never having been trained on the weapon. Twelve weeks after the incident, the navy bowed to pressure from African American organizations and identified Miller, awarding him the Navy Cross.[43] Skeptics have subsequently raised doubts about whether Miller accomplished the feats for which he was decorated, but he remained an important symbol for many African Americans. They noted that, consistent with navy policy at the time, Miller received no transfer to a combat position as a result of his heroism but continued serving food and drinks to white officers on the escort carrier *Liscome Bay* on which he died when that ship sank on November 24, 1943.[44]

Black soldiers sought positions in combat but found themselves relegated to roles as garrison troops at Efate in the New Hebrides, at Guadalcanal in the southern Solomons, and at Banika in the Russell islands. But Black soldiers from the First Battalion of the Twenty-fourth Infantry Regiment (which had been David Fagen's unit in the Philippines) and members of the all-Black Ninety-third Division eventually served with white soldiers in combat in March 1945 on Bougainville.[45] More than a million Black men and women served in the armed forces during the war, more than half of them overseas in Europe or the Pacific.

Despite clear evidence of African American loyalty to the Allied effort, counterintelligence officers made Black people special targets of surveillance, investigation, and harassment. Naval intelligence officials in Hawaii ranked "Negroes" second only to "Japanese" people as primary suspects of subversion.[46] The Federal Bureau of Investigation issued a wildly inflated estimate of more than 100,000 African American members of pro-Japanese organizations (perhaps counting those who escaped the draft in the way that Malcolm X did).[47] Yet while mass subversion by Blacks was largely a figment of J. Edgar Hoover's always active imagination, the racialized nature of U.S. policy and propaganda in relation to the Japanese did elicit strong responses from African Americans.

In *Lonely Crusade*, a postwar *roman a clef* based on his wartime experiences as an African American assembly-line worker, Chester Himes writes of the complicated relationship between Japan and his lead character, Lee Gordon. When navy training exercises make him think for a moment that a Japanese invasion is in progress, Gordon exults, "They're here! Oh, Goddammit, they're coming! Come on, you little bad bastards! Come on and take this city." Himes writes: "In his excitement he expressed a secret admiration for Japan that had been slowly mounting in him over the months of his futile search for work. It was as if he reached the conviction that if Americans did not want him the Japanese did. He wanted them to come so he could join them and lead them on to victory; even though he himself knew that this was only the wishful yearning of the disinherited."[48]

The Office of War Information (OWI) conducted a confidential survey of African Americans in 1942. Eighteen percent of the respondents indicated that they expected their personal condition to improve if Japan invaded the United States; 31 percent thought that their circumstances would remain the same; 26 percent had no opinion or refused to answer.[49] The OWI concluded that only 25 percent of African Americans supported the war effort wholeheartedly and that 15 percent had "pro-Japanese" inclinations. Yet a careful study of letters to the editor and editorials in the Black press showed that most African Americans neither particularly supported nor condemned Japan.[50]

Detroit journalist Gordon Hancock accused white government officials of "colorphobia" in their close surveillance of Japanese expansion in the Far East while virtually ignoring what Hancock saw as the manifestly greater dangers posed by German actions in Europe. Chester Himes worked his reaction to the Japanese internment into another mid-forties novel, *If He Hollers Let Him Go*, by having his narrator, Bob Jones, trace the roots of his rage against white supremacy to the Japanese internment: "Maybe it wasn't until I'd seen them send the Japanese away that I'd noticed it. Little Riki Oyana singing 'God Bless America' and going to Santa Anita [for internment] with his parents the next day. It was taking a man up by the roots and locking him up without a chance. Without a trial. Without a charge. Without even giving him a chance to say one word. It was thinking about if they ever did that to me, Robert Jones, Mrs. Jones's dark son, that started me to getting scared."[51]

Gloster Current, the NAACP's director of branches, noted how these countersubversive measures against Japanese Americans raised special concern in the Black community. When the government announced its plans to incarcerate more than 100,000 law-abiding Japanese Americans, Current observed, "Many a Negro throughout the country felt a sense of apprehension always experienced in the face of oppression: Today *them,* tomorrow *us.* For once the precedent had been established of dealing with persons on the basis of race or creed, none of us could consider ourselves safe from future 'security' measures."[52] This interethnic solidarity among aggrieved racial groups was one of the main products of the World War II experience and one of its most important postwar legacies.

Before the war, African Americans and Japanese Americans lived in close proximity in many western U.S. cities. On Jackson Street in Seattle, Japanese restaurants and Black barber shops catered to customers from both races as well as to customers of Filipinx, Chinese, and Mexican ancestry. White-owned hotels, restaurants, and motion picture theaters denied service to Black customers, but Japanese American entrepreneurs welcomed them.[53] In Los Angeles, African Americans and Japanese Americans shared several areas of the city, notably the neighborhood bounded by Silver Lake, Sunset, and Alvarado, the section near Vermont, Fountain, and Lucille, and the streets near Arlington, Jefferson, and Western. People in these neighborhoods shared experiences with discrimination as well; because of the "subversive" and "heterogeneous" nature of their communities, the Home Owners Loan Corporation Secret City Survey Files designated the property of homeowners in these districts undesirable for federal loan support.[54]

Less than a week after the attack on Pearl Harbor, Seattle's Black-owned and Black-edited newspaper, *Northwest Enterprise,* opposed plans to evacuate Japanese Americans from the West Coast. "Don't lose your head and commit crimes in the name of patriotism," a front-page editorial cautioned. In terms its African American readers well understood, the newspaper reminded them that "the same mob spirit which would single them [Japanese Americans] out for slaughter has trailed you through the forest to string you up at some crossroad."[55]

Personal relationships between Japanese Americans and members of other racialized groups motivated individual responses to the internment. Chicano playwright Luis Valdez remembers that the incarceration of Japanese Americans from California brought a temporary moment of prosperity to his family in Delano when the U.S. Army appointed his father manager of a farm previously run by Japanese Americans. Yet prosperity had its price. The Japanese farmer who lived on the land refused to go to the camps and hanged himself in the kitchen of the house that Valdez and his family would inhabit for the duration of the war. The playwright remembers being afraid to enter the kitchen late at night and recalls that during one evening of telling ghost stories he and his cousins thought they could see the farmer's body hanging from a lamp. After the war, the Valdez family returned to the fields and life as impoverished farmworkers.[56]

At the Manzanar Relocation Center in 1944, authorities discovered that one of the "Japanese Americans" incarcerated in their camp was actually Mexican American. Ralph Lazo decided to present himself as a Japanese American at the time of the internment in order to stay with his high school friends. "My Japanese-American friends at Belmont High School were ordered to evacuate the West Coast, so I decided to go with them," Lazo explained. "Who can say I haven't got Japanese blood in me? Who knows what kind of blood runs in their veins?" When embarrassed relocation officials ordered his release from Manzanar, Lazo enlisted in the army. An African American from Seattle drove a Japanese family to the train scheduled to take them to a relocation center and stood by them until it was time to get on board. An interpreter overheard the Black man tell a Japanese woman in the group, "You know that if there's ever anything I can do for you whether it be something big or something small, I'm here to do it."[57]

In the San Francisco Bay Area, the chair of the Alameda County Branch of the NAACP's legal committee wrote to the organization's national spokesperson, Walter White, in July 1942 to protest the "inhumane treatment of Japanese evacuees, and the simultaneously eased restrictions against white enemy aliens." Frank Crosswaith of the Negro Labor Committee criticized the Supreme Court's decision to uphold curfews on Japanese Americans on the West Coast as evidence of "the spread of Hitler's despicable doctrine of racism." When New York's usually liberal mayor Fiorello La Guardia objected to the placement of relocated Japanese Americans in that city in 1944, Roy Wilkins, editor of the NAACP's *The Crisis,* joined George Schuyler, then assistant editor of the *Pittsburgh Courier,* Fred Hoshiyama of the Japanese American Citizens League, and socialist Norman Thomas in addressing a mass protest rally. While Cheryl Greenberg is absolutely correct in arguing that the NAACP responded too timidly and too parochially to the internment—the organization attempted to take advantage of the internment by seeking to replace Japanese American farmhands in California's agricultural fields with Blacks—she also demonstrates that the organization did more than most other civil rights or ethnic groups to defend Japanese Americans. Especially in California, the NAACP offered aid to returned evacuees and supplied them with extensive legal assistance.[58]

In 1945, Charles Jackson condemned attacks in California against Japanese Americans returning from the internment camps in an editorial in *The Militant,* the organ of the Socialist Workers Party. Jackson urged his fellow Blacks to "go to bat for a Japanese-American just as quickly as we would for another Negro. These people are obviously being denied their full citizenship rights just as we are. They are pictured in the capitalist press as toothsome, 'brown-bellied bastards, and are described by the capitalist commentators as half-man and half beast.' This vicious type of prejudice indoctrination is familiar to every Negro."[59]

The interethnic identification between people with similar although not identical experiences with racism that characterizes Charles Jackson's response to the assaults on Japanese Americans proved important in reconfiguring racial politics during World War II. Members of racialized minority groups frequently found themselves identified with one another. Military officials and political leaders in California favored a plan to move urban Japanese Americans to farm work in rural areas, hoping that such a move would prevent the influx of "a lot of Negroes and Mexicans" into the farming regions. At the Poston internment camp, a staff person complained that many of the facility's officials knew little about Japanese Americans but "almost automatically transferred attitudes held about Negroes to the evacuees."[60]

When deployed in combat and support roles, African American service personnel were often confronted with the fear characteristic of colonial officials everywhere that contact between native peoples and armed troops of their own race might "contaminate" the population. When large numbers of Black U.S. troops arrived in Trinidad, British colonial officials on that island protested that the "self-assurance" of the troops would spread to the islanders and make them uncontrollable. The U.S. Department of State agreed with the British officials and consequently ordered the troops replaced by Puerto Ricans who spoke mostly Spanish and thus constituted less of a threat to fraternize with the Anglophone Black population.[61] The Puerto Rican presence in Hawaii, however, seemed to play a different role in race relations than it did in Trinidad. The 30,000 African American sailors, soldiers, and war workers who came to Hawaii during the war discovered that the Hawaii census classified people of African origin as Puerto Rican—and therefore "Caucasian"—to distinguish them from native and Asian inhabitants of the islands. Thus, by moving to Hawaii, Blacks became at least provisionally legally white. Native Hawaiians often displayed sympathy for Blacks in unexpected ways. One bus driver tried to help African Americans defeat their white tormentors when racial fights broke out on his vehicle. He kept the rear doors closed if Blacks were winning, but then opened the doors to let them slip away when the fights ended. As a Black war worker recalled, "There was what you would call an empathy from the local people as to what the black people had endured. They sort of, I guess, sympathized with us to a degree."[62] Nonetheless, military service in Hawaii hardly insulated Blacks from racism. During the war, brothels in Honolulu's Hotel Street district refused to admit African Americans or Hawaiians of color because white servicemen and war workers from the mainland objected to their presence. Continually warned against associating with Black men, local women sometimes viewed the African Americans with fear. One Chinese Hawaiian wrote, "I am very scared of these Negro soldiers here in Honolulu. They make my skin shrivel and my self afraid to go near them."[63]

Communities of color found their fates intertwined during the war; they could not isolate themselves from one another. When large numbers of African American workers from the South moved to war production centers on the West Coast, city officials, realtors, and military authorities saw to it that they found housing in the sections of Seattle, San Francisco, and Los Angeles left vacant by the Japanese internment rather than in white neighborhoods.[64] At the same time, some Mexican Americans felt more vulnerable to racist attacks after the Japanese relocation. "In Los Angeles, where fantasy is a way of life," observed liberal journalist Carey McWilliams, "it was a foregone conclusion that the Mexicans would be substituted as the major scapegoat group once the Japanese were removed." After mobs of white sailors attacked Mexican American youths wearing zoot suits in June 1943, the *Los Angeles Times* printed a caricature of Japanese premier Tojo riding on horseback and wearing a zoot suit.[65]

A 1942 Gallup Poll discovered that "American" respondents held slightly more favorable opinions of Mexicans than of Japanese people, but Lieutenant Edward Duran Ayers of the Los Angeles County Sheriff's Department proved an exception. He drew on many popular stereotypes and slurs in grand jury testimony where he paradoxically contrasted "violence-prone" Mexicans with "law abiding" Chinese and Japanese populations, of course not explaining why 100,000 law-abiding Japanese Americans had been shipped off to internment camps. Even more contradictorily, Ayers "explained" that the propensity toward violence that he discerned among Mexicans was a result of the "oriental" background of their pre-Columbian ancestors, which left them in his view with the "oriental" characteristic of "total disregard for human life."[66]

While racialized groups retained their separate (and sometimes antagonistic) interests and identities, panethnic antiracist coalitions emerged on occasion in support of Japanese Americans. Representatives of African American, Filipinx, and Korean community groups met with delegates from sixteen federal, state, and local agencies at the Palace Hotel in San Francisco in January 1945 to establish the Pacific Coast Fair Play Committee. They agreed that "any attempt to make capital for their own racial groups at the expense of the Japanese would be sawing off the limbs on which they themselves sat." Sometimes, identification came from a perception of common problems. In the novel *Lonely Crusade,* Chester Himes has his Black protagonist learn how Black, Mexican, and Asian American residents share similar experiences with white racism when he reads a newspaper that reports on "a white woman in a shipyard" who "accused a Negro worker of raping her," on a group of white sailors who "had stripped a Mexican lad of his zoot suit on Main Street before a host of male and female onlookers," and about a Chinese girl who had been mistaken for Japanese and "slapped on a crowded streetcar by a white mother whose son had been killed in the Pacific."[67]

By the end of the war, race had become a visible and clearly contested element in all areas of U.S. life. The humiliation and indignity imposed on Japanese Americans during their incarceration left lasting scars, demonstrating once again how state policy marked Asian Americans as permanently foreign in a manner quite dissimilar to every other immigrant group. During the war, Japanese Americans not only lost years of their lives and millions of dollars in property that went mostly to whites, but they suffered a systematic assault on their culture by incarceration, surveillance, and confiscation policies aimed at wiping out the key conduits of the Japanese language and Japanese culture in America.[68] In addition, a wave of violent attacks against Japanese American persons and property swept the West Coast toward the end of the war, and the leniency shown the perpetrators by law enforcement officials and juries portended permanent second-class status for Americans of Japanese ancestry.[69]

Yet Japanese Americans secured some victories in the postwar period. In 1948, California voters rejected efforts to institutionalize and extend the state's anti-Japanese Alien Land Law by a vote of 59 percent against and only 41 percent in favor. The 1952 McCarren-Walter Immigration Act reversed the ban on nonwhites becoming naturalized citizens, a prohibition that had been in effect since 1790, even though the national origins quotas in the act still displayed strong prejudice against immigrants from Asia. Large-scale migration by African Americans and Mexican Americans seeking work in war industries changed the composition of the region's nonwhite population during the war: California's Black population increased from 124,000 to 462,000, and the Black population of Seattle quadrupled between 1941 and 1945 as African Americans replaced Japanese Americans as the city's largest minority group.[70] In some ways, whites' hatred for Blacks and Mexicans eased some of the pressures on Japanese Americans. For example, as Roger Daniels points out, the same voters who rejected the 1948 Alien Land Law Referendum in California also voted overwhelmingly against a Fair Employment Practices measure aimed mainly at prohibiting job discrimination against African American and Mexican American workers.[71]

For African Americans, the Pacific war contributed to a new militancy. Struggles to secure high-paying jobs in defense industries and to get positions on the front lines in combat led logically to postwar activism, ranging from massive campaigns for voting rights in the South to struggles for access to jobs and housing in the North. A. Philip Randolph organized resistance to the draft among African Americans in the postwar period until President Truman capitulated and ordered the desegregation of the military in 1948.

But the war did more than incubate a certain amount of militancy; it taught lasting lessons about the inescapably racialized nature of power and politics in the United States.

African Americans responded with mixed emotions to what they had learned about white racism from their wartime experiences. In a postwar rumination, James Baldwin recalled, "The treatment accorded the Negro during the Second World War marks, for me, a turning point in the Negro's relation to America. To put it briefly, and somewhat too simply, a certain hope died, a certain respect for white Americans faded." John Hope Franklin had some of the same feelings. "Obviously I was pleased with the outcome of the war," he recalled, "but I was not pleased with certain policies pursued by our government. I wish that the government could have been less hypocritical, and more honest about its war aims. I wish that it could have won—and I believe it could have—without the blatant racism that poisoned the entire effort; without its concentration camps for our Japanese citizens, which smacked too much of Hitlerism; and without the use of the atomic bomb."[72]

A Black soldier stationed in the Philippines, Nelson Peery, drew a parallel between the postwar fate of African Americans and the destiny of the Filipinx people he had come to know during his time in the service: "I knew. No one had to tell me. I knew that America was going to beat us back into line when we got home. The Negro troops got a taste of racial equality in foreign lands. As they came home, that had to be beaten and lynched and terrorized out of them before they would go back to building levees and picking cotton. I could see no reason to expect that the Filipinos, also referred to as 'niggers,' were going to get any better treatment. It was the reason I felt such a deep sense of unity with, and loyalty to, the islands and their people." In a book published immediately after the surrender of Japan, Walter White observed that "World War II has given to the Negro a sense of kinship with other colored—and also oppressed—peoples of the world. Where he has not thought or informed himself on the racial angles of colonial policy and master-race theories, he senses that the struggle of the Negro in the United States is part and parcel of the struggle against imperialism and exploitation in India, China, Burma, South Africa, the Philippines, Malaya, the West Indies, and South America."[73]

The postwar period also served as a crucible for antiracist thought and action among members of other aggrieved racial groups. Chicanx scholar and author Americo Paredes (see Chapter 3) served as a Pacific staff correspondent and editor for the U.S. military's newspaper *Stars and Stripes* during the war. He entered Japan with the U.S. occupation forces and, after meeting and marrying a Japanese national, he remained in that country after the war to report on the trials of Japanese leaders charged with atrocities. The racial insults directed against the defendants by the U.S. military reminded Paredes of things he had heard said about people of Mexican origin back home in south Texas, and in that context he felt some affinity with the accused. Paredes went on to work as a journalist in Korea and China during the postwar years. His student and biographer Jose Limon notes that Paredes "developed an attachment to these Asian peoples and a conviction that racism had played a key role in the extension of American military power in that part of the world. This conviction was reinforced when he and his wife decided to return to the United States and encountered racist immigration quotas for Japanese designed to discourage marriages such as his."[74]

Malcolm X certainly embraced a similar anti-imperialism and internationalism after he converted to Islam in a Massachusetts prison in the late 1940s. When the Korean War broke out, he wrote a letter from prison (which he knew would be read by that institution's censors as well as by outside intelligence agents) explaining, "I have always been a Communist. I have tried to enlist in the Japanese Army last war, now they will never draft or accept me in the U.S. Army." Paroled in 1953, he secured employment moving truck frames and cleaning up after welders at the Gar Wood factory. FBI agents visited him at work demanding to know why he had not registered for the draft. He pretended that he did not know that ex-convicts had to register, and the FBI apparently believed him. His draft board in Plymouth, Michigan, denied his request for status as a conscientious objector but judged him "disqualified for military service" because of an alleged "asocial personality with paranoid trends."[75]

Black encounters with Asia became increasingly important between 1940 and 1975, as the United States went to war in Japan, the Philippines, Korea, China, Vietnam, Laos, and Cambodia. As examined in Chapter 4, these U.S. wars in Asia have played an important role in reconfiguring race relations in North America. They have augmented racist tendencies to conflate Asian Americans with the nation's external enemies, as evidenced most clearly by hate crimes against people of Asian origin in the wake of the war in Vietnam, and racist hostility to Asian nations in the wake economic competition between Asian and North American industries.[76] But U.S. wars in Asia have also repeatedly raised once again the kinds of contradictions faced by communities of color during World War II. For example, Gerald Horne and Mary L. Dudziak have shown how the Supreme Court's 1954 decision in *Brown v. Board of Education* responded in part to the imperatives of the Cold War because segregation made it difficult for the United States to present itself as the defender of freedom to emerging nations in Asia, Africa, and Latin America.[77]

In addition, U.S. wars in Asia and their costs to communities of color generated new critiques of the nation's domestic and foreign policies. Amiri Baraka (formerly LeRoi Jones) argues that the Korean conflict created many of the preconditions for the modern-day civil rights movement, and indeed many Korean War veterans, including James Foreman and Bobby Seale, played prominent roles in African American protest groups during the 1950s and 1960s.[78] Ivory Perry, a prominent community activist in St. Louis, always credited his service at Camp Gifu, Japan, and in combat in Korea as the crucible for his own subsequent activism. Meeting Japanese and Korean citizens who seemed refreshingly nonracist compared to the white Americans Perry had known helped him see that white supremacy was primarily a phenomenon of U.S. national history, not of human nature. In addition, the contrast between the freedoms he was sent overseas to defend and the freedoms he could not realize at home made him more determined than ever to bring about changes in his own country. As he remembers thinking on his return to the United States from the war, "I shouldn't have been in Korea in the first place because those Korean people they haven't ever did anything to Ivory Perry. I'm over there trying to kill them for something that I don't know what I'm shooting for. I said my fight is here in America."[79]

When Muhammad Ali (whose conversion to Islam involved the direct intervention and assistance of Malcolm X) refused to fight in the Vietnam War because "I ain't got no quarrel with them Viet Cong," his celebrated case not only brought to light the broad base of support that anti-imperialist and internationalist thinking had among African American but it also helped publicize, legitimate, and proselytize for an antiwar movement that was interracial in many significant ways.[80] As Edward Escobar, Carlos Munoz, and George Mariscal have shown, the Chicano Moratorium in Los Angeles in 1970 demonstrated mass opposition to the war among Mexican Americans, and it also played a crucial role in building the Chicano movement itself.[81] Antiwar protest among Chicanx held particular significance because it required them to oppose the official positions of important institutions in their community including the Catholic church, trade unions, and veterans groups.[82]

Just as U.S. wars in Asia brought to the surface the racial contradictions confronting African Americans and Mexican Americans, antiracist movements among Blacks and Chicanx helped Asian Americans address their unresolved grievances in respect to white supremacy in the United States. During the Vietnam War, militant Asian American political and cultural groups emerged as important participants in interethnic Third World coalitions. African American examples often guided these groups. Rie Aoyama, a Japanese American activist from Seattle explains, "We had no role models for finding identity. We followed what blacks did. Within the whole Asian American identity, part of the black identity came with it. Usually when you say Asian American, you are going to have some aspect of black experience too." Nancy Matsuda similarly attributes her politicization to her recognition while in high school of the parallels between Asian Americans and Blacks: "I realized how blacks were an oppressed people, and I saw how Asians were oppressed too. So for me, it was a complete turnaround from wanting to be associated with the whites to wanting to be associated with the blacks, or just a minority."[83] In 1968, Toru Sakahara, a Japanese American attorney and community leader in Seattle, organized a discussion group that brought representatives of the Black Panther Party in dialogue with members of the Japanese American Citizens League and Jackson Street business owners whose property had been damaged during a civil insurrection in that city.[84]

The racialized nature of the Pacific war has had enduring consequences for race relations in the United States. It exacerbated the antagonisms and alienations of race while at the same time instigating unexpected alliances and affinities across communities of color. Yet it is important to understand that fights between men of different races often involved competition for power over women or over access to them. The prophetic currents of African American and interethnic antiracist activity during World War II addressed important issues about race, nation, and class, but they did precious little to promote an understanding, analysis, or strategy about the ways in which hierarchies of gender initiated, legitimated, and sustained social inequalities and injustices.

The Black nationalist organizations that identified with Japan and other "nonwhite" nations during the 1920s and 1930s also advocated a rather consistent subordination of women to men. In some of these groups women did attain visibility as organizers and activists: government agents shadowed Mittie Maud Lena Gordon because of her work as head of the Peace Movement of Ethiopia, and they put Madame M.L.T. De Mena under surveillance because of her public association with Ashima Takis. Pearl Sherrod took over Satakota Takahishi's newspaper column in local papers after he was deported, and she also served as nominal leader of the society for the Development of Our Own. Takahishi himself spoke out forthrightly for women's rights, condemning the "peculiar ideas prevailing among a certain group of men, that the women should not hold any office in an organization, nor even have a voice at the meetings." Counseling respect between men and women, Takahishi reminded his followers that a woman held the post of international supervisor in his organization. That woman, however, did most of her speaking to white audiences that Takahishi refused to address. In addition, he demonstrated his own lack of respect for women by having an affair with a young female follower while Pearl Sherrod Takahishi ran his organization for him. This development led Sherrod to report her husband to the Immigration and Naturalization Service herself when he tried to return to the United States in 1939.[85]

The white servicemen who attacked Mexican American youths in Los Angeles in the 1943 Zoot Suit Riots justified their actions as a defense of white women from the predatory attentions of nonwhite "hoodlums." At the same time, many Mexican American youths saw the zoot suiters as heroic defenders of Mexican women from advances by white men. In an article about the riots for the NAACP journal, *The Crisis,* Chester Himes compared the sailors to storm troopers, dismissing them as uniformed Klansmen. But he portrayed the riots as primarily a fight about access to women. Condemning the "inexplicable" and "incomprehensible" ego that allows "southern white men" to believe that they are entitled to sex "with any dark skinned woman on earth," Himes explained that Mexican American and Black youths objected to white men dating women of their races because "they, the Mexican and negro boys, cannot go out in Hollywood and pick up white girls."[86]

Himes analyzed the ways in which the war in the Pacific emboldened white men about approaching women of color. He recounted an incident that he witnessed on a streetcar when three white sailors on leave from the "Pacific skirmishes" began talking loudly about "how they had whipped the Japs." Himes noted sarcastically, "It seems always to give a white man a wonderful feeling when he whips a Jap." One sailor boasted about his prowess in combat, and then bragged, "Boy, did those native gals go fuh us." Looking around the streetcar, one of them announced that a white man could get any woman he wanted, in a clear attempt to intimidate two "Mexican" youths in the company of an attractive girl. Himes complained that African American and Mexican American men could not protest remarks like these made to their wives and sweethearts by white men and, even worse, that unescorted Black women would "get a purely commercial proposition from every third unescorted white man or group of white men."[87] Although he fashioned a sensitive and perceptive critique of how official approval of the attacks on zoot suiters replicated the rule by riot that dominated the lives of Blacks in the South, Himes never identified the role played by gender in constructing racial identities, or the ways in which desires for equality based on equal male privileges over women undermined the egalitarian principles and hopes that he articulated elsewhere.

Part of the prejudice toward Black soldiers originated from white servicemen who warned the women they met about the dangers of being molested and raped by Black men. A Japanese American woman in Hawaii noticed how her views had been channeled in that direction one day after she shared an uneventful bus ride with four African American servicemen. Surprised that they had not accosted her, she wrote to a friend, "Gee, I was very frightened. . . . Funny isn't it how I am about them. One would be that way after hearing lots of nasty things about them."[88] On the home front and overseas, battles between Black and white war workers, service personnel, and civilians stemmed from struggles over sex—over rumors of rape, competition for dates, and symbolic and real violations of the privileges of white masculinity.[89]

In his important analysis of government distribution of pin-up photos among U.S. servicemen during World War II, Robert Westbrook shows how the maintenance of white male prerogatives and privileges involved much more than the regressive thinking or selfish behavior of individuals (see Chapter 4). Westbrook makes a persuasive case that the entire war effort had to be presented as a defense of middle-class male norms in order to solve some difficult ideological problems raised by the government's need for popular sacrifice. Westbrook explains that liberal capitalist states have difficulty providing compelling reasons for their citizens to go to war. Given its promises of insulating private property and personal happiness from demands by the state, how can the liberal capitalist state ask its subjects to surrender property, happiness, liberty, and life in pursuit of collective goals?

In the United States during World War II, Westbrook argues, the answer came from couching public obligations as private interests, by stressing military service as the defense of families, children, lovers, friends, and an amorphously defined but clearly commodity-driven "American Way of Life." Just as wartime advertisers' promises about the postwar period featured full freezers rather than the four freedoms, just as Hollywood films presented soldiers sacrificing themselves for apple pie, the Brooklyn Dodgers, and the girl they left behind rather than for the fight against fascism, the U.S. government chose to supply its fighting men with pictures of Betty Grable in a swimsuit as an icon of the private world of personal pleasure that would be restored to them when the war was won. Grable's identity as a blonde, white, wholesome, middle-class, and married beauty made her an appropriate symbol, fitting the war effort firmly into the conventions, history, aspirations, and imagery of middle-class European American life and culture.[90] Consequently, when white men engaged in racist violence against soldiers and civilians of color, they acted upon an understanding of their privileges and prerogatives that the government and other important institutions in their society had encouraged.

After World War II, U.S. economic expansion and military engagement in Asia led to a new stage of racial formation. The same propagandists who deployed alarmist images of violated white women as the reason to resist "yellow feet" on U.S. soil during the war now fashioned fables of romantic love between white U.S. servicemen and Asian women as allegories of empire. In his perceptive analysis of race as the "political unconscious" of American cinema, Nick Browne shows how World War II occasioned a displacement of some of the U.S. film industry's traditional images of African Americans onto Asia. In films including *The Teahouse of the August Moon* (1956) and *Sayonara* (1957), the U.S. presence in Asia becomes naturalized by a grid of sexual relations in which white males have general access to all women, white women are prohibited from sex with nonwhite men, nonwhite men have access to nonwhite women only, and nonwhite women submit to both nonwhite and white men. Consequently, in Browne's formulation, the social world created by the complicated intersections of race, gender, nation, and class attendant to the U.S. presence in Asia relies upon a unified "gender-racial-economic system built as much on what it prohibits as what it permits."[91] This use of gendered imagery to make unequal social relations seem natural and therefore necessary endures today as a particularly poisonous legacy of the Asia Pacific war, especially at a time when so much of the project of transnational capital depends upon the low-wage labor of exploited Asian women workers.

During World War II, African Americans found in Asia a source of inspiration and emulation whose racial signifiers complicated the binary Black–white divisions of the United States. They exposed the internationalist past and present of U.S. race relations, and they forged intercultural communications and contacts to allow for the emergence of antiracist coalitions and consciousness. Liberal narratives about multiculturalism and cultural pluralism to the contrary, race relations in the United States have always involved more than one outcast group at a time acting in an atomized fashion against a homogenous "white" center. Interethnic identifications and alliances have been powerful weapons against white supremacy. All racial identities are relational; communities of color are mutually constitutive of one another, not just competitive or cooperative.

The history of interethnic antiracist coalitions among even ostensibly essentialist and separatist Black nationalist groups points toward potentially effective strategies for the present. Yet to abstract race from the other social relations in which it is embedded would be to seriously misread the nature of racial formation and the social construction of identities. As Susan Jeffords points out, "The complex intersections between all of the manifestations of dominance in patriarchal structures will vary according to historical moments and location, and must be specified in each situation in order to be adequately understood and challenged."[92]

In our own time, when the rapid mobility across the globe of capital, commodities, images, ideas, products, and people creates fundamentally new anxieties about identities connected to nation, race, class, and gender, the relevance of transnational interracial identifications and alliances prefigured during World War II should be manifestly evident. Race is as important as ever; people are dying every day all around the world because of national narratives with racist preconditions. But at a time when women make up so much of the emerging low-wage world workforce, when patriarchal narratives continue to command the allegiance of killers for so many causes, it is also evident that the same imagination and ingenuity that allowed for unlikely coalitions across continents in the past on issues of race must now include a fully theorized understanding of gender as it intersects with identities based on narratives of nation, race, and class.

11

California

The Mississippi of the 1990s

*It is not true that people become liars without knowing it. A liar
always knows that he is lying, and that is why all liars travel in packs:
in order to be reassured that the judgment day will never come for
them. They need each other for the well-being, the health, the
perpetuation of their lie. They have a tacit agreement to guard each
other's secrets, for they have the same secret.*

—JAMES BALDWIN

During the 1960s, comedian Jackie "Moms" Mabley frequently told a
story about voting rights in Mississippi. According to her tale, an African American attorney attempts to get on the voting rolls at the local
registrar's office. Pulling out the literacy tests that had been used historically to disenfranchise Black voters in that state, the registrar asks the applicant to recite the names of all the books of the Bible in order—backward
and forward. The question is supposed to be impossible to answer, but being
a Black Baptist from Mississippi, the lawyer answers it easily. The next question asks him to interpret an arcane clause in the Mississippi state constitution. Most voters would be stumped here, but being a law school graduate
and a practicing attorney, the applicant answers that one correctly as well.
Finally, in frustration, the registrar pulls out a Chinese language newspaper,
throws it at the attorney, and commands sharply, "Tell me what that says!"
The attorney picks up the paper calmly, peruses it carefully, and says slowly,
"Oh, that's easy. This says that no matter *what* I do, you're not going to let me
vote here in Mississippi."[1]

A friend of mine often invokes Moms Mabley's story as a way of describing
the frustrations he faces in trying to get private businesses and government
agencies to obey civil rights laws and to implement the nondiscriminatory
policies they claim to support. Like the attorney in her story, he finds that
previously unannounced rules, regulations, and principles emerge mysteri-
ously whenever the possessive investment in whiteness is threatened. "How
did it go today?" someone will ask him in respect to a meeting about discrimination in housing or unfair employment and promotion practices. "They

handed me the Chinese newspaper," he'll reply. It sometimes seems as if the Chinese newspaper arrives every day, almost as if he has a subscription.

My friend is not deterred by his recognition of the innate unfairness of established bureaucratic procedures, of the stubborn resistance to substantive change, and the disingenuous disavowal of racial intent that he encounters. The humor in Moms Mabley's story comes from recognition, not resignation—from unmasking procedures that purport to be fair as actually unfair. Today this story invokes memories of a difficult but ultimately largely successful struggle in the past. We know in the 2010s that despite its limits, the civil rights movement of the 1960s won some lasting victories. Moms Mabley's joke raised the consciousness and the morale of participants in that movement, and today the attorney in her story would be able to vote. In fact, given the rapid emergence of alliances among aggrieved communities of color, that attorney today might even know how to read a Chinese newspaper.

Yet Mabley's metaphor also reveals the complexity and contradictions of whiteness. Being asked to read a Chinese newspaper is only absurd if China is figured as the master trope of foreignness, as the opposite of "American" identity. Literacy tests were not only devices used against Blacks but were also key mechanisms for denying entry and citizenship to immigrants.[2] Encoded in Mabley's joke is the assertion that no matter how despised they may be, Blacks are American and therefore entitled to the privileges denied them by white supremacy. Yet the operative assumption behind this assertion is that it is unreasonable to expect someone who is "American" to be able to read a Chinese newspaper. This is in no way to belittle the Black claim for inclusion contained in Mabley's story, only to warn that in the current multiracial and international context in which racial identities are made and unmade, a simple Black–white binary, or indeed any binary opposition, will not help us address or redress the possessive investment in whiteness.

As delineated in the previous chapter, the destinies and self-definitions of Asian Americans and African Americans have long been linked. Shortly after the Civil War, southern planters proposed importing large numbers of Chinese laborers to replace freed slaves as agricultural workers. They followed a well-established path with this proposal; throughout the Americas labor migrations from Asia and especially China followed soon after the abolition of slavery—in the West Indies and South America as well as in the United States.[3] Although only a small number of Chinese workers came to the southern United States, many of them settled in Mississippi, where their presence complicated the local racial economy. Some married African Americans and others conducted business in African American neighborhoods. Some cities required Chinese residents to attend separate segregated schools and be buried in their own cemeteries. Some of the Mississippi Chinese objected to these practices, filing lawsuits asking to have themselves declared "white."[4]

Informed audiences in the 1960s knew that Moms Mabley's story contained fact as well as fiction, at least in respect to literacy tests. The "understanding clause" of the Mississippi constitution of 1890 required prospective voters to demonstrate that they could read any section of the state constitution—or at least understand it when it was read to them by giving "a reasonable interpretation of it."[5] Although it did not specifically mention race, the clear intention of this clause since its inception in 1890 was to give registrars discretionary power to prevent Blacks from voting. They could ask questions like "how many bubbles are in a bar of soap" and then deny the franchise to applicants, claiming they got the answer wrong and therefore were not literate enough to vote. Like the poll tax, the grandfather clause, the white primary, and other features of civic life in the South outlawed by the 1965 Voting Rights Act, this clause in the state constitution was but one of many institutional practices designed to produce racially differentiated results while disavowing any racist intent.

Racially exclusive policies in Mississippi before the 1960s relied as much on covert as overt racism. No law said that African Americans could not vote in Mississippi, because no such law was needed. White people knew that registrars would protect the possessive investment in whiteness by finding nearly all of the Black applicants "unqualified" by pretending they could not pass the literacy test. Similarly, no state law barred people of color from attending the state's all-white universities because no such law was needed. When Clennon King, a thirty-seven-year-old Black teacher attempted to enroll in summer courses at the University of Mississippi at Oxford in 1958, highway patrol officers arrested him and had him committed to a state mental hospital, because "any nigger who tried to enter Ole Miss must be crazy." Authorities kept King in custody for two weeks, refusing to declare him competent to leave the institution until he promised to move to Georgia upon his release.

Similarly, in 1959, Clyde Kennard applied for admission to Mississippi Southern University in Hattiesburg. An African American army veteran who had successfully completed two years of study at the University of Chicago, Kennard sought to complete his education when he was compelled to return home to Mississippi to run the family farm after illness incapacitated his stepfather. School and state officials urged Kennard to withdraw his application, but he refused. Police officers, aware of a law that barred convicted felons from attending state colleges, then arrested Kennard and charged him with stealing chicken feed worth $25.00 from a warehouse. Despite what historian David M. Oshinsky describes as "clear evidence of a frame-up," a jury composed entirely of whites took only ten minutes to find the defendant guilty, and a state judge promptly sentenced Kennard to seven years at Parchman Prison Farm. In jail, the authorities denied him medical treatment and check-ups even though he had cancer of the colon. Kennard died of cancer in 1963, shortly after an international protest campaign secured his release from jail through a pardon from Governor Ross Barnett.[6]

State officials in Mississippi never admitted at the time that their refusal to admit Kennard and King to the state's white universities had anything to do with color. To do so would be to admit that the state was violating the Fourteenth Amendment to the Constitution. Instead, they argued that the problem with the two applicants was not the color of their skin but the content of their character. They claimed that King was crazy and that Kennard was a criminal. Of course, they knew these characterizations were lies. Their supporters, patrons, and benefactors knew they were lies. Certainly King, Kennard, and their allies knew they were lies. No one was fooled, but no one had to be. State officials were handing King and Kennard the Chinese newspaper.

The politicians who pursued these policies did not always enjoy undiluted popularity. Some white Mississippians felt guilty about their complicity with this system and many more experienced an uneasiness that made them avert their eyes and avoid knowing too much about the policies carried out in their names. Their leaders made them ashamed of themselves. But segregationist politicians knew they could always count on the possessive investment in whiteness; they could always secure support from a significant segment of the electorate by offering them the pleasures of participating in a game that was fixed, by salving the wounds of a competitive society by assuring whites that members of another race would always be beneath them. The sadistic pleasures offered to this constituency depended in no small measure on a cynical combination—disingenuous disavowal of racist intent coupled with pointed and deliberate deployment of policies having clearly racist consequences.

Most of the time, the majority of white Mississippians did not think of themselves as racists, yet they supported and sustained a white supremacist system. Most viewed themselves as moderates unfairly burdened by the legacy of past practices that they imagined they would have opposed had they been alive in those days. They believed themselves to be enlightened opponents of primitive racialist thinking but also practical realists who feared that rapid changes in race relations would give Blacks freedoms for which they were not prepared and consequently would undermine economic efficiency, burden taxpayers, and increase social disorder.

The combination of racism and disavowal that characterized Mississippi politics during the 1960s had distinct local inflections, but it evidenced a national problem of long standing. Disavowals of racist intent do not mean that racism is not in effect; on the contrary, that is often the way racism works most successfully. A paradoxical and nettling combination of racism and disavowal has always permeated the possessive investment in whiteness. In his excellent study of soldiers and civilians during World War II, historian

Takashi Fujitani identifies "the systematic disavowal of racism coupled with its ongoing reproduction" as the driving force behind the treatment of Japanese Americans in that era. He notes the curious rhetoric of Franklin Delano Roosevelt on February 1, 1943, in announcing the establishment of the 442nd Combat Team, a military unit composed exclusively of Japanese American soldiers. "No loyal citizen of the United States should be denied the democratic right to exercise the responsibilities of citizenship, regardless of his ancestry," the president proclaimed. He added, "The principle on which this country was founded and by which it has always been governed is that Americanism is a matter of the mind and the heart; Americanism is not, and never was, a matter of race or ancestry. A good American is one who is loyal to this country and to our creed of liberty and democracy."[7]

Roosevelt's invocation of antiracist ideals contradicted his racial practices. The president's speech came almost exactly one year after he issued Executive Order 9066 mandating the forced incarceration of more than 100,000 loyal Japanese American civilians and the confiscation or compulsory sale of their property. The 442nd Combat Team would be part of a military ruled by whites that routinely relegated African Americans to underequipped and poorly supported segregated units. Roosevelt's proclamation about race's irrelevance to the American creed did not motivate him to close the internment camps, offer reparations to the people incarcerated in them, or reverse U.S. laws restricting naturalized citizenship to "white" immigrants and banning immigration from Asian nations. The president took no action to oppose state laws that denied Japanese Americans the right to own property or to marry partners of their choice if they happened to be of another race. Instead, in a move characteristic of the possessive investment in whiteness, he extended to the members of the 442nd Combat Team the full responsibilities of citizenship without its rewards—the opportunity to fight and possibly die for a country that relegated them to second-class status precisely *because of* their ancestry and race. Roosevelt invoked antiracist principles, but only to perpetuate racist practices.

President Roosevelt's rhetoric about race no doubt reflected the pressures of practical politics as well as his own personal predispositions. He served as the leader of a political coalition that contained both open white supremacists and spokespersons for communities of color. Establishing the 442nd Combat Team enabled him to make a concession to Japanese Americans without offending the settled expectations or direct interests of whites. Roosevelt's allusions to the enduring traditions of inclusion in the United States may have been a tactical move to legitimate a progressive yet controversial policy, to incorporate within the contours of tradition changes emerging from the radical transformations in social relations engendered by the war.

Beyond Roosevelt's personal motivations, however, the practice of pursuing policies designed to have detrimental effects on nonwhites while at the same time disingenuously disavowing any racial intent is characteristic of traditional "Americanism." The framers of the U.S. Constitution coyly avoided referring to race directly in their document, but its passages about the slave trade and its formula for counting persons held in servitude to determine representation in Congress acknowledge racist realities that were seen as too divisive and discomforting to allow direct mention. The key legislative achievements of Roosevelt's own New Deal—the Federal Housing Act, the Wagner Act, and the Social Security Act—contained no overt racial provisions, but the racialized categories in FHA appraisers' manuals and the denial of Wagner Act and Social Security coverage to farmworkers, domestics, teachers, librarians, and social workers made these measures systematic subsidies to white males at the expense of people of color and all women.

Roosevelt's simultaneous disavowal and embrace of racism illustrates a broader pattern. By avoiding direct endorsement of white supremacy, by denying the salience of race in determining life chances and opportunities in the present and the past, by relegating racism to some previous era, civil rights rhetoric like Roosevelt's condones the promotion and extension of racist practices. Thus, Roosevelt's language in establishing the 442nd Combat Team ultimately tells us less about the personal hypocrisy of the president or the contradictions of the New Deal than about the limits of a civil rights rhetoric that waves the banner of inclusion while practicing exclusion, maintaining and extending the privileges attendant to the possessive investment in whiteness.

In the process of connecting whiteness with the maintenance of economic security, stability, and predictability, Mississippians of the 1960s resembled their parents and their grandparents more than they recognized. Their confidence in the progress that had already been made in race relations and their certainty that rapid change would bring chaos followed a well-worn path. Disapproval of yesterday's racism as ideological justification of today's was not new in the 1960s; it had characterized the entire history of the state's racial economy. James Baldwin identified the core contradictions within this mindset in his analysis of the racial philosophy of the great Mississippi writer William Faulkner. In Baldwin's view, Faulkner was "seeking to exorcise a history which is also a curse. He wants the old order, which came into existence through unchecked greed and wanton murder, to redeem itself without further bloodshed—without, that is, any further menacing of itself—without coercion. This, old orders never do, less because they would not than because they cannot. They cannot because they have always existed in relation to a force which they have had to subdue. Their subjugation is the key to their identity and the triumph and justification of their history, and it is also on this continued subjugation that their material well-being depends."[8]

Baldwin's diagnosis of Faulkner connects racial attitudes to economic interests. For more than a century the plantation system sustained Mississippi's economy and shaped the contours of its race relations. Whatever else white racism was in Mississippi, it was also a system for ensuring a predictable supply of docile low-wage workers for a labor-intensive economy. As the economy changed, earlier forms of racial subordination became obsolete and new forms emerged. Conflicts over racial identities in Mississippi during the 1960s touched on matters of conscience, but they also emanated from contradictions caused by the transformation from one economic order to another. The traditional low taxes, low wages, and management control over the point of production that Mississippians inherited from the preindustrial era sometimes helped their state attract northern capital as it began to industrialize during the 1960s. In that context, however, racial antagonisms, the power of local landowners, and the weaknesses of the state's social and industrial infrastructure inhibited growth and development. Northern corporations wanted to take advantage of the state's low wages, but Mississippi's social structure caused them problems. Their vulnerability to customer boycotts and stockholder protests made the presence of de jure segregation in southern states a potential economic liability for national and multinational firms like Woolworth's drug stores and the Crown-Zellerbach paper company.[9] The turmoil in Mississippi in the 1960s represented a settling of accounts from more than a century of racial subordination, but it also reflected a struggle for authority and power in the context of dramatic economic and social change. The question was how traditional racial categories would influence and shape that change. White racism in Mississippi during the 1960s reassured whites that they would retain the privileges to which they had become accustomed despite the upheavals caused by economic transformation and change.

National economic growth after World War II extended the reach of the industrial system to the remotest corners of Mississippi, a state still dominated in many ways by preindustrial institutions, and created a time of transition during the 1950s and 1960s from which new social relations emerged. Mississippi's political leaders during the 1960s did not prevent the dawn of a new day in their state, but in their ferocious resistance to change they defeated the radical democratic changes proposed by Fannie Lou Hamer and other grassroots activists in the Mississippi freedom movement. In a lesson that was not lost on whites in the rest of the nation, they demonstrated the ability to break the law successfully by resisting federal court orders. Their resistance laid the groundwork for northern resistance to school desegregation, for Richard Nixon's southern strategy, for the assault on civil rights and affirmative action that defined the Reagan coalition and the presidencies of Bush I and Bush II, and the timid abdication of leadership on issues of racial justice displayed by the liberals in the Clinton and Obama administrations.

In *Development Arrested*, Clyde Woods reveals how the politics of the plantation aristocracy in Mississippi have influenced race relations throughout the nation and the world. He argues that the racist practices that emerged originally to ensure that Mississippi's cotton barons would have a large, reliable, and docile labor force were not simply the result of an aberrant local culture. They stemmed, he explains, from a system sustained by the federal government's policies on transportation infrastructure and agricultural subsidies, by policies of both major political parties and regional and national business associations, by the desires of international financiers and investors, and by transnational alliances among elites. Woods shows that segregation in Mississippi emerged as a quintessentially modern strategy to control labor, to disperse and dilute the political power of the Black population, and to produce a police state built around the mutually constitutive powers of the plantation and the prison. By paying Black workers low wages and imposing obstacles to land ownership and asset accumulation, plantation owners made sure that they produced the unemployment that they condemned as vagrancy, the shattered families that they blamed on Black immorality, and the hopelessness and self-hatred that produced violence that could then be punished by imprisonment and forced unpaid labor that closely resembled slavery.[10]

Clyde Woods proves that the leaders of the plantation bloc were dependent on the very federal spending that they often condemned: spending that produced the local levee and rail systems, that made it profitable to leave land fallow, to mechanize production, and to evict sharecroppers. Federal subsidies assisted Mississippi planters in marketing their products overseas and gave them unearned advantages over global competitors. Woods details the specific federal policies that subsidized the activities of the Mississippi Valley Cotton Planters Association and the Delta Council, and explains how the Social Security Act, the Wagner Act, and the War on Poverty were expressly structured to preserve the power of the plantation elite at the expense of Mississippi's Black working class.

Thus, it is no accident that Mississippians Trent Lott and Haley Barbour emerged as leaders of the Republican Party by the 1990s, or that Democrat Bill Clinton's obeisance to the interests of planters and agri-business in Arkansas helped propel him to the presidency. The diehard white supremacists in the Mississippi Delta certainly felt they lost too many battles in the 1960s, but by preserving the value and strategic importance of whiteness, they actually triumphed. The rest of us have paid a terrible price for their victory.

The transformations that took place in Mississippi during the 1960s resonate with the rapid changes taking place today throughout the United States as a result of globalization, economic restructuring, computer-generated automation, and the planned shrinkage of social services provided by the state. Today too, demagogic politicians try to reassure white people that whatever else they may lose, they will retain the possessive investment in whiteness. The role that race played in social change in Mississippi in the middle of the twentieth century takes on special significance for contemporary political debates in the twenty-first century fueled by a resurgent white nationalism.

In 1997, Minnesota senator Paul Wellstone journeyed to Mississippi to retrace Robert Kennedy's much publicized tour of the state three decades earlier. Kennedy's visit in 1967 drew national attention to the nature and extent of poverty in the Mississippi Delta. Wellstone hoped to use his visit to "put the issues of race, gender, poverty, and children back on the public agenda." Although he pledged to travel the length and breadth of the country from Los Angeles to New York in future visits, Wellstone used the symbolic importance of Mississippi in the national imagination to dramatize his opposition to the draconian, mean-spirited, and inhumane welfare reform bill passed by Congress and signed by President Clinton in 1996, with its "disgraceful lack of concern for the downtrodden."[11]

As one might expect, the senator's allies applauded his gesture while his opponents attacked it. Bennie G. Thompson, Mississippi's sole Black representative to the U.S. Congress at the time, accompanied Wellstone on his tour of Tunica County and declared, "We have several thousand families that still don't have running water. This is one of the wealthiest countries in the world and if there are individuals who want to highlight the plight of these families, I can't say that person is doing anything but trying to help." Mississippi governor Kirk Fordice, on the other hand, in an unfortunate choice of words, complained that Wellstone was "using Mississippi as a whipping boy," adding, "I'm sick of it."[12] Fordice, however, did not indicate that he was sick of Mississippi having one of the worst records in the nation in respect to poverty, infant mortality, and illiteracy. In 1990, Black per capita income in Mississippi remained less than half of white per capita income, and for all citizens, the state ranked near the bottom in per capita income. Almost half of the state's 400,000 Black children lived in families whose income put them below the poverty line.[13] As of 2015, these numbers remain dismal: Black Mississippians' per capita income is barely more than half of whites', the state has moved to dead last in per capita income for all citizens together, and almost half of the roughly 300,000 Black children in the state live in poverty.[14]

Wellstone's allies and his opponents alike correctly understood the ways in which Mississippi's history made the state a highly charged setting for discussions about race and poverty. Yet it is hard to imagine how useful lessons about the present actually emerge through references to Mississippi, precisely because the state's image is so connected to the past. Governor Fordice was not wrong to say that Mississippi has become an easy target. The state's past has been so bad that it can be summoned up as the negative example against which any injustice elsewhere can easily be rationalized and accepted. If we are to learn the lessons that the historical Mississippi of the 1960s can teach us, we need to see beyond the rhetorical Mississippi of the

1960s that has been constructed in subsequent decades. Neither Wellstone's easy identification of Mississippi as a unique center of injustice nor Fordice's protestations of innocence allow us to understand the strong links between the racial order in Mississippi during the 1960s and the racial order in the United States and around the world today.

The Mississippi of the 1960s that has come down to us through political discourse, popular journalism, fiction, and motion pictures (especially *Mississippi Burning* and *Ghosts of Mississippi*) strips the struggle in that state of all context and complexity. It presents a simple story about the victory of good whites over bad ones, while submissive and cowed Blacks look on with fear, apprehension, and ultimately, gratitude. Vigilante violence by poor whites emerges as the main problem in this fictive 1960s Mississippi, while the disciplined and determined struggle by Blacks for jobs, education, housing, and political power disappears from view. Elite white protection of Black interests serves as a legitimating excuse to promote vicious and condescending stereotypes about working-class whites. This portrait distorts the past, to be sure, but it also distorts the present by confining all the worst evils of racism to the past and to poor whites—to one group of people in one state during one time period. It gives us a history that hides the present rather than illuminating it, that serves to protect present social relations from examination, analysis, and critique.

Hollywood actor James Woods, star of *Ghosts of Mississippi,* offers proof of the intellectual paralysis that the iconic status of Mississippi in the 1960s engenders. Woods played the role of Byron de la Beckwith in that motion picture, the fertilizer salesman who assassinated Medgar Evers but escaped punishment for more than thirty years until grassroots pressure finally forced a new trial leading to a conviction. Discussing his preparation for the role, the MIT-educated Woods told a reporter that he once encountered de la Beckwith but refused to meet with him "on moral grounds. I just don't like him, and I thought it would make him feel special, that I would further inflame his narcissism." Woods's contempt for de la Beckwith as an individual is understandable, but the actor's own understanding of racism leaves a lot to be desired. When asked if the South had changed since Evers's assassination, Woods replied, "Well, they convicted him. And California didn't convict O. J. Simpson did they?"[15]

Woods's answer ignores some important differences between the two cases. Police investigators discovered de la Beckwith's fingerprint on a rifle found in a vacant lot near the killing. They established that de la Beckwith owned a rifle and a scope like the one used in the murder. They produced two cab drivers who testified that de la Beckwith had inquired about Evers's address prior to the killing. During his first trial, the accused waved to friends in the courtroom, drank soda pop, sat with his legs on another chair, offered cigars to the prosecutor, and had to be escorted by a bailiff back to his chair when he strolled to the jury box to exchange pleasantries with the jurors. Members of the state-funded Mississippi Sovereignty Commission secretly helped the defense with jury selection. It took thirty-one years to get de la Beckwith convicted of a crime that he frequently bragged about committing.[16] Residents of de la Beckwith's hometown held a parade in his honor when the first jury announced it could not agree on a verdict. A second trial also resulted in a hung jury. After those two trials, local officials appointed Evers's murderer as an auxiliary police officer with full powers of law enforcement.[17]

In addition, James Woods surely knows that, however worthy they may have been as human beings, Simpson's alleged victims, Nicole Brown Simpson and Ron Goldman, were not murdered to silence a political movement and disenfranchise a whole race of people. Simpson's wealth rather than his color secured him the best defense money could buy. De la Beckwith, on the other hand, had only his whiteness to protect him from prison, but for thirty-one years that was enough. Yet Woods did not confine himself to comparing the Simpson and de la Beckwith cases; he went on to raise the issue of affirmative action. Responding to a question about whether the South had really changed since 1963, Woods opined, "I really think we've accomplished much more than we realize, but things like affirmative action are actually holding back progress, reducing dignity. I have a ton of black friends and they hate the idea that people might think they gained their position based on some kind of quota, rather than on the basis of their talent. It's insulting. It's like people keep adding on to and building their house, and they sometimes have to be told that it's done, it's time to live in the house. This country needs to shut up already and get going. Stop whining and start living. There's too much yakking and not enough thinking."[18]

His answer indicates that Woods could stand to do a little less yakking and a little more thinking (and reading) himself. Woods's analogy comparing affirmative action to needless tinkering with an already built house is seriously flawed. James Woods probably lives in a dwelling that needs no more fixing, but the nation at large still needs to get its house in order. At the time Woods gave this response, racial discrimination lowered the gross national product by nearly 2 percent every year—a total of more than $100 billion.[19] As of 2013, that percentage increased to 2.3 percent.[20] Such discrimination squanders the skills and talents of women and minority workers while providing an unearned bonus to white men by protecting them from the fullest possible field of competitors. For whom is the house finished, when Blacks hold less than 5 percent of the 32,900 newsroom jobs,[21] when only 2 percent of the partners in accounting firms are African American,[22] when Black attorneys make up only 3 percent of the lawyers employed by large law firms and less than 2 percent of the partners in these businesses?[23] Black people are twice as likely to be unemployed as whites with identical levels of education,[24] and a wealthy Black person is just as likely to live in a segregated neighborhood as a low-income Black person.[25]

In his reply to the reporter's question, Woods makes a rhetorical move common to many defenders of white privilege. He relegates Black grievances against whites to the past while situating white complaints about Blacks in the present. The actor deflects attention away from the racism practiced against African Americans in the South by raising corollary (and presumably equal) objections to what he presumes to be the special privileges enjoyed by O. J. Simpson and Black beneficiaries of affirmative action. Woods doesn't seem concerned that affirmative action remedies came into existence because of white resistance to desegregation, that the quotas he imagines to exist are illegal and nonexistent, and that weaknesses in the structure and enforcement of civil rights laws make affirmative action programs both necessary and desirable.

If Woods's "ton of black friends" really do "hate the idea that people might think they gained their position based on some kind of quota, rather than on the basis of talent," one wonders how insulted Woods's *white* friends must feel, especially those who inherited money from their parents; who got their jobs through family connections, fraternity brothers, or prep school contacts; who enjoyed the benefits of a healthy environment or a decent education because of their favored position in a discriminatory housing market. The stigma that is supposed to haunt those helped by affirmative action evidently does not apply to white people, to the 12 percent of Harvard undergraduates who receive preferential treatment because their parents were alumni, consequently increasing by four times their likelihood of admission compared to applicants not connected to the college through family ties.[26] It bears repeating: at Harvard, alumni children are more than four times as likely to be admitted as a Black student.[27] The class of 2014 at that institution included approximately 200 more applicants whose parents attended Harvard than would be expected if legacy applicants were accepted at the rate for all applications—a number only 20 percent lower than the total number of Black members of the class.[28] Apparently, advantages carry a stigma only when people of color receive them.

Minority students with slightly lower test scores or grade point averages are often *better* students than those who score above them because they achieve results under more difficult conditions. Minority students are concentrated in the schools with the lowest funding, the least experienced teachers, and the sparsest resources. They are less likely than their white counterparts to have the money to enable them to take standardized tests like the SAT and the GRE over and over again so that their scores improve, to hire tutors and purchase the expensive courses that private entrepreneurs offer to boost scores on standardized tests, and to be in schools that offer advanced placement and other enrichment courses that colleges value in making decisions about admissions. James Woods expresses no anguish about these inadequate schools, inexperienced teachers, or financial pressures, but he raises his voice against affirmative action programs that help members of minority groups succeed in spite of all the obstacles placed in their path.

The familiar arguments against affirmative action that James Woods articulates are the product of a pervasive propaganda campaign, the fruits of the public relations reach of a handful of wealthy corporations and the conservative think tanks they finance. For example, in the late winter of 1995, newspapers around California reported the start of a bold new initiative against affirmative action. A story on the front page of the March 30, 1995, *San Francisco Chronicle* attributed the genesis of this campaign to the private frustrations of one aggrieved individual. "After losing a coveted teaching job to a minority woman," the story began, "Tom Wood has turned his private frustration into a public crusade that threatens to end America's 30-year experiment with affirmative action." Wood explained that he had been a candidate for a position in the philosophy department at a California university, that he was clearly "the most qualified applicant" for the job, but that the hiring committee passed over him because he was not "the right race or the right sex."[29] Yet Wood refused to identify the position for which he applied, raising doubts about whether the incident had happened at all.

Wood presented himself as an apolitical individual, a liberal who believed in the teachings of Martin Luther King, Jr., and now an innocent white male victim of the excesses of affirmative action. He did not tell the press that he was affiliated with the conservative National Association of Scholars, a group created and funded lavishly by right-wing extremist foundations. (In 1992, the National Association of Scholars received $375,000 from the Scaife Foundation, $125,000 from a foundation connected to the Olin family, and $72,500 from the Bradley Foundation.)[30] When Wood described himself to the press as the most qualified candidate for the job that he did not receive, he did not disclose that he had not published any scholarly work in any venue in the fifteen years after he received his Ph.D.—a record of productivity that would disqualify him for employment at any serious research university. Portraying himself as "an academic," Wood did not reveal that he had never been employed in a permanent college teaching position, that except for two one-year positions as a visitor at different universities, he worked as a computer programmer in a San Francisco bank and as a part-time instructor at a psychology institute where he earned $1,200 a course. When the television newsmagazine *Dateline* looked into his case, they discovered that five jobs were listed for which Wood might have applied, and that four of these went to white male candidates. The fifth went to a woman who was far superior to Wood in academic achievement—as indeed nearly every candidate for all five of these positions must have been.[31]

Tom Wood's picture of himself as an innocent victim of affirmative action turned out to be false; the truth was that he was a white male who chose to blame women and minorities for his own shortcomings as a job candidate. Yet the special privileges he enjoyed as a white male and the massive amounts of money poured into his cause by right-wing foundations and the Republican Party led gullible reporters to write stories about the campaign that uncritically repeated his charges and read largely like press releases from the National Association of Scholars.[32] As planned, Wood soon picked up a powerful ally in Governor Pete Wilson, who saw an attack on affirmative action as a means of giving a distinctive slant to his campaign for the Republican nomination for the presidency. Acting in concert with his longtime African American ally, Ward Connerly, whom he had appointed to the University of California Board of Regents, Wilson broke a long tradition of leaving the university system free of political meddling. He mobilized Connerly and other regents that he had appointed to pass two measures banning affirmative action programs in student admissions, faculty hiring, and contracting.

Wilson and Connerly used the same combination of racism, disavowal, and dissembling that characterized Tom Wood's public posture in their campaign against the only proven effective tools for promoting diversity in the University of California system. Connerly contended that affirmative action was a form of "slavery" because "if we carefully examine the definition of slavery, we find its most important characteristics—'dependency' and 'under the domination of another'—present in affirmative action."[33] Purists might want to point out that Connerly's understanding of slavery ignores its history as a system of permanent, hereditary, racialized servitude reducing human persons to the status of property, legally defenseless against beatings, whippings, and rapes—surely a far cry from receiving fifty extra points out of 3,000 when applying for admission to college. But definitions aside, if Connerly was so concerned about dependency, one wonders why his whole political career depended on the largesse and insider connections provided by his patron Pete Wilson, or why Connerly followed Wilson's wishes in transforming the state university into a vehicle for the advancement of the governor's electoral ambitions.

Connerly had also been a beneficiary of affirmative action. Although he first denied to reporters that he had ever benefited from "minority preferences," Connerly soon conceded that he certified a firm he co-owned in equal partnership with his white wife as a 51 percent minority-owned company in order to win Energy Commission contracts worth more than $1 million. Connerly's long association with Wilson probably also did not hurt his chances of winning contracts from fifteen California communities to administer Community Development Block grants. This is an odd history for someone who favors ending others' access to support, who champions private enterprise as superior to working for the state, and who complains that affirmative action encourages dependency and makes Blacks "perpetuate the self-defeating and corrosive myth that we cannot do it without help from someone else—and we all too often don't even try."[34]

Wilson, Connerly, and their allies on the Board of Regents argued that affirmative action in student admissions gave special preferences to applicants from underrepresented groups, that these preferences were undeserved, and that they undermined the quality of the student body. Regent Leo Kolligan, an attorney from Fresno, announced that he voted for the resolutions introduced by Wilson and Connerly "because I believe in equal rights. To me, when you give preferential treatments you're not exercising equal rights. That's not what I understand the Constitution to be."[35] Yet Kolligan and the other regents took a different view when it came to the children of their friends and business associates. A few months before his vote against affirmative action in the University of California system, Kolligan privately contacted admissions officers at the University of California at Los Angeles (UCLA) and pressured them to admit the daughter of a white Fresno builder, a young woman who had taken no high school honors classes, who had scored an anemic total of 790 on standardized tests, and who compiled only a slightly above-average high school grade point average. Because of the regent's intervention on her behalf, the applicant secured admission, leapfrogging over more than 500 prospective students with credentials stronger than her own. Almost all of the regents who supported ending affirmative action, including Ward Connerly, had engaged in similar successful lobbying for personal friends and business associates. In one case, a student backed by one of the regents secured admission even though 6,000 candidates for admission had better test scores and grade point averages than he did. When student, faculty, and community groups protested against the gap between the regents' philosophy about what others should do and their own behavior, the regents complained that they felt persecuted by such criticism. Regent Stephen Nakashima worried that these protests were unfair to wealthy children because they made it sound as if having connections would now count against applicants. "It seems it would be ridiculous for a child of mine to apply to UC-Berkeley," he moaned, demonstrating precious little confidence that his children could succeed in a fair competition.[36]

In the summer of 1995, when they pushed their plan through the University of California regents meeting, Wilson and Connerly denied that their motives were political. Yet Wilson made his victory over affirmative action in the university system a prominent part of his campaign for the presidency. In December, Connerly announced that he would head the campaign effort to pass Proposition 209, the statewide ballot initiative launched by the National Association of Scholars and Tom Wood. While campaigning to "free" Blacks, minorities, and women from the "dependency" of affirmative action, Connerly did not disclose that he serves as a trustee of the National Association of Scholars and that the campaign on behalf of Proposition 209 depended upon infusions of cash from wealthy individuals and right-wing foundations who have never shown much interest in freeing the same groups from dependency on low wages, unsafe working conditions, or discrimination in education, employment, and housing.[37] Nor did Connerly address the fact that the supporters of Proposition 209 needed him to head the campaign precisely because his identity as an African American helped shield them from taking responsibility for the racist sentiments mobilized by their campaign. "It was like using affirmative action to defeat affirmative action," admitted Joe C. Gelman, who had been the campaign manager for Proposition 209 when Connerly was recruited to take his place. "We were being pretty cynical, I have to admit."[38]

As the November election approached, Wilson frantically lobbied business leaders in September to secure donations to the media campaign against affirmative action. In a confidential telephone conference call to prospective donors to the Republican Party, Wilson made no mention of slavery, fairness, equal opportunity, or even affirmative action but described the campaign as a "wedge issue" designed to divide the Democrats and to bring more Republican voters to the polls. Speaker of the House Newt Gingrich joined in on the call and described the ballot initiative as crucial to the hopes of the national Republican Party: "We have to be competitive in California to keep control of the House." As *Los Angeles Times* columnist Peter King observed, "The only thing shocking about all this is its utter nakedness, the absence of any semantical coyness."[39]

Yet even if Wood, Wilson, and Connerly treated it like a game, the fight against affirmative action has all too real social consequences. The cynical demagogues who secure short-term gain from fueling white resentment will not be the ones who have to face the consequences of their actions. Ending affirmative action cuts off avenues of upward mobility that have proven of great importance to aggrieved communities. Minority contractors cut off from entry into the construction business by overt discrimination, unfair lending practices, and covert exclusion from insider networks gain one of the few possible sources of asset accumulation available to minorities through affirmative action programs. The loyalty of minority medical school graduates to the communities from which they come provides one of the only hopes their communities have of receiving decent medical care. Affirmative action opens up opportunities for decent-paying jobs to groups traditionally excluded from them at every income level, and it provides one of the few effective mechanisms for offsetting the effects of continuing discriminatory practices in the public and private sectors alike. College students, professionals, and skilled workers are important role models in inner-city communities, expanding the range of possibilities for those around them. Schools, businesses, and governments also benefit from the presence of the broadest possible range of students, workers, and leaders because diversity is rewarding in itself but also because the greatest amount of talent always comes from the broadest possible pool.

The new admissions policies mandated by the University of California regents received their first test during the 1996 to 1997 academic year. Only fourteen African American applicants secured admission in a class of 792 students at the law school at the University of California at Berkeley. To make matters worse, all fourteen chose to go to other institutions in protest against the adoption of an admissions policy that elevated performance on often criticized standardized tests over demonstrated success in school. With one stroke of the pen, the regents turned the state's best law school into a provincial place unable to offer its students a cosmopolitan and diverse atmosphere. "That's the bad news, yes," conceded Ward Connerly, but then he protested that "no one talks about the good news, that fourteen black students were admissible and, if they had chosen to attend, no one would have questioned their right to be there."[40] He expressed no concern about driving talented future lawyers out of the state, about the loss to all of the students incurred by learning the law in a segregated environment, no concern over an admissions policy that demands that minority taxpayers subsidize the educations of those who successfully discriminate against them, and no concern that the $3.6 million that Connerly and his allies spent on Proposition 209 to protect the possessive investment in whiteness might have been better spent on improving the educational opportunities and resources available to minorities if better education had actually been their goal.

Connerly further embarrassed himself by citing the research of Professor Claude M. Steele as justification for Proposition 209. Steele's research has shown that Black students experience great anxiety in testing situations because they know that whites have negative opinions about Blacks and consequently fear that any mistakes they make will be interpreted as evidence of their inferiority. Connerly argued that Proposition 209 would lessen that anxiety by taking away "preferences" that he claimed reinforce the idea that Black students are inferior. In fact, it magnified the weight given to the very tests that Steele proved undervalued the abilities of Black students. Steele emphatically rejected Connerly's interpretation of his research, arguing that eliminating affirmative action would "almost certainly not" rid campuses of stereotypes, and called instead for mentoring programs and accelerated classes to demonstrate the state's trust in the potential of underachieving Black students.[41] At that point, Connerly lost interest in talking about research.

With the implementation of the regents' ban on affirmative action and the success of Proposition 209, young people of color interested in higher education in California faced a stark new reality. Already victimized by diminished state spending on recreation centers, libraries, counseling and health services, and schools, they now confronted a program targeted expressly against those among them who had the most ambition, who had studied the hardest, and who had stayed away from drugs and gangs. The success of previous students from these backgrounds in higher education and in the professions in the past now meant nothing. Students from underfunded inner-city schools now had to outperform their suburban rivals on standardized tests, completely unreliable indicators of how well these students will do once they arrive at college. If inner-city minority students drop out of school, take drugs, join gangs, and commit crimes, the state is willing to spend huge amounts of money on prisons for them. But if they work hard, succeed in school, and have ambition, the state is willing to hand them the equivalent of Moms Mabley's Chinese newspaper.

California's leaders advanced these regressive policies while patting themselves on the back about how much progress has been made and how much better things are today in the fight against racial discrimination. Ward Connerly claimed that the battle against discrimination was won in the early 1980s, that in California "we're at a 9 or a 10 with 10 being the best." Connerly contrasted California's record on discrimination with that of other states and concluded, "In other states, things are probably at a 7 or 8. I'm not sure a Mississippi is at the same point as a California."[42] Connerly agrees with James Woods about affirmative action, but argues that California is ahead of Mississippi; he disagrees with Paul Wellstone about affirmative action and welfare reform, but agrees that Mississippi provides the power of a negative example.

Yet the arguments advanced by Connerly and his patrons had far more in common with the defense of white supremacy in Mississippi in the past and present than they recognize. In their anti–affirmative action and anti-immigrant rhetoric, California's leaders in the 1990s deployed the same combination of racism and disavowal that proved so poisonous in Mississippi during the 1960s. Because their speeches rarely contain direct racist epithets, they may seem more benign than the Ross Barnetts and James Eastlands of yesterday. But in a new economic era where educational and technical training became more important than ever before in determining opportunities and life chances, Governor Wilson and his allies did more harm to more people in more permanent ways than Ross Barnett and his cohorts ever did in the 1960s.

The urgency of the crises of the 1990s and the need for presence of mind about it made it dangerous to compare the largely binary struggle between Blacks and whites in Mississippi in the 1960s with the intercultural conflict and cooperation that characterized California in the 1990s. What happened in Mississippi in the 1960s was that in a moment of crisis, elements of the state's past reappeared with a vengeance and undermined opportunities for peaceful, democratic, and egalitarian social change. That same dynamic appeared in

California and in other states around the nation in the 1990s. California became a new version of the Mississippi of the 1960s and an evil of its own—a
new bad example of how mobilizing white contempt against communities of
color, immigrants, low-wage workers, and people perceived as non-normative
could promise psychic reparations for the damage done to the quality of life by
decades of neoconservative and neoliberal policies.

California's harsh racial history rivals that of any state in the union, including Mississippi. Its Native American population fell from more than
300,000 when white settlers first entered the state to less than 150,000 when
California achieved statehood in 1850. White aggression cut the number to
less than 30,000 in the first decades of statehood through impressment of
Native Americans for labor gangs and outright physical assaults on them.
White settlers murdered at least 4,500 Native Americans in the state between 1848 and 1880. Shortly after statehood, the California legislature
passed a law forbidding testimony by Native Americans in legal proceedings
that involved whites, while another statute made it illegal to supply Indians
with firearms or ammunition. The legislature initially denied Native Americans admission to public schools; when forced to change the policy, the
legislature relegated Native American students to segregated schools and
classrooms.[43] Although slavery was outlawed by the state constitution of
1850, the legislature passed a law that allowed any white to arrest any Native
Americans not presently working for whites and force them to "work off" the
costs of bail through involuntary servitude. Many of the white miners who
struck it rich did so with the aid of unpaid Native American labor.[44]

As white Californians used legal and illegal means to compel Native
Americans to labor on their behalf, they used similar force against Chinese
immigrants to prevent them from working. In the 1860s and 1870s "Anti-
Coolie Clubs" lobbied for legislation to end Asian immigration to the United
States. They organized boycotts of goods made by Chinese workers in America, committed arson against factories suspected of hiring Chinese employees, and physically assaulted individual Chinese people in the streets.
Legislative acts prevented the Chinese from voting in California elections
and barred their participation in public works projects financed by state
funds.[45] A state court ruling in 1854 held that, like Native Americans, Blacks,
and mulattos, Chinese residents of California could not testify in court in
cases that involved whites.[46]

Through laws that did not expressly mention race but had clear racial
consequences, municipal and state authorities alike conspired to prevent the
Chinese from accumulating assets. San Francisco and other cities outlawed
the operation of laundries in wood buildings inside the city limits but enforced the act only against Chinese-owned businesses. In 1870, San Francisco enacted a "cubic air" ordinance requiring inexpensive lodging houses
to provide at least 500 cubic feet of clean air for each adult resident, then

enforced the act only in Chinatown. The 1890 San Francisco Segregation Ordinance designated all Chinese residents for removal from a residential area when speculators cast a covetous eye on the neighborhood near downtown (see Chapter 2). Even though many of these laws ultimately proved unconstitutional, they effectively hindered Chinese immigrants from accumulating assets, thereby granting a de facto subsidy to white business owners and workers who were not encumbered by either restrictive ordinances or the need to wage a long and costly legal struggle against them.

Despite the guarantees of the Treaty of Guadalupe Hidalgo, Mexicans in California also suffered from racial oppression. An early anti-vagrancy act defined vagrants as "all persons who [were] commonly known as 'Greasers' or the issue of Spaniards or Indian blood . . . and who [went] armed and [were] not peaceable and quiet persons," a definition that made resistance against Anglo incursions on land titles supposedly protected by the treaty all but impossible. A "Foreign Miner's Tax" that demanded $20.00 monthly from "foreign" but not "American" miners led to taxing U.S. citizens of Mexican ancestry as well Mexican immigrants, but not Anglos. When taxation proved too clumsy a means, Anglo miners used physical force and direct attacks to drive Mexican miners from the gold-producing regions of the state.[47] Although legal categories officially designated people of Mexican origin as "white" and extended the possible benefits of citizenship to them, concerted action among Anglos disarmed and disenfranchised many Mexicans, denied them opportunities for asset accumulation and education, and used legal and illegal means to relegate most people of Mexican origin to a segment of the workforce where they would be unable to compete with whites.

From the start, African Americans also faced institutionalized racism in California. The state constitution prevented Blacks from voting, holding public office, testifying in court in cases involving whites, serving on juries, attending public schools, or homesteading land.[48] As with other groups, denial of African American citizenship rights affected their opportunities to accumulate assets and made them susceptible to criminal action by whites. In the early 1860s, Rodney Schell, a white man, robbed a millinery shop owned by a Black proprietor. The store owner was powerless to complain to the police because state law prevented him from testifying in court in a case involving a white man. When African American civil rights activist George Gordon complained to the police about the case, Schell shot and killed Gordon. This incident and the political mobilization it spawned led to a change in the law and the granting of the right to testify in court in California to African Americans. Yet Blacks won this right at the expense of the state's Chinese population. They advanced their claims by arguing that respectable Christian and American Blacks should be allowed to testify in court and not be constrained by a law originally aimed at the Chinese, whom Black spokespersons derided for their "filthy habits," idolatrous religion, and loose sexual morality. Just as Chinese residents in Mississippi attempted to win some gains for themselves at the expense of Blacks by suing for "white" status, California Blacks fought for the right to testify in court by promoting themselves as allies in the defense of whiteness against the foreign Chinese.[49]

The long history of racial oppression and interracial conflict in California shows that Mississippi is not the only state with ghosts from its past and skeletons in its closet. California has long been a racialized state, systematically channeling opportunities for asset accumulation and the exercise of citizenship rights toward whites and away from communities of color. Dramatic events like the Japanese internment, the Zoot Suit Riots, the repeal of fair-housing legislation in 1964, Proposition 187, and Proposition 209 flow logically from a history of state protection for the possessive investment in whiteness. Yet just as the Mississippi that produced James Eastland, and Ross Barnett, and Byron de la Beckwith also produced Fannie Lou Hamer, Medgar Evers, and Bill Moore, Californians are also divided on issues of race, property, and politics.

In 1995, labor activists from the Korean Immigrant Worker Advocates group (KIWA) played a major role in exposing the existence of slave labor conditions facing Thai immigrant garment workers in an El Monte, California, sweatshop. KIWA shared offices with worker advocate groups serving Thai and Pilipinx workers. It had experience and skills useful to the Thai workers. The organization mobilized an interracial campaign to hold retailers accountable for the conditions in which their products are produced. The resulting publicity brought KIWA to the attention of Latinx sweatshop workers who asked the group for help in their battle with employers. The El Monte workers eventually won over $4 million from major retail outlets, all of whom initially denied culpability. The campaign helped fuel other interethnic antiracist coalitions in the garment industry that led to passage of a state law mandating fair wages for workers, and the establishment of centers serving immigrant workers from Asia and Latin America.[50]

There were many differences between California in the 1990s and the Mississippi of the 1960s, but one constant remained—the cowardice and craven opportunism of elected officials locally and nationally, eager to gain and retain power at any cost. These leaders showed themselves to be long on noble pronouncements but short on noble deeds. They preached the politics of inclusion, but they pursued policies of exclusion. They proclaimed their faith in the work ethic, but their politics declared war on working people and their institutions. They professed a desire to get government out of people's lives, but they perpetuated invasions of privacy through restrictions on reproductive rights, attacks on lesbian, gay, bisexual, transgender, and queer people, and proposals to mandate compulsory prayer in the schools. They promised to curtail government spending, but they deployed state power ruthlessly to promote capital accumulation and protect the property of the rich. They proposed new initiatives about education, but they spent their money on incarceration. They preached the love of God, but they practiced the love of gain.

Shortly before publishing the first edition of this book, I delivered a lecture about the possessive investment in whiteness at an eastern college. After my talk I was approached by a young student who was greatly disturbed by the things I had said. "I think you're too hard on white people," she offered. I told her that no one would be more delighted to be proven wrong about whiteness than I would, to find out that the possessive investment in whiteness is not as strong as I believe it to be. But I told her that this was not a matter for idle speculation. In the years ahead, I told her, we will have ample opportunities to see what white people are made of, to see whether we can transcend our attachments to the mechanisms that give whiteness its force and power. We need to learn why our history has been built so consistently on racial exclusion and why we continue to generate new mechanisms to increase the value of past and present discrimination. How can we account for the ways in which white people refuse to acknowledge the possessive investment in whiteness even while working to increase its value every day? We can't blame the color of our skin. It must be the content of our character.

12

Change the Focus and Reverse the Hypnosis

Learning from New Orleans

For it would seem that a certain category of exceptions never failed to make the world worse –that category, precisely, for whom power is more real than love.

—JAMES BALDWIN

In the wake of the terrible destruction of much of New Orleans by Hurricane Katrina, President Bush made a brief appearance on September 2, 2005, at the Louis Armstrong Airport in New Orleans to tell the nation what he did on his summer vacation. At a time when hundreds of thousands of residents had fled their homes in the city because of flooding, at a moment when tens of thousands of people left behind still suffered terribly from the effects of hunger, heat, and thirst, from disease spread by untreated sewage flowing through the streets and from shortages of medicine and medical care, the president attempted to link himself personally to the local situation. Predicting that the city would actually be improved by the hurricane, the president joked, "I believe the town where I used to come from Houston, Texas, to enjoy myself—occasionally too much—will be that very same town, that it will be a better place to come to."[1]

To the president, and perhaps to much of his core constituency, the meaning of New Orleans rests with wild times on Bourbon Street, a tourist zone characterized by excessive drinking, lurid sex shows, and music that simulates the golden age of Dixieland jazz. This New Orleans is a place to come *to* from somewhere else, not a place to live *in*, a spot for revelry that can be smirked about knowingly in retrospect after one's return to bourgeois respectability and domesticity elsewhere. That New Orleans is the only New Orleans that the president could imagine worthy of rebuilding.

Yet there is another New Orleans. That New Orleans has been the home of Mahalia Jackson, Louis Armstrong, and Jelly Roll Morton. It was the place where Homére Plessy and other creoles of Haitian ancestry had the temerity to challenge segregation by defying the Louisiana Separate Car Act in 1891. It was the city that served as the base of operations for Tom Dent, Richard and Oretha Castle Haley, Lolis Elie, and Jerome Smith as they organized opposition to Jim Crow segregation in the 1960s in the parts of Louisiana and Mississippi that Fannie Lou Hamer used to call "the land of the tree and the home of the grave."

That New Orleans persists today. It is a city where the streets have names like Melpomene, Erato, Tchoupitoulas, and Desire, where the smell of red beans and rice is always in the air, and where local musicians are still heard on the radio even when they do not have current hits or recording contracts. This New Orleans is a metropolis where Pleasure and Social clubs parade in the streets, where musicians cook meals on the job, and where for many years, Tim's Barber Shop on North Claiborne Avenue advertised itself as the place to get your hair "dyed, fried, and laid to the side."

New Orleans is home to thousands of Latinos and Asians. It is not only one of the most southern ports of the United States but also serves functionally as the northern-most appendage of the Caribbean. The city is a place that has been in continuous contact for centuries with ships, sailors, passengers, and cargo from Cuba, Haiti, Puerto Rico, Trinidad, and Mexico. Its pre-Lenten carnival celebrations evoke the cultures of Cuba, Trinidad, Haiti, and West Africa. Rara rhythms from Haiti and *habanera* beats from Cuba permeate the sounds made by many different kinds of musicians from the Crescent City. The legendary Jelly Roll Morton exemplified the pan-Caribbean identity of New Orleans. His parents came from Haiti, but he was raised by his godparents who were Cuban, and he learned to play *habanera* rhythms from his guitar teacher who was Mexican. When Cyril Neville moved from his native New Orleans to New York, he felt most comfortable with Puerto Rican, Haitian, and Jamaican musicians because they reminded him of home. His brother Art Neville enjoyed a productive collaboration in Trinidad with calypso singer the Mighty Sparrow. Cyril Neville claims that New Orleans has an "island" culture, pointing to the dreams, songs, and rhythms of Caribbean countries as crucial components of local life because the city shares that region's history of "the slave trade with Africa, souls being shipped and abandoned, cultures confused and commingled, the sense of oppression, the sense of relaxation, humid heat hanging over your head like a hammer, carnivals and rituals and a beat that goes from morning till night, drums that talk like singers and singers who sing like drums."[2]

The city of New Orleans shows strong traces of the history of Spanish colonial rule and Mexican migration. Between 1853 and 1855, Benito Juarez, a Zapotec Indian from Oaxaca, spent his time working as a cigar maker in the French Quarter by day and mobilizing political opposition to dictatorial rule in his native land by night. Juarez returned home and eventually became president of Mexico. The Mexican Army's Eighth Cavalry Military

Band made a triumphant appearance at the 1884 World's Cotton Exposition in New Orleans, and their melodies, harmonies, and rhythms quickly became part of the city's local musical culture.

New Orleans has been the home of incomparable artists and unparalleled artistry. This is the city where Blind Willie Johnson got arrested by New Orleans police officers in front of the Customs House building in 1929, not for panhandling or for disturbing the peace, but because he sang the gospel song "If I had My Way in This Wicked World I Would Tear This Building Down" so convincingly that he frightened the local authorities who had him arrested for inciting to riot. In this New Orleans, blind blues guitar virtuoso Snooks Eaglin played so well that jealous band members sometimes tried to confound him by detuning his guitar just before he went on stage. Yet without breaking stride, Eaglin always got back in tune within the first five bars of the first song. This is the New Orleans where Professor Jo Dora Middleton thought she could impress her young student, pianist James Booker, with the difficulty of playing classical music by handing him sheet music by J. S. Bach. Booker looked over the score and asked, "You want me to play this front to back or back to front?"

In this New Orleans, the magnificently talented Irma Thomas, the Soul Queen of New Orleans, graces the alto section of the First African Baptist Church Choir every Sunday. Thomas rarely gets to sing lead, however, because incredibly enough, the congregation assumes that several other members of the congregation sing just as well as she does. In this New Orleans, the histories of the piano playing by Professor Longhair and James Booker, the poetry of Brenda Marie Osbey and Sybil Kein, and the theatrical innovations of John O'Neal and Gilbert Moses stand as monuments to the beauty, intelligence, and moral power of the Black community. Their art has functioned, in the words of New Jersey hip-hop artist Lauryn Hill, as an "opus to reverse the hypnosis." It challenges the system that elevates white property over Black humanity by systematically following Hill's admonition to change "the focus from the richest to the brokest."[3]

The pleasures of New Orleans come from a crucible of undeniable pain. Ninth Ward poet and journalist Kalamu ya Salaam reminds us that "living poor and Black in the Big Easy is never as much fun as our music, food, smiles, and laughter make it seem."[4] George Landry (now deceased, but formerly Chief Jolly of the Wild Tchoupitoulas Mardi Gras Indian tribe, and the uncle of the musicians known as the Neville Brothers) was nearly beaten to death by police officers who accused him falsely of accosting a white woman. To make Landry confess, they positioned his testicles in a drawer and slammed it shut. Yet he still refused to comply with their demands.[5] As a youth, Landry's nephew Charles Neville witnessed a Black man bleed to death after being dragged along city streets behind a car driven by whites.[6] Charles's brother Cyril got in so many fights growing up in New Orleans that when he went for his Army pre-induction physical exam, he had a long scar on his neck, his elbow in a cast, and needed crutches to walk. One of his fellow draftees assumed Neville was returning from the war and asked him what Vietnam was really like. "I don't know," Cyril replied, "this shit is just from the 'hood."[7]

The perpetual struggle for dignity and self-determination waged by working-class Blacks in New Orleans took a dramatic turn in June 2005. Eight weeks before Hurricane Katrina hit the Louisiana mainland, eighty-two-year-old Allison "Tootie" Montana stood before the New Orleans City Council to speak up on behalf of some of the "brokest" residents of the Crescent City. Montana delivered his remarks in the wake of repeated incidents of police brutality and vigilante violence against Black people in New Orleans in the preceding six months. On New Year's Eve, four white men working as bouncers at the Razoo Club on Bourbon Street beat and killed Levon Jones, a vacationing Georgia Southern college student. Establishments in the French Quarter are notorious for their exclusionary policies. They charge Blacks higher cover charges and higher prices for drinks and selectively enforce unwritten "dress codes" as a way to discourage Black patronage. Managers at the Razoo Club claimed that Jones's attire did not conform to the club's dress code, so they used deadly force to evict him. On March 24, New Orleans police officers killed Jenard "Nordy" Thomas, a twenty-five-year-old T-shirt shop employee and part-time college student, in the 1500 block of Piety Street. They stopped Thomas as he was leaving a friend's house because they thought he looked suspicious. The officers claimed Thomas pulled a gun on them, but no gun was found on or near his bullet-riddled corpse. Several months later, Raymond Robair, a forty-eight-year-old roofer, was beaten, kicked, and killed by New Orleans police officers who encountered him outside the house of a friend he had been visiting in the Tremé neighborhood.

The focal point of Montana's ire was an attack by New Orleans police officers on St. Joseph's Day (March 19) at the corner of Lasalle Street and Washington Avenue. Officers dispersed a peaceful assembly of Mardi Gras Indian tribes—social clubs of Black men who masquerade as Plains Indians and parade through their neighborhoods in flamboyant costumes on Mardi Gras Day and St. Joseph's Day. The officers contended that the tribes were marching without a permit and needed to be dispersed. Representatives of the Indians contended that those assembled posed no threat to civic order, and they had never needed a permit before, even though their organizations had been parading every St. Joseph's Day for more than a century.

Montana spoke from his perspective as a resident of the Seventh Ward—the oldest continuous free Black neighborhood in the United States—and as a Black worker whose labor as a lather had helped build houses throughout the city of New Orleans. Montana made his living installing the wooden battens on which plaster hangs. A master craftsman, he sometimes entertained his fellow workers by blindfolding himself on the job and then driving nails into place perfectly. To add to the spectacle, he kept his supply of nails in his mouth, spitting them into his hands in succession as he needed them. Montana also served as the unofficial handy man on his block, performing a wide range of construction tasks for his neighbors, but never accepting a cent from them in return for his efforts. He explained that people in the Seventh Ward had always helped each other, that years ago they had even come together to build houses for one another.[8]

Yet for all his contributions as a worker and a neighbor, it was Montana's role as chief of the downtown Yellow Pocahontas Indian tribe—and as "Chief of Chiefs" of all the Mardi Gras Indians—that led to his appearance before the city council that night. Estabon Eugene, known as "Big Chief Peppy" of the uptown Golden Arrows Tribe, had actually signed up to be the first speaker, but he graciously stepped aside out of respect for his senior downtown rival. Montana delineated the long history of police harassment that he had witnessed with his own eyes going back decades. He condemned the St. Joseph's day action, especially the summons issued to Mardi Gras Indian Bertrand Butler and the arrest of Butler's daughter. He told the council members solemnly, "I want this to stop." Montana then paused, collapsed, and fell to the floor.[9] Police officers called for an ambulance and administered CPR as Montana's son Darryl held the Chief in his arms. City Council President Oliver Thomas adjourned the meeting and asked those present to pray. The Indians in the room began to sing, "Indian Red," a song that serves as a prayer traditionally voiced to honor the tribal chief. Montana died that night at Charity Hospital.

Tootie Montana died fighting for the right of Black people in New Orleans to occupy and traverse urban space. His final words "I want this to stop" speak volumes about the seriousness that lies beneath the surface of the Indians' colorful handmade costumes, festive dances, celebratory songs, and intricate language and lore. Often misunderstood and even condemned as a frivolous escape from serious political and economic problems, Indian masking by New Orleans Blacks serves important functions.[10] Especially in the post–civil rights and postindustrial era, when disinvestment, economic restructuring, and the co-optation of Black elected officials by powerful white elites has neutralized the ability of working-class Blacks in New Orleans to secure meaningful resources through the political system, the enduring utility of alternative academies like Mardi Gras Indian masking merits close attention. By themselves, alternative academies cannot produce substantive realignments of political or economic power, but as repositories of collective memory, sites of radical solidarity, and sources of moral and political instruction, they hold enormous potential for the development of collective mobilization and struggle.

In a city where decades of housing discrimination, environmental racism, urban renewal, and police harassment have relegated different races to different spaces, the ferocious theatricality and aggressive festivity of the Mardi Gras Indians hold great significance for the politics of place. Montana's Yellow Pocahontas tribe, like all Mardi Gras Indian groups, comes from a specific neighborhood and speaks for it. The corner of Lasalle and Washington where the Indians were not allowed to congregate on St. Joseph's Day 2005 is not just any corner. It is the location of the Dew Drop Inn, a venerable hotel and rhythm and blues nightclub where many New Orleans musicians played on weekends during the 1950s, 1960s, and 1970s. During those same years on weeknights, the Dew Drop hosted Drag Queen revues. Bobby Marchand would sing his national hit song "There's Something on Your Mind" at the club on weekends, but perform as a drag queen named Roberta on week nights.[11] The Indian tribes function in these neighborhoods as mutual aid societies. They help their members meet unexpected emergencies by paying medical bills and funeral expenses, financing urgent home repairs, or making up for lost wages caused by layoffs, illness, and injuries. These forms of self-help serve especially important functions because of the price that Black people in New Orleans pay for the racialization of space and the spatialization of race.

Systematic segregation and discrimination prevent Black people from freely acquiring assets that appreciate in value, from moving to desirable neighborhoods with better services and amenities, and from reaping the rewards of homeownership built into the tax code. Like suburban homeowners' associations and stakeholders in Common Interest Developments, inner city residents nurture a defensive localism. Unlike their counterparts in the suburbs, however—groups that have their private governments, exclusionary zoning, and tax subsidized privatism—inner-city residents can neither control the uses to which their neighborhoods are put nor secure increases in the exchange value of their homes. Their only recourse under these circumstances is to increase the use value of their neighborhoods by turning "segregation into congregation," fashioning ferocious attachments to place as a means of producing useful mechanisms of solidarity.[12]

The organized abandonment of poor and working-class Black people in New Orleans before the hurricane left them isolated in high-poverty neighborhoods, making them especially vulnerable to the effects of flooding. In the aftermath of Hurricane Katrina, they faced a concentrated campaign to disperse them to other regions, permanently removing them from New Orleans. These plans portended particularly vicious injuries because Blacks in New Orleans had come to depend so much on neighborhood support networks that provide what Mindy Fullilove describes as "emotional ecosystems" grounded in the solidarities of space, place, and race. Displaced residents of the Seventh, Ninth, and Thirteenth Wards stood to lose much more from Hurricane Katrina than did the owners of mansions, luxury apartments, office buildings, and hotels because they were resource poor but network rich.

The reconstitution of those networks and the spaces and social relations that nurtured and sustained them should have been the first priority of any rebuilding effort. They should have had the right to return, the right to rebuild, and the right to expect that Black dignity and humanity would be protected as diligently and as assiduously as white property. Instead, they faced a regime of dispossession and displacement, the latest in a long line of historical insults and injuries responsible for the conditions that make mutual aid societies like the Mardi Gras Indians so important in their lives.

The practical activities of mutual aid that the Indians conduct provide material resources for an aggrieved community. At the same time, however, they also offer cultural and ideological instruction. In contrast to the fantasy representations of pirates, birds, animals, and royalty played out by costumed members of the city's social elite riding along Canal Street on expensive floats on Mardi Gras Day, the Indians invert the imagery of western movies and wild west shows to celebrate the radical solidarity and defensive resistance of warriors defending their home territory against outside aggression. They position themselves as oppositional and embattled. They move beyond the Black–white binary that shapes the core categories of white supremacy in the United States to assert an affinity with another aggrieved racial group. Some members of these tribes have actual Indigenous ancestry; others including Cyril Neville have been inducted as honorary members of native nations. Yet the main appeal of Indian imagery in this tradition lies in its inversion of the hierarchies of the possessive investment in whiteness. On the day when the members of the city's social elite flamboyantly display their European heritage, the Mardi Gras Indians emphasize the new world realities of conquest and attempted genocide.[13]

Cyril Neville remembers learning about Indian masking from his uncle George Landry who served as Big Chief of the Wild Tchoupitoulas. "We don't need your fancy floats," Neville imagines the Indians saying to the downtown Mardi Gras. "We don't need floats at all. We have our own stories, our own music, our own drama. We'll make our own costumes according to our designs and we'll design our own parades." Neville recalls his uncle's moral authority as something rooted in their family's uptown Thirteenth Ward neighborhood, taking the name of his tribe from one local street and masking as an Indian to tell the world "This is who I am, this is where I'm from."[14] On the day when the official Mardi Gras parade enshrines Canal Street as the center of the city, the Indians parade proudly through their neighborhoods, calling communities into being through performance. As Cyril Neville explains, "The mythology of the tribes is based on territorial integrity—this is our plot of ground where we rule." He recalls Chief Jolly's sense of self-affirmation as something rooted in his uptown Thirteenth Ward neighborhood.

Civil rights activist and cultural visionary Jerome Smith recalls that watching Tootie Montana and the Yellow Pocahontas tribe parading through the streets of New Orleans helped shape the consciousness about race and politics that later enabled him to work for civil rights with the Student Nonviolent Coordinating Committee and the Congress of Racial Equality. Smith came from a working-class family. His grandfather was a militant in the Black long-shore workers' union and his parents raised him to respect and admire Black intellectuals and activists Mary McLeod Bethune and Paul Robeson. Yet Smith credits Tootie Montana as an important political influence as well because he

> unconsciously made statements about black power . . . the whole thing about excellence, about uniqueness, about creativity, about protecting your creativity—I learned that in those houses [of the Indians]. Police would try to run the Indians off the street, but we had a thing. You don't bow, you don't run from 'em, not black or white or grizzly grey.[15]

The New Orleans hit by Hurricane Katrina contained a dynamic community of struggle, a community capable and deserving of playing a central role in the reconstruction of the city. Yet this community and its vision for the future will continue to remain invisible unless people reverse the hypnosis and shift the focus from the richest to the brokest. From the perspective of the richest people, the richest corporations, and the most powerful politicians and media outlets in our society, New Orleans needed to be rebuilt for the convenience of investors, entrepreneurs, and owners. This process obscured from view the needs, demands, abilities, and aspirations for justice of people who, while often broke, have never been broken.

The perspective of the rich about the destruction and rebuilding of New Orleans is easy to see. In the wake of the devastation caused by Hurricane Katrina and his own administration's maliciously incompetent relief efforts, President Bush outlined a program of legalized looting to enable corporations to profit from the misfortunes of poor people. Just as he did with the occupation of Iraq, Bush viewed the emergency in New Orleans as an excuse for an exercise in neoliberal social engineering, as an opportunity to implement the free market fundamentalism that was not yet politically palatable in the rest of the country. Bush ordered the suspension of laws that require affirmative action in hiring and contracting, that mandate environmental protection, and that prescribe paying the prevailing union scale and minimum wage on federally funded rebuilding projects. The president offered lavish tax breaks to corporations by making the entire Gulf Coast a taxpayer-subsidized "enterprise zone," and he even exploited the emergency as an opportunity to advance his schemes to undermine public education by using taxpayer money to support vouchers to send children to private schools. The Obama administration followed that path dutifully, embracing the Bush playbook for rebuilding New Orleans resolutely and enthusiastically.

Bush's appointees to the Federal Emergency Management Agency failed miserably in carrying out even the simplest tasks related to the relief effort, but they took pains to suggest that private citizens make donations to a list of faith-based charities approved by the White House, many of which had no track record of any kind in disaster relief. Rather than allocating funds to the publicly accountable (at least in theory) National Guard and New Orleans Police Department to provide security for the people of New Orleans, the Bush administration immediately hired the private paramilitary Blackwater "security" firm to protect fully insured downtown property from looters. Consistent with the crony capitalism central to its policies in Iraq, the administration granted huge no-bid contracts to Halliburton and other politically connected corporations under the guise of "rebuilding New Orleans." At the very moment when unverified and almost uniformly untrue news reports sensationalized tales of alleged looting and violence by the poor in the aftermath of the hurricane, the legalized looting by the rich proposed and implemented by the president escaped media exposure and scrutiny.

The desires of the rich in respect to the rebuilding of New Orleans found direct expression in the words of Alphonso Jackson, George Bush's secretary of housing and urban development, and one of those Black conservatives who usually claims that discrimination has ended and that the time for color-blind policies has begun. Yet Jackson's approach to New Orleans was expressly color conscious. "New Orleans is not going to be as black as it was for a long time, if ever again," Jackson predicted. "I'm telling you, as HUD Secretary and having been a developer and a planner, that's how it's going to be."[16] Jackson did not specify exactly which principles of HUD administration and urban development require the removal of Black people from cities where they are the majority of the population.

Secretary Jackson could have said that while it would be unwise to build new houses in parts of the flood-prone mostly Black lower Ninth Ward, that new housing throughout the city would be made available to all residents of New Orleans as required by Fair Housing Act of 1968 and civil rights laws dating back to 1866. He did not explain why his administration considered it necessary to give students vouchers enabling them to leave public schools while failing to provide vouchers for temporary housing or subsidies to promote homeownership among people shut out of the housing market by illegal discrimination by the real estate, mortgage lending, and insurance industries. As secretary of housing and urban development, Jackson bore major responsibility for enforcing fair housing laws, yet he ignored the fifty to one hundred complaints per week about fair housing violations reported to the Greater New Orleans Fair Housing Action Council (GNOFHAC). Like his predecessors in the Clinton administration, Jackson took no action to address the findings of testing surveys showing that African Americans seeking apartments in the Crescent City encountered discrimination 77 percent of the time. Although attorneys representing GNOFHAC won more than $1 million in actual and punitive damages between 1995 and 2005 for victims of housing discrimination, the Bush administration's commitment to crime fighting never included protecting Black and Latinx citizens of New Orleans from illegal impediments to rentals and homeownership.[17]

Secretary Jackson's vision of forcing a decline in the Black population of New Orleans clearly corresponded to policies that had been pursued by both political parties in recent years. The Clinton administration supervised the destruction of thousands of public housing units in New Orleans without producing adequate replacement housing. The number of public housing units in the city dropped by 8,000 units between 1996 and 2002. The Convention Center stands near the site of the former St. Thomas project, which had housed more than 1,000 Black families. When Hurricane Katrina devastated much of the public housing remaining in New Orleans, Republican Representative Richard Baker from Baton Rouge announced jubilantly, "We finally cleaned up public housing in New Orleans. We couldn't do it, but God did."[18]

The observations by Secretary Jackson and Congressman Baker resonated with the sentiments of Jimmy Riess, a wealthy white developer who directs the New Orleans Regional Transportation Authority (NORTA). Riess told the *Wall Street Journal* that one part of the plan for rebuilding New Orleans should entail keeping poor people from returning to their neighborhoods. At Riess's urging, New Orleans Mayor Ray Nagin hosted a confidential meeting in Dallas less than two weeks after Hurricane Katrina hit so that wealthy investors (sarcastically dubbed the "forty thieves" by leaders of grassroots community organizations) could plan the city's future. To provide political protective cover for their plans, the meeting was chaired by Nagin, a nominal Democrat and an African American, but a politician whose main base of support at that time came from white developers and voters, who endorsed ultra-conservative Republican Bobby Jindal against the Democratic nominee (and eventual winner) Katherine Blanco in the state's 2003 gubernatorial election, and who appointed Riess to his position at NORTA. Participants at the meeting also included two Black business executives, one Black state senator, and musician Wynton Marsalis, who spoke to the group by telephone from New York.

There was no one present at the Dallas meeting likely to change the focus from the richest to the brokest—no representatives of the many grassroots groups working for justice in New Orleans. Jimmy Reiss and Ray Nagin excluded from their meeting representatives of the Douglass Community Coalition, a group attempting to turn the city's Frederick Douglass High School into a community learning center. The mayor and his business backers did not invite representatives from the Hands Off Iberville/C3 coalition, established to fight urban renewal and the destruction of housing for Black people in a neighborhood adjacent to the French Quarter. While willing to listen to Wynton Marsalis speaking on the telephone from New York, the organizers of the Dallas meeting had no interest in hearing from representatives of Community Labor United, a coalition of labor and community activists, from representatives of the Ernie K-Doe community center in the Treme Neighborhood, from the staff of Bob Moses's Algebra Project and Young People's Project or John O'Neal's Junebug Theatre. Mayor Nagin and the business elite conducted their deliberations without hearing from any residents of the downtown Ninth Ward devastated by flooding, from the uptown Black neighborhoods in the Thirteenth Ward, from the downtown Seventh Ward, or West Bank neighborhoods in Algiers.

The plans for reconstructing New Orleans by its richest residents revealed the terrible dearth of democracy in the city, the state of Louisiana, and the United States. They are part and parcel of a global system that values property more than people, that places the pursuit of profits ahead of the preservation of coastal wetlands and the prevention of global warming, that imposes austerity on the poor to promote prosperity for the rich. Changing the focus from the richest to the brokest, however, can reveal something quite different—the determination of working people unwilling to let democracy die. The Black working class in New Orleans has long refused to concede that white property is more important than Black humanity. Its long histories of struggle and self-affirmation are especially important today as the destruction and reconstruction of New Orleans compel us to confront the painful truth about how we have been actually governed in this society and to face up to the apocalypse on the installment plan that surrounds us as a result.

The late and sorely missed Clyde Woods, a scholar who worked closely with grassroots social movements in New Orleans, argued that the devastation and suffering experienced in that city in the wake of the hurricane did not occur because New Orleans was a primitive backwater left out of the benefits of modern development. On the contrary, Woods maintained, the policies that prevail in New Orleans are the harbingers of an emerging world shaped by the calculated cruelties and organized abandonments of neoliberal racial capitalism. Impacting different populations in different ways, this fragmented, delinked, privatized, and devolved model of the state refuses to meet human needs but assists investors in reaping the gains that flow from accumulation by dispossession.[19] He maintained that New Orleans is our future, a model of privatized plunder and predation being tested first in Ferguson and Flint, in Indian country and in Iraq, but intended for implementation across the nation and around the world.

Neoliberal policies for rebuilding New Orleans to benefit investors and owners at the expense of residents and workers have instigated a new Battle of New Orleans, a fight to control the story of what happened in the Crescent City after the hurricane and the lessons to be drawn from that history. As soon as the dimensions of the disaster became evident, pundits and politicians attempted to exploit the tragedy for their own ends. Less than ten days after the hurricane hit, *New York Times* columnist David Brooks seconded the call by HUD secretary Alphonso Jackson for ethnic cleansing of the city. "If we just put up new buildings and allow the same people to move back into their old neighborhoods, then urban New Orleans will become just as rundown and dysfunctional as before," Brooks counseled.[20] One week later educational entrepreneurs pressed the case for using the disaster as a pretext for privatizing public education. Chris Kinman of Freedom Works proposed that the rescue of people trapped by the storm required another rescue effort, "saving New Orleans school kids from their broken public-school system."[21] Brooks described privatization as Katrina's "silver lining," while Kinman called the storm "a golden opportunity."

Silver and gold were certainly at the center of their thoughts, but simply as plunder rather than as either lining or opportunity. Echoing Congressman Baker's celebration of the flood waters' destruction of public housing, a proclamation by the American Enterprise Institute one year after the storm crowed that Katrina "accomplished in a day" what "school reformers" failed to do for years—dismantle the city's public school system.[22] President Obama's secretary of education Arne Duncan concurred with these views, declaring in 2010 that Hurricane Katrina was "the best thing that happened to the education system in New Orleans" because it created the preconditions that made privatization possible.[23] Writing in the *New Yorker* a decade after the disaster, Malcolm Gladwell, the neoliberal gadfly for whom every problem has a technical rather than a political solution, celebrated the expulsion of New Orleans Blacks from their ancestral neighborhoods and support systems. He went on to scold those who protested this displacement. "The fact that you may have lived in a neighborhood for generations, or become attached to a set of longstanding educational traditions," Gladwell declared, "does not mean that you should always return to that neighborhood if you are displaced, or reconstruct those traditions."[24] In the most bizarre, shameless, and indecent commentary of all, *Chicago Tribune* columnist Kirsten McQueary, writing ten years after the hurricane, declared that she actually felt envious of New Orleans, She said she longed for a similar storm to hit her city. Without enumerating or describing the number of lives lost and permanently altered, the pollution and disease that emanated from the flooding, or the homes and neighborhoods destroyed, McQueary acknowledged that Hurricane Katrina brought "chaos, tragedy and heartbreak" to New Orleans. Yet it was all worth it, she declared, and worth replicating in Chicago, because the emergency enabled the city to slash the municipal budget, fire workers who belonged to unions, and replace public education with what McQueary described as a "free-market education system."[25]

These declarations of silver linings and golden opportunities ignored the actual causes of poverty and educational inequality in New Orleans. During the second half of the twentieth century when highway building and urban renewal devastated thriving Black neighborhoods and automated containerization eliminated many of the high-paying blue-collar jobs open to Black workers, government and business leaders in Louisiana worked together to create a state characterized by low wages, high profits, a shredded social safety net, and one of the highest rates of incarceration in the world. In short, the very "free-market" system that McQueary presented as the cure for the city's ills had actually been the cause of them. The state's elites deregulated businesses, provided tax subsidies to big corporations, and promoted ecologically unsound development. Along with failure to enforce fair housing laws, the impact of the 1996 cuts in federal welfare spending, and the predatory lending practices permitted by bank deregulation, these policies increased concentrated poverty and exacerbated its effects. Yet the post-Katrina propagandists ignored this history and blamed the problems of the Black poor and the Black working class on the existence of public housing, public schools, and the Black public.

The neoliberal "reforms" implemented in New Orleans and celebrated by both conservative and liberal politicians and pundits plundered public resources for private gain, but they did not improve the lives of Black students or the communities they inhabited. They produced a publicly funded private school system that produces its profits by creating schools characterized aptly by local educator Raynard Saunders as unaccountable and undemocratic, as cash cows yet chronic failures.[26] Subsidies for gentrification have attracted young white professionals to move to New Orleans, but that has only made housing for the working class and the poor more expensive and less available. Profit-based development projects continue to ignore the city's fragile ecosystem and contribute to the recurrent costs and crises that come from flooding.

Yet democracy is not dead in New Orleans. The seeds of democratic renewal are planted deeply in its soil—in the freedom dreams of its activists, artists, and intellectuals; in the mutuality, self-help, and solidarity of its working people; in the dynamism of its intercultural and interracial energy and imagination. The United Teachers of New Orleans, one of the first integrated unions in the South, continues to bring together teachers, parents, students, and community members to battle for educational equity and opportunity. Environmental justice organizations educate the public about the need to plant and replace trees as protection against flooding, while labor activists, opponents of police brutality, and groups committed to facilitating reentry into communities by the formerly incarcerated forge a new public sphere from the bottom up. Although they lack access to the mass-mediated neoliberal echo chamber that portrays disasters as silver linings and golden opportunities, they succeed every day in shifting the focus from the richest to the brokest. But it will take more than an opus to reverse this hypnosis. It requires hard work, sacrifice, and struggle. It entails confronting the people who actually run this country, facing up to the selfishness, sadism, greed, contempt, and corruption of what is probably the most disgruntled, embittered, and angry agglomeration of "haves" in the history of the world. It compels us to see the price all people pay for the possessive investment in whiteness. But the first step is to hear the words of Tootie Montana and to echo them, to look at what has been happening in New Orleans and elsewhere, and say "I want this to stop."

13

White Lives, White Lies

Because they think they are white, they do not dare confront the
ravage and the lie of their history.

—James Baldwin

On the morning of November 9, 2016, people residing in the United States
awakened to a frightening new understanding of the poisonous presence of the possessive investment in whiteness in the nation's political
culture. Overwhelming support from white voters enabled Donald Trump
to secure the presidency, largely by catering to their most vile and violent
impulses and aspirations.

Trump set the stage for his candidacy by proclaiming and incessantly
repeating a lie. He alleged that Barack Obama had been born in Kenya and
was therefore ineligible to be president. When that claim was clearly shown
to have always been untrue, Trump lied about the lie, claiming initially that
the real facts came out only because of pressure by him. Later he changed his
tune and alleged that it was Hillary Clinton and not Trump who had questioned Obama's birthplace and eligibility to be president. During the campaign, Trump continued his mendacity. Seventy percent of the statements
that he made while running for office were found to be false by PolitiFact,
while only 4 percent of his utterances were determined to be completely
true.[1] Trump's subsequent performance in his first months as president followed that pattern. He put forth a seemingly endless series of falsehoods,
fabrications, and fantasies. Trump lied about big things and about small
things; about the percentage of the votes he received in the election; about
the size of the crowds attending his inauguration;, about trade deficits, sur-
pluses, and the size of his privately held businesses. He claimed to have received supportive phone calls that had never been made and admiring letters

that had never been sent. Trump uttered at least one falsehood publicly every day during his first forty days as president.[2]

Most observers agree that Trump's chronic dishonesty reveals something significant about him as a person. Yet his success in the political system and his particular popularity with white voters prompts questions that go far beyond Trump's personal issues. Lurking beneath the surface of many of the little lies that may not matter to his constituency at all are Trump's big lies, and these matter to them a great deal. These are the lies inherent in the possessive investment in whiteness. Whiteness in this instance is not just an embodied identity or even solely a systematically structured social advantage but rather a way of knowing and perceiving the world that teaches people to live with evil, to accept it, and to learn to lie about it. It does this through three distinct mechanisms: (1) a methodological individualism that portrays social relations as simply the sum total of acts by individuals, not the product of interactions within complex practices, processes, systems, and structures; (2) a performed amnesia about history that presumes that past discrimination has nothing to do with today's differential racial outcomes; and (3) an insistence on seeing white people as innocent of racial discrimination and instead as victims of the unfair injury of reverse discrimination. These are false premises that lead to false conclusions. They are lies that require the production of ever more lies. They have been challenged and refuted by people of all races time and time again, yet they endure at the center of the national political culture, as Trump correctly assumed in shaping his campaign and his administration.

Trump assures his followers that they are victims of political correctness and reverse racism rather than the beneficiaries of a system rigged to subsidize them. He reinforces their core belief that when nonwhite people protest against racism, they are being racist. People of color are not seen as claimants for equality and justice but rather as deviant, dysfunctional, and dependent beings seeking special favors. Trump taps into a deep desire stoked by identification with whiteness that seeks to never be disadvantaged in relation to someone who is not white, to never be held accountable or responsible—individually or collectively—for the skewing of opportunities and life chances along racial lines.

In colloquial usage, a "white lie" is a trivial or harmless falsehood. Sometimes it refers to an untruth told to protect someone else's feelings. In contrast, the white lies that Trump taps into are neither trivial nor harmless. They stand at the center of the political culture of the United States, as the driving force akin to what performance theorist Diana Taylor calls "percepticide." In her study of spectacle and state violence by the ruling junta in Argentina in the 1970s and 1980s, Taylor argues that in order be thought of as good citizens "people were forced to focus on the given to be seen and ignore the atrocities-given-to-be invisible."[3] The possessive investment in whiteness teaches people to see and condemn Black football players kneeling in protest when the national anthem is played, but not to see the unprosecuted police killings of unarmed Black people that caused the protests in the first place. People are taught to see and honor the flag but pressured not to notice the illegal and unconstitutional policies enacted at home and abroad under the aegis of that banner. The spectacular and sadistic violence of white racism—its sordid legacy of lynchings, vigilante violence, arson, police beatings and shootings—are not incidental mechanisms of white rule but rather ends in themselves. They are not utilitarian acts, but rather expressive performances designed to compel oppressed people to witness the discretionary power over life and death maintained by their dominators.

The white nationalist politics that have flourished in the Age of Trump work to produce horrifying images and to provoke ugly emotions, to shock and intimidate, to compel people to look away, to suppress their senses, and to embrace wanting "not to know." They seek to make the public sphere so debased and degraded that decent people will retreat from it with revulsion and fear. Taylor shows that the spectacular cruelty, brutality, and dishonesty of the dictatorial regime in Argentina were not evidence of uncontrollable excess but rather carefully calculated technologies of domination. Percepticide spread through the populace, not as the product of irrationality but rather as part of a rationally planned practice designed to demoralize and demobilize opponents. We do not know if the Trump regime or future U.S. governments eventually will reach the level of repression that prevailed in Argentina, but we can be confident that the vulgarity, the hysteria, and the stoking of hatred and violence coming from the White House and its allies is not a departure from the plan. It is the plan itself.

Resorting to the grand lies of whiteness, however, always runs the risk of also exposing and unraveling them. President Trump demonstrated this dynamic during a falsehood-filled address to the National Boy Scout Jamboree some six months into his term as president. Speaking to a group of young people whose organizational pledge commits them to help others at all times, to remain morally straight, and to obey the Boy Scout "law" that tells them a scout is always trustworthy, helpful, kind, and thrifty, the president offered as example for the scouts to emulate the life and career of real estate developer William Levitt. Lauding the successful Levittown housing projects that the developer created in New York, New Jersey, Pennsylvania and Puerto Rico, Trump told the scouts triumphantly that Levitt "sold his company for a tremendous amount of money. And he went out and bought a big yacht."[4]

Trump neglected to tell the Boy Scouts that Levitt made his profits from a business that banned Blacks from living in its developments. He did not inform them that Levitt did not secure the capital from the private market but instead relied for the full costs of the developments' construction and sales on loans guaranteed by the federal government. As Levitt admitted in testimony at a congressional hearing in 1957, "We are 100 percent dependent on the government."[5] Citizens of all races paid the taxes that put the full faith and credit of the federal government behind these loans, but only whites could secure them to own homes in Levittown. As a result, Levitt made his money from an enterprise that funneled rewards for racism to whites in the form of privileged and exclusive access to assets that appreciated in value over time and were then handed down through inheritance inside white families. This was of course not a matter of concern to Donald Trump, who inherited his own wealth from his bigoted real estate owner father and who ran the family business in ways that led to it being accused of violating fair housing laws. The president did not mention that Levitt took thousands of dollars in deposits from prospective home buyers in Florida but never built the promised houses. He omitted the part of the developer's career when Levitt siphoned off $5 million illegally from his charitable foundation.[6] Trump did express deep concern, however, about the fact that by the end of his life Levitt had squandered most of the fortune he had made. The president asked the scouts to ponder Levitt's fallen fortunes, not as an object lesson about barring Blacks from neighborhoods, taking deposits on homes that were never built, or misallocating for personal use funds donated to a charitable foundation. Recalling an encounter at a cocktail party with Levitt after his fortunes had soured, Trump related that the developer informed him, "Donald, I lost my momentum. I lost my momentum."[7] The lesson the president drew from those words was that he, Donald Trump, could not lose his momentum. He informed the boy scouts that his momentum depended on people loyal to him, pontificating that "we could use some more loyalty, I will tell you that." Trump explained his own failure to get the Republican-controlled Congress to support the poorly conceived and poorly explained health care legislation he favored by blaming it on their disloyalty. For Trump, the tragedy of William Levitt's life was not that he made his money through expressly racist practices but that he failed to hang on to all of his money; not that he took deposits for homes he never built and took money from a charity for his own use but that he got caught doing it, and that getting caught led to his loss of momentum. For Trump, whose entire political persona came from the lies of whiteness, maintaining momentum requires race-based appeals to the settled expectations and grandiose aspirations of fragile and fearful people possessed by their investments in whiteness.

As president, Trump placed the nation's civil rights administration in the hands of Jeff Sessions, a man who had been rejected for a federal judgeship by Congress in the 1980s because of his blatant racism. As part of the successful challenge to that nomination, Coretta Scott King described Sessions as a man who as U.S. attorney had initiated groundless politically motivated prosecutions intended to intimidate elderly Blacks from voting. Senator Edward Kennedy had described the nomination of Sessions to a judgeship as a disgrace. When Senator Elizabeth Warren attempted to inject King's letter about Sessions' conduct into the debate about whether he should be confirmed as Trump's attorney general in 2017, Senate Republican majority leader Mitch McConnell did not bother to refute the charges against Sessions but simply silenced Warren, ruling that reading the words of Coretta Scott King on the Senate floor would be "out of order."

As attorney general, Sessions moved quickly to protect the possessive investment in whiteness, ending investigations of corrupt and violent police departments, approving fair housing settlements that had been previously found unacceptable, and making alleged discrimination against whites the focal point of his "civil rights" policy by challenging college affirmative action programs that have been found constitutionally sound by the courts over and over again. In keeping with Trump's understanding that his appeal to his followers rested on methodological individualism, historical denial, and affirmations of white innocence and white injury, the Department of Justice set in motion a program of producing ever more lies to justify and excuse those previously uttered.

Because of the possessive investment in whiteness, white lives become premised on white lies. As individuals, *white people* have the same capacity for truth and falsehood as anyone else. Honesty and dishonesty are equally represented in all racial groups. The ideology and practice of *whiteness*, however, relies on lie after lie after lie. The issue is not the credibility of any individual speaker but rather the ways in which the denials, disavowals, evasions, and occlusions of whiteness produce ways of knowing that make unrecognizable the actual social relations and social institutions by which we are governed. The lies told by individuals are significant and harmful, sometimes even deadly. But much worse are the core epistemological lies wedded to whiteness.

The Foundational Lies of the Possessive Investment in Whiteness

The pattern of living with evil, accepting it, and learning to lie about it has both a long history and a dangerous and deadly momentum in the present. From the start, the ideology of white possession has rested on fiction, fabrication, and outright fraud. In order to seize, occupy, possess, and exploit Indigenous lands, Europeans invented the legal lie of *terra nullius*, which means "empty land." This doctrine held that territory that had been inhabited by Indigenous peoples for thousands of years was actually unoccupied and unowned, that it had only been "discovered" by Europeans, not invaded by them.[8] It was not just speculators, swashbucklers, and settlers who orchestrated this lie. John Locke and other Enlightenment philosophers insisted

that Native peoples had no rights to their land, that they were indolent no-
mads and therefore could claim no property. In Locke's view, property rights
depended on written legal titles held by individual owners who labored to
increase the exchange value of land by making it ripe for capitalist exploitation and returns on investment. Indigenous people holding land collectively
and living in reciprocity with the natural world sought to coexist with nature, not turn it into surplus value. Therefore, Locke and others concluded
they had no right to the land, so whites could take it. Property became en-
shrined in law as defined by the particular beliefs of the conquerors, while
the particular beliefs of Indigenous cosmology were not acknowledged or
refuted, but simply dismissed outright. As the late Arthur Manuel of the
Neskonlith Indian Band of the Secwepemc Nation argued succinctly, the
European "doctrine of discovery" authorizing white possession of Indigenous land functioned as a fig leaf put in place to cover naked thievery.[9]

The lie of terra nullius fabricated to justify and excuse settler colonialism
found equivalents in the lies that legitimated slavery, especially the concept
of the captive taken in a just war. Once again, the ideas of John Locke played
a crucial role. During the years when Locke formulated his foundational
theses about individual liberty, he also invested money in the slave trade,
lived off the profits that his patron secured from enslaved plantation labor,
and helped write the constitution of the slaveholding South Carolina colony.
Like many other Enlightenment philosophers, Locke attempted to justify his
low desires with high ideals.[10] He resolved the contradiction between his
claims that freedom depended on property with his active participation in
denying freedom to people he classified as property by deploying a lie. Locke
claimed that the humans kidnapped from their African homes and subjected to racialized, permanent, and hereditary chattel slavery were prisoners
captured in a just war. In fact, no war had taken place. As Charles Mills
notes, the free contracting subject of the law celebrated by Locke depended
upon the discursive erasure of "the Red aborigine whose land had been taken
for the contractual construction of the white settler state" as well as the
"Black slave who has been contracted over by being bought and sold."[11]
Empty lands and just wars were invoked as noble creeds to cover up ignoble
deeds. From the start of European settlement in the western hemisphere,
philosophy, political theory, and statecraft depended on living with evil, accepting it, and lying about it.

Historian James Horton identifies an additional pattern of mendacity
central to the possessive investment in whiteness. Lies told originally to justify slavery outlived the slave system itself. They shaped the core contours of
subsequent racisms on the terrains of culture and belief, long after slavery
had been legally abolished. "In some ways, it would have been better," Horton explains, "if America had just looked the world in the eye and said 'Look,
we hold these people in slavery because we need their labor, and we have got

the power to do it.'"[12] This honest course, however, was not the path taken. Instead, defenders of and apologists for the slave system lied about Black people in order to legitimate the wealth secured from their bondage. Educated preachers, professors, and politicians claimed that African Americans were different, inferior, and not quite human, shaping the beliefs of a broader populace. These lies persisted long after the abolition of slavery. They festered and thrived inside what Horton describes as "that rationalization which we now recognize as what we call American racism."[13]

One of the rationalizations Horton references that started in the time of slavery but has survived long beyond it is the lie of race itself. Racialization has made racial identity a disastrous social fact, but race as an idea and an entity is simply a biological fiction. The Human Genome Project has established that humans are 99.9 percent the same. There are no races in the biological sense. Politically, however, race has come to matter a great deal because it is a lie that has proved itself useful to power and because many people believe in it. As Dorothy Roberts states crisply, "Race is not a biological category that is politically charged. It is a political category that has been disguised as a biological one."[14] Like the lies of terra nullius and just wars, the lie of biological race has been of enormous political and economic utility. The glaring inequalities and injustices attached to race would be hard to explain and justify as rational or humane social policy, but they escape scrutiny and justification when attached to lies about the natural order that depict oppressed people as innately inferior and unfit for freedom.

Lies attendant to the initial formation of the U.S. order generated the need for an ever expanding list of more falsehoods. Supreme Court Chief Justice Roger Taney displayed this dynamic clearly in the majority opinion that he authored deciding the 1857 *Dred Scott v. Sandford* case. Scott was a slave who filed suit in federal court seeking his freedom because he had been brought to Illinois and the Wisconsin territory where slavery was prohibited by law. Taney not only ruled that Scott must remain enslaved but that no Black person, slave or free, had any rights that white people were bound to respect. The chief justice held that the framers of the Constitution had considered Blacks an inferior race of people, and therefore that is how they must be treated by the law. He did not subject that belief to scrutiny and did not rule on whether evidence verified it. It was enough that a previous generation of white people believed in Black inferiority to inscribe that prejudice into law.[15]

The decision in Scott's case led to one of the most destructive civil wars in history. During and after the war, mass mobilization by newly free Black people and their allies sought to sever the link between rights and whiteness that Taney codified in 1857. They compelled Congress to pass the 1866 Civil Rights Act and the Thirteenth, Fourteenth, and Fifteenth amendments. These measures were designed to initiate a "new birth constitution," one that required the government to protect Black freedom and Black rights to the very same dimension and degree that it previously protected the slave system.[16] Yet very quickly, the nation's precarious democracy was undermined by its pervasive hypocrisy. Southern whites used restrictive new laws, mass incarceration, and vigilante violence to force free Blacks to remain a source of cheap and exploitable labor and to destroy the new democratic opportunities and institutions that emerged for the poor of all races in the wake of abolition democracy.

Lying loomed large as a legitimating practice for these new laws. The Thirteenth Amendment banned enforced servitude but made an exception for people imprisoned. Southern states used the prison system as a form of control over Black labor. Inmates who were Black comprised only 2 percent of the prison population of Alabama in 1850, but by 1870, three quarters of those incarcerated in the state's penal institutions were Black.[17] This spike in the prison population did not reflect a crime wave among newly freed Blacks. The "offenses" that most often led to Black incarceration in the jails and prisons of Alabama and other southern states were loitering and vagrancy. Workers not employed by whites for the wages and under the working conditions that whites wanted were jailed for loitering and having no visible means of support. Those workers who sought to move toward better employment opportunities were arrested for vagrancy. As Ruth Wilson Gilmore observes acerbically, this meant Blacks could be arrested no matter what they did. They were guilty if they moved around or if they stood still. Legalized slavery had ended, but much of the post-bellum South's public infrastructure was built by laborers coerced to work without compensation or choice.[18] By criminalizing Black poverty and using the law to deny the right to quit a job or seek a new one, the loophole in the Thirteenth Amendment became another stimulus for the enduring lie of chronic Black criminality.[19]

Northerners in the legislative, executive, and judicial branches of government joined forces with southerners to lie about the aims and intentions of the "new birth" Constitution and subvert its application. In the *Civil Rights Cases* of 1883, the Supreme Court declared the 1875 Civil Rights Act unconstitutional because opening up access to public accommodations by Blacks was construed as reverse discrimination against whites. Speaking for the 8–1 majority, Justice Joseph Bradley ruled that while it might have been necessary to ratify the Fourteenth Amendment in 1868 and the Fifteenth Amendment in 1870 to protect the rights of Blacks emerging from slavery, passing a bill protecting Black rights just five years later in 1875 in the wake of ferocious and unremitting anti-Black legal and extra-legal action amounted to giving Blacks special privileges and meting out undue punishments to whites by compelling them to do business with or tolerate the presence of Blacks in business establishments. "When a man has emerged from slavery," Bradley argued, "there must be some stage in the progress of his elevation when he takes the rank of a mere citizen and ceases to be a special favorite of the laws."[20] Few Blacks living in 1883 facing unremitting violence and oppression had any reason to consider themselves the "special favorite of the laws." Without the legal protections that the Court misrepresented as special favoritism, Blacks essentially became citizens without rights, deprived of the equal protection of the law supposedly guaranteed by the Fourteenth Amendment. In the name of equality and fighting against special favoritism, Justice Bradley's opinion once again established that Blacks had no rights that whites were bound to respect. Still cited and honored as legal precedent in part today, the *Civil Rights Cases* helped shape discourses and practices that require us to live in the midst of evil but lie about its existence.

Mendacity also subverted the Fifteenth Amendment. Legislators and registrars could not ban Black voting outright because of this constitutional provision, so they turned to the subterfuge of the Grandfather Clause. Pretending to be race-neutral, this legal measure restricted the franchise to people whose grandfathers had been voters. Virtually no Blacks were allowed to vote under the Grandfather Clause because their ancestors were not considered by the law to be citizens, voters, or even humans according to the laws that prevailed before the Civil War. These clauses remained in place and were fully enforced through the first decades of the twentieth century, at which point they were supplanted by other lies, especially voting restrictions designed to produce racist outcomes without announcing openly racist intent such as the poll tax, the white primary, and the literacy test.[21]

The Supreme Court's ruling in *Plessy v. Ferguson* in 1896 brought the logic of *Dred Scott v. Sandford* and the *Civil Rights Cases* to an even higher level of malicious mendacity. The Court's decision legitimated de jure Jim Crow segregation as the law of the land, yet this case did not really revolve around questions about the rights of Blacks, as is commonly thought. Instead, the matters decided in the *Plessy case* entailed competing notions about the rights of whites. Plaintiff Homére Plessy did not contend that segregated railroad cars were unfair to Black passengers. He argued instead that he was entitled to ride in the white car because he was a light-skinned mixed-race person whose ancestry was seven-eighths white. Plessy and the judges alike knew that he could not have boarded the train in the first place if he had been dark skinned and phenotypically Black, that he would likely have been assaulted and killed for attempting to cross the color line. Yet he had an accurate understanding of the law's protection and privileging of whiteness as property in making his case. As Cheryl Harris has established, Plessy claimed that his propertied interest in whiteness had been injured by a policy that compelled him to sit in a car reserved for Blacks.[22] The Court remanded the issue of Plessy's whiteness back to the courts in Louisiana, ruling instead that if he *were* Black as the state contended, no violation of his rights had occurred.

The majority opinion in the *Plessy* case was written by Justice Henry Brown. He ruled that assigning Blacks to separate railroad cars (and by extension to separate schools, bathrooms, and sections of theaters and restaurants) in no way "stamps the colored race with a badge of inferiority." He admitted that although laws like the Louisiana separate car statute prevented Blacks from occupying spaces reserved for whites, it equally prevented whites from occupying the spaces to which Blacks were relegated. Treating disingenuous fiction as a legal fact, Justice Brown and the Court majority pretended that the dirty and uncomfortable railroad cars to which Blacks were consigned were effectively equal to the clean and comfortable cars in which whites could ride. Segregated public accommodations, the Court ruled, were "separate but equal," even though everyone knew that they were separate and unequal. This majority opinion in *Plessy* used denial and subterfuge to support policies grounded in presumptions of Black inferiority and lesser citizenship.

Even the lone dissenter in *Plessy v. Ferguson* depicted the white race as superior. In a widely cited and celebrated dissent, Justice John Harlan argued that the Constitution should be color-blind. But in the sentences that preceded that declaration, sentences that are rarely cited, celebrated, or even quoted, Harlan wrote, "The white race deems itself to be the dominant race in this country. And so it is in prestige, in achievements, in education, in wealth and in power. So, I doubt not, it will continue to be for all time if it remains true to its great heritage and holds fast to the principles of constitutional liberty."[23] The disagreement between Harlan and the majority was not over whether the law should support white supremacy but rather about the best and most effective ways of supporting it. Despite proclaiming in 1896 that the Constitution is color-blind in his *Plessy* dissent, Harlan had no problem authoring the opinion of a unanimous Supreme Court in 1899 that upheld segregation by color in schools in the case of *Cumming v. Board of Education*.[24]

Conventional legal histories generally claim that Justice Henry Brown's ruling in *Plessy v. Ferguson* was overturned by the unanimous opinions of the Court in another "Brown" decision—*Brown v. Board of Education I* and *II* in 1954 and 1955.[25] Yet there are important continuities between Justice Brown's 1896 opinion in *Plessy* and the 1954 and 1955 *Brown I* and *Brown II* decisions. In *Plessy v. Ferguson*, the majority treated segregation as a device to maintain order because it presumed that whites would not want to associate with Blacks and that they had a right not to. If whites reacted violently to laws that created integration, it would be the law that was to blame. In *Brown I*, the Court held that separate facilities were inherently unequal, that school segregation stamped Blacks with the stigma of inferiority. Yet, like the majority in *Plessy*, the justices in *Brown* worried that desegregation would provoke white violence. As a result, as discussed in Chapter 2, in *Brown II*, the Court left the pace of ending segregation to the whim of whites. In the U.S. constitutional system, rights are supposed to be personal and present.

People are supposed to have rights and be able to exercise them. Yet the Court's order in *Brown II* to desegregate "with all deliberate speed" meant that for Black people, rights were to be secured on the installment plan, with only a few granted now in hopes that the rest could be provided later. Fear of white resistance became a self-fulfilling prophecy as the phrase "all deliberate speed" produced much deliberation but very little speed. Ten years after *Brown v. Board I*, only 2 percent of the schools covered by the decision had started any kind of desegregation. At that pace, full integration would have taken 500 years. As the evidence and arguments in Chapter 2 of this book demonstrate, by the time of the *Parents Involved in Community Schools* cases outlawing successful local school desegregation programs in Seattle and Louisville, Supreme Court justices claimed that using race in order to desegregate schools was as racist as using it to segregate them. In the face of unremitting evil, the Court chose to accept it and to lie about it.

Describing Nonwhites as Unfit for Freedom as a Technology of White Racist Rule

The apologists for conquest who formulated the doctrine of discovery and the principle of terra nullius did not really believe that the lands of the Americas were empty. They spoke frequently about Indigenous people. They did so, however, only to declare them to be unfit for inclusion in the category of what they termed civilized humanity. Enlightenment thinkers could not really sustain the claim that enslaved Africans were captives taken in a just war, so they formulated discourses that make white racial domination appear natural, necessary, and inevitable. The founder of Western moral philosophy, Immanuel Kant, contended that the Indigenous peoples of the Americas could not be educated, while Blacks might be educable, but only as servants.[26] Philosopher of history G.W.F. Hegel claimed that Blacks lacked the capacity for reason and were devoid of morals or ethics. Colonialism and slavery were not acts of aggression and plunder by Europeans, in Hegel's view, but were favors performed for the benefit of Africans by soldiers and missionaries generously bringing to them the gifts of order and morality.[27] John Locke believed that African women had conceived babies with apes and were not fully human, that slaves could kill themselves if they disliked slavery but had no right to rebel. He counseled a friend that when confronted with injustice and inequality, "You should feel nothing at all of others' misfortune."[28]

Justifying racial subordination by claiming that Blacks are unfit for freedom has been a central and enduring mechanism of the possessive investment in whiteness. Justice Taney did not rule that Dred Scott and all other Blacks had to be silenced and suppressed because the profits and stability of the slave system depended on their oppression. He argued instead that it was their innate inferiority that relegated Blacks to the status of beings without rights. Confronted with the 1875 Civil Rights Act granting Blacks equal access to market transactions, Justice Bradley ignored the relentless anti-Black racism that made passage of the law necessary and claimed that granting equality to Blacks would elevate them over whites as the "special favorites of the law." In *Brown v. Board I*, the Supreme Court ruled that school classrooms were key sites for the creation and preservation of democratic citizenship and that therefore school segregation violated the constitutional rights of Black children. In *Brown II* and a series of subsequent decisions described in Chapter 2 of this book, however, the Court held that those constitutional rights were less important than the comfort and convenience of whites seeking to hoard educational advantages for children of their race.

The declaration in *Brown II* that desegregation could take place with "deliberate" speed led to a whole series of subterfuges grounded in fictions about Black unfitness and inferiority. Authorities in Louisiana, for example, argued after *Brown* that segregated schools remained necessary, not for reasons of racism or the protection of white privileges, but rather to save innocent white children, especially girls, from having to sit side by side with Black classmates who they described as uniformly diseased, immoral, and depraved.[29] Additional efforts to describe Blacks as unfit for freedom came from the Louisiana legislature in the form of laws expressly intended to inflate the statistics of Black common law marriages and out-of-wedlock births. The statutes made marriage licenses dependent on documents that poor and working-class Blacks were not likely to have, such as original birth certificates and health forms filled out by licensed physicians in the previous ten days. Another new law restricted the issuing of marriage licenses to the time between 8 A.M. and noon on weekdays, hours when working people had to be on the job. The legislature mandated that unless newborn babies had birth certificates issued within five days of their birth they would be considered illegitimate. It passed legislation that banned the long-established practice in the state of common law marriages, required legal documentation that any previous marriages had been dissolved, limited the numbers of people who could perform marriage ceremonies, and insisted that all people who wished to be married provide the state with official documents certifying them as free of venereal disease. These requirements were intended to impose impractical and onerous demands on a population whose members were largely unable to afford medical care, were excluded routinely from segregated clinics and hospitals, had low levels of literacy, and moved often because of housing insecurity or in efforts to find employment. Yet loopholes in the new laws gave poor and working-class whites options that Blacks did not have. Couples wishing to wed could secure needed documents by making a personal visit to the home of a county official on any day and any time.

Because of voter suppression, all of these officials were white and were all but certain to consider allowing Blacks into their homes to be highly inappropriate.

The behavior of Black people in Louisiana did not change after *Brown v. Board*, but the new laws gave the appearance of rampant Black deviance and dysfunction that provided a new pretext for resisting the implementation of the *Brown* decision. State officials led by Governor Jimmie Davis dropped indigent Blacks from the welfare rolls, claiming that their "immoral behavior" made them ineligible for the public support routinely secured by impoverished whites. Davis denied 20,000 needy Black children support from the state with the claim that all of the mothers of these thousands of children were "professional prostitutes."[30]

In the wake of the *Brown I* decision, the legislatures of both Louisiana and Mississippi passed laws that allowed state officials to deny welfare payments and other kinds of support to children who lived in "morally unsuitable" homes, a definition that encompassed a home where a mother had received aid to dependent children previously and where the parents were unmarried. Soon, claims of "bad moral character" emerged as a reason to disqualify potential voters. Louisiana authorized local registrars to deny the right to vote to men who fathered a child out of wedlock. The state of Mississippi devised a convenient form of voter suppression with a statute that empowered any voter to challenge another's right to vote by charging bad moral character. Governor Orville Faubus of Arkansas and his supporters defied the president and the Supreme Court in 1957 by refusing to integrate the schools in the city of Little Rock. Whites complained that they objected to desegregation because it would mean that white girls would have to shower with Black girls after gym classes and be exposed to venereal diseases by using the same bathrooms as Black girls. They predicted that white parents would soon be confronted with the humiliation of having Black grandchildren.[31] These arguments about Black dysfunction as a justification for segregation had already been refuted in footnote eleven of *Brown I* where the Court explained that even if real, the deficiencies attributed to Black children by these claims stemmed from the very segregation that relegated them to poverty, bad health, and lack of education. The results of segregation, the Court declared, could not be used as justification for its continuation.[32]

The fantasies of Black deviance and dysfunction mobilized to resist implementation of *Brown v. Board* became repackaged as responses to and refutations of the imperatives of subsequent civil rights measures. Instead of working to implement the full language and intent of laws and court decisions mandating educational equity, fair hiring, and fair housing, government social policies starting with the Johnson administration's Moynihan Report in 1965 blamed Black poverty not on white racism but on the alleged weaknesses of the Black family and the putative malfeasance of Black women as mothers. For Moynihan and those he influenced, the question was not what obstacles are placed in the path of Black progress by the possessive investment in whiteness but rather how the structure of the Black family inhibits opportunities and life chances. The policies that proceeded from those premises include ending anti-poverty programs, launching the war on drugs, instituting broken windows policing, slashing social welfare spending, and creating programs designed to give Black boys and men advantages over Black girls and women. Because they proceeded from false premises, each of these policies exacerbated most of the conditions they purported to prevent. As the late Clyde Woods asserted, "The portrayal of working-class African Americans and their communities as deviant and pathological is the product of a deviant and pathological strain deeply embedded in American thought. It is a sickness masquerading as science."[33]

The long history of lies fabricated as historical excuses for segregation and white racial domination continues in the present. Nowhere has this continuity been more evident than in Ferguson, Missouri, where protests against the killing of an unarmed teenager revealed policies and practices that deployed discourses of Black deviance to relegate Black people to unlivable destinies while augmenting the rewards and privileges of the possessive investment in whiteness.

The White Racial Frame in Ferguson

The pattern of prevarication present in both the ruling opinion written by Judge Henry Brown in *Plessy v. Ferguson* and in the concessions made to white resistance in *Brown v. Board II* illuminates another series of lies connected to the name "Brown": the falsehoods required to excuse and justify the killing of Michael Brown in Ferguson, Missouri, on August 9, 2014. From the first moment that police and municipal authorities learned that Officer Darren Wilson had shot and killed unarmed teenager Michael Brown, they inverted the facts, treating the dead youth as the aggressor and portraying the officer who repeatedly shot at him and killed him as the victim. Police officers left Michael Brown's bullet-riddled body to fester in the street under the hot summer sun for four and a half hours. Wilson's supervisors did not secure or photograph his gun. They allowed him to drive himself to the police station and wash the blood off his hands. Officer Wilson made no effort to find out whether Brown remained alive after the shooting nor did he call for an ambulance. Police investigators took their time speaking with witnesses, waiting as long as two months after the shooting to gather eyewitness testimony.[34] The police department hid Wilson's identity from the public for as long as possible, and when induced to give out his name it released at the same time a videotape of an incident involving Brown at a local market in an attempt to defame the victim. The chief of police denied that this move was designed to help Officer Wilson, contending that his department had to release the video because of a Freedom of Information Act request. It soon became apparent, however, that there had been no such request,

The St. Louis County prosecutor Robert McCulloch manipulated, contorted, and distorted the grand jury process to protect Officer Wilson from the questions he would have had to answer at a preliminary hearing. Grand jury proceedings are designed to consider all the evidence that would justify an indictment and subsequent trial, but McCulloch inverted this mission and slanted the deliberations so that Officer Wilson would not be held accountable for his actions or even have to answer questions about them in the adversarial context of a trial. McCulloch solicited and presented testimony to the grand jury from witnesses he knew were lying. Immediately before Officer Wilson's scheduled testimony, prosecutors distributed to jurors copies of a state law authorizing a standard of evidence that the Supreme Court had previously ruled to be unconstitutional. During his grand jury testimony, Wilson asserted that he stopped Brown initially because he had received a report about a robbery at a local market. Yet when he spoke with another officer immediately after the killing, Wilson said he did not know anything about the alleged incident at the store. McCulloch and staff did not question Wilson about this contradiction at all, but they repeatedly belittled and questioned the credibility of witnesses whose testimony contradicted the fables that Wilson concocted during the weeks he was preparing to appear before the grand jury.[35] The officer claimed that he had to fire his gun over and over again because he had been punched by Brown and feared for his life. Yet immediately after the shooting the officer's body showed no cuts, bruises, or broken blood vessels.

By focusing primarily on the ninety-second street encounter between Wilson and Brown, city, county, and state officials attempted to hide what a subsequent Department of Justice investigation (provoked by the exemplary work of the public interest lawyers from Arch City Defenders) established clearly: that the aggressive policing of minor violations like jaywalking exemplified in Officer Wilson's stop of Michael Brown stemmed from a coordinated policy to finance city activities through fines imposed on Ferguson's poorest residents, who are disproportionately Black.

The municipal courts in Ferguson and adjacent suburbs in North St. Louis County require the racialized poor to subsidize the rich. The systematic nature of this exploitation was fully documented in the comprehensive investigation of the area's police practices, court conditions, fines, and finances conducted by the Department of Justice. Blacks driving in these cities are stopped repeatedly by police officers on suspicion of having expired automobile tax stickers or license plate tags, of driving without proof of insurance, or of passing in no passing zones. When the "probable cause" for detainment does not produce credible charges, officers fish for outstanding

warrants and provoke arguments that enable them to bring charges of ob-
structing justice or resisting arrest. Small suburban municipalities in St.
Louis County derive significant portions of their operating expenses from
racially profiling the Black motorists who pass through them by fining them
for "poverty violations." The St. Louis area's inadequate transportation system and the spatial mismatch between areas where Blacks can live and the
jobs open to them make it necessary for them to drive to work through numerous municipalities replete with speed traps. The low wages that Black
workers receive often leave them with insufficient funds to pay insurance
costs and registration fees, much less court fees and fines. Several of these
local governments derive as much as 40 percent of their annual revenues
from these fines and fees, in clear violation of state law. The inability of defendants to afford counsel leads to fines they cannot afford to pay; nonpay-
ment leads to more fines as punishment. When people do not show up for
court dates because they know they cannot pay the fees and fines, warrants
are issued, which means they can be arrested by officers of any municipality
at any time. Jail sentences for outstanding warrants can lead to unemployment and eviction, which makes it even less likely that the fines can be paid.
Each conviction has unknown but often extensive collateral consequences.
For example, residency in the city of Berkeley, Missouri, entails purchase of
an occupancy permit. The city requires a valid driver's license as proof of
identity. If a license has been suspended because of outstanding warrants, its
holder cannot move into the city. But such persons are also then likely to be
stopped and cited for driving with a suspended license or driving a vehicle
with expired tags or inspection stickers. They can be stopped in each municipality and written up for the same offense every time, leaving them owing
fines for the same "crime" in many different municipalities.

Homeowners and renters in the Black neighborhoods of North County
suburbs are cited, convicted, and fined for failure to remove leaf debris, high
grass, and weeds, and for having unpainted back porches. Pedestrians are
stopped, questioned, frisked, and charged with jaywalking, wearing saggy
pants, or playing boomboxes too loud.[36] This draconian policing in the municipalities of the North County has structural causes and motivations. The
state of Missouri's fiscal and taxation policies function to subsidize the
state's wealthiest citizens and cities. Local property tax abatements and tax
relief mandated by state law, sparse levels of state aid to counties and cities,
and laws that allow wealthy municipalities to protect sales tax revenues from
being used by the state's general fund create opportunity hoarding for the
rich and inequality and deprivation for the working class and the poor.
Housing segregation makes the Black poor particularly vulnerable to predatory policing. In 2014, when Michael Brown was killed, whites made up 29
percent of the population of Ferguson but accounted for only 12.7 percent of
motorists stopped by police officers. Blacks made up two thirds of the city's

population but represented 86 percent of those detained. Blacks in Ferguson were nearly twice as likely to be searched and twice as likely to be arrested as whites, even though searches of Blacks found contraband 21.7 percent of the time while searches of whites found contraband 34 percent of the time. Fines and court fees provided the city of Ferguson with more than $2 million in revenue. In 2013 alone, Ferguson's municipal court handled approximately three warrants and 1.5 cases per household.[37]

The Department of Justice investigation found that Ferguson's white elected officials, administrators, police officers, prosecutors, judges, and clerks engaged in systematic and coordinated violations of the laws and the constitutional rights of the city's Black citizens. Yet rather than accepting responsibility for their actions, they claimed that they were compelled to run the system as they did because Black residents of Ferguson lacked personal responsibility. The perpetrators of an illegal system of for-profit racial profiling, fining, and jailing maintained that they had to act as they did to make Black people behave like proper suburban dwellers. In fact, the Justice Department investigation found that the Black citizens of Ferguson went to extraordinary lengths to be responsible, to attempt to answer every summons, and to pay fines. Some came back again and again to request their legal right to have the courts assign them community service as a means of working off fines they could not afford to pay, but their requests were denied. In addition, officers wrote incorrect times and dates for court appearances on tickets. Clerks mailed summonses to wrong addresses. Public notices stated that fines could be paid until 5 P.M., but the windows closed at 4:30. Defendants were given a start time for court hearings, but judges began proceedings and locked the courthouse doors thirty minutes before that time.[38] At one point, a member of the Ferguson City Council complained to other municipal officials that Judge Ronald Brockmeyer routinely failed to listen to testimony, to review reports, or read the record of the criminal histories of defendants, or even to let relevant witnesses testify. Yet a reply came back that the revenues that flowed from these procedures in Judge Brockmeyer's court were needed by the city, so the judge's behavior could not be questioned.[39]

While justifying their actions by referring to the alleged lack of personal responsibility among Blacks, Ferguson's city clerks, judges, attorneys, and officers—all of whom were white—demonstrated precious little responsibility of their own. A Ferguson Police Department patrol supervisor was cited for speeding twice in a nearby municipality, but before the case could come to court, the city prosecutor in Ferguson made a phone call and "fixed" the tickets. The city's mayor persuaded the prosecuting attorney to quash a ticket issued to an employee of a charity that the mayor's wife supported. Court clerks in Ferguson and Hazelwood fixed some twelve tickets at each other's request. The court clerk in Ferguson made a relative's two tickets "disappear" and quashed one issued to the wife of a coworker's friend. A former police chief of Ferguson and the current collector of revenue did not have to pay fines in neighboring municipalities because the Ferguson clerk persuaded clerks in those cities to ignore the offenses. Judge Ronald Brockmeyer fixed a ticket for a Ferguson court clerk in Breckenridge (where he also serves as a judge), and he got the Ferguson prosecuting attorney to quash a ticket Brockmeyer was issued in Hazelwood.[40] When Blacks in Ferguson could not pay fines, Judge Brockmeyer ordered them to be incarcerated in overcrowded cells where they were denied soap, toothpaste, and toothbrushes; where the walls were smeared with mucus and blood; and where they were subjected to the constant stench of excrement and refuse. But Brockmeyer himself owes the Internal Revenue Service more than $170,000 in back taxes and has never spent a day in jail for his failure of personal responsibility.[41]

Taxes and fines levied against Blacks in Ferguson helped pay the salary of white city court clerk Mary Ann Twitty. The Department of Justice investigation found that she routinely circulated racist anti-Black emails to supervisors of the city's police and court operations. One described a Black woman receiving an abortion as a crime control measure. Another featured a picture of Ronald Reagan feeding a chimpanzee connected to a caption that described the picture as Ronald Reagan babysitting Barack Obama in 1962. Twitty explained that she thought the emails were funny. Conceding that "they look racist," she said they were only jokes and that she meant no harm to anyone or anybody. "I didn't send them out because I was racist, because I am not," Twitty insisted. When the Department of Justice investigation made her emails public knowledge, the city fired her. Twitty did not feel this episode revealed her to be lacking in personal responsibility, however. Instead, she expressed outrage at losing her job. "They ruined my life for the sake of what was going on in Ferguson. I think it's sickening. It just really upset me." When asked about her role in practices that unfairly targeted Blacks for fines to generate revenue for the city, Twitty replied, "I set no fines. I just abided by them." Returning to the issue of losing her municipal job for circulating racist emails about Blacks during working hours, Twitty complained, "It took me a while to get over the feeling of being raped and being thrown under the bus."[42] Here there was no discourse about how punishment is needed to teach personal responsibility. Twitty saw no connection between her jokes and the climate in the city that sent Blacks to confinement in fetid jails for simply being poor. The city clerk—who expressed no sympathy for Michael Brown's parents whose son's life was taken by a Ferguson police officer for the crime of "manner of walking in roadway" and who had to witness his dead body lying in that roadway like the carcass of an animal for four hours—described herself as feeling raped and thrown under the bus. Mary Ann Twitty, however, was soon hired as municipal court clerk in Vinita Park, another North County municipality.

The white power structure in Ferguson learned how to live with evil, accept it, lie about it, and even profit richly from it. Yet when held accountable for their actions they presented themselves as persecuted innocents. Moreover, they claimed that their critics were the true liars. Witnesses at the scene and before the grand jury testified that Michael Brown had his hands up in a position of surrender when he was shot. This testimony became transformed into a symbol used by demonstrators to protest the killing. As they marched on the streets of Ferguson and other cities, protestors held their hands high above their hands and chanted "Hands up. Don't shoot." The prosecutor's office in response claimed that its investigation showed that Brown did not have both hands above his head, that only one arm and one hand were in that position. Ferguson municipal and police officials and their supporters seized on this claim to contend that the entire "hands up" story was a lie. Yet Michael Brown had a two-centimeter hole in his punctured lung, had a broken arm, and had been shot in the hand. The prosecutors' own evidence showed that Brown was in a posture of surrender whether he had one hand up or two. But even if his hands had not been up at all, he was still not a mortal threat to Officer Wilson.

The lies told about the killing of Michael Brown represented an act of police aggression as a noble effort at self-defense. Police officers dispatched to the scene of the shooting felt no obligation to comfort Michael Brown's grieving parents or to treat his dead body with dignity. Instead, they launched a massive show of force designed to intimidate and further humiliate those who believed that Michael Brown's death was cause for sorrow. The predatory policing and fining of Black residents in Ferguson was not acknowledged as an act of plunder but instead attributed to the lack of personal responsibility on the part of the poor people whose fines contributed more than four times as much to the municipality's budget than the property taxes assessed on Emerson Electric, a Fortune 500 company located in Ferguson.[43] Like the white lies told to justify Indigenous dispossession, slavery, and segregation, the falsehoods that shaped the conflict in Ferguson revolved around consistent depictions of nonwhite people as unfit for freedom.

The Patterns of the Past and the Problems of the Present

Many little lies were needed to prop up the white racial frame in Ferguson. Also evident in the controversy, however, was a systematic suppression of the truth by the frame itself. The possessive investment in whiteness's methodological individualism, historical amnesia, and insistence on white innocence and injury hid the origins, evolution, and meaning of the incident. Inside the ways of knowing promoted by the possessive investment in whiteness, questions about the killing centered on the ninety-second incident that took place on August 9, 2014, but not on the ninety-year history of race and place that preceded and shaped it. The press, politicians, prosecutors, and much of the public focused on the motivations and actions of the officer who did the killing and of the youth he killed, not on the structures of their lives that placed them in antagonistic opposition to each other on that fatal day. By making the personal culpability of Officer Wilson the issue, investigators and commentators missed the opportunity to explore larger questions about collective responsibility and accountability.

For more than one hundred years before Ferguson became a flashpoint for racial antagonism, the St. Louis area had been the scene of institutionalized racial segregation and stratification through racial zoning, restrictive covenants, mortgage redlining, and government housing policies that have promoted white homeownership and asset accumulation while relegating Blacks to means-tested public housing and vouchers. A persistent and consistent pattern of white violence and white lawlessness in St. Louis functioned to place people of different races in different places, places with radically different amenities, opportunities, hazards, and dangers. In the early twentieth century, an explicit racial zoning ordinance made it illegal to purchase a home on a block where more than 75 percent of the residents were of another race.[44] Restrictive covenants written into deeds bound whites together in a racial cartel pledged to keep dwellings in white hands in perpetuity. Whites used mob violence to prevent Blacks from moving into white neighborhoods or from using publicly funded facilities. In 1949, more than 200 white men waving weapons and screaming racial epithets attacked a group of thirty Black children attempting to swim in a municipally funded and operated swimming pool.

Public policy and private practices in the St. Louis area worked regularly to restrict, regulate, and rig economic exchanges in favor of whites. Redlining policies supported and administered by the government subsidized white flight to the suburbs while denying loans to mixed or Black neighborhoods. Highways built to lessen commuting time from the suburbs to downtown increased the value of homes in white suburbs while demolishing inner-city housing, contributing to the already artificially constrained housing market open to Blacks. Seventy-five percent of the people displaced by the construction of new highway interchanges in downtown St. Louis were Black.[45] Twenty thousand Black residents of the Mill Creek Valley were forced out of their homes by urban renewal projects, creating new overcrowded slums in the few areas of settlement subsequently open to them. These projects displaced businesses, undermined property values in Black neighborhoods, and led to higher tax burdens on inner-city residents.[46] All subsequent development and urban policy in the region flowed from the imperative of protecting this racialized understanding of place. As historian Colin Gordon concludes, racial prejudice provided "the ethical and effective foundation of local incorporation, zoning, taxation and redevelopment policies in St. Louis and its suburbs."[47]

St. Louis city officials concentrated subsidized public housing in ghetto neighborhoods, while government bodies in adjacent St. Louis County used exclusionary zoning to resist public housing and minimize the number of units available to low-income home seekers. The city of St. Louis and the state of Missouri were found guilty in federal court of maintaining segregated schools in clear violation of *Brown v. Board*. Yet political leaders from both the Republican and Democratic parties pandered to white resentments by resisting court orders and portraying desegregation as reverse racism against whites. Republican John Ashcroft as attorney general and governor resisted court orders, filed repeated appeals on minor and trivial issues to delay their implementation, and opposed every magnet school proposal. Ashcroft falsely claimed that the state had never been found guilty of any wrongdoing by the federal courts when in fact the clear and consistent finding of the federal judiciary was that the state was obligated to pay most of the costs of desegregation in St. Louis precisely because its policies played a primary role in creating separate and unequal schools. Ashcroft's policies expended $4 million of state money in the 1980s and 1990s to fight desegregation.

In a 1998 friendly interview with the white supremacist *Southern Partisan* magazine, Ashcroft hailed the "honor" of the leaders of the slaveholding Confederacy. He depicted as a noble enterprise their treasonous insurgency against the U.S. government that sought to preserve the profits they secured from forced unpaid labor, whippings, rapes, selling humans, and breaking up families. Ashcroft hailed Jefferson Davis, Stonewall Jackson, and Robert E. Lee as patriots, and in a revealing Freudian slip praised them for risking their lives "and subscribing their sacred fortunes and honor" to the cause. Ashcroft probably meant to say their fortunes and their sacred honor, but maybe not. After all, giving property sacred status is the point of the possessive investment in whiteness.[48]

Democrat Jay Nixon who succeeded Ashcroft as attorney general and later as governor, followed the same pattern. As attorney general, he dissolved the desegregation plans implemented in St. Louis and Kansas City, describing them as unwarranted burdens on the state rather than as legally mandated accountability for the continuing effects of the state's past actions.[49] As governor during the Ferguson upheaval, Nixon condemned the protests but not the launching of tear gas, chemical irritants, rubber and plastic bullets, stun grenades, chemical irritants, and long-range acoustic devices at demonstrators. The commander of the National Guard units reporting to Governor Nixon referred to the citizens exercising their constitutional rights of assembly and protest in Ferguson as "enemy forces" and "adversaries" of the state.[50]

This long history led Michael Brown and Darren Wilson to Canfield Drive in Ferguson on August 9, 2014. Racialized land-use policies concentrated the Black population of St. Louis on the city's north side. The serial destruction of Black neighborhoods enacted by urban renewal, the tax policies that encourage segregation and opportunity hoarding in the suburbs while depriving the city of the tax base required to fund necessary services and the massive white resistance to enforcing the 1968 Fair Housing Act and adhering to its mandate to affirmatively further fair housing made inner-city residents desperate to move to more favored places. Yet discrimination, redlining, racially motivated zoning, and the artificially limited amount of affordable housing units leave low-income Blacks with few options to improve their living conditions. Blacks moving out of the conditions that segregation created in the northern parts of the city of St. Louis encounter a similarly segregated and stratified environment in newly desegregated north St. Louis County neighborhoods, including southeast Ferguson where Michael Brown lived and died. Blacks moving from the city mainly entered areas characterized by already declining property values.[51] Eager to own property and move out of declining ghetto neighborhoods, many Black first-time homeowners pinned their hopes for upward mobility on purchasing houses in Ferguson. Yet the collapse of the home mortgage industry and the ruinous consequences of fraudulent and predatory lending practices caused a massive drop in property values, a severe spike in foreclosures, and a spate of evictions. Seventy percent of the 300 Ferguson homes on the market in 2015 were in the process of foreclosure, and property values dropped to 40 percent below what they had been in 2006.[52]

Many Ferguson residents are renters, some of whom pay exorbitantly high monthly amounts to speculators who bought multiple dwellings for cash in the wake of the home mortgage foreclosure crisis of 2008, a crisis that was itself propelled by racially motivated predatory lending.[53] Some renters hold Section 8 vouchers that make up the difference between the market rent and what the voucher holder can afford. These vouchers guarantee that landlords will receive the full rental amount on time every month, but fair housing regulations that allow discrimination based on source of income mean that landlords do not have to admit Section 8 voucher holders into their buildings. Those who do tend to cluster the new tenants in particular complexes in particular neighborhoods where they become quickly stereotyped and stigmatized by city officials, white property owners, and police officers. The artificially constrained housing market open to Blacks means that absentee landlords have a captive population, that they can charge more money for rent and spend less on maintenance and repairs. It also means that residents of areas replete with Section 8 housing are particularly vulnerable to predatory policing. Legal scholar Priscilla Ocen argues that while restrictive covenants are no longer legally permissible because of the 1968 Fair Housing Act, administration of Section 8 vouchers functions as a de facto form of restrictive covenant.[54]

When Black youths like Michael Brown move to the suburbs, they do not receive the benefits of the neighborhood race effects generally associated with suburbia. They attend schools that spend less per pupil than the county average, even though the municipalities in which they live have higher than average tax rates.[55] The Normandy High School that Michael Brown attended drew its students from twenty-nine different municipalities.[56] The school had low graduation rates, gave out a large number of in-school and out-of-school disciplinary suspensions, and lost its accreditation by the state because of low scores on standardized tests.[57] Laws passed by the state legislature to limit the property tax obligations of affluent residents and policies under which the state government gives minimally to local school districts rig the game, ensuring that the most money is spent on the students who need it the least and the smallest amount is expended on behalf of those who need it the most.

Long before the violence that took his life on August 9, 2014, Michael Brown was already the victim of the slow violence of displacement, dispossession, and disposability that has characterized the racial ecology of St. Louis and the United States for centuries. An act like jaywalking that goes unnoticed, unpoliced, and unprosecuted in white neighborhoods provokes aggressive police action in Ferguson to protect the property system from which whites benefit. This action uses the historical claim that Blacks are unfit for freedom as a pretext to make the Black poor pay for the city services designed to protect white property owners and corporate interests.

The protests that erupted in Ferguson on August 9, 2014, did not take place because the killing of Michael Brown was so unusual. They took place because it was so ordinary, because it distilled and crystallized in one incident decades of displacement, dispossession, disempowerment, demonization, and dehumanization. It displayed in vivid relief the lies of whiteness, the workings of a system of calculated cruelty and mean-spirited mendacity. The display of force implemented to intimidate and silence witnesses produced instead a collective response among differently situated people linked by relegation to a shared unlivable destiny.

This battle continues to rage. One website keeping track of police killings in the United States reported police officers shot and killed at least 2,900 people in the first three years following the killing of Michael Brown.[58] This grim reality puts into relief an exchange of words nearly fifty years ago between a white police official and a Black civil rights worker. In the midst of civil rights protests in Albany, Georgia, in 1962, the white chief of police Laurie Pritchett told demonstrator Charles Sherrod why the chief had no compunction about sending Sherrod and other nonviolent activists to local jails where they were routinely beaten. "It's just a matter of mind over matter," the chief proclaimed, informing Sherrod that "you don't matter" and "I don't mind."[59] A half-century later, this battle continues. Living with evil, accepting it, and learning to lie about it proceed persistently through the frames of methodological individualism, historical amnesia, and affirmations of white innocence and injury. Yet millions of people have now taken direct action in the streets to make the nation mindful of how and why Black Lives Matter.

Living with Evil and Being Taught to Accept It and to Lie about It

The nightmare from which we cannot wake up did not begin on November 8, 2016. Donald Trump's electoral victory was largely unexpected, but Trumpism comes as no surprise. Robin Kelley reminds us that the rage of white nationalism reflects the avarice and desires of the haves, not the cry of justice from the have-nots. The median income of Trump voters was more than $70,000 per year.[60] A third of his voters had yearly incomes between $50,000 and $100,000 and another third had incomes that exceed $100,000 per year. Whites without college degrees made up a disproportionate share of the Trump electorate, but nearly 60 percent of these voters had incomes that placed them in the top half of earners and 20 percent of the non–college educated Trump voters had household income exceeding $100,000.[61] Large numbers of poor and working-class voters did not vote. In part, this was due to coordinated voter suppression efforts made possible by the Supreme Court's evisceration of the Voting Rights Act in its 2013 *Shelby v. Holder* decision. Yet voters may also have stayed home because Hillary Clinton committed herself to defending and continuing the policies of the Clinton and Obama administrations of mass incarceration and mass deportation, of increasing concentrated poverty by cutting social programs and failing to enforce fair housing laws, of deregulating the banking industry and bailing out its fraudsters but not their victims. We have two political parties in the United States. The Republicans have been shameless in pandering to the possessive investment in whiteness. Yet the Democrats have been spineless in response.[62] Leaders of both parties have promoted programs and deployed discourses deeply steeped in the empirical and epistemological lies of whiteness. These lies cannot be wished away or even voted away, at least not in the short run. But they can be undermined, opposed, and overcome by activists, artists, and academics committed to refusing an unlivable destiny, to rejecting the fatal triad of living with evil, accepting it, and learning to lie about it. As W.E.B. Du Bois wrote nearly a century ago, "Nations reel and stagger on their way; they make hideous mistakes; they commit frightful wrongs; they do great and beautiful things. And shall we not best guide humanity by telling the truth about all this, so far as the truth is ascertainable?"[63]

Notes

PREFACE: BILL MOORE'S BODY

The epigraph is from James Baldwin, *The Devil Finds Work* (New York: Dell, 1976), 7.

1. See, for example, Daniel T. Lichter, Domenico Parisi, and Michael C. Taquino, "Toward a New Macro-Segregation? Decomposing Segregation within and between Metropolitan Cities and Suburbs," *American Sociological Review* 80, 4 (2015): 843–873, available at doi:10.1177/0003122415588558; Peter K. Enns and Christopher Wlezien, eds., *Who Gets Represented?* (New York: Russell Sage Foundation, 2011); Daria Roithmayr, *Reproducing Racism: How Everyday Choices Lock in White Advantage* (New York: New York University Press, 2014).

2. Harvard Sitkoff, *The Struggle for Black Equality, 1954–1980* (New York: Hill and Wang, 1981), 124.

3. Congress of Racial Equality [CORE] Papers, State Historical Society, University of Wisconsin, MSS14, box 5, folder 40, p. 3.

4. "White Foe of Segregation Slain on a Protest Trek in Alabama," *New York Times,* April 25, 1963.

5. Sitkoff, *The Struggle for Black Equality,* 135; CORE Papers, MSS14, box 5, folder 40, page unnumbered, "White Foe of Segregation."

6. Foster Hailey, "Alabama Holds Two in Hiker's Slaying," *New York Times,* May 2, 1963.

7. "White Foe of Segregation."

8. Claude Sitton, "Dozen to Resume Slain Postman's Walk Tomorrow," *New York Times,* April 30, 1963.

9. "Alabama Jury Refuses to Indict in Murder of Hiking Postman" and "One Negro on Jury," *New York Times,* September 14, 1963.

10. Taylor Branch, *Parting the Waters: America in the King Years, 1954–63* (New York: Touchstone, 1988), 750.

11. Foster Hailey, "8 Negroes Seized in Alabama Walk," *New York Times,* May 2, 1963.

12. Sitton, "Dozen to Resume Slain Postman's Walk Tomorrow."

13. Stephan Lesher, *George Wallace: American Populist* (Reading, MA: Addison Wesley, 1990), 180.

14. Sitkoff, *The Struggle for Black Equality*, 135–136; John Hope Franklin, *From Slavery to Freedom: A History of Negro Americans*, 4th ed. (New York: Knopf, 1974), 483.

15. Claude Sitton, "11 Seized Trying Postman's Walk," *New York Times*, May 20, 1963.

16. Foster Hailey, "Alabama Holds 2 in Hiker's Slaying," *New York Times*, April 26, 1963.

17. Claude Sitton, "March to Continue," *New York Times*, April 28, 1963.

18. Sitkoff, *The Struggle for Black Equality*, 151; Franklin, *From Slavery to Freedom*, 483. This is the incident dramatized in the 1996 film *Ghosts of Mississippi*.

19. Franklin, *From Slavery to Freedom*, 483.

20. Sitkoff, *The Struggle for Black Equality*, 176.

21. John Dittmer, *Local People: The Struggle for Civil Rights in Mississippi* (Urbana: University of Illinois Press, 1995), 109.

22. Bob Zellner, *The Wrong Side of Murder Creek: A White Southerner in the Freedom Movement* (Montgomery, AL: New South Books) 2008; Michael Westgate with Ann Vick-Westgate, *Gale Force: Gail Cincotta The Battles for Disclosure and Community Reinvestment* (Cambridge, MA: Harvard Bookstore, 2011); Christina Caron, "Heather Heyer, Charlottesville Victim Recalled as a 'Strong Woman,'" *New York Times*, August 13, 2017, available at https://www.nytimes.com/2017/08/13/us/heather-heyer-charlottesville-victim.html?mcubz=0, accessed August 20, 2017.

23. CORE Papers, MSS 14, letter from Gordon Carey to Bill Moore, March 20, 1963; "White Foe of Segregation."

24. Kay Mills, *This Little Light of Mine: The Life of Fannie Lou Hamer* (New York: Penguin, 1993), 87; Erich Harrison, "Secret Files to Shed Light on State-Sanctioned Racism," *Los Angeles Times*, August 18, 1997, sec. A.

25. James W. Silver, *Mississippi: The Closed Society* (New York: Harcourt, Brace and World, 1966); Chad Mitchell Trio, "We're Going to Miss Ole Miss"; Phil Ochs, "Here's to the State of Mississippi"; Nina Simone, "Mississippi Goddamn."

26. Charles Payne, *I've Got the Light of Freedom: The Organizing Tradition and the Mississippi Freedom Struggle* (Berkeley: University of California Press, 1996), 340.

27. Mills, *This Little Light of Mine*, 51.

28. Sitkoff, *The Struggle for Black Equality*, 181.

29. Mills, *This Little Light of Mine*, 125.

30. Payne, *I've Got the Light of Freedom*.

31. Dittmer, *Local People*, 23.

32. Proposition 209 was a state ballot resolution banning affirmative action policies by state institutions. Proposition 187 was aimed against immigrants. SP 1 and SP 2 were resolutions adopted by the University of California Board of Regents banning the use of race as a consideration in hiring and admissions decisions.

INTRODUCTION TO THE TWENTIETH ANNIVERSARY EDITION: THE CHANGING SAME

The epigraph is from James Baldwin, *The Fire Next Time* (New York: Vintage, 1993), 5.

1. Mikhail Bakhtin, *The Dialogic Imagination* (Austin: University of Texas Press, 1981).

2. Barbara Tomlinson and George Lipsitz, "American Studies as Accompaniment," *American Quarterly* 65, 1 (March 2013): 1–30.

3. Particularly influential were W.E.B. Du Bois, James Baldwin, Cedric Robinson, Cheryl Harris, Robin Kelley, Toni Morrison, Richard Dyer, Michael Rogin, Jill Quadagno, Melvin Oliver, Thomas Shapiro, Toni Cade Bambara, David Roediger, Vicki Ruiz, David Theo Goldberg, Lisa Lowe, Theodore Allen, Eric Lott, and Joe Feagin.

4. These include Anna Julia Cooper, Frances E. W. Harper, Amiri Baraka, Joel Kovel, Stan Weir, Alessandro Portelli, Johnny Otis, Gregory Squires, Dorothy Roberts, Christopher Small, Michael Omi, and Howard Winant.

5. Chuck Morse, "Capitalism, Marxism and the Black Radical Tradition: An Interview with Cedric Robinson," *Perspectives on Anarchist Theory* 3, 1 (Spring 1999). In this interview Robinson states, "Whiteness Studies deconstruct and decenter whiteness, showing that it is an artifice, that it has a history and one that does not go back very far. The best of the work (like George Lipsitz's *The Possessive Investment in Whiteness*) is an extension of radical Black Studies," available at http://www.hartford-hwp.com/archives/45a/568.html, accessed August 12, 2017. The connection that Robinson recognizes here is evident to me from my discussions of racial formation and racial projects in writings that preceded *The Possessive Investment in Whiteness*, especially *A Life in the Struggle: Ivory Perry and the Culture of Opposition, Rainbow at Midnight: Labor and Culture in the 1940s*, and *Time Passages*. The segregation of scholarly disciplines and subdisciplines, however, has masked those connections for many readers who view whiteness studies as its own silo.

6. Martin Luther King, Jr., "A Time to Break Silence," in *A Testament of Hope: The Essential Writings and Speeches of Martin Luther King Jr.*, ed. James M. Washington (San Francisco: Harper, 1991), 243.

7. National Community Reinvestment Coalition, "2017 Policy Agenda: Investing in a Just Economy" (Washington, DC: National Community Reinvestment Coalition, 2017), available at www.nscr.org.

8. *United States v. Southeastern Community and Family Services, Inc.*, 2016; *United States v. Piekarsky & Donchak*, 2010; *Kennedy v. City of Zanesville*, 2008.

9. Robert G. Schwemm, "Fair Housing Litigation after *Inclusive Communities*: What's New and What's Not," 115 *Columbia Law Review Sidebar* 106 (2015), available at http://columbialawreview.org/content/fair-housing-litigation-after-inclusive-communities-whats-new-and-whats-not/, accessed August 12, 2017.

10. Irene Bloemraad and Kim Voss, "The Protests of 2006: What Were They, How Do We Understand Them, Where Do We Go?" in *Rallying for Immigrant Rights: The Fight for Inclusion in the 21st Century*, ed. Kim Voss and Irene Bloemraad (Berkeley: University of California Press, 2011), 3–43.

11. Jodi Rios, "Flesh in the Street," *Kalfou* 3, 1 (Spring 2016): 63–78; Keeanga-Yamahtta Taylor, *From #BLACKLIVESMATTER to Black Liberation* (Chicago: Haymarket, 2016); African American Policy Forum, "Say Her Name: Resisting Police Brutality against Black Women" (New York: African American Policy Forum, 2015), available at http://static1.squarespace.com/static/53f20d90e4b0b80451158d8c/t/560c068ee4b0af26f72741 df/1443628686535/AAPF_SMN_Brief_Full_singles-min.pdf, accessed August 11, 2017.

12. Steven H. Marshall, *The City on a Hill from Below: The Case of Prophetic Black Politics* (Philadelphia: Temple University Press, 2011), 35.

13. Sunni Patterson, "We Know This Place" *American Quarterly* 61, 3 (September 2009): 719–721.

14. Cedric J. Robinson, *Black Movements in America* (New York: Routledge, 1997), 11.

15. Martin Luther King, Jr., in *A Testament of Hope*, ed. James Washington (New York: HarperOne, 2003), 315.

16. Sunni Patterson, "We Know This Place."

CHAPTER 1. THE POSSESSIVE INVESTMENT IN WHITENESS

The epigraph is from James Baldwin, *The Devil Finds Work* (New York: Dell, 1976), 1.

1. Raphael Tardon, "Richard Wright Tells Us: The White Problem in the United States," *Action,* October 24, 1946. Reprinted in Keneth Kinnamon and Michel Fabre, *Conversations with Richard Wright* (Jackson: University Press of Mississippi, 1993), 99. Malcolm X and others used this same formulation in the 1960s, but I believe that it originated with Wright, or at least that is the earliest citation I have found.

2. Toni Morrison points out the ways in which African Americans play an essential role in the white imagination, how their representations both hide and reveal the terms of white supremacy upon which the nation was founded and has been sustained ever since. See *Playing in the Dark: Whiteness in the Literary Imagination* (Cambridge, MA: Harvard University Press, 1992).

3. Richard Dyer, "White," *Screen* 29, 4 (Fall 1998): 44.

4. I thank Michael Schudson for pointing out to me that since the passage of civil rights legislation in the 1960s whiteness dares not speak its name, cannot speak in its own behalf, but rather advances through a color-blind language radically at odds with the distinctly racialized distribution of resources and life chances in U.S. society.

5. Walter Benjamin, "Madame Ariane: Second Courtyard on the Left," in *One-Way Street* (London: New Left Books, 1969), 98–99.

6. Aileen Moreton-Robinson, *The White Possessive: Property, Power, and Indigenous Sovereignty* (Minneapolis: University of Minnesota Press, 2015), xiii, xix.

7. See Lisa Lowe, *Immigrant Acts: On Asian American Cultural Politics* (Durham, NC: Duke University Press, 1996), 11–16; Gary B. Nash, *Red, White, and Black: The Peoples of Early America* (Englewood Cliffs, NJ: Prentice-Hall, 1974); Ronald Takaki, *A Different Mirror: A History of Multicultural America* (Boston: Little, Brown, 1993), 177–183.

8. Nash, *Red, White, and Black,* 292–293.

9. Clyde Woods, *Redevelopment Drowned and Reborn: The Blues and Bourbon Restorations in Post-Katrina New Orleans* (Athens: University of Georgia Press, 2017), 11–12.

10. Tiya Miles, *Ties That Bind: The Story of an Afro-Cherokee Family in Slavery and Freedom* (Berkeley: University of California Press, 2005), 32; Howard R. Lamar, *Texas Crossings: The Lone Star State and the American Far West, 1836–1986* (Austin: University of Texas Press, 1991), xiii.

11. Quintard Taylor, *In Search of the Racial Frontier: African Americans in the West, 1528–1990* (New York: W. W. Norton 1999), 164–191; Pekka Hämäläinen, *The Comanche Empire* (New Haven, CT: Yale University Press, 2008), 321–341.

12. Ian Haney Lopez, *White by Law: The Legal Construction of Race* (New York: New York University Press, 2006); Laura Gomez, *Manifest Destinies: The Making of the Mexican American Race* (New York: New York University Press, 2007).

13. Bernard C. Nalty, *Strength for the Fight* (New York: Simon and Schuster, 1989).

14. Nash, *Red, White, and Black,* 294.

15. Woods, *Development Drowned and Reborn,* 13; Cedric Robinson, *Black Movements in America* (New York: Routledge, 1997), 41–44.

16. Takaki, *A Different Mirror,* 187–188; Peter Narvaez, "The Influences of Hispanic Music Cultures on Afro-American Blues Music," *Black Music Research Journal* 14, 2 (Fall 1994): 206; Ernest V. Allen, "'When Japan Was Champion of the Darker Races'; Satokata Takahishi and the Flowering of Black Messianic Nationalism," *Black Scholar* 24, 1 (1994): 27–31.

17. Jill Quadagno, *The Color of Welfare: How Racism Undermined the War on Poverty* (New York: Oxford, 1994), 91; Kenneth Jackson, *Crabgrass Frontier: The Suburbanization of the United States* (New York: Oxford University Press, 1985); Douglas S. Massey and Nancy A. Denton, *American Apartheid: Segregation and the Making of the Underclass* (Cambridge, MA: Harvard University Press, 1993).

18. I thank Phil Ethington for pointing out to me that these aspects of New Deal policies emerged out of political negotiations between the segregationist Dixiecrats and liberals from the North and West. My perspective is that white supremacy was not a gnawing aberration within the New Deal coalition but rather an essential point of unity between southern whites and northern white ethnics.

19. Records of the Federal Home Loan Bank Board of the Home Owners Loan Corporation, City Survey File, Los Angeles, 1939, Neighborhood D-53, National Archives, Box 74, RG 195.

20. Kenneth Jackson, *Crabgrass Frontier: The Suburbanization of the United States* (New York: Oxford University Press, 1985), 210–211.

21. John R. Logan and Harvey Molotch, *Urban Fortunes: The Political Economy of Place* (Berkeley: University of California Press, 1987), 182.

22. Logan and Molotch, *Urban Fortunes*, 114; Mindy Thompson Fullilove, *Root Shock: How Tearing Up City Neighborhoods Hurts America, and What We Can Do about It* (New York: Ballantine Books, 2004), 20.

23. Arlene Zarembka, *The Urban Housing Crisis: Social, Economic, and Legal Issues and Proposals* (Westport, CT: Greenwood, 1990), 104.

24. Quadagno, *The Color of Welfare*, 91, 92.

25. Logan and Molotch, *Urban Fortunes*, 130.

26. See Gary Gerstle, "Working-Class Racism: Broaden the Focus," *International Labor and Working Class History* 44 (Fall 1993): 36.

27. Logan and Molotch, *Urban Fortunes*, 168–169.

28. Troy Duster, "Crime, Youth Unemployment, and the Underclass," *Crime and Delinquency* 33, 2 (April 1987): 308, 309.

29. Massey and Denton, *American Apartheid*, 55.

30. Christopher Bonastia, *Knocking on the Door: The Federal Government's Attempt to Desegregate the Suburbs* (Princeton, NJ: Princeton University Press, 2010), 132–133.

31. Robert D. Bullard, "Environmental Justice for All," in *Unequal Protection: Environmental Justice and Communities of Color,* ed. Robert Bullard (San Francisco: Sierra Club, 1994), 9–10.

32. City of Houston Planning and Development Department, *Race\Ethnicity: 1980–2010, City of Houston*, 2012, available at http://www.houstontx.gov/planning /Demographics/docs_pdfs/Cy/coh_race_ethn_1980-2010.pdf, accessed 30 July 2017.

33. Robert D. Bullard, "Environmental Justice and the Politics of Garbage: The Mountains of Houston," *Cite 93* (2014), available at http://drrobertbullard.com/wp-content /uploads/2014/07/Final-2014-Bullard-Cite-Article.pdf, accessed July 30, 2017.

34. Marianne Lavelle, and Marcia Coyle, "Unequal Protection: The Racial Divide in Environmental Law, a Special Investigation," *National Law Journal*, 15 (1992), available at http://www.ejnet.org/ej/nlj.pdf, accessed July 22, 2017.

35. Robert D. Bullard, Paul Mohai, Robin Saha, and Beverly Wright, *Toxic Wastes and Race at Twenty: 1987–2007* (United Church of Christ, 2007), available at http://www .ejnet.org/ej/twart-light.pdf, x.

36. Robert J. Sampson and Alix S. Winter, "The Racial Ecology of Lead Poisoning," *Du Bois Review: Social Science Research on Race*, 13 (2016): 261–283.

37. Amanda Starbuck and Ronald White, *Living in the Shadow of Danger: Poverty, Race, and Unequal Chemical Facility Hazards* (Washington DC: Center for Effective Government, 2016).

38. Kyle Crowder and Liam Downey, "Inter-Neighborhood Migration, Race, and Environmental Hazards: Modeling Micro-Level Processes of Environmental Inequality," *American Journal of Sociology*, 115 (2010): 1110–1149.

39. Bullard et al., *Toxic Wastes and Race at Twenty: 1987–2007*, xii.

40. Crowder and Downey, "Inter-Neighborhood Migration, Race, and Environmental Hazards."

41. Evan J. Ringquist, "Assessing Evidence of Environmental Inequities: A Meta-Analysis," *Journal of Policy Analysis and Management* 24, 2 (2005): 223–247.

42. Robert D. Bullard, "Environmental Racism and the Environmental Justice Movement," in *Global Environmental Politics: From Person to Planet*, ed. Simon Nicholson and Paul Wapner (New York: Routledge, 2016), 238–245.

43. K. M. Schmit, Z. Wansaula, R. Pratt, S. F. Price, and A. J. Langer, "Tuberculosis—United States," *Morbidity and Mortality Weekly Report* 66 (2017): 289–294.

44. Jamie Vickery and Lori M. Hunter, "Native Americans: Where in Environmental Justice Research?" *Society & Natural Resources* 29, 1 (2016): 36–52, available at https://doi.org/10.1080/08941920.2015.1045644.

45. Laurel Morales, "For the Navajo Nation, Uranium Mining's Deadly Legacy Lingers," NPR.org, 2016, available at http://www.npr.org/sections/health-shots/2016/04/10/473547227/for-the-navajo-nation-uranium-minings-deadly-legacy-lingers, accessed July 30, 2017.

46. Mitchell Landsberg, "Wide Ethnic Disparities Found in County," *Los Angeles Times*, July 25, 2000, B7; Peter S. Wenz, "Just Garbage," in *Faces of Environmental Racism: Confronting Issues of Global Justice*, ed. Laura Westra and Peter S. Wenz (Lanham, MD: Rowman and Littlefield, 1996), 66; Robert D. Bullard, "Decision Making," in *Faces of Environmental Racism: Confronting Issues of Global Justice*, ed. Laura Westra and Peter S. Wenz (Lanham, MD: Rowman and Littlefield, 1996), 8.

47. Machiko Yasuda, "California Pollution Map: LA Has 3 of the Most Polluted ZIP Codes," Southern California Public Radio, 2013, available at http://www.scpr.org/news/2013/04/23/36934/map-3-los-angeles-neighborhoods-among-most-pollute/, accessed July 30, 2017, pulling data from CalEnviroScreen; James L. Sadd et al., "Playing It Safe: Assessing Cumulative Impact and Social Vulnerability through an Environmental Justice Screening Method in the South Coast Air Basin, California," *International Journal of Environmental Research and Public Health* 8, 12 (2011): 1441–1459, available at https://doi.org/10.3390/ijerph8051441; Environmental Health Coalition, "New Data Show San Diego's Low-Income Communities of Color Remain among Most Heavily Polluted in California," *Environmental Health Coalition*, 2017, available at http://www.environmental health.org/index.php/en/media-center/press-releases/606-february-7-2017-new-data-show-san-diego-s-low-income-communities-of-color-remain-among-most-heavily-polluted-in-california, accessed July 30, 2017; Environmental Health Coalition, "Environmental Justice," Environmental Health Coalition, 2011, available at http://www.environmental health.org/index.php/en/who-we-are/mission/environmental-justice, accessed July 30, 2017; Martha Matsuoka, *Building Healthy Communities from the Ground UP: Environmental Justice in California*, 2003, available at http://www.environmentalhealth.org/images/PDF/PDFs_Archive/EJReport.pdf pdf, accessed July 30, 2017.

48. George Lipsitz, *How Racism Takes Place* (Philadelphia: Temple University Press, 2011), 7.

49. Javier M. Rodriguez et al., "Black Lives Matter: Differential Mortality and the Racial Composition of the U.S. Electorate, 1970–2004," *Social Science & Medicine* 136 (2015): 193–199, available at https://doi.org/10.1016/j.socscimed.2015.04.014.

50. Kaiser Family Foundation, "Distribution of Medicare Beneficiaries by Race /Ethnicity," Henry J. Kaiser Family Foundation, 2016, available at http://www.kff.org /medicare/state-indicator/medicare-beneficiaries-by-raceethnicity/, accessed July 30, 2017; Samantha Artiga et al., *Racial and Ethnic Disparities in Access to and Utilization of Care among Insured Adults*, Henry J. Kaiser Family Foundation, 2015, available at https://www.chausa.org/docs/default-source/diversity-and-disparities/issue-brief-racial -and-ethnic-disparities-in-access-to-and-utilization-of-care-among-insured-adults.pdf? sfvrsn=0, accessed July 30, 2017.

51. Gail Wadsworth, Thea Rittenhouse, and Sarah Cain, *Assessing and Addressing Farm Worker Food Security: Yolo County, 2015* (Davis, CA: California Institute for Rural Studies, 2016), available at http://www.cirsinc.org/phocadownload/assessing%20 and%20addressing%20farm%20worker%20food%20security.pdf, accessed July 30, 2017.

52. Duane F. Alwin and Linda A. Wray, "A Life-Span Developmental Perspective on Social Status and Health," *The Journals of Gerontology: Series B*, 60, Special_Issue_2 (2005): S7–14, available at https://doi.org/10.1093/geronb/60.Special_Issue_2.S7, np.

53. Center for Behavioral Health Statistics and Quality, *2015 National Survey on Drug Use and Health: Detailed Tables* (Rockville, MD: Substance Abuse and Mental Health Services Administration, 2016), 232.

54. American Civil Liberties Union, "Race and Criminal Justice," 2017, available at https://www.aclu.org/issues/racial-justice/race-and-criminal-justice.

55. Todd R. Clear, *Imprisoning Communities: How Mass Incarceration Makes Disadvantaged Neighborhoods Worse* (New York: Oxford, 2007), 8, 14; Bruce Western, *Punishment and Inequality in America* (New York: Russell Sage, 2006), 47.

56. Eva Bertram, Morris Blachman, Kenneth Sharpe, and Peter Andreas, *Drug War Politics: The Price of Denial* (Berkeley: University of California Press, 1996), 38–42; American Civil Liberties Union, "Racial Disparities in Sentencing," Submission to the Inter-American Commission on Human Rights, 153rd Session (October 2014), 8.

57. Michelle Alexander, *The New Jim Crow: Mass Incarceration in the Age of Colorblindness* (New York: New Press, 2012).

58. Raymond Paternoster et al., *An Empirical Analysis of Maryland's Death Sentencing System with Respect to the Influence of Race and Legal Jurisdiction* (College Park: University of Maryland, 2003), available at http://www.aclu- 16 August 16, 2017.

59. National Association for the Advancement of Colored People, "Criminal Justice Fact Sheet," NAACP, 2017, available at http://www.naacp.org/criminal-justice-fact-sheet/, accessed July 24, 2017; United States Sentencing Commission, *Report on the Continuing Impact of* United States v. Booker *on Federal Sentencing* (U.S. Sentencing Commission, 2012), available at https://www.ussc.gov/sites/default/files/pdf/news/congressional-testi mony-and-reports/booker-reports/2012-booker/Part_A.pdf, accessed August 16, 2017, 108.

60. Eva Bertram, Morris Blachman, Kenneth Sharpe, and Peter Andreas, *Drug War Politics: The Price of Denial* (Berkeley: University of California Press, 1996), 41.

61. Massey and Denton, *American Apartheid*, 61.

62. Gertrude Ezorsky, *Racism and Justice: The Case for Affirmative Action* (Ithaca, NY: Cornell University Press, 1991), 25.

63. Chenoa A. Flippen, "Unequal Returns to Housing Investments? A Study of Real Housing Appreciation among Black, White and Hispanic Households," *Social Forces* 82, 4 (2004): 1543.

64. Caitlin Knowles Myers, "Discrimination and Neighborhood Effects: Understanding Racial Differentials in US Housing Prices," *Journal of Urban Economics* 56, 2 (2004): 279–302, available at https://doi.org/10.1016/j.jue.2004.03.006; Chenoa A. Flippen, "Unequal Returns to Housing Investments? A Study of Real Housing Appreciation among Black, White and Hispanic Households," *Social Forces* 82, 4 (2004): 1543.

65. Paul Ong and J. Eugene Grigsby III, "Race and Life-Cycle Effects on Home Ownership in Los Angeles, 1970 to 1980," *Urban Affairs Quarterly* 23, 4 (June 1988): 605; Jim Campen, "Lending Insights: Hard Proof that Banks Discriminate," *Dollars and Sense,* January–February 1991, 17; Mitchell Zuckoff, "Study Shows Racial Bias in Lending," *Boston Globe,* October 9, 1992.

66. Massey and Denton, *American Apartheid,* 108.

67. Andra C. Ghent, Rubén Hernández-Murillo, and Michael T. Owyang, "Differences in Subprime Loan Pricing across Races and Neighborhoods," *Regional Science and Urban Economics* 48 (2014): 199–215, available at https://doi.org/10.1016/j.regsciurbeco.2014.07.006.

68. Drew DeSilver and Kristen Bialik, *Blacks and Hispanics Face Extra Challenges in Getting Home Loans* (Washington DC: Pew Research Center, 2017); Patrick Bayer, Fernando Ferreira, and Stephen L. Ross, *Race, Ethnicity and High-Cost Mortgage Lending* (Cambridge, MA: National Bureau of Economics Research, 2014); William C. Apgar and Allegra Calder, "The Dual Mortgage Market: The Persistence of Discrimination in Mortgage Lending," in *The Geography of Opportunity: Race and Housing Choice in Metropolitan America,* ed. de Souza Briggs Xavier (Washington, DC: Brookings Institution Press, 2005). For a review of the literature on the targeting of subprime mortgages to people of color, see Jacob S. Rugh and Douglas S. Massey, "Racial Segregation and the American Foreclosure Crisis," *American Sociological Review* 75, 5 (2010): 629–651.

69. Sarah Burd-Sharps and Rebecca Rasch, *Impact of the US Housing Crisis on the Racial Wealth Gap across Generations* (American Civil Liberties Union, 2015), available at http://webarchive.ssrc.org/pdfs/DiscrimLend_ACLU_SSRC.pdf, accessed July 30, 2017.

70. Melvin Oliver and Thomas Shapiro, *Black Wealth/White Wealth: A New Perspective on Inequality* (New York: Routledge, 1995).

71. Richard Rothstein, *The Color of Law: A Forgotten History of How Our Government Segregated America* (New York: Liveright, 2017), 111.

72. Patrick Bayer, Fernando Ferreira, and Stephen L. Ross, "What Drives Racial and Ethnic Differences in High Cost Mortgages? The Role of High Risk Lenders," *National Bureau of Economic Research Working Paper* n. 22004, Cambridge, MA, February 2016.

73. Gregory Squires, "Runaway Plants, Capital Mobility, and Black Economic Rights," in *Community and Capital in Conflict: Plant Closings and Job Loss,* ed. John C. Raines, Lenora E. Berson, and David McI. Gracie (Philadelphia: Temple University Press, 1983), 70.

74. Gertrude Ezorsky, *Racism and Justice* (Ithaca, NY: Cornell University Press, 1991), 15. See, e.g., Lou Adler, "New Survey Reveals 85% of All Jobs Are Filled Via Networking," *LinkedIn Pulse,* 2016, available at https://www.linkedin.com/pulse/new-survey-reveals-85-all-jobs-filled-via-networking-lou-adler, accessed July 30, 2017.

75. Gary Orfield and Carol Ashkinaze, *The Closing Door* (Chicago: University of Chicago Press, 1991), 225–226.

76. City of St. Louis, *City of St. Louis Economic Development Incentives PFM Report,* 2016, available at https://www.stlouis-mo.gov/government/departments/sldc/documents/city-of-st-louis-economic-development-incentives-pfm-report.cfmm accessed July 30,

2017; St. Louis Post Dispatch Editorial Board, "Editorial: Demand Transparency on Property Tax Abatements in St. Louis," *St. Louis Post Dispatch*, 2016, available at http://www.stltoday.com/opinion/editorial/editorial-demand-transparency-on-property-tax-abatements-in-st-louis/article_4cbb6372-c175-5fca-a7ec-f5e8f1e838f4.html, accessed July 30, 2017.

77. Grant Driessen, *Tax-Exempt Bonds: A Description of State and Local Government Debt* (Congressional Research Service, 2016), available at https://fas.org/sgp/crs/misc/RL30638.pdf, accessed July 31, 2017, 9; see, e.g., Jonathan Roenker, Emily Spurlock, and Mark Clark, *The Impact of Industrial Revenue Bonds on Property Taxes and School Funding* (Legislative Research Commission, Program Review and Investigations Committee, 2011), available at http://www.lrc.ky.gov/lrcpubs/RR401.pdf, accessed July 31, 2017; Peter Downs, "Tax Abatements Don't Work," *St. Louis Journalism Review*, February 1997, 16.

78. Citizens for Tax Justice, *Who Pays Taxes in America in 2016?*, 2016, available at http://ctj.org/ctjreports/taxday2016.pdf, accessed July 31, 2017; Mac Taylor, *Common Claims about Proposition 13* (California Legislative Analyst's Office, 2016), available at http://lao.ca.gov/reports/2016/3497/common-claims-prop13-091916.pdf, 2, 9–10, 19, 22, 25.

79. William Chafe, *The Unfinished Journey* (New York: Oxford University Press, 1986), 442; Noel J. Kent, "A Stacked Deck: Racial Minorities and the New American Political Economy," *Explorations in Ethnic Studies* 14, 1 (January 1991): 11; Bureau of Labor Statistics, U.S. Department of Labor, *Economics Daily*, Median weekly earnings by educational attainment in 2014, available at https://www.bls.gov/opub/ted/2015/median-weekly-earnings-by-education-gender-race-and-ethnicity-in-2014.htm, accessed July 25, 2017. Weekly earnings multiplied by 52 to approximate yearly earnings.

80. Carey Goldberg, "Hispanic Households Struggle as Poorest of the Poor in the U.S.," *New York Times*, January 30, 1997, sec. A.

81. Kent, "A Stacked Deck," 13.

82. Melvin Oliver and James Johnson, "Economic Restructuring and Black Male Joblessness in United States Metropolitan Areas," *Urban Geography* 12, 6 (November–December 1991); Gerald David Jaynes and Robin M. Williams, Jr., eds., *A Common Destiny: Blacks and American Society* (Washington, DC: National Academy Press, 1989); Reynolds Farley and Walter R. Allen, *The Color Line and the Quality of Life in America* (New York: Russell Sage Foundation, 1987); Melvin Oliver and Tom Shapiro, "Wealth of a Nation: A Reassessment of Asset Inequality in America Shows at Least One-Third of Households Are Asset Poor," *Journal of Economics and Sociology* 49, 2 (April 1990); Jonathan Kozol, *Savage Inequalities: Children in America's Schools* (New York: Crown, 1991); Cornell West, *Race Matters* (Boston: Beacon, 1993).

83. Economic Policy Institute, *African Americans: State of Working America* (Economic Policy Institute, 2017), available at http://www.stateofworkingamerica.org/fact-sheets/african-americans/, accessed July 30, 2017; Pew Research Center, *Demographic Trends and Economic Well-Being* (Pew Research Center, 2016), available at http://www.pewsocialtrends.org/2016/06/27/1-demographic-trends-and-economic-well-being/, accessed July 30, 2017.

84. Michael I. Norton and Samuel R. Sommers, "Whites See Racism as a Zero-Sum Game That They Are Now Losing," *Perspectives on Psychological Science* 60, 2 (May 2012): 215–218.

85. Charles Gallagher, "'The End of Racism' as the New Doxa: New Strategies for Researching Race," in *White Logic, White Methods: Racism and Methodology*, ed.

Eduardo Bonilla-Silva and Tukufu Zuberi (Lanham, MD: Rowman and Littlefield, 2008), 167.

86. Douglas S. Massey, *Categorically Unequal: The American Stratification System* (New York: Russell Sage Foundation, 2007), 66.

87. Lawrence D. Bobo et al., "The Real Record on Racial Attitudes," in *Social Trends in American Life: Findings from the General Social Survey since 1972*, ed. Peter V. Marsden (Princeton, NJ: Princeton University Press, 2012), 60.

88. Data from the 2008 General Social Survey, reported in Claude S. Fischer, "It's the 50th Anniversary of the Civil Rights Act—Race Still Matters," *Boston Review*, July 2, 2014, available at http://bostonreview.net/blog/claude-fischer-civil-rights-race, accessed July 30, 2017.

89. Data from the 2012 General Social Survey, reported in Nate Silver and Allison McCann, "Are White Republicans More Racist Than White Democrats?" *FiveThirtyEight*, 2014, available at https://fivethirtyeight.com/features/are-white-republicans-more-racist -than-white-democrats/, accessed July 30, 2017.

90. Mary D. Edsall and Thomas Byrne Edsall, *Chain Reaction: The Impact of Race, Rights, and Taxes on American Politics* (New York: W. W. Norton & Company, 1992).

91. Rogena Schuyler, "Youth: We Didn't Sell Them into Slavery," *Los Angeles Times*, June 21, 1993, sec. B.

92. Jim Newton, "Skinhead Leader Pleads Guilty to Violence, Plot," *Los Angeles Times*, October 20, 1993, sec. A.

93. Jia Tolentino, "All the Greedy Young Abigail Fishers and Me," *Jezebel*, June 28, 2016, available at http://jezebel.com/all-the-greedy-young-abigail-fishers-and-me-1782508801, accessed August 27, 2017; Nikole Hannah-Jones, "What Abigail Fisher's Affirmative Action Case Was Really About," *Pro Publica*, June 23, 2016, available at https://www.pro publica.org/article/a-colorblind-constitution-what-abigail-fishers-affirmative-action-case -is-r, accessed August 27, 2017.

94. Sugar Land, Texas, City Data, available at http://www.city-data.com/city/Sugar -Land-Texas.html, accessed August 27, 2017.

95. Antonin Scalia, "The Disease as Cure," *Washington University Law Quarterly* 147 (1979): 153–154, quoted in Cheryl I. Harris, "Whiteness as Property," *Harvard Law Review* 106, 8 (June 1993): 1767.

96. Harris, "Whiteness as Property," 993.

97. The rise of a black middle class and the setbacks suffered by white workers during deindustrialization may seem to subvert the analysis presented here. Yet the black middle class remains fragile, far less able than other middle-class groups to translate advances in income into advances in wealth and power. Similarly, the success of neoconservatism since the 1970s has rested on securing support from white workers for economic policies that do them objective harm by mobilizing countersubversive electoral coalitions against busing and affirmative action, while carrying out attacks on public institutions and resources by representing "public" space as black space. See Oliver and Shapiro, "Wealth of a Nation." See also Logan and Molotch, *Urban Fortunes*.

98. Johnny Otis, *Upside Your Head! Rhythm and Blues on Central Avenue* (Hanover, NH: Wesleyan/University Press of New England, 1993). Mobilizations against plant shutdowns, for environmental protection, against cutbacks in education spending, and for reproductive rights all contain the potential for panethnic antiracist organizing, but too often neglect of race as a central modality for how issues of employment, pollution, education, or reproductive rights are experienced isolates these social movements from their broadest possible base.

99. Benjamin, "Madame Ariane," 98, 99.

CHAPTER 2. LAW AND ORDER: CIVIL RIGHTS
LAWS AND WHITE PRIVILEGE

The epigraph is from James Baldwin, *The Devil Finds Work* (New York: Dell, 1976), 69.

1. Charles McClain, *In Search of Equality: The Chinese Struggle against Discrimination* (Berkeley: University of California Press, 1994), 223–233.

2. Richard Rothstein, *The Color of Law: A Forgotten History of How Our Government Segregated American* (New York: Liveright, 2017), 47.

3. The realtors' national code and local rules are described in Dennis R. Judd and Todd Swanstrom, *City Politics: Private Power and Public Policy* (New York: HarperCollins, 1994), 198.

4. Thomas Sugrue, "Crabgrass-Roots Politics: Race, Rights, and the Reaction against Liberalism in the Urban North: 1940–1964," *Journal of American History* 82, 2 (September 1995): 551–578; Arnold Hirsch, "Massive Resistance in the Urban North," *Journal of American History* 82, 2 (September 1995): 522–550.

5. David Theo Goldberg, *Racist Culture: Philosophy and the Politics of Meaning* (London: Blackwell, 1993), 195.

6. Douglas S. Massey and Nancy A. Denton, *American Apartheid: Segregation and the Making of the Underclass* (Cambridge, MA: Harvard University Press, 1993), 188.

7. Arlene Zarembka, *The Urban Housing Crisis: Social, Economic, and Legal Issues and Proposals* (Westport, CT: Greenwood, 1990), 101–103.

8. Jill Quadagno, *The Color of Welfare: How Racism Undermined the War on Poverty* (New York: Oxford, 1994), 98–99.

9. Massey and Denton, *American Apartheid*, 189–190, 191–192.

10. Quadagno, *The Color of Welfare*, 99.

11. Quadagno, *The Color of Welfare*, 9.

12. Massey and Denton, *American Apartheid*, 196–200.

13. Massey and Denton, *American Apartheid*, 196.

14. Massey and Denton, *American Apartheid*, 190.

15. The Office of Fair Housing and Equal Opportunity, *FY 2006 Annual Report on Fair Housing* (U.S. Department of Housing and Urban Development, 2007), available at https://www.hud.gov/offices/fheo/fy2006rpt.pdf, accessed August 2, 2017, 31.

16. National Fair Housing Alliance, *The Crisis of Housing Segregation: 2007 Fair Housing Trends Report* (National Fair Housing Alliance, 2007), available at http://nation alfairhousing.org/wp-content/uploads/2017/04/2007_fair_housing_trends_report.pdf, accessed August 2, 2017, 26.

17. Massey and Denton, *American Apartheid*, 190.

18. Quadagno, *The Color of Welfare*, 109–110. Richard Rothstein, *The Color of Law: A Forgotten History of How Our Government Segregated America* (New York: Liveright, 2017), 125–126. Rothstein's discussion of the Black Jack case reveals another dimension of white resistance, refusal, and renegotiation. Although the municipality of Black Jack was defeated in court, the developers were forced to sue, and this delayed the project to a time when interest rates had risen and it became financially unfeasible. Fair housing litigation against St. Bernard Parish in Louisiana and Westchester County in New York entailed similar delays that preserved discriminatory practices, raised the stakes for fair housing proponents, and invited outside support for segregation. In the Westchester case, the Trump administration accepted a settlement proposed by Westchester County that had been found seriously inadequate by the previous administration.

19. Zarembka, *The Urban Housing Crisis*, 16–17.

20. Massey and Denton, *American Apartheid*, 105.

21. Zarembka, *The Urban Housing Crisis,* 103.

22. Zarembka, *The Urban Housing Crisis,* 129.

23. Massey and Denton, *American Apartheid,* 206.

24. John Hope Franklin, *The Color Line: Legacy for the Twenty-First Century* (Columbia: University of Missouri Press, 1993), 20.

25. Massey and Denton, *American Apartheid,* 207–208.

26. Zarembka, *The Urban Housing Crisis,* 106; Quadagno, *The Color of Welfare,* 114.

27. Zarembka, *The Urban Housing Crisis,* 8.

28. Amaad Rivera et al., *Foreclosed: State of the Dream* (Boston: United for a Fair Economy, 2008), 1, 17.

29. Ping Cheng, Zhenguo Lin, and Yingchun Liu, "Racial Discrepancy in Mortgage Interest Rates," *Journal of Real Estate Finance and Economics* 51, 1 (2015): 101–120, available at https://doi.org/10.1007/s11146-014-9473-0. Mean mortgage rates and median loan amounts are on page 12. The $16,000 figure referenced here assumes the median loan amount given to Blacks in this study, $105,000 and a thirty-year fixed rate mortgage.

30. Chenoa A. Flippen, "Unequal Returns to Housing Investments? A Study of Real Housing Appreciation among Black, White and Hispanic Households," *Social Forces* 82, 4 (2004): 1543.

31. Cheryl I. Harris, "Whiteness as Property," *Harvard Law Review* 106, 8 (June 1993), 1754.

32. Harris, "Whiteness as Property," 1755.

33. Nathaniel R. Jones, "Civil Rights after *Brown*: 'Stormy the Road We Trod,'" in *Race in America: The Struggle for Equality,* ed. Herbert Hill and James E. Jones, Jr. (Madison: University of Wisconsin Press, 1993), 100.

34. Wiley A. Branton, "Race, the Courts, and Constitutional Change in Twentieth-Century School Desegregation Cases after *Brown*," in *African Americans and the Living Constitution,* ed. John Hope Franklin and Genna Rae McNeil (Washington, DC: Smithsonian Institution Press, 1995), 86; Harris, "Whiteness as Property," 1756.

35. Lawrence Tribe quoted by Richard Thompson Ford, "The Boundaries of Race: Political Geography in Legal Analysis," in *In Pursuit of a Dream Deferred: Linking Housing and Education Policy,* ed. John A. Powell, Gavin Kearney, and Vina Kay (New York: Peter Lang, 2001), 244.

36. Stephen Breyer, quoting *San Antonio v. Rodriguez* ruling in "Dissenting, 551 U.S. Supreme Court of the United States, Nos. 05-908 and 05-915, *Parents Involved in Community Schools v. Seattle School District No., 1 et al.,* 2007, 48.

37. Peter Irons, *Jim Crow's Children* (New York: Penguin Books, 2004), 238.

38. Irons, *Jim Crow's Children,* 242–243.

39. Breyer, "Dissenting," 48.

40. James T, Patterson, *Brown v. Board of Education: A Civil Rights Milestone and Its Troubled Legacy* (New York: Oxford University Press, 2001), 178–181.

41. Jamin B. Raskin, *Overruling Democracy: The Supreme Court vs. the American People* (New York: Routledge, 2003), 160.

42. Quadagno, *The Color of Welfare,* 30.

43. Quadagno, *The Color of Welfare,* 127.

44. Gary Orfield, "School Desegregation after Two Generations: Race, Schools, and Opportunity in Urban Society," in *Race in America: The Struggle for Equality,* ed. Herbert Hill and James E. Jones, Jr. (Madison: University of Wisconsin Press, 1993), 240.

45. Orfield, "School Desegregation," 245, 240, 237.

46. Recent research indicates Orfield's comments are still applicable. For a few examples, see Pew Research Center, *On Views of Race and Inequality, Blacks and Whites*

Are Worlds Apart (Pew Research Center, 2016), available at http://www.pewsocialtrends .org/2016/06/27/on-views-of-race-and-inequality-blacks-and-whites-are-worlds-apart/, accessed August 3, 2017, 4–6; Pew Research Center, *Optimism about Black Progress Declines: Blacks See Growing Values Gap Between Poor and Middle Class* (Pew Research Center, 2007), available at http://www.pewsocialtrends.org/files/2010/10/Race-2007.pdf pdf, accessed August 3, 2017, 10; Sam Dillon, "Merger of Memphis and County School Districts Revives Challenges," *New York Times*, November 5, 2011, section Education, available at https://www.nytimes.com/2011/11/06/education/merger-of-memphis -and-county-school-districts-revives-challenges.html, accessed August 3, 2017; Erica Frankenberg and Rebecca Jacobson, "Trends—School Integration Polls," *Public Opinion Quarterly* 75, 4 (2011): 790; Dillon, "Merger of Memphis and County School Districts Revives Challenges."

47. Thomas Shapiro discusses cases like these in the Orinda, California and Copley Township, Ohio school districts in *Toxic Inequality: How America's Wealth Gap Destroys Mobility, Deepens the Racial Divide & Threatens Our Future* (New York: Basic Books, 2017), 80–83.

48. U.S. Government Accountability Office, Report to Congressional Requesters, "K-12 Education: Better Use of Information Could Help Agencies Identify Disparities and Address Racial Discrimination" April 2016, available at www.gao.gov/products/GAO -16-345, accessed December 19, 2017.

49. Charles Lawrence III and Mari J. Matsuda, *We Won't Go Back: Making the Case for Affirmative Action* (New York: Houghton Mifflin, 1997), 45.

50. Carter A. Wilson, "Exploding the Myths of a Slandered Policy," *Black Scholar* (May/June 1986): 20; Harris, "Whiteness as Property," 1770.

51. Harris, "Whiteness as Property," 1773.

52. David W. Bishop, "The Affirmative Action Cases: Bakke, Weber, and Fullilove," *Journal of Negro History 67*, 3 (Fall 1982): 231.

53. Justin C. Worland, "Legacy Admit Rate at 30 Percent," *Harvard Crimson* (Cambridge, MA, 2011), section News, available at http://www.thecrimson.com/article /2011/5/11/admissions-fitzsimmons-legacy-legacies/, accessed July 30, 2017.

54. Daniel Golden, "The Story behind Jared Kushner's Curious Acceptance into Harvard," *Pro Publica*, November 18, 2016, available at https://www.propublica.org/article /the-story-behind-jared-kushners-curious-acceptance-into-harvard, accessed August 3, 2017.

55. Ary Spatig-Amerikaner, *Unequal Education: Federal Loophole Enables Lower Spending on Students of Color* (Center for American Progress, 2012), available at https:// www.americanprogress.org/issues/education/reports/2012/08/22/29002/unequal-edu cation/, accessed August 1, 2017, 7–8.

56. Gary Orfield and others, *Brown at 60: Great Progress, a Long Retreat and an Uncertain Future* (Civil Rights Project, 2014), available at https://www.civilrightsproject .ucla.edu/research/k-12-education/integration-and-diversity/brown-at-60-great-progress -a-long-retreat-and-an-uncertain-future/Brown-at-60-051814.pdf, accessed July 31, 2017, 10.

57. Harris, "Whiteness as Property," 1731; Barbara Kersley et al., *Inside the Workplace: Finds from the 2004 Workplace Employment Relations Survey* (New York: Routledge, 2006), 73.

58. See Michele Pellizzari, "Do Friends and Relatives Really Help in Getting a Good Job?" *Industrial and Labor Relations Review* 63, 3 (2010): 495, for a review of the literature.

59. Truman F. Bewley, *Why Wages Don't Fall during a Recession* (Cambridge, MA: Harvard University Press, 1999), 333, 368.

60. Pellizzari, "Do Friends and Relatives Really Help in Getting a Good Job?" 495.

61. Quadagno, *The Color of Welfare*, 23.

62. George Lipsitz, *Rainbow at Midnight: Labor and Culture in the 1940s* (Urbana: University of Illinois Press), 1994.

63. Herbert Hill, "Black Workers, Organized Labor, and Title VII of the 1964 Civil Rights Act: Legislative History and Litigation Record," in *Race in America: The Struggle for Equality*, ed. Herbert Hill and James E. Jones, Jr. (Madison: University of Wisconsin Press, 1993), 263.

64. William H. Harris, *The Harder We Run: Black Workers since the Civil War* (New York: Oxford University Press, 1983), 123–137.

65. Quadagno, *The Color of Welfare*, 64.

66. George Lipsitz, *A Life in the Struggle: Ivory Perry and the Culture of Opposition* (Philadelphia: Temple University Press, 1995), 84–85.

67. John Hope Franklin, *From Slavery to Freedom* (New York: McGraw-Hill, 1999), 483.

68. Peter B. Levy, "The Civil Rights Movement in Cambridge, Maryland, during the 1960s," *Vietnam Generation* 6, 3–4 (1995): 101.

69. Quadagno, *The Color of Welfare*, 63, 67.

70. Hill, "Black Workers, Organized Labor," 267.

71. Helene Slessarev, *The Betrayal of the Poor* (Philadelphia: Temple University Press, 1997), 39–41.

72. Hill, "Black Workers, Organized Labor," 269–270, 170.

73. Quadagno, *The Color of Welfare*, 64–65.

74. Slessarev, *The Betrayal of the Poor*, 70, 74.

75. Quadagno, *The Color of Welfare*, 73–75.

76. Alphonso Lumpkins to James F. Conway, September 5, 1980, James F. Conway Papers, records group 7, series 2, box 11, Civil Rights Enforcement Agency File, Washington University Libraries, St. Louis, MO.

77. Edward H. Kohn, "Judges Called Adverse to Anti-Bias Suits," *St. Louis Post-Dispatch*, February 11, 1980.

78. Gertrude Ezorsky, *Racism and Justice: The Case for Affirmative Action* (Ithaca: Cornell University Press, 1991), 25.

79. Richard Child Hill and Cynthia Negry, "Deindustrialization and Racial Minorities in the Great Lakes Region, USA," in *The Reshaping of America: Social Consequences of the Changing Economy*, ed. D. Stanley Eitzen and Maxine Baca Zinn (Englewood Cliffs, NJ: Prentice-Hall, 1989), 168–178.

80. Harris, "Whiteness as Property," 1783.

81. Harris, "Whiteness as Property," 1778; Derrick Bell, "Remembrances of Racism Past: Getting beyond the Civil Rights Decline," in *Race in America: The Struggle for Equality*, ed. Herbert Hill and James E. Jones, Jr. (Madison: University of Wisconsin Press, 1993), 80.

82. Robert L. Carter, "Thirty-five Years Later: New Perspectives on *Brown*," in *Race in America: The Struggle for Equality*, ed. Herbert Hill and James E. Jones, Jr. (Madison: University of Wisconsin Press, 1993), 86, 88.

83. Carter, "Thirty-five Years Later," 86.

84. Bell, "Remembrances of Racism Past," 76.

85. Charles Mills, *The Racial Contract* (Ithaca, NY: Cornell University Press, 1997), 18.

86. John C. Roberts, "Opinion of Roberts, C.J.," 51, US 2007 Supreme Court of the United States Nos. 05-908 and 05-915 *Parents Involved in Community Schools v. Seattle School District No.1 et al.*, 37.

87. Clarence Thomas, "J. Concurring," 551 US 2007 Supreme Court of the United States, Nos. 05-908 and 05-915 *Parents Involved in Community Schools v. Seattle School District No. 1 et al.*, 3.

88. Drew Days III, "The Current State of School Desegregation Law: Why Isn't Anybody Laughing?" in *In Pursuit of a Dream Deferred*, ed. John A. Powell, Gavin Kearney, and Vina Kay (New York: Peter Lang, 2001), 159–181.

89. Days, "The Current State of School Desegregation Law," 175.

90. Amy Stuart Wells and Robert L. Crain, *Stepping over the Color Line: African American Students in White Suburban Schools* (Berkeley: University of California Press, 1997), 259.

91. R. D. Taub, D. G. Taylor, and J. A. Dunham, *Paths of Neighborhood Change: Race and Crime in Urban America* (Chicago: University of Chicago Press, 1984); Craig St. John and Nancy A. Bates, "Racial Composition and Neighborhood Evaluation," *Social Science Research* 19, 1 (1990): 47–61.

92. Thomas M. Shapiro, *The Hidden Cost of Being African-American* (New York: Oxford University Press, 2004), 271.

93. Richard Rothstein, *The Color of Law: A Forgotten History of How Our Government Segregated America* (New York: Liveright, 2017).

94. Meredith Lee Bryant, "Combatting School Resegregation through Housing: A Need for Reconceptualization of American Democracy and the Rights It Protects," in *In Pursuit of a Dream Deferred*, ed. John A. Powell, Gavin Kearney, and Vina Kay (New York: Peter Lang, 2001), 56–58.

95. Bryant "Combatting School Resegregation."

96. Bell, "Remembrances of Racism Past," 80.

97. *The Life and Death of Malcolm X*, Sitmar Entertainment VHS 2768, videocassette.

CHAPTER 3. IMMIGRANT LABOR AND IDENTITY POLITICS

The epigraph is from James Baldwin, *The Devil Finds Work* (New York: Dell, 1976), 134.

1. Quoted in Lawrence Levine, *The Opening of the American Mind: Canons, Culture, and History* (Boston: Beacon Press, 1996), 123.

2. Kitty Calavita, "The New Politics of Immigration: 'Balanced Budget Conservatism' and the Symbolism of Proposition 187," *Social Problems* 43, 3 (August 1996): 284–306.

3. Mark Potter, "San Diego: City of Shame," *San Diego Reader* 25, 32 (August 8, 1996): 1, 8–10.

4. Holly Sklar, *Chaos or Community? Seeking Solutions, Not Scapegoats for Bad Economics* (Boston: South End, 1995), 96.

5. Patrick J. McDonnell, "Immigrants a Net Economic Plus, Study Says," *Los Angeles Times*, May 18, 1997, sec. A.

6. David Bacon, "Labor Slaps the Smug New Face of Union-Busting," *Covert Action Quarterly* 60 (Spring 1997): 38–39; Angela Stuesse, *Scratching Out a Living: Latinos, Race, and Work in the Deep South* (Berkeley: University of California Press, 2016).

7. Lisa Lowe repeats the basic contours of this argument in *Immigrant Acts: On Asian American Cultural Politics* (Durham: Duke University Press, 1996), 20, 174–175.

8. Potter, "San Diego," 8–10.

9. Julianne Hing, "Tucson's Ousted Mexican-American Studies Director Speaks: 'The Fight's Not Over,'" *Color Lines* (April 27, 2012), available at http://www.colorlines.com/articles/tucsons-ousted-mexican-american-studies-director-speaks-fights-not-over, accessed August 29, 2017.

10. Christine Sleeter, "Commentary," *Education Week*, February 15, 2012, available at http://www.edweek.org/ew/articles/2012/02/15/21sleeter.h31.html, accessed August 29, 2017.

11. United States District Court, District of Arizona, *Gonzalez v. Douglas*, Case 4:10-cv-00623-AWT Document 468, 3. August 22, 2017.

12. United States District Court, District of Arizona, *Gonzalez v. Douglas*, Case 4:10-cv- 00623-AWT Document 468, 3. August 22, 2017, 38–42.

13. Automotive News, "North America Car and Truck Assembly Plants—as of 1-22-15," *Automotive News* (2015), available at https://www.autonews.com/assets/PDF /CA98053122.pdf, accessed August 11, 2017; Jorge Eduardo Mendoza, "The Effect of the Chinese Economy on Mexican Maquiladora Employment," *International Trade Journal* 24, 1 (2010): 60; Jesus Cañas, Roberto Coronado, and Robert W. Gilmer, *Texas Border: Employment and Maquiladora Growth, The Face of Texas: Jobs, People, Business, Change* (Dallas, TX: Federal Reserve Bank of Dallas, 2005), 28; Vera Pavlakovich-Kochi, *IMMEX—Mexico's Export-Oriented Manufacturing and Services* (Arizona's Economy: Economic and Business Research Center, 2015), available at https://www.azeconomy .org/2015/03/featured/immex-mexicos-export-oriented-manufacturing-and-services/.

14. For average Mexican wages in export-oriented manufacturing along the U.S./Mexican border, see Hunt Institute for Global Competitiveness, *Paso Del Norte Economic Indicator Review* (University of Texas at El Paso, 2015), http://huntinstitute .utep.edu/wp-content/uploads/2014/04/Paso-del-Norte-Economic-Indicator-Review -No-1-April-20151.pdf, accessed August 13, 2017. For hours and wages of nonsupervisory manufacturing employees in the United States (including back data for 2014), Bureau of Labor Statistics, "Industries at a Glance: Manufacturing: NAICS 31–33," United States Department of Labor, Bureau of Labor Statistics, 2017, available at https://www.bls.gov /iag/tgs/iag31-33.htm, accessed August 13, 2017.

15. Rafael Perez-Torres, *Chicano Poetry* (New York: Cambridge University Press, 1995), 101.

16. Janice Shields, "Social Dumping in Mexico under NAFTA," *Multinational Monitor*, April 1995, 24.

17. Shields, "Social Dumping in Mexico under NAFTA," 22.

18. Iván N. Pérez-Maldonado et al., "Exposure Assessment of Polybrominated Diphenyl Ethers (PBDEs) in Mexican Children," *Chemosphere* 75, 9 (2009): 1215–1220, available at https://doi.org/10.1016/j.chemosphere.2009.01.083; Alana Semuels, "Upheaval in the Factories of Juarez," *The Atlantic*, January 21, 2016, available at https://www.theatlantic.com/business/archive/2016/01/upheaval-in-the-factories-of -juarez/424893/, accessed August 14, 2017.

19. Christopher A. Shores et al., "Sources and Transport of Black Carbon at the California–Mexico Border," *Atmospheric Environment* 70 (2013): 490–499, available at https://doi.org/10.1016/j.atmosenv.2012.04.031; City of San Diego, "Maquiladoras/Twin Plants," *Economic Development*, n.d., available at https://www.sandiego.gov/economic -development/sandiego/trade/mexico/maquiladoras, accessed August 14, 2017.

20. Claudia Schatan and Liliana Castilleja, "The Maquiladora Electronics Industry on Mexico's Northern Border and the Environment," *International Environmental Agreements: Politics, Law and Economics* 7, 2 (2007): 109–135, available at https://doi .org/10.1007/s10784-007-9039-1.

21. Emilio Godoy, "Mexico: Maquiladora Factories Manufacture Toxic Pollutants | Inter Press Service," Inter Press Service News Agency, 2011, available at http://www

.ipsnews.net/2011/08/mexico-maquiladora-factories-manufacture-toxic-pollutants/ /, accessed August 14, 2017.

22. Shields, "Social Dumping in Mexico under NAFTA," 22.

23. Yen Le Espiritu, *Asian American Women and Men: Labor, Laws, and Love* (Gender Lens) (Thousand Oaks, CA: Sage, 1997).

24. Lowe, *Immigrant Acts,* 60–83.

25. Juan Flores, "'Que Assimilated, Brother, Yo Soy Assimilao': The Structuring of Puerto Rican Identity in the·U.S.," *Journal of Ethnic Studies* 13, 3 (1985): 1–16; Jack D. Forbes, *Black Africans and Native Americans: Color, Race, and Caste in the Evolution of Red-Black Peoples* (Oxford: Basil Blackwell, 1988); Gary Y. Okihiro, *Margins and Mainstreams: Asians in American History and Culture* (Seattle: University of Washington Press, 1994), 31–63; Peter Narvaez, "The Influences of Hispanic Music Cultures on Africa-American Blues Musicians," *Black Music Research Journal* 14, 2 (Fall 1994): 206; Kevin Gaines, *Uplifting the Race: Black Leadership, Politics, and Culture in the Twentieth Century* (Chapel Hill: University of North Carolina Press, 1996), 56; James Howard, *Shawnee! The Ceremonialism of a Native Indian Tribe and Its Cultural Background* (Athens: University of Ohio Press, 1981), 21–23. I thank Rachel Buff for calling Howard's work to my attention and for her own superb scholarship, which has influenced my understanding of panethnic antiracism in significant ways.

26. Teresa de Lauretis, "Eccentric Subjects," *Feminist Studies* 16, 1 (Summer 1990):115–151.

27. Ramon Gutierrez, *When Jesus Came, the Corn Mothers Went Away* (Stanford, CA: Stanford University Press, 1990).

28. George Sanchez, *Becoming Mexican American* (New York: Oxford University Press, 1993).

29. Vicki Ruiz, *Cannery Women/Cannery Lives: Mexican Women, Unionization, and the California Food Processing Industry, 1930–1950* (Albuquerque: University of New Mexico Press, 1987); David Montejano, *Anglos and Mexicans in the Making of Texas, 1836–1986* (Austin: University of Texas Press, 1987); Neil Foley, *The White Scourge* (Berkeley: University of California Press, 1997); Rosaura Sanchez, *Telling Identities: The Californio Testimonios* (Minneapolis: University of Minnesota Press, 1995).

30. David Gutierrez, *Walls and Mirrors: Mexican Americans, Mexican Immigrants, and the Politics of Ethnicity* (Berkeley: University of California Press, 1995).

31. Jose David Saldivar, *Border Matters* (Berkeley: University of California Press, 1997); Carl Gutierrez-Jones, *Rethinking the Borderlands: Between Chicano Culture and Legal Discourse* (Berkeley: University of California Press, 1995); Ramón Saldivar, *Chicano Narrative: The Dialectics of Difference* (Austin: University of Texas Press, 1990), 7.

32. Rosa Linda Fregoso, *The Bronze Screen* (Minneapolis: University of Minnesota Press, 1994); Chela Sandoval, *Methodology of the Oppressed* (Minneapolis: University of Minnesota Press, 2000); Gloria Anzaldua, *Borderlands: La Frontera: The New Mestiza* (San Francisco: Spinsters/Aunt Lutte, 1987), 30; Jose Limon, *Dancing with the Devil: Society and Cultural Poetics in Mexican-American South Texas* (Madison: University of Wisconsin Press, 1994).

33. Yvonne Yarbro-Bejarano, "The Female Subject in Chicano Theatre: Sexuality, 'Race,' and Class," *Theatre Journal* 38, 4 (December 1986): 389–407; Norma Alarcón, "Chicana's Feminist Literature: A Revision through Malintzin/or Malintzin: Putting Flesh Back on the Object," in *This Bridge Called My Back: Writings by Radical Women of Color,* ed. Cherrie Moraga and Gloria Anzaldua (Watertown, MA: Persephone,

1981), 182–189; Steven Loza, *Barrio Rhythm: Mexican American Music in Los Angeles* (Urbana: University of Illinois Press, 1993); James Diego Vigil, *Barrio Gangs: Street Life and Identity in Southern California* (Austin: University of Texas Press, 1988), 117, 121; Brenda Bright, "Remappings: Los Angeles Low Riders," in *Looking High and Low,* ed. Brenda Bright and Liza Bakewell (Tucson: University of Arizona Press, 1995).

34. I must add here out of deference to Bob Marley that while he shot the sheriff, he did not shoot the deputy.

35. Americo Paredes, *With His Pistol in His Hand* (Austin: University of Texas Press, 1958), 171–172.

36. Robert Farris Thompson, *The Flash of the Spirit* (New York: Oxford University Press, 1984).

37. Renato Rosaldo, *Culture and Truth: The Remaking of Social Analysis* (Boston: Beacon, 1989), 150–155 (quote on p. 151). See also Limon, *Dancing with the Devil,* 76–94.

38. Lowe, *Immigrant Acts.*

39. *CAAAV Voice* 9, 1 (Winter 1997): 3; *CAAAV Voice* 9, 2 (Summer 1997): 11.

40. Lowe, *Immigrant Acts,* 165–166; Jennifer Ji-ye Chun, George Lipsitz, Young Shin, "Intersectionality as a Social Movement Strategy: Asian Immigrant Women Advocates," *Signs* 38, 4 (Summer 2013): 917–940.

41. Mike Davis, "Kajima's Throne of Blood," *The Nation,* February 12, 1996, 18–21.

42. Eric Mann and Chris Mathis, "Civil Rights Consent Decree? Legal Tactics for Left Strategy," *Ahora Now* 4 (1997): 1–11.

43. James Baldwin, *No Name in the Street* (New York: Dial, 1972), 129.

CHAPTER 4. WHITENESS AND WAR

The epigraph is from James Baldwin, *The Fire Next Time* (New York: Vintage, 1993), 52–53.

1. Jodi A. Byrd, *Transit of Empire: Indigenous Critiques of Colonialism* (Minneapolis: University of Minnesota Press, 2015), xx.

2. Winona LaDuke, *The Militarization of Indian Country* (East Lansing: Michigan State University Press, 2012), xvi–xvii.

3. Democracy Now, "Native American Activist Winona LaDuke on Use of 'Geronimo' as Code for Osama bin Laden: The Continuation of the Wars against Indigenous People," May 6, 2011, available at https://www.democracynow.org/2011/5/6/native_american_activ ist_winona_laduke_on, accessed August 29, 2017.

4. Kelly Lytle Hernandez, *Migra! A History of the U.S. Border Patrol* (Berkeley: University of California Press, 2010), 38–39.

5. Mark Barnes, *The Spanish-American War and the Philippine Insurrection, 1898–1902* (New York: Routledge, 2010).

6. Stephen Kinzer, *The True Flag: Theodore Roosevelt, Mark Twain and the Birth of the American Empire* (New York: Henry Holt, 2017), 175.

7. Yen Le Espiritu, *Asian American Panethnicity: Building Institutions and Identities* (Philadelphia: Temple University Press, 1992), 141–143; see also the film directed by Renee Tajima and Christine Choy, *Who Killed Vincent Chin?* (New York: Film News Now Foundation, 1987).

8. Helen Zia, "Violence in Our Communities: 'Where Are the Asian Women?'" in *Making More Waves: New Writing by Asian American Women,* ed. Elaine H. Kim, Lilia V. Villaneuva, and Asian Women United of California (Boston: Beacon, 1997), 208.

9. Darrell Y. Hamamoto, *Monitored Peril: Asian Americans and the Politics of TV Representation* (Minneapolis: University of Minnesota Press, 1994), 165; Espiritu *Asian American Panethnicity*, 155–156.

10. Hamamoto, *Monitored Peril*, 166–167; Mike Clary, "Rising Toll of Hate Crimes Cited in Slaying," *Los Angeles Times*, October 10, 1992, sec. A.

11. Lisa Lowe, *Immigrant Acts: On Asian American Cultural Politics* (Durham: Duke University Press, 1996) 6–22; Yen Le Espiritu, *Asian American Women and Men: Labor, Laws, Love (Gender Lens)* (Thousand Oaks: Sage, 1997), 9–13; Gary Y. Okihiro, *Margins and Mainstreams* (Seattle: University of Washington Press, 2014).

12. Espiritu, *Asian American Women and Men*, 90; Dorothy Manevich, *Americans Have Grown More Negative toward China over the Past Decade* (Pew Research Center, 2017), available at http://www.pewresearch.org/fact-tank/2017/02/10/americans-have -grown-more-negative-toward-china-over-past-decade/, accessed August 4, 2017.

13. Reginald Horsman, *Race and Manifest Destiny: The Origins of American Anglo-Saxonism* (Cambridge, MA: Harvard University Press, 1981); David Roediger, *Towards the Abolition of Whiteness: Essays on Race, Politics, and Working-Class History* (New York: Verso, 1994).

14. Michael Rogin, *Ronald Reagan, the Movie: And Other Stories in Political Demonology* (Berkeley: University of California Press, 1987).

15. Kathleen Hall Jamieson, *Eloquence in an Electronic Age* (New York: Oxford University Press, 1988), 162, 163.

16. Lefty Frizzell, "Mom and Dad's Waltz," Columbia Records 20837, appears in *Billboard* on August 18, 1951, and stays on the charts for twenty-nine weeks; Joel Whitburn, *Top Country Hits, 1944–1988* (Menomonee, WI: Record Research, 1989), 107; Robert Westbrook, "'I Want a Girl Just Like the Girl that Married Harry James': American Women and the Problem of Political Obligation in World War II," *American Quarterly* 42, 4 (December 1990): 587–615; Amy Kaplan, "Romancing the Empire: The Embodiment of American Masculinity in the Popular Historical Novel of the 1890s," *American Literary History* 2, 4 (Winter 1990): 659–690.

17. Robert Westbrook, "Private Interests and Public Obligations in World War II," in *The Power of Culture: Critical Essays in American History*, ed. Richard Wightman Fox and T. J. Jackson Lears (Chicago: University of Chicago Press, 1993), 195–222.

18. Benedict Anderson, *Imagined Communities* (New York: Verso, 1983).

19. Hobson, quoted in Kaplan, "Romancing the Empire," 677.

20. Francis X. Clines, "Military of U.S. 'Standing Tall,' Reagan Asserts," *New York Times*, December 13, 1983.

21. Kevin Bowen, "Strange Hells: Hollywood in Search of America's Lost War," in *From Hanoi to Hollywood: The Vietnam War in American Film*, ed. Linda Dittmar and Gene Michaud (New Brunswick, NJ: Rutgers University Press, 1991), 229.

22. James William Gibson, "The Return of Rambo: War and Culture in the Post-Vietnam Era," in *America at Century's End*, ed. Alan Wolfe (Berkeley: University of California Press, 1991), 389, 390.

23. William Adams, "Screen Wars: The Battle for Vietnam," *Dissent* (Winter 1990): 65.

24. See Lynne Cheney, "Report," in *On Campus* 7, 3 (November 1987): 2, as well as Lynne Cheney, "Report to the President, the Congress, and the American People," *Chronicle of Higher Education* 35, 4 (September 21, 1988): A18–19.

25. It was reported that the *Mayaguez* carried only paper supplies for U.S. troops, but as a container ship, its cargo could have included much more sensitive material for

surveillance or combat, which may account for the vigorous government reaction to its capture. See Marilyn Young, *The Vietnam Wars, 1945–1990* (New York: Harper Collins, 1991), 301; see also Thomas J. McCormick, *America's Half Century: United States Foreign Policy in the Cold War* (Baltimore: Johns Hopkins University Press, 1989), 178–179.

26. "A Force Reborn," *U.S. News and World Report*, March 18, 1991, 30; Harry G. Summers, Jr., "Putting Vietnam Syndrome to Rest," *Los Angeles Times*, March 2, 1991, sec. A; E. J. Dionne, Jr., "Kicking the 'Vietnam Syndrome,'" *Washington Post*, March 4, 1991, sec. A; Kevin P. Phillips, "The Vietnam Syndrome: Why Is Bush Hurting if There Is No War?" *Los Angeles Times*, November 25, 1990.

27. Robert McKelvey, "Watching Victory Parades, I Confess Some Envy: Vietnam Vets Weren't Feted by Parades," *Los Angeles Times*, June 16, 1991, sec. M; James S. Barron, "A Korean War Parade, Decades Late," *New York Times*, June 26, 1991, sec. B.

28. Young, *The Vietnam Wars*, 314. Per the Chicago Council on Global Affairs Poll conducted in May 2014, 58 percent of Americans continue to view the U.S. role in the Vietnam War as a "dark moment" in American history: Dina Smeltz, *Foreign Policy in the Age of Retrenchment: Results of the 2014 Chicago Council Survey of American Public Opinion and US Foreign Policy*, Chicago Council Surveys (Chicago: Chicago Council on Foreign Affairs, 2014), 8.

29. George C. Herring, *America's Longest War* (New York: Wiley, 1968), George McT. Kahin, *Intervention* (New York: Knopf, 1986), and Stanley Karnow, *Vietnam: A History* (New York: Viking, 1984) present different perspectives on the war, but their cumulative evidence reveals the untenable nature of any hypothesis blaming internal division in the United States for the war's outcome.

30. Thomas Ferguson and Joel Rogers, *Right Turn: The Decline of the Democrats and the Future of American Politics* (New York: Hill and Wang, 1986), 79, 80.

31. Katherine S. Newman, "Uncertain Seas: Cultural Turmoil and the Domestic Economy," in *America at Century's End*, ed. Alan Wolfe (Berkeley: University of California Press, 1991), 116.

32. Newman, "Uncertain Seas," 116–117, 121; William Chafe, *The Unfinished Journey* (New York: Oxford University Press, 1986), 449.

33. See Michael I. Luger, "Federal Tax Incentives as Industrial and Urban Policy," in *Sunbelt/Snowbelt: Urban Development and Regional Restructuring*, ed. Larry Sawers and William K. Tabb (New York: Oxford University Press, 1984), 201–234.

34. Christian G. Appy, *Working Class War: American Combat Soldiers and Vietnam* (Chapel Hill: University of North Carolina Press, 1993), 6, 11.

35. There were, of course, important exceptions to this pattern. Antiwar activists supported coffeehouses, draft counseling centers, and antiwar newspapers at dozens of military bases. Many local peace coalitions united trade unionists, intellectuals, suburban liberals, students, and poor people, and—especially after 1970—the antiwar counterculture had a substantial working-class presence. But almost nowhere did any of this produce a class-based critique of why the war was fought and who had to fight it. Of course, the antiwar movement emerged as an ad hoc coalition based on college campuses with few other institutional resources. McCarthyism's destruction of the Old Left and the timidity of social democrats left the work of radicalism to politically inexperienced children of the middle class.

36. Billy Joel, "Allentown," Columbia Records 03413, entered *Billboard* charts on November 27, 1982, rose as high as number seventeen, and remained on the charts twenty-two weeks; Bruce Springsteen, "Born in the USA," Columbia Records 04680, entered *Billboard* charts November 10, 1984, rose to number nine, and remained on the charts

seventeen weeks; see Joel Whitburn, *Top Pop Singles* (Menomonee Falls, WI: Record Research, 1987), 266, 475; Bobbie Ann Mason, *In Country* (New York: Perennial Library, 1985).

37. Adams, "Screen Wars," 71–72.

38. Frank Burke, "Reading Michael Cimino's *The Deer Hunter*: Interpretation as Melting Pot," *Film and Literature Quarterly* 20, 3 (1992): 252–253.

39. Adams, "Screen Wars," 72; Gaylin Studlar and David Dresser, "Never Having to Say You're Sorry: Rambo's Rewriting of the Vietnam War," in *From Hanoi to Hollywood: The Vietnam War in American Film,* ed. Linda Dittmar and Gene Michaud (New Brunswick, NJ: Rutgers University Press, 1991), 111, 108; Stephen Prince, *Vision of Empire: Political Imagery in Contemporary American Film* (New York: Praeger, 1992), 66, 69.

40. Susan Jeffords, *The Remasculinization of America: Gender and the Vietnam War* (Bloomington: Indiana University Press, 1989).

41. Lynda Boose, "Techno-Muscularity and the 'Boy Eternal': From the Quagmire to the Gulf," in *The Cultures of United States Imperialism,* ed. Donald Pease and Amy Kaplan (Durham, NC: Duke University Press, 1994), 588–599, 600, 602.

42. Jeffords, *The Remasculinization of America,* 180; Philip Slater, *A Dream Deferred: America's Discontent and the Search for a New Democratic Ideal* (Boston: Beacon, 1991).

43. Cole and LaHaye are quoted in Michael Lienesch, *Redeeming America: Piety and Politics in the New Christian Right* (Chapel Hill: University of North Carolina Press, 1993), 60, 54, 58.

44. "Talk Radio Lowlights," *Extra! Update* (newsletter), December 1996, 2.

45. Chaim F. Shatan, "'Happiness Is a Warm Gun'—Militarized Mourning and Ceremonial Vengeance: Toward a Psychological Theory of Combat and Manhood in America, Part III," *Vietnam Generation* 3, 4 (1989): 147.

46. Jamieson, *Eloquence in an Electronic Age,* 161.

47. Hobson quoted in Kaplan, "Romancing the Empire," 679.

48. Shatan, "'Happiness Is a Warm Gun,'" 140–141.

49. O'Brien is quoted in Young, *The Vietnam Wars,* 329.

50. George Mariscal "'Our Kids Don't Have Blue Eyes, but They Go Overseas to Die': Chicanos in Vietnam," paper read at the conference "America and Vietnam: From War to Peace," University of Notre Dame, South Bend, IN, December 4, 1993.

51. Kitty Calavita, "The New Politics of Immigration: 'Balanced Budget Conservatism' and the Symbolism of Proposition 187," *Social Problems* 43, 3 (August 1996): 284–306.

52. See, for example, Rita Chaudry Sethi, "Smells Like Racism: A Plan for Mobilizing against Anti-Asian Bias," in *the State of Asian America: Activism and Resistance in the 1990s,* ed. Karen Aguilar-San Juan (Boston: South End, 1994), 235–250.

53. Timothy J. Dunn, *The Militarization of the U.S.-Mexico Border, 1978–1992* (Austin, TX: Center for Mexican American Studies, 1996), 87–89.

54. Mark Dow, "Behind the Razor Wire: Inside INS Detention Centers," *Covert Action Quarterly* 57 (Summer 1996): 35.

55. Jesse Katz, "Marine Is Cleared in Texas Border Death," *Los Angeles Times,* August 15, 1997, sec. A; Sam Howe Verhovek, "Pentagon Halts Drug Patrols after Border Killing," *New York Times,* July 31, 1997, sec. A.

56. W.E.B. Du Bois, *Black Reconstruction in America, 1860–1880* (New York: Touchstone, 1992), 696.

57. Anthony D. Romero, "Living in Fear: How the U.S. Government's War on Terror Impacts American Lives," in *Lost Liberties: Ashcroft and the Assault on Individual Freedom,* ed. Cynthia Brown (New York: New Press, 2003), 115.

58. Robert E. Pierre, "Victims of Hate, Now Feeling Forgotten," *Washington Post,* September 14, 2002, A01.

59. Robert Pear, "Teachers Union Called Terrorist," *San Francisco Chronicle,* February 24, 2004, 1.

60. Anthony Romero, "Living in Fear," 119.

CHAPTER 5. HOW WHITENESS WORKS:
INHERITANCE, WEALTH, AND HEALTH

The epigraph is from James Baldwin, *The Devil Finds Work* (New York: Dell, 1976), 68.

1. Karyn D. McKinney, *Being White: Stories of Race and Racism* (New York: Routledge, 2005), 192–193. See also Peggy McIntosh, "White Privilege: Unpacking the Invisible Knapsack," in *Race, Class and Gender: An Anthology,* 5th ed., ed. Margaret Andersen and Patricia Hill Collins (Belmont, CA: Thompson/Wadsworth, 2004), 103–108.

2. Emmanuel Saez and Gabriel Zucman, "Wealth Inequality in the United States since 1913: Evidence from Capitalized Income Tax Data," *Quarterly Journal of Economics* 131, 2 (May 2016): 552, available at doi:10.1093/qje/qjw004.

3. Edward N. Wolff, "Household Wealth Trends in the United States, 1962 to 2013: What Happened over the Great Recession?" *Russell Sage Foundation Journal of the Social Sciences* 2, 6 (2016): 30. See Table 2 for (1) wealth controlled by the wealthiest 20 percent, (2) income earned by the highest earning 1 percent compared to the lowest earning 60 percent of the country, and (3) income earned by the lowest earning 90 percent.

4. Thomas M. Shapiro, *Toxic Inequality: How America's Wealth Gap Destroys Mobility, Deepens the Racial Divide, and Threatens Our Future* (New York: Basic Books, 2017), 103.

5. Estelle Sommeiller, Mark Price, and Ellis Wazeter, "Income Inequality in the U.S. by State, Metropolitan Area, and County" (Washington, DC: Economic Policy Institute, 2016), 1, 3, available at http://www.epi.org/files/pdf/107100.pdf.

6. Wolff, "Household Wealth Trends in the United States," 30.

7. Thomas M. Shapiro, *The Hidden Cost of Being African American: How Wealth Perpetuates Inequality* (New York: Oxford University Press, 2005), 190.

8. Jill Quadagno, *The Color of Welfare: How Racism Undermined the War on Poverty* (New York: Oxford University Press, 1994), 91–92.

9. Amy Traub et al., "The Asset Value of Whiteness: Understanding the Racial Wealth Gap," *Demos* (2017): 8.

10. Thomas M. Shapiro, *Toxic Inequality* 135, 138.

11. Thomas Shapiro, Tatjana Meschede, and Sam Osoro, *The Roots of the Widening Racial Wealth Gap: Explaining the Black-White Economic Divide* (Waltham, MA: Institute for Assets and Social Policy, 2013), 5.

12. Rebecca Tippett et al., *Beyond Broke: Why Closing the Racial Wealth Gap Is a Priority for National Economic Security* (Durham, NC: Center for Global Policy Solutions, Duke University, 2014), 8.

13. Pew Research Center, *Demographic Trends and Economic Well-Being* (Pew Research Center, 2016), available at http://www.pewsocialtrends.org/2016/06/27/1-demo graphic-trends-and-economic-well-being/. Compare median white income to median Black income ($71,300 to $43,300) and white net worth ($144,200) to Black (listed as one thirteenth that of whites').

14. Daria Roithmayr, *Reproducing Racism: How Everyday Choices Lock in White Advantage* (New York: New York University Press, 2014), 2.

15. Julia Isaacs, "Economic Mobility of Black and White Families" (Economic Mobility Project of The Pew Charitable Trusts, 2016), 6, available at https://www.brookings.edu/wp-content/uploads/2016/06/11_blackwhite_isaacs.pdf.

16. United States Census Bureau, "Quarterly Residential Vacancies and Homeownership, Second Quarter 2017" (United States Census Bureau, 2017), available at https://www.census.gov/housing/hvs/files/currenthvspress.pdf.

17. Laura Sullivan et al., "The Racial Wealth Gap: Why Policy Matters" (Demos and The Institute on Assets and Social Policy, 2015): 2, available at http://www.demos.org/sites/default/files/publications/RacialWealthGap_1.pdf.

18. Shapiro, *The Hidden Cost,* 53–56. x

19. See Chapter 2, note 29.

20. Sullivan et al., "The Racial Wealth Gap," 2. This number represents the combined effect of eliminating the gap in homeownership and the gap in return on investment in homeownership between Blacks and whites.

21. Oliver and Shapiro, *Black Wealth/White Wealth: A New Perspective on Racial Inequality* (New York; Routledge, 1995), 9.

22. Gregory Acs et al., "The Cost of Segregation: National Trends and the Case of Chicago, 1990–2010" (Urban Institute, 2017), available at https://www.metroplanning.org/uploads/cms/documents/cost-of-segregation-urban.pdf, 38–39.

23. Center for Responsible Lending, "The Nation's Housing Finance System Remains Closed to African-American, Hispanic, and Low-Income Consumers Despite Stronger National Economic Recovery in 2015" (Center for Responsible Lending, 2016): 1, available at http://responsiblelending.org/sites/default/files/nodes/files/research-publication/2015_hmda_policy_brief_2.pdf.

24. Amy Higgins, "2015 Mortgage Lending Trends in New England," Community Development Issue Brief (Boston: Federal Reserve Bank of Boston, 2016): 11.

25. Debbie Gruenstein Bocian et al., "Lost Ground, 2011: Disparities in Mortgage Lending and Foreclosures" (Center for Responsible Lending, 2011): 21, available at http://alabamaabc.org/dnld/pac518b501861f36167/5-Lost-Ground-2011.pdf.

26. California Reinvestment Coalition, "Stolen Wealth: Disparities in California's Subprime Mortgage Market," prepared by Kevin Stein and Margaret Libby, executive summary, 5, November 2001, San Francisco.

27. United States Department of Justice, "Justice Department Reaches $21 Million Settlement to Resolve Allegations of Lending Discrimination by Suntrust Mortgage," United States Department of Justice, 2012, available at https://www.justice.gov/opa/pr/justice-department-reaches-21-million-settlement-resolve-allegations-lending-discrimination; United States Department of Justice, "Justice Department Reaches Settlement with Wells Fargo Resulting in More Than $175 Million in Relief for Homeowners to Resolve Fair Lending Claims," United States Department of Justice, 2012, available at https://www.justice.gov/opa/pr/justice-department-reaches-settlement-wells-fargo-resulting-more-175-million-relief.

28. Shapiro, *Toxic Inequality,* 9; Richard Rothstein, *The Color of Law: A Forgotten History of How Our Government Segregated America* (New York: Liveright, 2017), 111.

29. Marjery Austin Turner et al., "Housing Discrimination against Racial and Ethnic Minorities 2012" (United States Department of Housing and Urban Development, 2013), xv–xvii, available at https://www.huduser.gov/portal/Publications/pdf/HUD-514_HDS2012.pdf.

30. Benjamin Edelman, Michael Luca, and Dan Svirsky, "Racial Discrimination in the Sharing Economy: Evidence from a Field Experiment," *American Economic Journal: Applied Economics* 9, 2 (April 2017): 1–22, available at doi:10.1257/app.20160213.

31. National Center for Health Statistics, "Health, United States, 2016: With Chartbook on Long-Term Trends in Health" (Hyattsville, MD: U.S. Department of Health and Human Services, 2017): 263, 29, 265, available at https://www.cdc.gov/nchs/data/hus/hus16.pdf#015; Office of Minority Health, "Heart Disease and African Americans," U.S. Department of Health and Human Services Office of Minority Health, 2016, available at https://minorityhealth.hhs.gov/omh/browse.aspx?lvl=4&lvlid=19.

32. Philip Goodney et al., "Variation in the Care of Surgical Conditions: Diabetes and Peripheral Arterial Disease," a Dartmouth Atlas of Health Care Series (Dartmouth Institute for Health Policy and Clinical Practice, 2014): 15, available at http://www.dartmouthatlas.org/downloads/reports/Diabetes_report_10_14_14.pdf; Samantha Artiga et al., "Key Facts on Health and Health Care by Race and Ethnicity—Section 2: Health Access and Utilization" (Henry J. Kaiser Family Foundation, 2016): Exhibit 2.2, available at http://www.kff.org/report-section/key-facts-on-health-and-health-care-by-race-and-ethnicity-section-2-health-access-and-utilization/.

33. Office of Minority Health, "Diabetes and African Americans," U.S. Department of Health and Human Services Office of Minority Health, 2016, available at https://minorityhealth.hhs.gov/omh/browse.aspx?lvl=4&lvlid=18; Office of Minority Health, "Heart Disease and African Americans," U.S. Department of Health and Human Services Office of Minority Health, 2016, available at https://minorityhealth.hhs.gov/omh/browse.aspx?lvl=4&lvlid=19; Office of Minority Health, "Stroke and African Americans," U.S. Department of Health and Human Services Office of Minority Health, 2016, available at https://minorityhealth.hhs.gov/omh/browse.aspx?lvl=4&lvlid=28; Office of Minority Health, "Cancer and African Americans," U.S. Department of Health and Human Services Office of Minority Health, 2016, available at https://minorityhealth.hhs.gov/omh/browse.aspx?lvl=4&lvlid=16.

34. Office of Minority Health, "Cancer and African Americans."

35. National Center for Health Statistics, "Health, United States, 2016: With Chartbook on Long-Term Trends in Health" (Hyattsville, MD: U.S. Department of Health and Human Services, 2017): 116, available at https://www.cdc.gov/nchs/data/hus/hus16.pdf#015.

36. Maternal and Child Health Bureau, "Child Health USA 2014" (Rockville, Maryland: U.S. Department of Health and Human Services Health Resources and Services Administration, 2015): 76, available at https://mchb.hrsa.gov/chusa14/dl/chusa14.pdf.

37. Dolores Acevedo-Garcia, Theresa Osypuk, and Nancy McArdle, "Racial/Ethnic Integration and Child Health Disparities," in *The Integration Debate: Competing Futures for American Cities*, ed. Chester Hartman and Gregory Squires (New York: Routledge, 2010), 135.

38. Centers for Disease Control and Prevention, "Vaccination Coverage among Children Aged 19–35 Months—United States, 2014" (Centers for Disease Control and Prevention, 2015): Table 2, available at https://www.cdc.gov/mmwr/preview/mmwrhtml/mm6433a1.htm.

39. "Pregnancy Mortality Surveillance System" (Centers for Disease Control and Prevention, 2016), available at https://www.cdc.gov/reproductivehealth/maternalinfanthealth/pmss.html.

40. Deidre M. Anglin et al., "Racial Discrimination Is Associated with Distressing Subthreshold Positive Psychotic Symptoms among U.S. Urban Ethnic Minority Young Adults," *Social Psychiatry and Psychiatric Epidemiology* 49, 10 (2014): 1545–1555, available at doi:10.1007/s00127-014-0870-8.

41. Mario Sims et al., "Perceived Discrimination and Hypertension among African Americans in the Jackson Heart Study," *American Journal of Public Health* 102, Suppl 2 (May 2012): S258–65, available at doi:10.2105/AJPH.2011.300523.

42. Elizabeth A. Pascoe and Laura Smart Richman, "Perceived Discrimination and Health: A Meta-Analytic Review," *Psychological Bulletin* 135, 4 (July 2009): 531–554, available at doi:10.1037/a0016059.

43. Bernard Rosner et al., "Blood Pressure Differences by Ethnic Group among United States Children and Adolescents," *Hypertension* 54, 3 (September 1, 2009): 502–508, available at doi:10.1161/HYPERTENSIONAHA.109.134049; Office of Minority Health, "Heart Disease and African Americans."

44. Lianne Tomfohr et al., "Everyday Discrimination and Nocturnal Blood Pressure Dipping in Black and White Americans," *Psychosomatic Medicine* 72, 3 (April 2010): 266–272, available at doi:10.1097/PSY.0b013e3181d0d8b2.

45. Sid Kirchheimer, "Racism Should Be a Public Health Issue," *Medscape,* January 9, 2003, article 44757.

46. Christina A. Clarke et al., "'Racial and Social Class Gradients in Life Expectancy in Contemporary California,'" *Social Science and Medicine* (1982) 70, 9 (May 2010): 1373–1380, available at doi:10.1016/j.socscimed.2010.01.003.

47. National Center for Health Statistics, "Health, United States, 2016: With Chartbook on Long-Term Trends in Health" (Hyattsville, MD: U.S. Department of Health and Human Services, 2017): 116, available at https://www.cdc.gov/nchs/data/hus/hus16 .pdf#015; Office of Minority Health, "Heart Disease and African Americans"; Office of Minority Health, "Stroke and African Americans."

48. Elizabeth Sweet et al., "Relationships between Skin Color, Income, and Blood Pressure among African Americans in the CARDIA Study," *American Journal of Public Health* 97, 12 (December 2007): 2253–2259, available at doi:10.2105/AJPH.2006.088799.

49. Emily A. Benfer, "Contaminated Childhood: How the United States Failed to Prevent the Chronic Lead Poisoning of Low-Income Children and Communities of Color," *Harvard Environmental Law Review* 4 (2017), available at https://papers.ssrn.com /sol3/papers.cfm?abstract_id=2977465.

50. U.S. Department of Health and Human Services, "Use of Selected Clinical Preventive Services to Improve the Health of Infants, Children, and Adolescents—United States, 1999–2011," *Centers for Disease Control and Prevention Morbidity and Mortality Weekly Report, Supplement* 63, 2 (2014): 39, available at https://www.cdc.gov /mmwr/pdf/other/su6302.pdf.

51. Michigan Civil Rights Commission, "The Flint Water Crisis: Systemic Racism through the Lens of Flint" (Michigan Civil Rights Commission, 2017): 1, available at http:// www.michigan.gov/documents/mdcr/VFlintCrisisRep-F-Edited3-13-17_554317_7.pdf.

52. Mona Hanna-Attisha et al., "Elevated Blood Lead Levels in Children Associated with the Flint Drinking Water Crisis: A Spatial Analysis of Risk and Public Health Response," *American Journal of Public Health* 106, 2 (February 2016): 283–290, available at doi:10.2105/AJPH.2015.303003.

53. Michigan Civil Rights Commission, "The Flint Water Crisis."

54. Joshua Schneyer, "Reuters Investigates: Lead's Hidden Toll Is Felt across L.A.," Reuters, 2017, available at http://www.reuters.com/investigates/special-report/usa -lead-la/; Eric M. Roberts et al., "Assessing Child Lead Poisoning Case Ascertainment in the US, 1999–2010," *Pediatrics,* April 27, 2017, available at doi:10.1542/peds.2016 -4266. Centers for Disease Control and Prevention, "Childhood Lead Poisoning Data,

Statistics, and Surveillance," Centers for Disease Control and Prevention, 2016, available at https://www.cdc.gov/nceh/lead/data/index.htm.

CHAPTER 6. WHITE FRAGILITY, WHITE FAILURE, WHITE FEAR

The epigraph is from James Baldwin, *The Fire Next Time* (New York: Vintage, 1993), 44.

1. W.E.B. Du Bois, *Black Reconstruction in America, 1860–1880* (New York: Free Press, 1992), 700–701.

2. Michael Rogin, *Blackface, White Noise: Jewish Immigrants in the Melting Pot* (Berkeley: University of California Press, 1998).

3. Du Bois, *Black Reconstruction in America*, 357–358.

4. Chana Kai Lee, *For Freedom's Sake: The Life of Fannie Lou Hamer* (Urbana: University of Illinois Press, 2000), 135.

5. John Bracey, "How Racism Harms White Americans," Media Education Foundation, available at http://www.mediaed.org/transcripts/How-Racism-Harms-White-Americans-Transcript.pdf, accessed July 27, 2017.

6. Du Bois, *Black Reconstruction in America*, 701.

7. Karen Workman and Andrea Kannapell, "The Charleston Shooting: What Happened," *New York Times*, June 18, 2105; "Here are the 19 Heinous Words Charleston Shooter Allegedly Told Victims Before Opening Fire," available at http://www.western journalism.com/here-are-the-19-heinou-words-charleston-shorter-alle, accessed August 30, 2105.

8. Lizette Alvarez and Alan Blinder, "Recalling Nine Spiritual Mentors, Gunned Down during Night of Devotion, *New York Times*, June 18, 2015, available at http://www .nytimes.com/2015/06/19/us/nine-victims-of-charleston-church-shooting-remembered, accessed August 30, 2015.

9. Associated Press, "Charleston Shooting Suspect Dylann Roof Feared 'Blacks Were Taking Over the World,'" *New Orleans Times-Picayune*, June 19, 2015, available at http:// blog.nola.com/crime_impact/print.html?entry=/2015/06/charleston_gunman_roof_ra, accessed August 30, 2015.

10. David Remnick, "Mercy and a Manifesto in Charleston," *New Yorker* June 20, 2015, available at http://www.newyorker.com/news/news-desk/mercy-and-a-manifesto -in-charleston; Lenny Bernstein, Sari Horwitz, and Peter Holley, "Dylann Roof's Racist Manifesto: 'I Have no Choice,'" *Washington Post*, June 20, 2015, available at http:// www.washingtonpost.com/national/health-science/authorities-investigate-whether-ra, accessed August 30, 2015.

11. Bernstein, Horwitz, and Holley, "Dylann Roof's Racist Manifesto."

12. Bernstein, Horwitz, and Holley, "Dylann Roof's Racist Manifesto."

13. Pierre Thomas and Jack Colherty, "Dylann Roof Indicted on Federal Hate Crime Charges in Charleston Church Massacre, Court Documents Say," *ABC News* 2015, available at http://abcnews.go.com/US/dylann-roof-hit-federal-hate-crime-charges-charleston /print?id=, accessed August 30, 2015.

14. Vincent Harding, *There Is A River: The Black Struggle for Freedom in America* (San Diego: Harcourt Brace, 1981), 67.

15. Douglas Eggerton, "The Long Troubled History of Charleston's Emanuel AME Church," *New Republic*, June 18, 2015.

16. Jonathan Weisman, "Killings Add a Painful Chapter in Storied History of Charleston," *New York Times*, June 18, 2015; Harding, *There Is a River*, 65–72.

17. Associated Press, "Charleston Shooting Suspect Dylann Roof Feared 'Blacks Were Taking Over the World.'"

18. Remnick, "Mercy and a Manifesto in Charleston."

19. Charles Murray and Richard Herrnstein, *The Bell Curve: Intelligence and Class Structure in American Life* (New York: Free Press, 1994); James Q. Wilson and Richard Herrnstein, *Crime and Human Nature: The Definitive Study of the Causes of Crime* (New York: Simon and Schuster), 1985; Daniel Goleman, "Richard Herrnstein, 64, Dies; Backed Nature over Nurture," *New York Times*, September 16, 1994, available at http://www.nytimes.com/1994/09/16/obituaries/richard-herrnstein-64-dies-backed-nature-over-nurture.html, accessed August 6, 2107.

20. Frances Robles, "Dylann Roof Had AR-15 Parts during Police Stop in March, Record Shows," *New York Times*, June 26, 2015.

21. Jean Marbella, "James Jackson Indicted for Murder as Act of Terrorism, Hate crime in Stabbing of Black Man in New York," *Baltimore Sun*, March 27, 2017, available at http://www.baltimoresun.com/news/maryland/crime/bs-md-jackson-indicted-20170327-story.html, a Accessed July 17, 2017.

22. Matthew Haad and Jacey Fortin, "Two Killed in Portland While Trying to Stop Anti-Muslim Rant, Police Say," *New York Times*, May 27, 2017, available at https://www.nytimes.com/2017/05/27/us/portland-train-attack-muslim-rant.html, accessed July 18, 2017.

23. Gaby Del Valle, "Accused Killer of Black Soldier Liked Pro-Trump, Pro-White Memes," *Daily Beast*, May 22, 2017, available at http://www.thedailybeast.com/accused-killer-of-black-soldier-liked-pro-trump-pro-white-memes, accessed July 22, 2017; Carrie Wells, "Police, FBI Investigating University of Maryland Killing as Possible Hate Crime." *Baltimore Sun*, May 21, 2017, available at http://www.baltimoresun.com/news/maryland/crime/, accessed July 22, 2017.

24. Matt Stevens, "Kansas Man Indicted on Hate Crime Charges in Shooting of Indian Immigrants," *New York Times*, June 9, 2017.

25. Steven Yaccino, Michael Schwartz, and Marc Santora, "Gunman Kills 6 at a Sikh Temple Near Milwaukee," *New York Times*, August 5, 2012, available at www.nytimes.com/2012/08/06/shooting-reported-at-temple-in-wisconsin.html?_r=1&pagewanted=...; Erica Goode and Serge F. Kovlaeski, "Wisconsin Killer Fed and Was Fueled by Hate Driven Music," *New York Times*, August 6, 2012, available at www.nytimes.com/2012/06/07/us/army-veteran-identified-as-suspect-in-wisconsin-shooting.html?pagewanted=all, accessed August 18, 2012.

26. James McPherson, *The Illustrated Battle Cry of Freedom: The Civil War Era* (New York: Oxford University Press, 2003), 118.

27. David Wiegel, "The Joe Wilson 'You Lie' AR-15 Lower Receiver," *Slate* January 12, 2011, available at http://www.slate.com/blogs/weigel/2011/01/12/the_joe_wilson_you_lie_ar_15_lower_receiver.html, accessed August 5, 2017.

28. Richard Rothstein, *The Color of Law* (New York: Liveright, 2017), 40–41.

29. "Representative Peter King: There Are 'Too Many Mosques in This Country," *Politico Live*, available at www.politico.com/blogs,tehcrypt/0907/Rep_King_There_are_too_,many_mosques_in_this_country_.html, accessed July 14, 2012. Representative King later contended that he had been quoted out of context by the conservative blog Politico and that his position was that there are too many mosques that do not cooperate with law enforcement. The video of his statement, however, shows that King clearly said "There are too many mosques in this country, too many people sympathetic to radical Islam."

30. Scott Rothschild, "Kansas Legislator Suggests Using Hunters in Helicopters to Control Illegal Immigration, Likens Immigrants to Feral Hogs," *Lawrence Journal -World*, March 14, 2011, available at www2.ljworld.com/news/2011/mar/14/legislators -comment-illegal-immigration-critcized/, accessed July 14, 2012.

31. Because the initial police report was incorrect, many media outlets described Martin as carrying Arizona iced tea when in fact it was a fruit drink of that brand.

32. Lisa Bloom, *Suspicion Nation: The Inside Story of the Trayvon Martin Injustice and Why We Continue to Repeat It* (Berkeley, CA: Counterpoint, 2014), 85–87.

33. Carol Anderson, "Ferguson Isn't about Black Rage Against cops. It's white rage against Progress," *Washington Post*, August 29, 2014.

34. Bloom, *Suspicion Nation*, 27.

35. Bloom, *Suspicion Nation*, 71.

36. Bloom, *Suspicion Nation*, 103.

37. Mark Geragos, "Trayvon Was Black. It Matters," July 17, 2013, available at http:// www.geragos.com/blog/?p=13, accessed July 27, 2017.

38. Jonathan Capehart, "George Zimmerman's Relevant past," *Washington Post*, May 28, 2013, available at https://www.washingtonpost.com/blogs/post-partisan/wp/2013/05/28/ george-zimmermans-relevant-past/?utm_term=.a8bc9d9b52b0, accessed July 28, 2017.

39. Matthew Lysiak, "George Zimmerman Lost job as Party Security Guard for Being too Aggressive, Ex-Co-Worker Says," *New York Daily News*, March 29, 2012.

40. Capehart, "George Zimmerman's Relevant Past."

41. Antonia Blumberg, "George Zimmerman Says Killing Trayvon Martin Was God's 'Plan,' but These Christians Don't Agree," *Huffington Post*, March 25, 2015, available at http://www.huffingtonpost.com/2015/03/25/george-zimmerman-gods-plan _n_6938456.html, accessed July 29, 2017.

42. Gideon Resnick, "George Zimmerman Taunts Trayvon Martin's Parents: They Didn't Raise Their Son Right," *Daily Beast*, May 17, 2016, available at http://www.thedai lybeast.com/george-zimmerman-taunts-trayvon-martins-parents-they-didnt-raise-their -son-right, accessed July 29, 2017.

43. Frances Robles, "Records Show George Zimmerman Got D's in Criminal Justice Classes," *Miami Herald*, August 9, 2012, available at http://www.miamiherald.com/latest -news/article1941880.html, accessed July 29, 2017.

44. Holly Yan, "George Zimmerman's Encounters with the Law and Public Spotlight," CNN, May 12, 2015, available at http://www.cnn.com/2015/05/12/us/george-zimmerman -timeline/.

45. Igor Volsky, "7 Mind Blowing Moments from Zimmerman Juror B37's First Interview," *Think Progress*, July 16, 2013, available at https://thinkprogress.org/7-mind -blowing-moments-from-zimmerman-juror-b37s-first-interview-cfcc43d3974a, accessed July 28, 2017.

46. Charles Payne, *I've Got the Light of Freedom: The Organizing Tradition and the Mississippi Freedom Struggle* (Berkeley: University of California Press, 2007), 153.

47. "Trayvon Martin Gun Range Targets Were Sold Online 'to Make Money Off the Controversy,' Report Says," CBS News, available at www.cbs.news.com/.../trayvon -martin-gun-range-targets-were sold-online-to-make-money-off-the controv, accessed July 14, 2012.

48. Bloom, *Suspicion Nation*,180.

49. Bloom, *Suspicion Nation*, 251.

50. Zimmerman's father was white and his mother was a Peruvian immigrant. One member of the six-person jury was a Latina. Zimmerman often described himself as

Latino. His zeal to protect white property from the presence of Blacks, even though the subdivision where he lived was 20 percent Black, demonstrated the possessive investment in whiteness. Similarly, the Latina juror felt overwhelmed by the certainty of the five jurors who were white. Because for me whiteness is not a skin color but a condition of structured advantage and a culture of condoning that advantage, Zimmerman's Peruvian mother and Daniel Holtzclaw's Japanese mother do not exempt them from the possessive investment in whiteness any more than Clarence Thomas's skin and phenotype do. The object of inquiry in this book is a whiteness that is not reducible to white people.

51. Gilbert C. Gee and Chandra L. Ford, "Structural Racism and Health Inequities," *Du Bois Review* 8, 1 (2011): 116.

52. Rainbow Push Press Release, "Charleston Shootings Reflect Terrorism—Not Its Origins," June 18, 2015, available at http://rainbowpush.org/news/single/charleston_shootings_reflect_terrorism_-_not_its_origins.

53. Moon-kie Jung, *Beneath the Surface of White Supremacy: Denaturalizing U.S. Racisms Past and Present* (Stanford, CA: Stanford University Press, 2015), 43–44.

54. Gilbert C. Gee and Chandra L. Ford, "Structural Racism and Health Inequities," *Du Bois Review* 8, 1 (2011): 116.

55. For the concept of slow violence in a slightly different context, see Rob Nixon, *Slow Violence and the Environmentalism of the Poor* (Cambridge, MA: Harvard University Press, 2013).

56. Satcher quoted in Martin Frazier, "Health Care Racism Kills 83,000 Yearly," *Peoples World*, May 13, 2005, available at http://peoplesworld.org/health-care-racism-kills-83,000-yearly/, accessed August 31, 2015; D. Satcher et al., "What if We Were Equal? A Comparison of the Black-White Mortality Gap in 1960s and 2000," *Health Affairs* 24, 2 (March–April 2005): 459–464.

57. Martin Frazier, "Health Care Racism Kills 83,000 Yearly," *Peoples World*, May 13, 2005, available at http://peoplesworld.org/health-care-racism-kills-83,000-yearly/, accessed August 31, 2015.

58. Annie Sweeney, "Inside the Failed Prosecution of Chicago Detective Dante Servin," *Chicago Tribune*, July 3, 2015.

59. Victoria Law, "Why Is Marissa Alexander Still Being Punished for Fighting Back?" *The Nation*, January 28, 2015.

60. Associated Press, "Final Charge Dropped against Detroit Cop in Fatal Raid," *New York Times*, January 30, 20; George Hunter, "Cop in Aiyana Stanley-Jones Shooting Back on Job," *Detroit News*, April 17, 2015.

61. Christopher Maag, "Police Shooting of Mother and Infant Exposes a City's Racial Tension," *New York Times*, January 30, 2008, available at http://www.nytimes.com/2008/01/30/us/30lima.html, accessed July 26, 2017.

62. Michelle Dean, "'Black Women Unnamed': How Tanisha Anderson's Bad Day Turned into Her Last," *The Guardian*, June 5, 2015, available at https://www.theguardian.com/us-news/2015/jun/05/black-women-police-killing-tanisha-anderson, accessed September 10, 2017.

63. Christine Hauser, "Sandra Bland's Family Settles $1.9 Million Civil Suit, Lawyer Says," *New York Times*, September 15, 2016, available at https://www.nytimes.com/2016/09/16/us/sandra-bland-family-settlement-19-million-lawsuit.html, accessed September 10, 2017.

64. George Lipsitz, *How Racism Takes Place* (Philadelphia: Temple University Press, 2011), 42–43.

65. Dorothy Roberts, "Prison and Foster Care: The Systemic Punishment of Black Mothers," *UCLA Law Review* 59, 6 (2012): 1476–1500.

66. George Lipsitz, "'In an Avalanche Every Snowflake Pleads Not Guilty': The Collateral Consequences of Mass Incarceration and Impediments to Women's Fair Housing Rights," *UCLA Law Review* 59, 6 (2012): 1747–1809.

67. Joey Mogul, Andrea Ritchie, and Kay Whitlock, *Queer (In)Justice: The Criminalization of LGBT People in the United States* (Boston: Beacon, 2011), xii, 47.

68. Ben Fenwick and Alan Schwarz, "In Rape Case of Oklahoma Officer, Victims Hope Conviction Will Aid Cause," *New York Times*, December 12, 2015, available at https://www.nytimes.com/2015/12/12/us/daniel-holtzclaw-oklahoma-police-rape-case.html, accessed July 26, 2017.

69. Andrea J. Ritchie, "A Warrant to Search Your Vagina," *New York Times*, July 21, 2017, available at https://www.nytimes.com/2017/07/21/opinion/sunday/black-women-police-brutality.html, accessed July 26, 2017.

70. Holtzclaw's father is white and his mother is Japanese. He clearly thought of himself as white, however, as evidenced by invoking his possessive investment in whiteness as he committed his crimes against Black women. See Goldie Taylor, "Cop Used Whiteness as His Weapon to Rape Black Women," *Daily Beast*, December 11, 2015, available at http://www.thedailybeast.com/goldie-taylorcop-used-whiteness-as-his-weapon-to-rape-black-women, accessed July 26, 2017.

71. Dave Phillips, "Former Oklahoma City Police Officer Found Guilty of Rapes," *New York Times*, December 10, 2105, available at https://www.nytimes.com/2015/12/11/us/former-oklahoma-city-police-officer-found-guilty-of-rapes.html, accessed July 26, 2017.

72. Ben Fenwick and Alan Schwarz, "In Rape Case of Oklahoma Officer, Victims Hope Conviction Will Aid Cause," *New York Times*, December 12, 2015, available at https://www.nytimes.com/2015/12/12/us/daniel-holtzclaw-oklahoma-police-rape-case.html, accessed July 26, 2017.

73. Ben Fenwick and Alan Schwarz, "In Rape Case of Oklahoma Officer, Victims Hope Conviction Will Aid Cause," *New York Times*, December 12, 2015, available at https://www.nytimes.com/2015/12/12/us/daniel-holtzclaw-oklahoma-police-rape-case.html, accessed July 26, 2017.

74. Albert Memmi, *The Colonizer and the Colonized* (Boston: Beacon Press, 1965), 73.

75. Bernstein, Horwitz, and Holley, "Dylann Roof's Racist Manifesto."

76. Ian Haney Lopez, *White by Law* (New York: New York University Press, 2006), 82.

77. Jessica Garrison, "County Records Show Unpaid Tax Lien on Donnelly's Former Business," *Los Angeles Times,* March 19, 2014, available at http://www.latimes.com/local/la-me-tim-donnelly-20140320-story.html, accessed July 29, 2017.

78. Yasha Levine, "Tim Donnelly, Weimar Republican . . . and next Governor of California?" available at https://pando.com/2014/05/19/tim-donnelly-weimar-republican-and-next-governor-of-california/, accessed July 29, 2017.

79. Leo Chavez, *The Latino Threat: Constructing Immigrants, Citizens and the Nation* (Stanford, CA: Stanford University Press, 2008); Dominic Vitiello and Thomas J. Sugrue, eds., *Immigration and Metropolitan Revitalization in the United States* (Philadelphia: University of Pennsylvania Press, 2017); Julie A. Dowling and Jonathan Xavier Inda, eds., *Governing Immigration through Crime: A Reader* (Stanford, CA: Stanford University Press, 2013); Veronika Bondarenko and Skye Gold, "Despite Trump's Speech,

Immigrants Commit Far Fewer Crimes than Native-Born Americans," *Business Insider*, March 1, 2017, available at http://www.businessinsider.com/immigrants-commit-less -crime-than-native-born-americans-trump-speech-2017-3, accessed July 30, 2017.

80. Ruth Wilson Gilmore, *Golden Gulag: Prisons, Crisis, Surplus and Opposition in Globalizing California* (Berkeley: University of California Press, 2007); Mike Davis, *City of Quartz: Excavating the Future in Los Angeles* (New York: Verso, 2006); Sidney Plotkin and William Scheuerman, *Private Interests, Public Spending: Balanced Budget Conservatism and the Fiscal Crisis* (Boston: South End, 1999); Kitty Calavita, "The New Politics of Immigration: 'Balanced Budget Conservatism' and the Symbolism of Proposition 187," *Social Problems* 43, 3 (August 1996): 284–305.

81. Jessica Garrison, "Tim Donnelly Sees His Business Failure as Asset in Governor's Race," *Los Angeles Times*, May 21, 2014, available at http://www.latimes.com/local/politics /la-me-donnelly-20140522-story.html, accessed July 29, 2017.

82. Garrison, "Tim Donnelly Sees His Business Failure as Asset in Governor's Race."

83. Garrison, "Tim Donnelly Sees His Business Failure as Asset in Governor's Race."

84. Gene Maddaus, "Tim Donnelly's Revolution," *LA Weekly*, October 28, 2010, available at http://www.laweekly.com/news/tim-donnellys-revolution-2167556, accessed July 29, 2017.

85. Levine, "Tim Donnelly, Weimar Republican."

86. Jessica Garrison, "County Records Show Unpaid Tax Lien on Donnelly's Former Business," *Los Angeles Times*, March 19, 2014, available at http://www.latimes.com/local /la-me-tim-donnelly-20140320-story.html, accessed July 29, 2017.

87. Levine, "Tim Donnelly, Weimar Republican."

88. Harel Shapira, *Waiting for Jose: The Minutemen's Pursuit of America* (Princeton, NJ: Princeton University Press, 2013), 146.

89. Shapira, *Waiting for Jose*, 145.

90. Martin Wisckol, "Minutemen to Patrol Border in 4 States," *Orange County Register*, March 30, 2006, http://www.ocregister.com/2006/03/30/minutemen-to-patrol -border-in-4-states/, accessed August 2, 2017.

91. Martin Wisckol, "Gilchrist Staying the Course in Congressional District Bid," *Orange County Register*, December 2, 2005, available at http://www.ocregister .com/2005/12/02/gilchrist-staying-the-course-in-congressional-district-bid/, accessed August 1, 2017.

92. Jerry Seper, "Minutemen not Watching over Funds," available at http://www .washingtontimes.com/news/2006/jul/19/20060719-091346-2988r/, accessed August 2, 2017.

93. David Holthouse, "Jim Gilchrist Fired by Minuteman Project," *Intelligence Report,* Southern Poverty Law Center, July 1, 2007, available at https://www.splcenter.org /fighting-hate/intelligence-report/2007/jim-gilchrist-fired-minuteman-project, accessed August 1, 2007.

94. Elvia Malagon, "Man in Arizona Slayings Was Violent Polk Teen," *The Ledger,* May 8, 2012, available at http://www.theledger.com/news/20120508/man-in-arizona-slay ings-was-violent-polk-teen, accessed August 1, 2017; Sarah Lynch, "Mesa Parade Panel Weighs Ready Military Record," *East Valley Tribune,* September 28, 2006, available at http://www.eastvalleytribune.com/local/mesa/mesa-parade-panel-weighs-ready-military -record/article_7e1ad521-f81d-5fb0-a3d9-5a14b3eb5005.html, accessed August 1, 2017.

95. Michael Muskal, "Border Guard Founder J. T. Ready Blamed in Arizona Murder-Suicide," *Los Angeles Times*, May 3, 2012, available at http://articles.latimes.com/2012 /may/03/nation/la-na-nn-arizona-shooting-20120503, accessed August 2, 2017.

96. Jerry Seper, "Border Activist in Hiding from Court," *Washington Times*, June 14, 2010, available at http://www.washingtontimes.com/news/2010/jun/14/border-activist-in-hiding-from-court/, accessed August 1, 2017.

97. Christine Hauser, "Minuteman Co-Founder Sentenced to 19½ years for Molesting 5-Year-Old," *New York Times*, July 12, 2106, available at https://www.nytimes.com/2016/07/13/us/minuteman-christopher-simcox-sentenced-for-child-molestation.html, accessed August 1, 2017; Stephen Lemons, "Chris Simcox's Three Daughters Testify against Him in Child Molestation Trial," *Phoenix New Times*, May 24, 2016, available at http://www.phoenixnewtimes.com/news/chris-simcoxs-three-daughters-testify-against-him-in-child-molestation-trial-8319223, accessed August 1, 2017.

98. Kevin Wadlow, "Charleston Shooter Roof Left Little Fingerprint on the Keys," *Florida Keys News*, July 27, 2015, available at http://www.flkeysnews.com/news/article79615597.html, accessed August 3, 2017.

99. Chris Dixon and Kevin Sack, "A Friend Lied about Dylann Roof's Massacre Plan. Now He'll Go to Prison," *New York Times*, March 21, 2017, available at https://www.nytimes.com/2017/03/21/us/joey-meek-dylann-roof-charleston-church-shooting.html?mcubz=3, accessed August 18, 2017.

100. Herbert Blumer, "Race Prejudice as a Sense of Group Position," *Pacific Sociological Review* 1 (1958): 4.

101. Blumer, "Race Prejudice as a Sense of Group Position," 6.

102. United States Department of Labor, *The Negro Family, the Case of National Action* (Washington, DC: United States Government Printing Office, 1965). In the Johnson administration, Moynihan proposed some remedial action to shore up what he perceived to be the imperiled Black family, mainly, service in the military (which at that time meant in the Vietnam War) as a way to expose Black men to patriarchal male leadership and save them from what Moynihan perceived to be the excessive power of Black women. The misogynist and racist elements in his thought expanded over time. As an official in the Nixon administration, he moved away from advocating remedial policies to instead champion what he cruelly described as "benign neglect." See Stephen Steinberg, "The Moynihan Report at Fifty: The Long Reach of Intellectual Racism," *Boston Review*, June 24, 2015, available at http://bostonreview.net/us/stephen-steinberg-moynihan-report-black-families-nathan-glazer, accessed August 5, 2017.

103. Kent A. Ono and John M. Sloop, *Shifting Borders: Rhetoric, Immigration and California's Proposition 187* (Philadelphia: Temple University Press, 2002), 30.

104. Samuel P. Huntington, *Who Are We? The Challenges to America's National Identity* (New York: Simon and Schuster, 2004).

105. Jason Richwine and Robert Rector, "The Fiscal Cost of Unlawful Immigrants and Amnesty to the U.S. Taxpayer," The Heritage Foundation, May 6, 2013, available at http://www.heritage.org/immigration/report/the-fiscal-cost-unlawful-immigrants-and-amnesty-the-us-taxpayer, accessed August 5, 2017.

106. W. W. Houston, "The Richwine Affair," Democracy in America, *The Economist*, May 14, 2013, available at https://www.economist.com/blogs/democracyinamerica/2013/05/immigration-and-iq-0, accessed August 5, 2017.

107. Houston, "The Richwine Affair."

108. Craig Steven Wilder, *Ebony & Ivy: Race, Slavery and the Troubled History of America's Universities* (New York: Bloomsbury Press, 2013), 11.

109. Lauren Berlant, "Cruel Optimism," University of Pittsburgh Humanities Center, available at http://www.humcenter.pitt.edu/sites/default/files/Berlant%20Intro_Chapter%201.pdf, accessed August 5, 2017.

110. Here, I am paraphrasing a line from Toni Cade Bambara's novel *The Salt Eaters*.

CHAPTER 7. A PIGMENT OF THE IMAGINATION

The epigraph is from James Baldwin, *The Devil Finds Work* (New York: Dell, 1976), 71–72.

1. Thom Weildlich, "Executive Life; The Younger Face of the Boardroom," *New York Times*, February 2, 2003, available at http://www.nytimes.com/2003/02/02/business/exec utive-life-the-younger-face-of-the-boardroom.html?mcubz=0, accessed August 21, 2017.

2. Business Day, "Editors' Note," *New York Times*, February 9, 2003, available at http://www.nytimes.com/2003/02/09/business/editors-note.html?mcubz=0, accessed August 21, 2017.

3. Dominic Gates, "In Person; Boeing's Nicole Piasecki—Born into Aerospace Engineering," *Seattle Times*, June 28, 2011, available at http://www.seattletimes.com/busi ness/in-person-boeings-nicole-piasecki-8212-born-into-aerospace-engineering/, accessed August 21, 2017.

4. Gates, "In Person; Boeing's Nicole Piasecki."

5. Luke Charles Harris, *Nightline* interview, January 24, 2007, "Camden" transcript, Media Transcripts Inc. Transcript in author's possession courtesy of Luke Charles Harris.

6. *Nightline*, January 26, 2007, available at http://abcnews.go.com/2020/Video/player Index?id=2816480, accessed August 21, 2017.

7. Winona LaDuke, *All Our Relations* (San Francisco: Haymarket Books, 2017), 118, 119.

8. Roger Hayter, "'The War in the Woods': Post-Fordist Restructuring, Globalization, and the Contested Remapping of British Columbia's Forest Economy," *Annals of the Association of American Geographers* 93, 3 (September 2003): 706–729.

9. Richard Rothstein, *The Color of Law: A Forgotten History of How Our Government Segregated America* (New York: Liveright, 2017), 80.

10. Rothstein, *The Color of Law*, 166.

11. Harris, *Nightline* interview.

12. Douglas S. Massey and Nancy A. Denton, *American Apartheid* (Cambridge, MA: Harvard University Press,1993), 55.

13. Richard Rothstein, "Lessons: How Tax Code Worsens Education Gap," *New York Times*, April 25, 2001, available at http://www.nytimes.com/2001/04/25/nyregion /lessons-how-tax-code-worsens-education-gap.html, accessed August 21, 2017. Camden did receive direct Title 1 finding for poor children, which Princeton did not. But by allowing Princeton parents to deduct property tax payments from their federal returns, the federal government effectively subsidized the economic resources available to the Princeton school district.

14. Richard Rothstein, *The Color of Law: A Forgotten History of How Our Government Segregated America* (New York: Liveright, 2017), 129.

15. John Eligon, "Michael Brown Spent Last Weeks Grappling with Problems and Promise," *New York Times*, August 25, 2014, available at https://www.nytimes.com/2014 /08/25/us/michael-brown-spent-last-weeks-grappling-with-lifes-mysteries.html?mcubz=0, accessed August 21, 2017.

16. Paula Young Lee, "Robert Dear, 'Gentle Loner': The New York Times Reveals a Load of Biases in Early Round of Colorado Springs Planned Parenthood Coverage," *Salon*, November 30, 0215, available at http://gawker.com/new-york-times-decides-not -to-use-the-word-gentle-to-de-1745124689, accessed August 21, 2017.

17. Carol Anderson, *White Rage: The Unspoken Truth of Our Racial Divide* (New York: Bloomsbury, 2015), 3; Kimberly Jade Norwood, "From *Brown* to Brown: Sixty-Plus Years of Unequal Education," in *Ferguson's Fault Lines: The Race Quake That Rocked a Nation*, ed. Kimberly Jade Norwood (Chicago: American Bar Association, 2016), 98.

18. Jeff Chang, *We Gon' Be Alright: Notes on Race and Representation* (New York: Picador, 2016), 133.

19. This formulation comes from Jeff Chang, an astute observer of hip-hop and its detractors.

20. Julie Turkewitz, Richard Fausset, Alan Blinder, and Benjamin Mueller, "Robert Dear, Suspect in Colorado Killings, 'Preferred to Be Left Alone,'" *New York Times*, November 28, 2015, available at https://www.nytimes.com/2015/11/29/us/robert-dear -suspect-in-colorado-killings-preferred-to-be-left-alone.html?mcubz=3, accessed August 23, 2017.

21. Lee, "Robert Dear, 'Gentle Loner.'"

22. Turkewitz et al., "Robert Dear, Suspect in Colorado Killings, 'Preferred to Be Left Alone.'"

23. Turkewitz et al., "Robert Dear, Suspect in Colorado Killings, 'Preferred to Be Left Alone,'" 7.

24. In Philadelphia this practice is referred to as the "nickel ride." See Craig R. McCoy, "'Nickel Ride' Form of Police Abuse Persists," *Philadelphia Inquirer*, April 29, 2015, available at http://www.philly.com/philly/news/20150429_By_many_names_-__nickel _ride____rough_ride__-_entrenched_form_of_police_abuse_persists.html, accessed August 25, 2017.

25. Joseph Tanfani, "In Baltimore and Other Cities, Police Have Used 'Rough Rides' as Payback in the Past," *Los Angeles Times*, May 1, 2015, available at http://www.latimes .com/nation/nationnow/la-na-baltimore-rough-rides-20150501-story.html, accessed August 24, 2017. A state law capping settlement amounts led to a reduction in the award to Johnson.

26. Keeanga-Yamahtta Taylor, *From #Blacklivesmatter to Black Liberation* (Chicago: Haymarket Books, 2016), 76.

27. Carimah Townes, "Texas Senator Blamed Violence In Baltimore on 'Absent Fathers,' Has Nothing to Say about Waco Massacre," *Thinkprogress*, May 20, 2015, available at https://thinkprogress.org/texas-senator-blamed-violence-in-baltimore -on-absent-fathers-has-nothing-to-say-about-waco-massacre-fd0e7c154fda/, accessed August 24, 2017.

28. U.S. Department of Justice, Civil Rights Division, "Investigation of the Baltimore City Police Department," August 10, 2016, available at https://www.justice.gov/crt/file /883296/download, accessed August 24, 2017; Jay Stanley, "Baltimore Police Caught by Their Own Body Cameras Planting Evidence: Lessons," *ACLU*, August 7, 2017, available at https://thinkprogress.org/texas-senator-blamed-violence-in-baltimore-on-absent -fathers-has-nothing-to-say-about-waco-massacre-fd0e7c154fda/, accessed August 24, 201; Connor Friedersdorf, "The Brutality of Police Culture in Baltimore," *The Atlantic*, April 22, 2015, available at https://www.theatlantic.com/politics/archive/2015/04/the -brutality-of-police-culture-in-baltimore/391158/, accessed August 24, 2017.

29. Friedersdorf, "The Brutality of Police Culture in Baltimore."

30. U.S. Department of Justice, Civil Rights Division "Investigation of the Baltimore City Police Department."

31. George Lipsitz, *How Racism Takes Place* (Philadelphia: Temple University Press, 2011), 95–113; Harold McDougall, *Black Baltimore: A New Theory of Community* (Philadelphia: Temple University Press, 1993); W. Edward Orser, *Blockbusting in Baltimore: The Edmonson Village Story* (Lexington: University Press of Kentucky, 1994); Samuel Kelton Roberts, *Infectious Fear: Politics, Disease and the Health Effects of Segregation* (Chapel Hill: University of North Carolina Press, 2009); Rhonda Y. Williams,

The Politics of Public Housing: Black Women's Struggles against Urban Inequality (New York: Oxford, 2004).

32. Justin Fenton, "Report: Sandtown-Winchester Leads State in Number of People Incarcerated," *Baltimore Sun*, November 26, 2016, available at http://www.baltimoresun.com/news/maryland/crime/.

33. Keith Wallington and Diamonte Brown, "Structural Accountability after Freddie Gray," *Baltimore Sun*, May 5, 2015, available at http://www.baltimoresun.com/news/opinion/bs-ed-freddie-gray-legacy-20150505-story.html.

34. My preference, of course, would be that the aggrieved and suffering residents of Baltimore deploy nonviolent means of education, agitation, organization, and mobilization. The work I have done with the African American Policy Forum, the Woodstock Institute, and the National Fair Housing Alliance has focused on trying to augment collective capacity for peaceful change. Yet as Martin Luther King, Jr., and others have taught us, nonviolence is not simply the absence of violence. It requires the presence of justice. If we wish to make violence unacceptable, we have to make peaceful change plausible and present.

35. George Rawick, *From Sundown to Sunup: The Making of the Black Community* (Westport, CT: Greenwood Press, 1972), 125–149; Khalil Gibran Muhammad, *The Condemnation of Blackness: Race, Crime and the Making of Modern Urban America* (Cambridge, MA: Harvard University Press, 2010); Stephen Steinberg, *Turning Back: The Retreat from Racial Justice in American Thought and Policy* (Boston: Beacon Press, 1995).

36. Marco Williams, director, *Banished* (documentary film), Two Tone Productions and the Center for Investigative Reporting, 2007.

37. Kenneth J. Neubeck and Noel A. Cazenave, *Welfare Racism* (New York: Routledge, 2001).

38. Charles M. Blow, "Black Dads Are Doing Best of All," *New York Times*, June 8, 2015, available at https://www.nytimes.com/2015/06/08/opinion/charles-blow-black-dads-are-doing-the-best-of-all.html?mcubz=3, accessed August 26, 2017.

39. Jo Jones and William Mosher, "Fathers' Involvement with Their Children: United States, 2006–2010," National Health Statistics Reports, U.S. Department of Health and Human Services, Centers for Disease Control and Prevention, National Center for Health Statistics, n.71 December 20, 2013.

40. Justin Wolfers, David Leonhart, and Kevin Quealy, "1.5 Million Missing Black Men," *New York Times*, April 20, 2015, available at https://www.nytimes.com/interactive/2015/04/20/upshot/missing-black-men.html?mcubz=3.

41. Moon-kie Jung, *Beneath the Surface of White Supremacy: Denaturalizing U.S. Racisms Past and Present* (Stanford, CA: Stanford University Press, 2015), 145–167.

42. Peter Stallybrass and Allon White, *The Politics and Poetics of Transgression* (Ithaca, NY: Cornell University Press, 1986).

43. Ralph Ellison, *Invisible Man* (New York: Vintage Books, 1995), 200.

44. James Baldwin, *The Fire Next Time* (New York: Vintage Books, 1993), 92.

CHAPTER 8. WHITE DESIRE: REMEMBERING ROBERT JOHNSON

The epigraph is from James Baldwin, *The Devil Finds Work* (New York: Dell, 1976), 147.

1. "Every Crossroads Has a Story," *Living Blues,* November/December 1996, back cover.

2. Michael Schumacher, *Crossroads: The Life and Music of Eric Clapton* (New York: Hyperion, 1995), 19, 63, 99–100; Harry Shapiro, *Eric Clapton: Lost in the Blues* (New York: Da Capo, 1992), 11, 14.

3. Peter Guralnick, *Searching for Robert Johnson* (New York: Dutton, 1982); Francis Davis, *The History of the Blues: The Roots, the Music, the People, from Charley Patton to Robert Cray* (New York: Hyperion, 1995), 126; Marla C. Berns, ed., *"Dear Robert, I'll See You at the Crossroads": A Project by Renee Stout* (Santa Barbara, CA: University Art Museum, 1995); Walter Mosley, *RJ's Dream* (New York: Simon and Schuster, 1994); Walter Hill (director), *Crossroads,* Columbia Pictures, 1986; Ben Cromer, "Robert Johnson Tapes Found: Set Remastered," *Billboard,* December 7, 1996, 39.

4. Robert Farris Thompson, *Flash of the Spirit: African and Afro-American Art and Philosophy* (New York: Oxford, 1984), 19, 93.

5. Thompson, *Flash of the Spirit,* 19; see also Samuel A. Floyd, *The Power of Black Music: Interpreting Its History from Africa to the United States* (New York: Oxford University Press, 1995), 74, and Robert Palmer, *Deep Blues* (New York: Penguin, 1981), 59.

6. Hill, *Crossroads.*

7. Mosley, *RJ's Dream,* 143.

8. Nancy Rosenblum, "Romanticism," in *A Companion to American Thought,* ed. Richard Wightman Fox and James T. Kloppenberg (Oxford: Basil Blackwell, 1995), 601.

9. Shapiro, *Eric Clapton,* 14, 13.

10. Schumacher, *Crossroads,* 18, 19.

11. Schumacher, *Crossroads,* 205, 206; Shapiro, *Eric Clapton,* 145.

12. Guralnick, *Searching for Robert Johnson,* 15.

13. Guralnick, *Searching for Robert Johnson,* 17.

14. Palmer, *Deep Blues,* 113.

15. Guralnick, *Searching for Robert Johnson,* 12.

16. Palmer, *Deep Blues,* 57, 101.

17. Guralnick, *Searching for Robert Johnson,* 10–11.

18. Palmer, *Deep Blues,* 112.

19. Guralnick, *Searching for Robert Johnson,* 11, 20.

20. Palmer, *Deep Blues,* 59.

21. Palmer, *Deep Blues,* 62, 122.

22. Davis, *The History of the Blues,* 128; Palmer, *Deep Blues,* 80.

23. Palmer, *Deep Blues,* 119.

24. Lawrence Levine, *Black Culture and Black Consciousness: Afro-American Folk Thought from Slavery to Freedom* (New York: Oxford University Press, 1977), 10–11.

25. Edward Krehbiel, *Afro-American Folk Songs: A Study in Racial and National Music* (New York: Schirmer, 1914). I thank Jon Cruz for calling this information to my attention.

26. Guralnick, *Searching for Robert Johnson,* 31.

27. Palmer, *Deep Blues,* 120–121, 113, 175.

28. Chris Waterman, "'Corrine Corrina' and the Excluded Middle of the American Racial Imagination," in *Music and the Racial Imagination,* ed. P. Bohlman and R. Radano (Chicago: University of Chicago Press, 1998); B. B. King with David Ritz, *Blues All Around Me* (New York: Avon, 1996), 23.

29. Marla Berns, "On Love and Longing: Renee Stout Does the Blues," in Berns, *"Dear Robert, I'll See You at the Crossroads": A Project by Renee Stout* (Santa Barbara: University Art Museum, 1995), 42.

30. Holland Cotter, "Art That's Valued for What It Can Do," *New York Times,* July 18, 1993, sec. H.

31. Michael D. Harris, "Resonance, Transformation, and Rhyme: The Art of Renee Stout," in *Astonishment and Power,* ed. Wyatt MacGaffey and Michael D. Harris (Washington, DC: National Museum of African Art/Smithsonian Institution, 1993), 109.

32. Paul Gilroy, *Ain't No Black in the Union Jack* (Chicago: University of Chicago Press, 1987), 156, 158, 159.

33. George Rawick, *From Sundown to Sunup* (Westport, CT: Greenwood, 1972); Sterling Stuckey, *Slave Culture: Nationalist Theory and the Foundations of Black America* (New York: Oxford University Press, 1987).

34. Herman Gray, *Watching Race: Television and the Struggle for "Blackness"* (Minneapolis: University of Minnesota Press, 1995), quoted in Leland Ferguson, *Uncommon Ground: Archaeology and Early African America, 1650–1800* (Washington, DC: Smithsonian Institution Press, 1992), xiv.

35. Robert Farris Thompson, "The Song That Named the Land: The Visionary Presence of African-American Art," in *Black Art Ancestral Legacy: The African Impulse in African-American Art,* ed. Alvia Wardlaw (Dallas: Dallas Museum of Art, 1989), 97, 102, 127, 132.

36. Charles Joyner, *Down by the Riverside* (Urbana: University of Illinois Press, 1984), xxi.

37. Stuckey, *Slave Culture*; Sterling Stuckey, *Going through the Storm: The Influence of African American Art in History* (New York: Oxford University Press, 1994); Joseph E. Holloway and Winifred K. Vass, *The African Heritage of American English* (Bloomington: Indiana University Press, 1993); Melville Herskovitz, *The Myth of the Negro Past* (Boston: Beacon, 1958); LeRoi Jones, *Blues People* (New York: Morrow, 1963); Ben Sidran, *Black Talk* (New York: Holt, Rinehart, and Winston, 1971); John F. Szwed and Morton Marks, "The Afro-American Transformation of European Set Dances and Dance Suites," *Dance Research Journal* 20, 1 (Summer 1998): 29–36.

38. Arthur Schlesinger, Jr., *The Disuniting of America: Reflections on a Multicultural Society* (New York: Norton, 1991), 15, 82, 83, 85.

39. Of course, some Afrocentrists do work that conforms to Schlesinger's caricatures. But his citations of them are largely from journalistic sources; he offers little evidence that he has actually read their work. Moreover, his ignorance about the African presence in America leaves him poorly equipped to answer even these arguments, a circumstance he could have avoided simply by consulting the outstanding research of such writers as Sterling Stuckey, Lawrence Levine, Peter Wood, Robert Farris Thompson, Margaret Washington Creel, and George Rawick.

40. Carter G. Woodson, *The Negro in Our History* (Washington, DC: Associated Publishers, 1922), 628, quoted in Stuckey, *Going through the Storm,* 127.

41. Herskovitz, *Myth of the Negro Past*; Rawick, *Sundown to Sunup*; Jones, *Blues People*; Sidran, *Black Talk*; for a more recent discussion, see Mellonee V. Burnim and Portia K. Maultsby, *African American Music: An Introduction* (New York: Routledge, 2014), especially chapters 1 and 7.

42. Lawrence Levine, "Clio, Canons, and Culture," *Journal of American History* 80, 3 (December 1993): 849–867. See also the exchange of letters between Levine and Schlesinger in *Journal of American History* 81, 1 (June 1994): 367–368.

43. Arthur M. Schlesinger, Jr., "The Cult of Ethnicity, Good and Bad: A Historian Argues that Multiculturalism Threatens the Ideal that Binds America," *Time,* July 8, 1991, 21.

44. Renee Stout quoted in Julia Barnes Mandle, "Artists in the Exhibition/Interviews," in *Sites of Recollection: Four Altars and a Rap Opera,* ed. Williams College Museum of Art (Williamstown, MA: Williams College, 1992), 85.

45. Harris, "Resonance, Transformation, and Rhyme," 11, 114, 149.

46. Robert Farris Thompson, "Illuminating Spirits: 'Astonishment and Power' at the National Museum of African Art," *African Arts* 26 (October 1993): 66.

47. Harris, "Resonance, Transformation, and Rhyme," 114.

48. Harris, "Resonance, Transformation, and Rhyme," 111, 114, 149.

49. Florence Rubenfeld, "Renee Stout," *Arts Magazine,* May 1991, 79.

50. Thompson, "Song That Named the Land," 132, 131.

51. Thompson, "Illuminating Spirits," 68.

52. Harris, "Resonance, Transformation, and Rhyme," 111.

53. Thompson, "Song That Named the Land," 103.

54. Gylbert Coker, "African Art and the Black Folk Artist," in *African American Art,* ed. San Antonio Museum of Art (San Antonio, TX: San Antonio Museum of Art, 1994), 41.

55. Alvia J. Wardlaw, "Private Vision," in *Black Art Ancestral Legacy: The African Impulse in African-American Art,* ed. Alvia Wardlaw (Dallas: Dallas Museum of Art, 1989), 188.

56. Jontyle Theresa Robinson, "Recent Exhibitions: Black Art Ancestral Legacy," *African Arts* 24, 1 (January 1991): 29; Alvia J. Wardlaw, "Reclamations," in *Black Art Ancestral Legacy: The African Impulse in African-American Art,* ed. Alvia Wardlaw (Dallas: Dallas Museum of Art, 1989), 231.

57. Curtia James, "Astonishment and Power: Kongo Minkisi and the Art of Renee Stout," *Art News* 92, 8 (October 1993): 171.

58. Harris, "Resonance, Transformation, and Rhyme," 142, 151–154.

59. Stuckey, *Slave Culture,* 11.

60. Julia Barnes Mandle and Deborah Menaker Rothschild, eds., "Renee Stout," in *States of Recollection: Four Altars and a Rap Opera* (Williamstown, MA; Williams College Museum of Art, 1992), exhibition catalogue; Harris, "Resonance, Transformation, and Rhyme," 120; Thompson, "Song That Named the Land," 292.

61. Mandle, "Renee Stout," 91.

62. Mandle, "Renee Stout," 85.

63. Thompson, "Song That Named the Land," 100.

64. Gylbert Coker, "Nineteenth-Century African Art," in *African American Art,* ed. San Antonio Museum of Art (San Antonio: San Antonio Museum of Art, 1994), 8.

65. Alvia J. Wardlaw, "A Spiritual Libation: Promoting an African Heritage in the Black College," in *Black Art Ancestral Legacy: The African Impulse in African-American Art,* ed. Alvia Wardlaw (Dallas: Dallas Museum of Art, 1989), 54.

CHAPTER 9. *LEAN ON ME*: BEYOND IDENTITY POLITICS

The epigraph is from James Baldwin, *The Devil Finds Work* (New York: Dell, 1976), 134–135.

1. Jeffrey Page, "Joe Clark Faults Black Leaders," *Bergen Record,* November 15, 1989, sec. A.

2. Mike Kelly, "Time for the Boot," *Bergen Record,* November 14, 1989, sec. B.

3. Jeffrey Page, "Clark Asks Workers' Compensation," *Bergen Record,* September 6, 1990, sec. B.

4. Ronald Weitzer and Steven A. Tuch, "Race and Perceptions of Police Misconduct," *Social Problems* 51, 3 (2004): 315; James W. Buehler, "Racial/Ethnic Disparities in the Use of Lethal Force by US Police, 2010–2014," *American Journal of Public Health* 107, 2 (2016): 296.

5. Matthew J. Hickman, *Law Enforcement Management and Administrative Statistics: Citizen Complaints about Police Use of Force* (Washington, DC: U.S. Department of Justice, 2006), available at https://www.bjs.gov/content/pub/pdf/ccpuf.pdf, accessed

August 10, 2017, 2. Further, reliable data on police use of force is notoriously hard to come by: the paltry information available on police use of force over the last twenty years is plagued by serious methodological flaws, and has been critiqued as incomplete even by those who write the Bureau of Justice Statistics reports. See Matthew J. Hickman and Jane E. Poore, "National Data on Citizen Complaints about Police Use of Force: Data Quality Concerns and the Potential (Mis) Use of Statistical Evidence to Address Police Agency Conduct," *Criminal Justice Policy Review* 27, 5 (2016): 455–479; James J. Fyfe, "Too Many Missing Cases: Holes in Our Knowledge about Police Use of Force," *Justice Research and Policy* 4, 1–2 (2002): 87–102.

6. See, e.g., Callie Harbin Burt, Ronald L. Simons, and Frederick X. Gibbons, "Racial Discrimination, Ethnic-Racial Socialization, and Crime: A Micro-Sociological Model of Risk and Resilience," *American Sociological Review* 77, 4 (2012); Ruth D. Peterson and Lauren J. Krivo, "Macrostructural Analyses of Race, Ethnicity, and Violent Crime: Recent Lessons and New Directions for Research," *Annual Review of Sociology* 31, 1 (2005).

7. Judith R. Blau and Peter M. Blau, "The Cost of Inequality: Metropolitan Structure and Violent Crime," *American Sociological Review* 47, 1 (1982): 126.

8. John Hope Franklin, *The Color Line: Legacy for the Twenty-First Century* (Columbia: University of Missouri Press, 1993), 15, 16, 36, 37; Jane Mayer and Jill Abramson, *Strange Justice: The Selling of Clarence Thomas* (New York: Plume, 1995), 163.

9. Chester Himes, *If He Hollers Let Him Go* (New York: Thunder's Mouth Press, 1986), 41.

10. In this summary of Rawick's work I draw upon David Roediger's characteristically insightful essay, "Notes on Working Class Racism," in his indispensable collection *Towards the Abolition of Whiteness* (London: Verso, 1994), 61–68. I have also learned much from Paul Buhle's "Preface: Visions of Emancipation—Daniel De Leon, C.L.R. James, and George Rawick," in *Within the Shell of the Old: Essays on Workers' Self-Organization,* ed. Don Fitz and David Roediger (Chicago: Kerr, 1990), 1–4.

11. Lizabeth Cohen, *Making a New Deal* (Cambridge: Cambridge University Press, 1990), 323–361.

12. Roger Daniels, *Coming to America: A History of Immigration and Ethnicity in American Life* (New York: Harper, 1990), 282.

13. Baldwin, *The Devil Finds Work* (New York: Dial Press, 1976), 29–30.

14. Ruiz, *Cannery Women, Cannery Lives: Mexican Women, Unionization, and the California Food Processing Industry, 1930–1950* (Albuquerque: University of New Mexico Press, 1987); Robin D. G. Kelley, *Hammer and Hoe: Alabama Communists during the Great Depression* (Chapel Hill: University of North Carolina Press, 1990), 138–151.

15. Michael Rogin, *Blackface/White Noise: Jewish Immigrants in the Hollywood Melting Pot* (Berkeley: University of California Press, 1998), 253.

16. Patricia J. Williams, *The Rooster's Egg: On the Persistence of Prejudice* (Cambridge, MA: Harvard University Press, 1996), 65.

17. David Roediger, "Black Freedom and the WPA Slave Narratives: Dave Roediger Interviews George Rawick," in *Within the Shell of the Old: Essay on Workers' Self-Organization,* ed. Don Fitz and David Roediger (Chicago: Kerr, 1990), 10.

18. Toni Cade Bambara quoted in Darlene Clark Hine, Elsa Barkley Brown, and Rosalyn Terborg-Penn, eds., *Black Women in America: An Historical Encyclopedia* (Bloomington: Indiana University Press, 1993), 80.

19. W.E.B. Du Bois, *The Philadelphia Negro: A Social Study* (Philadelphia: University of Pennsylvania Press, 1995), 394.

CHAPTER 10. "FINDING FAMILIES OF RESEMBLANCE: 'FRANTIC TO JOIN . . . THE JAPANESE ARMY'"

The epigraph is from James Baldwin, *The Devil Finds Work* (New York: Dell, 1976), 100–101.

1. Arnold Shankman, *Ambivalent Friends: Afro-Americans View the Immigrant* (Westport, CT: Greenwood, 1982); Rosaura Sanchez, *Telling Identities: The Californio Testimonies* (Minneapolis: University of Minnesota Press, 1995), 50–95; Phil Ethington, *The Public City: The Political Construction of Urban Life in San Francisco, 1850–1990* (New York: Cambridge University Press, 1994), 170–206.

2. Malcolm X and Alex Haley, *The Autobiography of Malcolm X* (New York: Grove, 1965), 104–105, 106. Robin D. G. Kelley's adroit analysis of this incident in his splendid and indispensable book *Race Rebels* (New York: Free Press, 1994), 171, directed my attention to the significance of Malcolm's story. FBI Surveillance File on Malcolm X, November 30, 1954, quoted in Ferruccio Gambino, "Malcolm X, Laborer: From the Wilderness of the American Empire to Cultural Self Identification," Colloque 1984 de L'Association Francaise d'Eatudes Americaines Dourdan 25–27 Mai, 1984," unpublished manuscript in the author's possession, 17.

3. John Hope Franklin, "Their War and Mine," *Journal of American History 77*, 2 (September 1990): 576–577, 578.

4. Brenda Gayle Plummer, *Rising Wind: Black Americans and U.S. Foreign Affairs, 1935–1960* (Chapel Hill: University of North Carolina Press, 1996), 74–75. Plummer's comprehensive, persuasive, and fascinating book makes a major contribution to rethinking the roles of race and nation in the United States, past and present.

5. On the African American trickster tradition, see George Rawick, *From Sundown to Sunup: The Making of the Black Community* (Westport: Greenwood Press, 1972), 98. For the definitive analysis of the racialized nature of the Pacific war, see John Dower, *War without Mercy: Race and Power in the Pacific War* (New York: Pantheon, 1986).

6. Robin Kelley, *Hammer and Hoe: Alabama Communists during the Great Depression* (Chapel Hill: University of North Carolina Press, 1990).

7. Paul Gilroy, *The Black Atlantic* (Cambridge: Harvard University Press, 1993); Joseph E. Holloway, ed., *Africanism in American Culture* (Bloomington: Indiana University Press, 1991); George Lipsitz, *Dangerous Crossroads* (London: Verso, 1994).

8. Laura Mulvey, "Myth, Narrative, and Historical Experience," *History Workshop* 23 (Spring 1984): 3–19.

9. Gary Y. Okihiro, *Margins and Mainstreams* (Seattle: University of Washington Press, 1994), 44, 45; Daniel Rosenberg, "The IWW and Organization of Asian Workers in Early Twentieth-Century America," *Labor History 36*, 1 (Winter 1995): 77–87; Richard White, *It's Your Misfortune and None of My Own* (Tulsa: University of Oklahoma Press, 1991).

10. On exclusion acts, see Lisa Lowe, *Immigrant Acts: On Asian American Cultural Politics* (Durham: Duke University Press, 1996), 180–181. On the importation of Asian immigrant labor, reconstruction, and exclusion, see Okihiro, *Margins and Mainstreams*, 46–48.

11. Michael C. Robinson and Frank N. Schubert, "David Fagen: An Afro-American Rebel in the Philippines, 1899–1901," *Pacific Historical Review* 64, 1 (February 1975): 71, 72.

12. Robinson and Schubert, "David Fagen," 75, 81–82.

13. Nelson Peery, *Black Fire: The Making of an American Revolutionary* (New York: New Press, 1994), 277–278.

14. Tony Martin, *The Pan-African Connection: From Slavery to Garvey and Beyond* (Dover, MA: Majority, 1983), 64.

15. Garvey, quoted in Ernest V. Allen, "When Japan Was 'Champion of the Darker Races': Satokata Takahishi and the Flowering of Black Messianic Nationalism," *Black Scholar* 24, 1 (1995): 29.

16. Allen, "When Japan Was 'Champion of the Darker Races.'"

17. Michiko Hase, "Race, Status, and Culture in Trans-Pacific Perspective: African American Professionals in Japan," paper presented at the American Studies Association meetings, Nashville, TN, October 28, 1994, 9–10 (manuscript in the author's possession); W.E.B. Du Bois, *Dark Princess* (Jackson: University Press of Mississippi, Banner Books, 1995). See also Gilroy, *Black Atlantic.*

18. Du Bois, *Black Reconstruction in America* (see chap. 4, n. 49), 706, 704.

19. David J. Hellwig, "Afro-American Reactions to the Japanese and the Anti-Japanese Movement, 1906–1924," *Phylon* 37, 1 (1977): 94–96.

20. Quintard Taylor, "Blacks and Asians in a White City: Japanese Americans and African Americans in Seattle, 1890–1940," *Western Historical Quarterly* 23, 4 (November 1991): 426.

21. Karl Evanzz, *The Judas Factor: The Plot to Kill Malcolm X* (New York: Thunder's Mouth, 1992), 22.

22. E. U. Essien-Udom, *Black Nationalism: A Search for Identity in America* (Chicago: University of Chicago Press, 1962), 44–45, 74–75; Rony Martin, *Race First: The Ideological and Organizational Struggles of Marcus Garvey and the Universal Negro Improvement Association* (Westport, CT: Greenwood, 1976), 74–77; Humphrey J. Fischer, *Ahmadiyah* (Oxford: Oxford University Press, 1963); Gambino, "Malcolm X, Laborer," 25–26.

23. Dominic J. Capeci, Jr., *Race Relations in Wartime Detroit: The Sojourner Truth Housing Controversy of 1942* (Philadelphia: Temple University Press, 1984), 53; Evanzz, *The Judas Factor,* 24, 138; Dower, *War without Mercy,* 174.

24. Capeci, *Race Relations in Wartime Detroit,* 53.

25. The record of the Federal Bureau of Investigation in counterintelligence is such that any document the organization releases should be met with suspicion. Yet even if fabricated, this document at the very least shows the anxiety felt at high levels of government about the possibility of African Americans feeling allegiance to Japan because it was a nonwhite country. Evanzz, *The Judas Factor,* 138.

26. Ernest Allen, Jr., "Waiting for Tojo: The Pro-Japan Vigil of Black Missourians," *Gateway Heritage* 15, 2 (Fall 1994): 19, 26.

27. Robert A. Hill, ed., *The Marcus Garvey and UNIA Papers* (Berkeley: University of California Press, 1983), 596; Bob Kumamoto, "The Search for Spies: American Counterintelligence and the Japanese American Community, 1931–1942," *Amerasia Journal* 6, 2 (1979): 50.

28. Hill, *Marcus Garvey and UNIA Papers,* 506–507.

29. Allen, "When Japan Was 'Champion,'" 37.

30. Hill, *Marcus Garvey and UNIA Papers,* 506, 507.

31. Allen, "When Japan Was 'Champion,'" 25.

32. Gary Y. Okihiro, *Cane Fires: The Anti-Japanese Movement in Hawaii, 1865–1945* (Philadelphia: Temple University Press, 1991), 116–117.

33. Kumamoto, "The Search for Spies," 54.

34. Dabney, quoted in Dower, *War without Mercy,* 173–174.

35. Allen, "When Japan Was 'Champion,'" 37.

36. Capeci, *Race Relations in Wartime Detroit,* 54.

37. Allen, "Waiting for Tojo," 27, 28, 19.

38. Essien-Udom, *Black Nationalism*, 48–49, 67.

39. Malcolm X and Haley, *The Autobiography of Malcolm X*, 107.

40. Beth Bailey and David Farber, *The First Strange Place: Race and Sex in World War II Hawaii* (Baltimore, MD: Johns Hopkins University Press, 1992), 133; James Boggs, *The American Revolution: Pages from a Negro Worker's Notebook* (New York: Monthly Review, 1963), 79. I thank Suzanne Smith for calling my attention to this quote.

41. Walter White and Thurgood Marshall, *What Caused the Detroit Riot? An Analysis by Walter White and Thurgood Marshall* (New York: National Association for the Advancement of Colored People, 1943), 15; Roger Daniels, *Concentration Camps USA: Japanese Americans and World War II* (New York: Holt, Rinehart, and Winston, 1971), 36.

42. George Lipsitz, *Rainbow at Midnight: Labor and Culture in the 1940s* (Urbana: University of Illinois Press, 1994), 73–83; Bernard C. Nalty, *Strength for the Fight: A History of Black Americans in the Military* (New York: Free Press, 1986), 143–203.

43. Dennis Denmark Nelson, "The Integration of the Negro into the United States Navy, 1776–1947," master's thesis, Howard University, 1948, 28–29; Otto Lindenmeyer, *Black and Brave: The Black Soldier in America* (New York: McGraw-Hill, 1970), 88; Robert Ewell Greene, *Black Defenders of America, 1775–1973* (Chicago: Johnson, 1974), 202.

44. Nalty, *Strength for the Fight*, 186.

45. Nalty, *Strength for the Fight*, 166, 169.

46. Bailey and Farber, *The First Strange Place*, 159.

47. Cheryl Greenberg, "Black and Jewish Responses to Japanese Internment," *Journal of American Ethnic History* 14, 2 (Winter 1995): 22.

48. Chester Himes, *Lonely Crusade* (New York: Thunder's Mouth Press, 1986), 46.

49. Allen, "When Japan Was 'Champion,'" 37.

50. Dower, *War without Mercy*, 174.

51. Capeci, *Race Relations in Wartime Detroit*, 53; Himes, *If He Hollers Let Him Go*, 3 (see chap. 7, n. 6).

52. Greenberg, "Black and Jewish Responses," 19–20.

53. Taylor, "Blacks and Asians," 408, 413.

54. Records of the Federal Home Loan Bank Board of the Home Owners Loan Corporation, City Survey File, Los Angeles, 1939, Neighborhood D-50, D-33, D-30, Washington, DC; National Archives, Box 74, RG 195.

55. Taylor, "Blacks and Asians," 425.

56. Luis Valdez, *Envisioning California*, Keynote Address Publications Series, publication no. 3 (Sacramento: Center for California Studies, 1995), 7.

57. Beatrice Griffith, *American Me* (Cambridge, MA: Houghton Mifflin, 1948), 321; Taylor, "Blacks and Asians," 424.

58. Greenberg, "Black and Jewish Responses," 15, 18, 16, 18, 19.

59. Charles Jackson, "Plight of Japanese Americans," *Militant*, March 10, 1945, reprinted in C.L.R. James, George Breitman, and Edgar Keemer, *Fighting Racism in World War II* (New York: Monad, 1980), 342.

60. Daniels, *Concentration Campus USA*, 59, 105.

61. Nalty, *Strength for the Fight*, 167.

62. Bailey and Farber, *The First Strange Place*, 139, 161.

63. Bailey and Farber, *The First Strange Place*, 103, 162.

64. Daniels, *Concentration Camps USA*, 163.

65. Quoted in Mauricio Mazon, *The Zoot-Suit Riots: The Psychology of Symbolic Annihilation* (Austin: University of Texas Press, 1984), 19, 52. On the "zoot suit" riots, see Lipsitz, *Rainbow at Midnight*, 83–86 (see chap. 2, n. 44).

66. Mazon, *The Zoot-Suit Riots,* 23.

67. Daniels, *Concentration Camps USA,* 158; Himes, *Lonely Crusade,* 207. I thank Lisa Lowe for reminding me of the ways in which anti-Asian racism entails this rendering of Asian Americans as "permanently foreign."

68. Kumamoto, "The Search for Spies," 66–68.

69. Daniels, *Concentration Camps USA,* 159, 168.

70. Daniels, *Concentration Camps USA,* 162; Taylor, "Blacks and Asians," 428.

71. Daniels, *Concentration Camps USA,* 170. See also Kevin Allen Leonard, "'Is That What We Fought For?' Japanese Americans and Racism in California: The Impact of World War II," *Western Historical Quarterly* 21, 4 (November 1990): 480.

72. Baldwin, *The Fire Next Time* (New York: Dial, 1993), 63; Franklin, "Their War and Mine," 579.

73. Peery, *Black Fire,* 200; Walter White quoted in Dower, *War without Mercy,* 177–178.

74. Jose Limon, *Dancing with the Devil: Society and Cultural Poetics in Mexican American South Texas* (Madison: University of Wisconsin Press, 1994), 78.

75. Gambino, "Malcolm X, Laborer," 18, 19.

76. Yen Le Espiritu, *Asian American Panethnicity: Building Institutions and Identities* (Philadelphia, Temple University Press, 1992), 134–160.

77. Mary L. Dudziak, "Desegregation as Cold War Imperative," in *Critical Race Theory,* ed. Richard Delgado (Philadelphia: Temple University Press, 1995), 110–121.

78. LeRoi Jones, *Blues People* (New York: Morrow, 1963).

79. George Lipsitz, *A Life in the Struggle: Ivory Perry and the Culture of Oppositon* (Philadelphia: Temple University Press, 1995), 63.

80. Thomas R. Hietala, "Muhammad Ali and the Age of Bare Knuckle Politics," in *Muhammad Ali: The People's Champ,* ed. Elliott J. Gorn (Urbana: University of Illinois Press, 1995), 138; Franklin, *From Slavery to Freedom,* 474 (see introduction, n. 14).

81. Edward Escobar, "The Dialectics of Repression: The Los Angeles Police Department and the Chicano Movement, 1968–1971," *Journal of American History* 74, 4 (March 1993), 1483–1504; Carlos Munoz, *Youth, Identity, Power: The Chicano Movement* (London: Verso, 1989).

82. George Mariscal, "'Chale Con La Draft': Chicano Antiwar Writings," *Vietnam Generation* 6, 3–4 (1995):130.

83. Yasuko II Takezawa, *Breaking the Silence: Redress and Japanese American Ethnicity* (Ithaca, NY: Cornell University Press, 1995), 147, 148–149. See also David Gutierrez, *Walls and Mirrors: Mexican Americans, Mexican Immigrants, and the Politics of Ethnicity* (Berkeley: University of California Press), 1995. (see chap. 3, n. 20), for a discussion of how the Chicano movement grew from a similar desire to identify with blacks rather than with whites.

84. Quintard Taylor, *The Forging of a Black Community: Seattle's Central District from 1870 through the Civil Rights Era* (Seattle: University of Washington Press, 1994), 225–226.

85. Allen, "When Japan Was 'Champion,'" 33–37, 25.

86. Chester B. Himes, "Zoot Riots Are Race Riots," *The Crisis,* July 1948, 200.

87. Himes, "Zoot Riots Are Race Riots," 200, 201.

88. Bailey and Farber, *The First Strange Place,* 162.

89. Lipsitz, *Rainbow at Midnight,* 81–86 (see chap. 2, n. 44).

90. Robert Westbrook, "'I Want a Girl Just Like the Girl that Married Harry James': American Women and the Problem of Political Obligation in World War II," *American Quarterly* 42, 4 (December 1990): 587–615.

91. See Nick Browne's significant "Race: The Political Unconscious of American Film," *East-West Journal* 6, 1 (1992): 9.

92. Susan Jeffords, *The Remasculinization of America: Gender and the Vietnam War* (Bloomington: Indiana University Press, 1989), 180.

CHAPTER 11. CALIFORNIA: THE MISSISSIPPI OF THE 1990S

The epigraph is from James Baldwin, *No Name in the Street* (New York: Dial Press, 1972), 186 (see chap. 3, n. 33).

1. I thank Melvin Oliver for calling this story—and its significance—to my attention. John H. Burma presents a story similar to Mabley's as an example of folk humor deployed as a technique in race conflict by African Americans, and it seems likely that Mabley derived her joke from this story. See John H. Burma, "Humor as a Technique in Race Conflict," in *Mother Wit from the Laughing Barrel: Readings in the Interpretation of Afro American Folklore*, ed. Alan Dundes (New York: Garland, 1981), 624.

2. Hyung-chan Kim, *A Legal History of Asian Americans, 1790–1990* (Westport, CT: Greenwood, 1994), 104, 111.

3. Mary E. Young, *Mules and Dragons: Popular Culture Images in the Selected Writings of African-American and Chinese Women Writers* (Westport, CT: Greenwood, 1996), 2.

4. James W. Loewen, *The Mississippi Chinese: Between Black and White*, 2nd ed. (Prospect Heights, IL: Waveland, 1988).

5. John Dittmer, *Local People: The Struggle for Civil Rights in Mississippi* (Urbana: University of Illinois Press, 1995), 6.

6. David M. Oshinsky, *"Worse than Slavery": Parchman Farm and the Ordeal of Jim Crow Justice* (New York: Free Press, 1996), 231–232.

7. Takashi Fujitani, "Nisei Soldiers as Citizens: Japanese Americans in U.S. National Military and Racial Discourses," paper presented at the Conference on the Politics of Remembering the Asia/Pacific War, East–West Center, Honolulu, Hawaii, September 8, 1995, 5.

8. James Baldwin, *No Name in the Street* (New York: Dial, 1972), 46.

9. I make this argument at greater length in *A Life in the Struggle* (Philadelphia: Temple University Press, 1995).

10. Clyde Woods, *Development Arrested: The Blues and Plantation Power in the Mississippi Delta* (London: Verso, 1998).

11. Edwin Chen, "Senator Becomes Road Warrior in Battle against Poverty," *Los Angeles Times*, May 30, 1997, sec. A.

12. Tom Hamburger, "Some Mississippians Not Thrilled about Wellstone's 'Poverty' Tour," *Minneapolis Star-Tribune*, May 21, 1997, sec. A; Chen, "Senator Becomes Road Warrior."

13. Dittmer, *Local People*, 427.

14. United States Census Bureau/American FactFinder. "B19301B: Per Capita Income in the Past 12 Months (In 2015 Inflation-Adjusted Dollars) (Black or African American Alone)," *2006–2010 American Community Survey*, U.S. Census Bureau's American Community Survey Office, 2015, available at http://factfinder2.census.gov; United States Census Bureau/American FactFinder, "B19301A: Per Capita Income in the Past 12 Months (In 2015 Inflation-Adjusted Dollars) (White Alone)," *2011–2015 American Community Survey*, U.S. Census Bureau's American Community Survey Office, 2015, available at http://factfinder2.census.gov; United States Census Bureau/

American FactFinder; "DP03: Selected Economic Characteristics," *2011–2015 American Community Survey,* U.S. Census Bureau's American Community Survey Office, 2015, available at http://factfinder2.census.gov; National Center for Children in Poverty, "Mississippi Demographics of Poor Children," *National Center for Children in Poverty,* 2017, available at http://www.nccp.org/profiles/MS_profile_7.html.

15. Henry Cabot Beck, "Woods Noted for MIT Intellect," *Newark Star-Ledger,* January 3, 1997, Ticket section, 5.

16. Charles Payne, *I've Got the Light of Freedom: The Organizing Tradition and the Mississippi Freedom Struggle* (Berkeley: University of California Press, 1996), 288–289.

17. Payne, *I've Got the Light of Freedom,* 323.

18. Beck, "Woods Noted for MIT Intellect."

19. Walter J. Updegrave, "Race and Money," *Money,* December 1989, 152–162.

20. Ani Turner, *The Business Case for Racial Equity* (W. K. Kellogg Foundation and Altarum Institute, 2013), available at http://www.wkkf.org/resource-directory/resource /2013/10/the-business-case-for-racial-equity, 4.

21. Pew Research Center, *State of the News Media 2016* (Pew Research Center, 2016), available at http://assets.pewresearch.org/wp-content/uploads/sites/13/2016/06 /30143308/state-of-the-news-media-report-2016-final.pdf, accessed August 8, 2017, 82.

22. Scott Moore, *2013 Trends in the Supply of Accounting Graduates and the Demand for Public Accounting Recruits* (American Institute of CPAs, 2013), available at http://www.aicpa.org/InterestAreas/AccountingEducation/NewsAndPublications /DownloadableDocuments/2013-TrendsReport.PDF,accessed August 8, 2017, 31.

23. The American Lawyer, "The 2017 Diversity Scorecard: The Rankings," *American Lawyer,* 2017, available at http://www.americanlawyer.com/id=1202786839599.

24. Elise Gould and Tanyell Cooke, *Unemployment for Young Black Grads Is Still Worse than It Was for Young White Grads in the Aftermath of the Recession* (Economic Policy Institute, 2016), available at http://www.epi.org/publication/unemployment-for -young-black-grads-is-still-worse-than-it-was-for-young-white-grads-in-the-aftermath -of-the-recession/.

25. Douglas S. Massey, *Categorically Unequal: The American Stratification System* (New York: Russell Sage, 2007). Massey reviews the literature on this topic on pages 75 and 76.

26. Justin C. Worland, "Legacy Admit Rate at 30 Percent," *Harvard Crimson* (Cambridge, MA, 2011), section News, available at http://www.thecrimson.com/article /2011/5/11/admissions-fitzsimmons-legacy-legacies/, accessed July 30, 2017.

27. For the legacy admit rate, see Worland, "Legacy Admit Rate at 30 Percent." For the black admit rate, see "Black First-Year Students at the Nation's Leading Research Universities," *Journal of Blacks in Higher Education,* 2014, available at https://www.jbhe .com/2014/12/black-first-year-students-at-the-nations-leading-research-universities/.

28. Legacy applicants were accepted at a rate of roughly 30 percent in 2010 and made up a conservative estimate of 12 percent of the student body (and therefore, presumably, of each incoming class), according to Worland, "Legacy Admit Rate at 30 Percent." Reported by the *Harvard Gazette* ("A Historic Year for Harvard Admissions," *Harvard Gazette,* 2010, available at http://news.harvard.edu/gazette/story/2010/04/a-historic -year-for-harvard-admissions/).

29. *San Francisco Chronicle* quote from Peter H. King, "Story of a Story," *Los Angeles Times,* April 5, 1995, sec. A.

30. Jean Stefancic and Richard Delgado, *No Mercy* (Philadelphia: Temple University Press, 1996), 126.

31. "Affirmative Reaction," correspondent Josh Mankiewicz, prod. Cathy Singer, *Dateline,* NBC News, original broadcast January 24, 1996, program #2828–01, transcript.

32. See, for example, Steve Schmidt, "Scholars in Liberal Bastion Plot to End Legacy of 1960s," *San Diego Union-Tribune,* March 19, 1995, sec. A.

33. Ward Connerly, "Affirmative Action Has Outlived Its Usefulness," *Black Enterprise,* November 1995, 157.

34. Connerly, "Affirmative Action Has Outlived Its Usefulness."

35. Ralph Frammolino, Mark Gladstone, and Amy Wallace, "Some Regents Seek UCLA Admissions Priority for Friends," *Los Angeles Times,* March 16, 1996, sec. A.

36. Amy Wallace, "VIPS Do Influence Some Admissions, UC Provost Says," *Los Angeles Times,* May 17, 1996, sec. A.

37. Stefancic and Delgado, *No Mercy,* 128.

38. Barry Bearak, "Questions of Race Run Deep for Foe of Preferences," *New York Times,* July 27, 1997, 11.

39. "Private Call by Wilson Beckons Prop. 209 Votes," *San Francisco Examiner,* September 8, 1996, sec. B; Peter King, "The Curtain Pulled Back, for a Moment," *Los Angeles Times,* September 11, 1996, sec. A.

40. Bearak, "Questions of Race Run Deep," 10.

41. Claude M. Steele, "Student Self-Doubts Are No Reason to End Minority Preferences," *New York Times,* August 3, 1997, sec. E; Bearak, "Questions of Race Run Deep," 10.

42. Bearak, "Questions of Race Run Deep," 10.

43. Tomas Almaguer, *Racial Fault Lines: The Historical Origins of White Supremacy in California* (Berkeley: University of California Press, 1994), 133.

44. Richard White, *It's Your Misfortune and None of My Own* (Tulsa: University of Oklahoma Press, 1991), 338–339.

45. White, *It's Your Misfortune,* 341.

46. Almaguer, *Racial Fault Lines,* 162.

47. Ronald Takaki, *A Different Mirror: A History of Multicultural America* (Boston: Little, Brown, 1993), 178, 179.

48. Almaguer, *Racial Fault Lines,* 38.

49. Phil Ethington, *The Public City: The Political Construction of Urban Life in San Francisco, 1850–1990* (New York: Cambridge University Press, 1994), 185–188.

50. Miriam Ching Yoon Louie, *Sweatshop Warriors: Immigrant Women Workers Take on the Global Factory* (Boston: South End, 2001).

CHAPTER 12. CHANGE THE FOCUS AND REVERSE THE HYPNOSIS: LEARNING FROM NEW ORLEANS

The epigraph is from James Baldwin, *The Fire Next Time* (New York: Vintage, 1993), 72.

1. George Bush, "President Remarks on Hurricane Recovery Efforts," Louis Armstrong New Orleans International Airport, Kenner, Louisiana, September 2, 2005, *The White House.*

2. Art Neville, Aaron Neville, Charles Neville, and Cyril Neville with David Ritz, *The Brothers Neville: An Autobiography* (Boston: Little, Brown, 2000), 233.

3. "Final Hour," track 7 on Lauryn Hill, *The Miseducation of Lauryn Hill,* Ruffhouse Records, 1998.

4. Kalama ya Salaam, "Banana Republic," *Cultural Vistas* 4, 3 (1993): 40–49. Salaam comes from New Orleans' Ninth Ward.

5. Neville et al., *The Brothers Neville,* 33.

6. Neville et al., *The Brothers Neville,* 31.

7. Neville et al., *The Brothers Neville,* 214.

8. Katy Reckdahl, "Chief of Chiefs," *Gambit Weekly,* July 5, 2005; Michael Perlstein, "Doubts Raised in Police Killing in N.O.," *Times Picayune,* March 26, 2005.

9. Reckdahl, "Chief of Chiefs."

10. For more thorough analysis of the significance of the Indians, see George Lipsitz, *Time Passages* (Minneapolis: University of Minnesota Press, 1990), 233–253; and George Lipsitz, *Dangerous Crossroads* (London: Verso, 1994), 71–77. For another view, see Adolph Reed, Jr., "Demobilization in the New Black Political Regime," in *The Bubbling Cauldron: Race, Ethnicity, and the Urban Crisis,* ed. Michael Peter Smith and Joe. R. Feagin (Minneapolis: University of Minnesota Press, 1995), 202.

11. Dr. John, *Under a Hoodoo Moon: The Life of the Night Tripper* (New York: St. Martin's, 1994), 48, 72.

12. Earl Lewis, *In Their Own Interests: Race, Class, and Power in Twentieth Century Norfolk, Virginia* (Berkeley: University of California Press, 1991), 91–92.

13. Enslaved Blacks sometimes sought refuge in Indian territory in Louisiana, and there is a long history of intermarriage between Native Americans and Blacks. The Mardi Gras Indians, however, started as an African American inversion of the images presented by Wild West shows and western movies. Some Mardi Gras Indians do feel a kinship with Indigenous people, however, and attempt to learn from them and ally with them. George Landry distributed copies of Vine Deloria's *Custer Died for Your Sins* and Dee Brown's *Bury My Heart at Wounded Knee* to his family and worked with solidarity groups in Indigenous cultural survival issues.

14. Neville et al., *The Brothers Neville,* 245.

15. Kim Lacy Rodgers, *Righteous Lives* (New York: New York University Press, 1993), 111–112.

16. Lori Rodriguez and Zeke Minaya, "New Orleans' Racial Makeup in the Air," *Houston Chronicle,* September 29, 2005.

17. Nayita Wilson, "Housing Discrimination Is Significant in New Orleans," *Louisiana Weekly* 79, 3 (March 7–March 13, 2005): 1A, 18A.

18. *Wall Street Journal Washington Wire,* September 9, 2005, posted on *The Stakeholder: Democratic Congressional Campaign Committee Weblog.*

19. Clyde Woods, "Les Misérables of New Orleans: Trap Economics and the Asset Stripping Blues, Part 1," *American Quarterly* 61, 3 (2009).

20. David Brooks, "Katrina's Silver Lining," *New York Times,* September 8, 2005, available at http://www.nytimes.com/2005/09/08/opinion/katrinas-silver-lining.html?mcubz=0, accessed August 31, 2017.

21. Adam Johnson, "Katrina's 'Golden Opportunity': 10 Years of Corporate Media Celebrating Disaster," *Fair,* August 28, 2015, available at http://fair.org/home/katrinas-golden-opportunity-10-years-of-corporate-media-celebrating-disaster/, accessed August 31, 2017.

22. Veronique de Rugy and Katherine G. Newmark, "Hope after Katrina," American Enterprise Institute, October 1, 2006, available at http://www.aei.org/publication/hope-after-katrina/, accessed August 31, 2017; Johnson, "Katrina's 'Golden Opportunity.'"

23. Nick Anderson, "Education Secretary Duncan calls Hurricane Katrina Good for New Orleans Schools," *Washington Post,* January 30, 2010, available at http://www.washingtonpost.com/wp-dyn/content/article/2010/01/29/AR2010012903259.html.

24. Malcom Gladwell, "Starting Over," *New Yorker*, August 24, 2015, available at http://www.newyorker.com/magazine/2015/08/24/starting-over-dept-of-social-studies -malcolm-gladwell, accessed August 31, 2017.

25. Kristen McQueary, "Chicago, New Orleans, and Rebirth," *Chicago Tribune*, August 13, 2015, available at http://www.chicagotribune.com/news/opinion/commentary/, accessed August 31, 2017.

26. Raynard Saunders, "New Orleans Publicly Funded Private School System: Unbelievable Claims, Undemocratic, Unmasked Inequity, Unaccountable Cash Cow Schools and Chronic Failure All under the Guise of School Reform," *Souls* 17, 3–4 (July–December 2015): 201–210. See also Cedric Johnson, "Gentrifying New Orleans: Thoughts on Race and the Movement of Capital," *Souls* 17, 3–4 (July–December 2015): 175–200, and Marta Jewson, "State Ratings for New Orleans Schools Are on a Three-year Slide," *Louisiana Weekly* December 4, 2017, available at www.louisianaweekly.com/state -ratings-for-new-orleans-schools-are-on-a-three-year-slide/.

CHAPTER 13. WHITE LIVES, WHITE LIES

The epigraph is from James Baldwin, "On Being 'White' and Other Lies," in *Black on White: Black Writers on What It Means to Be White*, ed. David Roediger (New York: Schocken, 1998), 180.

1. Maria Konnikova, "Trump's Lies vs. Your Brain," *Politico*, January/February 2017, available at http://www.politico.com/magazine/story/2017/01/donald-trump-lies-liar -effect-brain-214658, accessed August 16, 2017.

2. David Leonhardt and Stuart A. Thompson, "Trump's Lies," *New York Times*, July 21, 2017, available at https://www.nytimes.com/interactive/2017/06/23/opinion/trumps -lies.html, accessed August 16, 2017.

3. Diana Taylor, *Disappearing Acts: Spectacles of Gender Nationalism in Argentina's 'Dirty War'* (Durham: Duke University Press, 1997), 119.

4. Amy Davidson Sorkin, "Donald Trump Tramples on Boy Scout Values," *New Yorker*, July 25, 2017, available at http://www.newyorker.com/news/amy-davidson-sorkin /donald-trump-tramples-on-boy-scout-values, accessed August 16, 2017.

5. Richard Rothstein, *The Color of Law: A Forgotten History of How Our Government Segregated America* (New York: Liveright, 2017), 72.

6. Eric Page, "William J. Levitt, 86, Pioneer of Suburbs, Dies," *New York Times*, January 29, 1994, available at http://www.nytimes.com/1994/01/29/obituaries/william -j-levitt-86-pioneer-of-suburbs-dies.html, accessed August 16, 2017.

7. Amy Davidson Sorkin, "Donald Trump Tramples on Boy Scout Values," *New Yorker*, July 25, 2017, available at http://www.newyorker.com/news/amy-davidson-sorkin /donald-trump-tramples-on-boy-scout-values, accessed August 16, 2017.

8. Aileen Moreton-Robinson, *The White Possessive: Property, Power, and Indigenous Sovereignty* (Minneapolis: University of Minnesota Press, 2015), 5.

9. Arthur Manuel, *Unsettling Canada: A National Wake-Up Call* (Toronto: Between the Lines, 2015), 3.

10. I take this deft formulation from Joel Kovel, *White Racism: A Psychohistory* (New York: Columbia University Press, 1984), 96.

11. Charles Mills, "White Time: The Chronic Injustice of Ideal Theory," *Du Bois Review* 11, 1 (2014): 33.

12. California Newsreel, "Interview with James O. Horton," *Race—The Power of an Illusion*, available at http://www.pbs.org/race/000_About/002_04-about-02.htm, accessed August 12, 2017.

13. California Newsreel, "Interview with James O. Horton."

14. Dorothy Roberts, *Fatal Invention: How Science, Politics, and Big Business Re-Create Race in the Twenty-first Century* (New York: New Press, 2011), 4.

15. *Dred Scott v. Sandford* 60 U.S. 393 (1857).

16. Nathan Newmark and J. J. Gass, *A New Birth of Freedom: The Forgotten History of the 13th, 14th, and 15th Amendments* (New York: Brennan Center for Justice, 2004).

17. Dorothy Roberts, "Constructing a Criminal Justice System Free of Racial Bias: An Abolitionist Framework," *Columbia Human Rights Law Review* 39 (2008): 261–266.

18. Ruth Wilson Gilmore, *Golden Gulag: Prisons, Surplus, Crisis and Opposition in Globalizing California* (Berkeley: University of California Press, 2006), 12.

19. Khalil Gibran Muhammad, *The Condemnation of Blackness: Race, Crime, and the Making of Modern Urban America* (Cambridge, MA: Harvard University Press 2010).

20. *Civil Rights Cases* 109 U.S. 3 (1883).

21. Michael J. Klarman, *From Jim Crow to Civil Rights: The Supreme Court and the Struggle for Racial Equality* (New York; Oxford, 2004), 8–60. Klarman notes that the Grandfather Clause was also used to excuse whites from taking the literacy test.

22. Cheryl I. Harris, "Whiteness as Property," in *Critical Race Theory: The Key Writings That Formed the Movement*, ed. Kimberle Crenshaw, Neil Gotanda, Gary Peller, and Kendall Thomas (New York: New Press, 1995), 276–291.

23. *Plessy v. Ferguson* 163 U.S.537 (1896).

24. Ian Haney Lopez, *White by Law* (New York: New York University Press, 2006), 218.

25. *Brown v. Board of Education of Topeka* 347 U.S.483 (1954).

26. Emmanuel Chukwudi Eze, "The Color of Reason: The Idea of 'Race' in Kant's Anthropology," in *Postcolonial African Philosophy: A Critical Reader*, ed. Emmanuel Chukwudi Eze (Cambridge: Blackwell, 1997), 116.

27. Emmanuel Chukwudi Eze, "Introduction: Philosophy and the (Post) Colonial," in *Postcolonial African Philosophy: A Critical Reader*, ed. Emmanuel Chukwudi Eze (Cambridge: Blackwell, 1997), 8–10.

28. Ibram X. Kendi, *Stamped from the Beginning: The Definitive History of Racist Ideas in America* (New York: Nation Books, 2016), 49–50.

29. Anders Walker, "Legislating Virtue: How Segregationists Disguised Racial Discrimination as Moral Reform following *Brown v. Board of Education*," *Duke Law Journal* 47, 2 (1997): 418.

30. Walker, "Legislating Virtue," 410–416.

31. Phoebe Godfrey, "Bayonets, Brainwashing and Bathrooms: The Discourse of Race, Gender and Sexuality in the Desegregation of Little Rock's Central High," *Arkansas Historical Quarterly* 62, 1 (2003): 51–52.

32. *Brown* 347 U.S. at 494 & n.11; Walker, "Legislating Virtue," 403.

33. Clyde Woods, "Les Misérables of New Orleans: Trap Economics and the Asset Stripping Blues, Part 1," in *In the Wake of Hurricane Katrina: New Paradigms and Social Visions*, ed. Clyde Woods (Baltimore, MD: Johns Hopkins University Press, 2010), 345.

34. Nicholas Mirzoeff, "The Murder of Michael Brown: Reading the Ferguson Grand Jury Transcripts," *Social Text* 34, 1 (2016): 64, 66.

35. Katherine Goldwasser, "The Prosecution, the Grand Jury, and the Decision Not to Charge," in *Ferguson's Fault Lines: The Race Quake That Rocked a Nation*, ed. Kimberly Jade Norwood (Chicago: American Bar Association, 2016), 37–56.

36. Radley Balko, "How Municipalities in St. Louis County, MO. Profit from Poverty," *Washington Post*, September 3, 2014; Arch City Defenders, "Municipal Courts White Paper," available at http://03a5010.netsolhost.com/WordPress/wp-content/uploads/2014/08/ArchCity-Defenders-Municipal-Courts-Whitepaper.pdf, accessed November 9, 2014;

United States Department of Justice, Civil Rights Division, *Investigation of the Ferguson Police Department* (Washington, DC: Department of Justice, 2015); Jodi Rios, "Flesh in the Street," *Kalfou* 3, 1 (2016).

37. Arch City Defenders, "Municipal Courts White Paper," http://www.archcitydefend ers.org/archcity-defenders-municipal-courts-whitepaper-2/, accessed August 13, 2017.

38. Balko, "How Municipalities in St. Louis County, MO., Profit from Poverty." Arch City Defenders, "Municipal Courts White Paper," accessed November 9, 2014.

39. United States Department of Justice, Civil Rights Division, *Investigation of the Ferguson Police Department*, 15.

40. United States Department of Justice, Civil Rights Division, *Investigation of the Ferguson Police Department*, 74, 75.

41. Jon Swaine, "Ferguson Judge behind Aggressive Fines Policy Owes $170,000 in Unpaid Taxes," *The Guardian,* March 6, 2015.

42. Dan Greenwald, "Former Ferguson City Court Clerk Who Sent Racist Emails Speaks Out," *KMOV.com*, April 8, 2015.

43. Walter Johnson, "What Do We Mean When We Say 'Structural Racism'? A Walk Down West Florissant Avenue, Ferguson, Missouri," *Kalfou* 3, 1 (Spring 2016): 36–62.

44. Jeff Chang, *We Gon' Be Alright: Notes on Race and Resegregation* (New York: Picador, 2016), 74.

45. Colin Gordon, *Mapping Decline: St. Louis and the Fate of the American City* (Philadelphia: University of Pennsylvania Press, 2008), 206.

46. Clarence Lang, *Grassroots at the Gateway: Class Politics and the Freedom Struggle in St. Louis, 1946–1975* (Ann Arbor: University of Michigan Press, 2009), 139–140.

47. Gordon, *Mapping Decline*, 8.

48. Ray Hartman, "Is John Ashcroft a Racist or Does He Just Play One on TV?" *Riverfront Times*, October 13, 1999, 3.

49. Dennis Judd, "The Role of Government Policies in Promoting Residential Segregation in the St. Louis Metropolitan Area," *Journal of Negro Education* 66, 3 (1997): 214–215.

50. Joanna Walters, "Troops Referred to Ferguson Protestors as 'Enemy Forces' Emails Show," *The Guardian*, April 17, 2015, available at https://www.theguardian.com/us -news/2015/apr/17/missouri-national-guard-ferguson-protesters-email, accessed August 18, 2017.

51. Judd, "The Role of Government Policies in Promoting Residential Segregation," 224.

52. Thomas Shapiro, *Toxic Inequality: How America's Wealth Gap Destroys Mobility, Deepens the Racial Divide, and Threatens Our Future* (New York: Basic Books, 2017), 85.

53. Peter Downs, "Ferguson: A String of Betrayals," *Labor Notes*, August 20, 2014, available at http://labornotes.org/blogs/2014/08/ferguson-string-betrayals, accessed August 16, 2017; Jacob Rugh and Douglas Massey, "Racial Segregation and the American Foreclosure Crisis," *American Sociological Review* 75, 5 (2010); Gary A. Dymski, "Racial Exclusion and the Political Economy of the Subprime Crisis," *Historical Materialism* 17 (2009).

54. Priscilla A. Ocen, "The New Racially Restrictive Covenant: Race, Welfare and the Policing of Black Women in Subsidized Housing," *UCLA Law Review* 59, 6 (2012).

55. Judd, "The Role of Government Policies in Promoting Residential Segregation," 226.

56. Gordon, *Mapping Decline*, 45.

57. Rebecca Klein, "Michael Brown's High School Is an Example of the Major Inequalities in Education," *Huffington Post*, August 21, 2014, available at http://www

.huffingtonpost.com/2014/08/21/michael-brown-high-school_n_5682852.html, accessed August 16, 2017.

58. Kelly Macias, "Three Years after Mike Brown's Death, Police Continue to Take Black Lives without Accountability," *Huffington Post*, August 11, 2017, available at https://www.dailykos.com/stories/2017/8/11/1688663/-Three-years-after-Mike-Brown-s-death -police-continue-to-take-black-lives-without-accountability, accessed August 17, 2017.

59. Eyes on the Prize, "Interview with Charles Sherrod," Washington University Digital Gateway, available at http://digital.wustl.edu/cgi/t/text/text-idx?c=eop;cc=eop;r gn=main;view=text;idno=she0015.0205.094, accessed August 16, 2017.

60. Robin D. G. Kelley, "After Trump," *Boston Review*, November 15, 2016, available at http://bostonreview.net/forum/after-trump/robin-d-g-kelley-trump-says-go-back-we -say-fight-back, accessed August 16, 2017.

61. Nicholas Carnes and Noam Lupu, "It Is Time to Bust the Myth: Most Trump Voters Were Not Working Class," *Washington Post*, June 6, 2017, available at https://www .washingtonpost.com/news/monkey-cage/wp/2017/06/05/its-time-to-bust-the-myth-most -trump-voters-were-not-working-class/?utm_term=.0abd97441320, accessed August 17, 2017.

62. This pairing of spineless and shameless to the best of my knowledge originated with Julian Bond in his capacity as chairman of the NAACP.

63. W.E.B. Du Bois, *Black Reconstruction in America, 1860–1880* (New York: Free Press, 1992), 714.

Acknowledgments

My debts to others are endless, and the space available for acknowledgments is limited. I wish I were eloquent enough to express fully the deep gratitude I feel toward everyone who has helped to educate me, but I know that no matter what I say I will never be able to say enough or say it well enough to do justice to the care, concern, and kindness that others have shown me. I am grateful to Sara Cohen and Aaron Javsicas of Temple University Press for the opportunity to publish a revised twentieth-anniversary edition of this book. I remain deeply indebted to the wise and wonderful Janet Francendese who was my press editor on the first edition and on my previous books at Temple. For this edition, Anna Chatillon-Reed has done exemplary work as my research assistant. Her comments, criticisms, and research findings have contributed greatly to the final book, and I very much look forward to the impact and influence of her own scholarly projects now in progress on issues of racial and gender justice. Barbara Tomlinson's sharp editorial eye and attention to evidence always enhances my writing and thinking.

I greatly appreciate the many things I have learned from work with the African American Policy Forum, the Woodstock Institute, the National Fair Housing Alliance, Students at the Center, Asian Immigrant Women Advocates, and Facing History and Ourselves. Martha Gonzalez, Quetzal Flores, and Ruben Guevara remind me that virtually everything I need to know I learned in East Los Angeles. As director of the Center for Black Studies Research and as a member of the editorial board of *Kalfou*, Diane Fujino has been an inspirational and invaluable interlocutor. I am grateful as well to the faculty and students from the departments of Black Studies and Sociology at the University of California, Santa Barbara, for the cultures of collegiality, work, and achievement they enable and encourage.

Walter Johnson, Doris Sommer, Arlene Davila, Robert Stam, Ella Shohat, Rachel Buff, and Joe Austin have contributed greatly to my understanding of the world and of my responsibilities in it. Robert Warrior's invitation to enter into a dialogue about whiteness with Aileen Moreton-Robinson, Kim Tallbear, and Cheryl Harris has provoked me to recognize how much more I need to learn about Indigenous dispossession. Like everyone else who works on whiteness in our society, I owe a tremendous debt to David Roediger, whose pioneering research established the categories with which we work. David is also a valued friend, ally, and confidant, someone who offers a moral and political compass for the rest of us. Over the years it has also been a privilege to read research and secure greatly needed assistance and insight from Michael Rogin, Sterling Stuckey, David Theo Goldberg, Joe Feagin, Clyde Woods, and Sherry Ortner. None of my research on whiteness would have existed had it not been for the inspiration, advice, and example of Melvin Oliver, whose fine book, *Black Wealth/White Wealth*, coauthored with Tom Shapiro, sets the standard of excellence in the field. In addition, everything that I write about race profits from the things that I learned from Ivory Perry and George Rawick.

The American Studies Association (ASA) has emerged as the most important academic site for the study of social identities, culture, and power. I am grateful for the leadership shown on these issues by my good friend Jan Radway, former president of the ASA, and by ASA members including Lucy Maddox, Barry Shank, Susan Douglas, Earl Lewis, George Sanchez, Paul Lauter, David W. Noble, Jose Saldivar, Sharon O'Brien, Wahneema Lubiano, Amy Kaplan, Mary Helen Washington, Robyn Wiegman, Jack Tchen, Ned Blackhawk, Chandra Mohanty, Stelamaris Coser, Jay Mechling, Herman Gray, and Rosa Linda Fregoso. I have also learned a great deal from exchanges with Don Brenneis, Daniel Segal, David Thelen, Kimberlé Crenshaw, Cheryl Harris, Devon Carbado, Luke Harris, and Patricia Williams. Old and trusted friends deserve acknowledgment too: Elizabeth Long, Ed Hugetz, Ed Robbins, Michael M. J. Fischer, Paul Buhle, Mari Jo Buhle, Maria Damon, Richard Leppert, and Nick Browne. Dan Czitrom has no popular-front illusions. Johnny Otis, Preston Love, Marisela Norte, and Stan Weir have been unique and awesome role models. This particular book has been especially enriched from interventions by Brenda Bright, Tom Dumm, Gayle Plummer, James Horton, Austin Sarat, John Bodnar, Wendy Kozol, Marla Berns, Bennetta Jules-Rosette, Denis Constant-Martin, and Gordon Hutner.

Toni Morrison, Stuart Hall, and Catherine Hall have inspired me in ways beyond my capacity for expression. Susan McClary and Rob Walser provide sweet harmony and rhythms that Freddie Greene would envy. Tricia Rose knows what needs to be said, why, and when; her friendship and support are greatly appreciated. Ann duCille blends intellectual brilliance, moral passion, and life-affirming wit; I count myself very lucky to know her. Robin D. G. Kelley deserves the last word. He is the O. G., the original Gramscian, whose writing breaks everything down for us, from Malcolm to Monk, from EPMD to E. P. Thompson. But his best work doesn't even appear in his own books; it makes itself manifest mainly through the ways he empowers and inspires others. On behalf of many of us, I want to say thanks.

Some parts of individual chapters have been published previously, in different versions, in the following articles and chapters. I thank those publishers for permission to reprint.

"The Possessive Investment in Whiteness: Racialized Social Democracy and the 'White Problem' in American Studies," *American Quarterly* 47, 3 (September 1995).

"Diasporic Intimacy in the Art of Renee Stout," in *Dear Robert: I'll See You at the Crossroads,* ed. Marla C. Berns (Santa Barbara, CA: University Art Museum, 1995).

"Dilemmas of Beset Nationhood: Patriotism, the Family, and Economic Change in the 1970s and 1980s," in *Bonds of Affection: Americans Define Their Patriotism*, ed. John Bodnar (Princeton, NJ: Princeton University Press, 1996).

"'Frantic to Join . . . the Japanese Army': The Asia Pacific War in the Lives of African American Soldiers and Civilians," in *The Politics of Culture in the Shadow of Capital*, ed. Lisa Lowe and David Lloyd (Durham, NC: Duke University Press, 1997).

"Separate and Unequal: Big Government Conservatism and the Racial State," in *State of White Supremacy: Racism, Governance and the United States*, ed. Moon-kie Jung, João H. Costa Vargas, and Eduardo Bonilla-Silva (Stanford, CA: Stanford University Press, 2011), 110–129. Copyright (c) 2011 by the Board of Trustees of the Leland Stanford Jr. University. All rights reserved. Used by permission of the publisher, Stanford University Press, sup.org.

"From Plessy to Ferguson," *Cultural Critique* #90, 2015, 119–139.

"The Changing Same," *Social Identities* Online, April 2017, 1–5.

Index

George Lipsitz is a Professor of Black Studies and Sociology at the University of California, Santa Barbara. His previous books include *How Racism Takes Place* and *A Life in the Struggle: Ivory Perry and the Culture of Opposition* (both Temple). Lipsitz serves as Chair of the boards of Directors of the African American Policy Forum and of the Woodstock Institute and is senior editor of the comparative and relational ethnic studies journal *KALFOU*.